Civil Service Systems in Western Europe

CIVIL SERVICE SYSTEMS IN COMPARATIVE PERSPECTIVE

General Editors: Hans A.G.M. Bekke, *Professor of Public Administration and* Frits M. van der Meer, *Associate Professor of Public Administration, Leiden University, The Netherlands*

This series provides the perfect arena for discussing developments taking place in civil service systems throughout the world. It addresses issues at the heart of modern public administration from a comparative perspective.

Focusing on different country groupings, leading experts analyse the changes in structure and functioning of today's civil service systems, considering institutional frameworks, performance and legitimacy. The importance attached to these issues is reflected in the urge for civil service reform which has assumed global proportions.

Titles in the series include:

Civil Service Systems in Central and Eastern Europe
Edited by Tony Verheijen

Civil Service Systems in Western Europe
Edited by Hans A.G.M. Bekke and Frits M. van der Meer

Civil Service Systems in Asia
Edited by John P. Burns and Bidhya Bowornwathana

Civil Service Systems in Western Europe

Edited by

Hans A.G.M. Bekke and
Frits M. van der Meer
Department of Public Administration, Leiden University

CIVIL SERVICE SYSTEMS IN COMPARATIVE PERSPECTIVE

Edward Elgar
Cheltenham, UK • Northampton, MA, USA

Published by
Edward Elgar Publishing Limited
Glensanda House
Montpellier Parade
Cheltenham
Glos GL50 1UA
UK

Edward Elgar Publishing, Inc.
136 West Street
Suite 202
Northampton
Massachusetts 01060
USA

A catalogue record for this book
is available from the British Library

Library of Congress Cataloguing in Publication Data

Civil service systems in Western Europe / edited by Hans J.G.M. Bekke and Frits M. van der Meer.
   —(Civil service systems in comparative perspective)
   Includes bibliographical references and index.
   1. Civil service—Europe, Western—Congresses. 2. Europe, Western—Politics and government—1989—Congresses. I. Bekke, A.J.G.M. II. Meer, F.M. van der (Frits M.), 1957– III. Series.

   JN94.A67 C586 2001
   351.4—dc21

                                             00–062288
ISBN 1 84064 607 1

Printed and bound in Great Britain by MPG Books Ltd, Bodmin, Cornwall

Contents

v

List of figures

List of tables

List of contributors

Bekke, Hans A.G.M., Department of Public Administration, Leiden University, the Netherlands

Christensen, Tom, Department of Political Science, University of Oslo, Norway

Dijkstra, Gerrit S.A., Department of Public Administration, Leiden University, the Netherlands

Fry, Geoffrey K., Department of Politics, University of Leeds, Great Britain

Goetz, Klaus H., Department of Government, London School of Economics, London, Great Britain

Hondeghem, Annie, Catholic University of Leuven, Belgium

Lewansky, Rudolf, Faculty of Political Science, University of Bologna, Italy

McKevitt, David, Department of Management and Marketing, College of Business, University of Limerick, Ireland

Meer, Frits M. van der, Department of Public Administration, Leiden University, the Netherlands

Meininger, Marie-Christine, International Institute for Public Administration, Paris, France

Millar, Michelle, Centre for Public Policy, Department of Political Science & Sociology, National University of Ireland, Galway, Ireland

Parrado Díez, Salvador, Department of Political and Sociological Sciences, University Carlos III of Madrid, Spain

Acknowledgements

A comparative study presenting extensive empirical research cannot be but the outcome of concerted effort. We are very appreciative of the care with which the contributors have accepted and completed the challenge the Civil Service Systems in Comparative Perspective project presented them. Conceived in 1989 as a joint effort coordinated by the Department of Public Administration of the University of Leiden and the School for Public and Environmental Affairs of Indiana University, the ensuing 1991 conference in the Netherlands resulted in a framework for analysis which was published in 1996. This served as the foundation for the empirical studies presented in a second conference in 1997 in the USA. The volume on Civil Service Systems in Central and Eastern Europe was published in 1999. This is the second volume in a series that will ultimately include Asia, Africa, and the Anglo-Saxon world.

We would like to thank the Dutch Ministry of the Interior since their financial assistance was crucial for organising this project. We also like to thank the Netherlands Institute of Government for their support. In addition the invaluable help of our assistants Hetty Hessels and Claudia Keijzers has to be mentioned. Julie Bivin Raadschelders and Anne van der Zwalmen each have done much to improve the text.

Hans A.G.M. Bekke and Frits M. van der Meer

Leiden, May 2000

1. Civil Service Systems in Western Europe: An Introduction

Hans A.G.M Bekke and
Frits M. van der Meer

'In a very real sense, public employees put flesh on the bare bones of government.'

Richard Rose, *Understanding Big Government*

EUROPEAN CIVIL SERVICE SYSTEMS

This observation by Richard Rose points to the reliance of government on the professional qualities of the public workforce: civil servants. In the past, the role and supposed power of civil servants in the policymaking process have been discussed and questioned by many in the political and the scientific communities. Assessments vary from the (in)ability of bureaucracy in Weberian terminology to a *Beamtenherrschaft* (rule by bureaucrats). Contrary to normative aspects of bureaucratic involvement, empirical research in the structure and functioning of civil service systems has been less profuse. Additional in-depth knowledge of civil service systems is nowadays more important than ever.

First, civil service systems are a basic constituent part of our systems of government. A better understanding of government implies that salient attributes of civil service systems have to be determined. To determine those attributes and to put them into perspective, a comparative approach is needed.

A second reason to pursue comparative civil service research can be found in the ongoing process of public sector reform. For more than a century, policies have been directed at reforming the public sector, in fact, public sector reform has almost become institutionalised. Although there is a certain bias towards emphasising temporary and national singularities, administrative reform is not confined to a few isolated countries. Since modern government very much depends on civil servants, the implications and demands for civil service reform are immense. Government reform, and especially initiatives pertaining to the reform of the civil service, has been placed high on the political agenda. Two important elements stand out in the debate on civil service system reform: the need for improving performance and the necessity of enhancing the legitimacy of the civil service (Perry and Raadschelders 1995). Before attempting to reform civil service systems, we must first know what to reform. As a 'bench mark' approach is increasingly used, comparative knowledge of civil service systems is mandatory.

Notwithstanding the manifest interest in civil service reform, in-depth comparative analyses of civil service systems are rather rare. The step of defining the nature and development of civil service systems is omitted with some unfortunate consequences for the quality of the reform proposals. In order to fill some voids in the current state of the art of civil service research, a comparative study of Western European civil service systems is presented here.

Comparative civil service research requires a framework to define the issues involved and the theoretical stance taken. The development of such a framework has been an integral part of the civil service project, which was designed in 1991 with the creation of a 'civil service research consortium'. The purpose of the consortium is to stimulate international comparative research on civil service systems. The consortium has been coordinated by the School of Public and Environmental Affairs of Indiana University (USA) and the Department of Public Administration of Leiden University. The Directorate General of Public Administration of the Dutch Home Office is also a participant in the project.

This research project has been conceived as a two-stage project from the beginning; the first stage is conceptual and the second stage is empirical. During the first phase, the basic concepts and the framework for conducting the comparative work were produced. Indiana University Press published the results under the editorship of Hans A.G.M. Bekke, James L. Perry and Theo A.J. Toonen as *Civil Service Systems in Comparative Perspective* in 1996. The theoretical framework serves as a guideline for empirical country studies encompassing major regions of the world (Asia, Western Europe, Central and Eastern Europe, Africa and the Anglo-Pacific rim). In 1999, a first volume on Central and Eastern European civil service systems edited by Tony Verheijen was published.

In this introductory chapter, the outline and the approach used in this volume on Western European civil service systems will be defined. First, the neo-institutional framework used in the different chapters will be explained. This will be followed by a more in-depth exploration of the comparative nature of this study. Finally, attention is focused on the structural dimension of civil service systems. This structural dimension will be explored in themes such as internal labour markets, reform and diffusion. The interface of civil service systems and their political and societal environment is studied by looking at issues such as representativeness, politicisation and public opinion. The dynamic nature of civil service systems is emphasised by examining the historical development of civil service systems.

A NEO-INSTITUTIONAL APPROACH TO CIVIL SERVICE SYSTEMS RESEARCH

The core concept in the research design used in this book is 'civil service systems'. Civil service systems are described as '... mediating institutions that mobilise human resources in the service of the affairs of the state in a given territory' (Morgan and Perry 1988). By using civil service systems instead of, for instance, the better known concept of bureaucracy, some common misconceptions can be avoided. Bureaucracy has a manifold meaning even when used in a classical Weberian sense (a form of organisation, a state of societal development and a staff of officials supporting the implementation of authority). Besides this Weberian plurality of notions, in everyday life, bureaucracy has acquired – rightly or wrongly – a pejorative meaning. In his concise study of the bureaucratic concept, Martin Albrow suggests that it is perhaps better to drop the name (Albrow 1970).

Using the concept of 'civil service systems' implies a number of things. This definition implies that an institutional approach is used (Bekke et al. 1996). The crucial words in our definition are 'mediating institutions'. To avoid any misunderstanding, institutions are not considered identical to organisations as was the case in previous institutional theory. Likewise, as the title 'Civil Service Systems in Comparative Perspective' reveals, it refers to a comparative neo-institutional approach. Douglass North argues that institutions have to be separated from organisations (North 1990). Institutions are the driving forces behind organisations in that they direct organisational behaviour. Civil service systems are to be seen as systems of rules and authority relations, which shape the behaviour of the members of civil services. A rule contains norms about prescribed behaviour and constitutes a point of convergence for the expectations of the actors involved (Bekke et al. 1996; Kiser and Ostrom 1982; Krasner 1983). 'Shape' implies that it adds to the continuation of certain modes of that behaviour.

Those formal and informal rules embodied in civil service systems can pertain to what has been called by Kiser and Ostrom, the three worlds of action. A first level has been termed the operational level. What is actually done in a civil service system context? With respect to the operational rules in the personnel management system, it concerns how people are recruited, promoted, rewarded and so on.

A second level of institutional analysis refers to the collective choice level. This level relates to the what, why, when and how civil service systems reform. According to these collective choice rules, the latitude possessed by civil servants to participate in decision-making procedures is also determined.

The third level, the constitutional level, of institutional analysis relates to civil service systems as symbols for interpreting actions involving the general public, members of the civil service itself and third parties (March and Olsen 1984, 1989; Bekke et al. 1996). The open character of recruitment in certain civil service systems according to the merit principle can be viewed as a symbol representing basic values in society itself. As this last example makes clear, these three levels are closely intertwined.

Using a neo-institutional approach, the specific nature and development of civil service systems are emphasised. We have to look at how these systems evolved, and more specifically, what factors have been influencing their development. The main question to be answered is, how do rules and authority relationships influence the behaviour of the members of the civil service over time? An institutional analysis of civil service systems seeks to identify:

1. The social and legal rules (that is prescribed behaviour and implicit and explicit norms) that determine the nature of a civil service system;
2. The origins of those rules; and
3. Why they endure (Perry and Raadschelders 1995).

COMPARATIVE CIVIL SERVICE SYSTEM RESEARCH

Considering the importance of civil service systems and the global nature of the reform efforts, it is quite remarkable that comparative (empirical) research on civil service systems has been relatively scarce. There are some well-known exceptions. Particularly the higher civil service has received much attention (Aberbach et al. 1981; Dogan 1975; Rose 1985; Pierre 1995; Farazmand 1997). With the exception of Rose, these works mainly concentrate on the interface between the 'political' and the 'administrative' systems. Recently, the OECD (PUMA and SIGMA), the IMF and the World Bank have taken a keen interest in generating information on civil service systems. Their (reform) angle (perhaps excluding SIGMA's work on Central and Eastern Europe) has placed a heavy emphasis on the export of New Public Management concepts. While these studies may be informative and valuable, there is still scope for 'truly' comparative studies of civil service systems in general. Given the ongoing changes in the structure and functioning of civil service systems, a wide knowledge gap needs still to be filled.

'Truly comparative studies' might sound a little presumptuous. As Ridley stated in 1975, three levels of comparative work can be distinguished. First, comparisons can be made without paying too much attention to theoretical implications. Peters has termed this approach the stamps, flags and coins approach (1988). This phraseology might sound somewhat denigrating, but voyeurism, at least confined to social science, doesn't need to be condemned outright (Peters 1988, 1996). Information gathering to satisfy curiosity has a meaning on its own. There is one difficulty involved: collecting the flags, stamps and coins implies that definitions or descriptions of these collectibles are given. As such, even this kind of comparative work is not free of theoretical concepts and choices. The real problem is that these choices are often implicit.

The same difficulty holds true for a second normative inspired approach. Often comparisons are made for reasons of evaluating (in the sense of ranking) (seemingly) related phenomena. To give a simple example, as a tourist, do we prefer Greece to the Maldives as a holiday destination? Is the Dutch system of water management to be preferred over that of Bangladesh? The latter example points to the applied dimension of this normative comparison in public administration. Even while making a normative statement about cross-national variation, it could be argued that an explicit explanation for the differences is not necessary. Nevertheless, this normative inspired comparison implies some standards for evaluation.

Only in the third and final case of trying to find an explanation for cross-national variation, is theory-guided research explicitly needed. As remarked by Pierre, while studies of individual cases may generate general findings, which may very well be of interest in their own right, their theoretical significance and value can only be assessed in a comparative context (Pierre 1995).

Some severe difficulties are encountered when trying to use a comparative, theoretical based analysis. Some of the issues involve what we want to compare (the dependent variables) and whether those features or systems are really comparable. Without going too deeply into this subject matter, we take a position of concentrating on a focused comparison aimed at middle-range theory (Peters 1988). In this book on Western European civil service systems, a deliberate theoretical framework is used. Given the methodological problems surrounding comparative research, some preliminary remarks about the nature of the framework are necessary.

A flexible framework has the advantage of accommodating national differences concerning conceptual meanings. But in using such a flexible approach, the equivalence problem can become acute. Is what we are trying to compare really the same (or different)? On the other hand, a rigid framework may lead to a 'procrustean' approach. Reality is stretched or compressed according to the conceptual needs of the framework involved. Do we lose some essential features of the component that has to be compared by extending or reducing reality?

Both questions are perhaps erroneous. The essential requirement of a comparative framework is that it helps to discover the salient features, in this case, of a civil service system, by highlighting a certain societal and cultural context. Similarities and differences are therefore not only related to (parts of) civil service systems under examination, but also to their political and social setting. That setting helps to understand the prevailing differences and similarities between key parts of different civil service systems. In this context, the neo-institutional approach will serve us well.

THEMES

Having defined the need for a neo-institutional and comparative framework for civil service analysis, a final concern is the themes that will be addressed in the country chapters. These themes comprise:

- the development (history) of the civil service system;
- internal labour market;
- representativeness;
- politicisation;
- public opinion;
- reform and diffusion.

Internal labour markets, reform and diffusion pertain mainly to the structure of civil service systems. Although not exclusively confined to these issues the 'managerial' dimension is most prominent here. The relations of the civil service systems with their political and societal environments are dealt with in the sections on politicisation, representativeness and public opinion. As follows from our discussion, the interconnection between the structural dimension of civil service systems and their positioning in the relevant political and societal environments is essential for understanding the dynamics of these systems. Ample attention will be paid to this interface in the section on historical development.

Above, we mentioned that the main purpose of using an institutional approach is to obtain an idea of how rules and authority relationships shape the behaviour of members of the civil service. By employing, for instance, rules and belief systems, institutions determine patterns of behaviour over a longer period of time. It serves as an organisational memory (Douglas 1982, 1986). At the same time, institutions come into existence and change over the course of time. Using an neo-institutional approach implies that we have to put emphasis on the historical development of civil service systems. Time and history as such are empty and meaningless concepts. To put it more strongly, arguing that 'forces of history' account for a certain event is changing 'time' into a metaphysical concept. During the course of history, during a certain period of time, 'things' happen. Those events are shaped during that period of time. We have to explain what those forces are. A historical analysis of civil service systems can provide us deeper insight into those forces shaping institutional development.

A historical analysis is, therefore, not only important to clarify the social and legal rules which determine the character of a civil service system, but at the same time it requires a look into the reasons for both institutional change and persistence. Major questions include: How did the civil service system develop? Which historical dynamics account for expansion or decline, change or persistence, structure and character of civil service systems over time (Perry and Raadschelders 1995)? As a starting point for this historical analysis, most authors have used the model designed by Raadschelders and Rutgers who propose 5 phases in the development of civil service systems namely,

1. civil servants as personal servants;
2. civil servants as state servants;
3. civil servants as public servants;
4. the civil service as protected service; and
5. the civil service as professional service.

In trying to explain the evolution (a term used by Raadschelders and Rutgers) of civil service systems, they suggest the following as explanatory factors:

- the importance of nation state building;
- the demarcation between the public and private domains of life;
- the creation of a separate civil service identity with respect to, amongst others, their legal status;
- the expansion of government tasks; and
- the increasing professionalism of the civil service.

In the following chapters, these issues are taken up and the extent to which these factors can help explain the development in the various countries is examined.

Mobilising human resources in the service of the state implies that a primary function of civil service systems is that of personnel systems. Those personnel systems can be perceived as more or less closed system for managing human resources or, to use a different term, internal labour markets. Lois

Wise argues that internal labour markets involve administrative policies and practices that determine the way human resources are used and rewarded within an organisation. These policies and procedures relate to the (formal and informal) rules pertaining to job definition or classification, deployment (including mobility) and staff development, job security and membership, and reward structures and wage rules (Wise 1996). Since these rules are interrelated, they define the particular nature of the internal labour market of a civil service system. Change occurring in one part of the internal labour market will have consequences for other parts. To give only one example, changing the system of recruitment from a job system to a career system can have major implications for management development and training practices.

While internal labour markets and personnel systems put emphasis on the 'internal' aspects of civil service systems, representativeness relates to the relationship of the civil service system to society. Civil servants are both members of an organisation and members of society. Their behaviour is partly influenced by the civil service structures they belong to and partly by the societal, cultural and economic environment (Peters 1996).

One can speak of representativeness in an empirical and normative way. The latter emphasises the importance of policies directed at increasing the level of representativeness in a civil service system. Van der Meer and Roborgh stress that by examining the importance attached to the issue of representativeness, we can obtain a deeper insight into the role and position of a civil service system in a particular political, administrative and societal context (Van der Meer and Roborgh 1996). The question of whether to pursue representativeness pertains directly to views on how the legitimacy of government and the responsiveness of the public service can be enhanced. In this volume, the differences between, for instance, France and the Netherlands, are illustrative. In the former, representativeness as a policy issue is neglected while in the latter case, it is positioned high on the policy agenda. As will be explained later, the view on the position and role of the state in society is crucial for understanding these differences.

Closely related to the issue of representativeness is the politicisation of the civil service. The relation between politics and the civil service has drawn much attention in European public administration, particularly since the 1960s. This is particularly the case with the issue of politicisation of the civil service or, conversely, the bureaucratisation of politics. Although the politics-administration dichotomy has been rebutted time and again, the issue of the demarcation between the political and administrative domains remains as alive as ever. However perplexing the interface between the political and administrative systems may be, an examination of that interface remains a important issue, not only with respect to the efficiency and effectiveness of government, but also given the importance attached to issues such as the legitimacy and responsiveness of government.

Politicisation is a complex issue, and it can have many different meanings. Two of the most recurring dimensions are the politicisation of recruitment and the politicisation of behaviour. With respect to the last, the question can be raised what the ideal-type is, which dominates within the civil service system. This refers to the normative aspect. To use two extremes: is the emphasis still on a neutral civil service implementing political decisions or is a more symbiotic relationship fostered? What does this mean for recruitment? With respect to the empirical side, we have to look at the actual interdependency between the political and administrative systems and the practice of including political criteria in the recruitment and selection criteria.

Public opinion concerns the external perception of the civil service system. The legitimacy and performance of a civil service system is dependent on the views of the general public and the elite. Public opinion research on the civil service invariably reveals a negative attitude toward the civil service. There is frequently a more negative general perception than direct contact with a civil servant would suggest. Nevertheless, variation does exist. What are the reasons for the more negative general attitude on the one hand, and the less negative attitude for specific civil service action? Second, how can the cross-national variations be explained?

To even the most casual observer it is clear that in the last two decades massive reorganisations have ripped through all levels of government and its personnel. These reorganisations coincided with a fundamental rethinking of the role and functioning of bureaucracy and we have come to know them under the label of New Public Management (NPM). While NPM in the 1980s was primarily focused on promoting a more efficient and effective government service, the attention in the 1990s included issues such as equity, integrity and so forth. This was conceptualised as 'good governance'. Reports of international organisations such as the OECD, the IMF, the World Bank, and the EU support programmes PHARE and TACIS for central and eastern European countries are illustrative of this more inclusive focus. The various chapters in this volume pay ample attention to civil service reform.

In our concluding chapter, we compare the different civil service systems discussed in the book according to the issues mentioned above. A first group of questions relate to issues such as: Can we distinguish some patterns in the historical development of civil service systems or are the national experiences unique? What designs and processes of redesigning internal labour markets can be observed? Is it possible to form some clusters? What are the cross-national variations in the representativeness of these European civil service systems, both in an empirical and a normative perspective? The same questions can be raised relating to the issues of politicisation and public opinion. A second group of questions relates to the possible explanations for these similarities and differences among these civil service systems.

BIBLIOGRAPHY

Aberbach, J.D., R.D. Putnam and B.A. Rockham (1981), *Bureaucrats and Politicians in Western Democracies*, Cambridge, Ma: Harvard University Press.

Albrow, M. (1970), *Bureaucracy*, London: Macmillan.

Bekke, A.J.G.M., J.L. Perry and Th.A.J. Toonen (1993), 'Comparing civil service systems', *Research in Public Administration,* **3**: 191–211.

Bekke, A.J.G.M., J.L. Perry and Th.A.J. Toonen (eds) (1996), *Civil Service Systems in Comparative Perspective*, Bloomington: Indiana University Press.

Dogan, M (ed.) (1975),*The Mandarins of Western Europe: The Political role of Top Civil Servants*, New York: Sage.

Douglas, M. (1982), *In the Active Voice*, London: Routledge & Kegan Paul.

Douglas, M. (1986), *How Institutions Think,* Syracuse, NY: Syracuse University Press.

Farazmand, A. (ed.) (1997), *Modern Systems of Government: Exploring the Role of Bureaucracy*, Thousand Oaks, Ca: Sage.

Hood, C. (1998), *The Art of the State: Culture, Rhetoric and Public Management,* Oxford: Clarendon Press.

Kiser, L.L. and E. Ostrom (1982), 'The three world of action: a meta-theoretical synthesis of institutional approaches', in E. Ostrom (ed.) *Strategies of Political Enquiry, Beverly Hills: Sage*: 179–222.

Krasner, S.D. (ed.) (1983), *International Regimes*, Ithaca, NY: Cornell University Press.

March, J.G. and J.P. Olsen (1984), 'The new instititutionalism: organizational factors in political life', *American Political Science Review,* **78**: 734–49.

March, J.G. and J.P. Olsen (1989), *Rediscovering Instititutions: The Organizational Basis of Politics,* New York: Free Press.

Meer, F.M. van der and L.J. Roborgh (1996), 'Civil servants and representativeness', in A.J.G.M. Bekke, J.L. Perry and Th.A.J. Toonen (eds.), *Civil Service Systems in Comparative Perspective*, Blookington: Indiana University Press

Meer, F.M. van der and J.C.N. Raadschelders (eds) (1998), *L'Entourage Administratif du Pouvoir Executif: Administering the Summit*, Brussels: Bruylant.

Morgan, E.P and J.L. Perry (1988), 'Re-orienting the comparative study of civil service systems', *Review of Public Personnel Administration,* **8**: 84–95.

North, D.C. (1990), *Institutions: Institutional Change and Economic Performance*, New York/Cambridge: Cambridge University Press.

Perry, J.L. and J.C.N. Raadschelders (1995), *Protocol for Comparative Studies of National Civil Service Systems*, Bloomington/Leiden.

Peters, B.G. (1988), *Comparing Public Bureaucracies: Problems of Theory and Method*, Tuscaloosa: University of Alabama Press.

Peters, B.G., 'Theory and methodology', in A.J.G.M. Bekke, J.L. Perry and Th.A.J. Toonen (eds.), *Civil Service Systems in Comparative Perspective*, Blookington: Indiana University Press

Pierre, J. (ed.) (1995*),* *Bureaucracy in the Modern State: An Introduction to Comparative Administration,* Aldershot: Edward Elgar.

Raadschelders, J.C.N. (1998), *Handbook of Administrative History,* New Brunswick, NJ: Transaction.

Ridley, F.F. (1975), *The Study of Government: Political Science and Public Administration*, London: Allen & Unwin.

Rose, R. (1984), *Understanding Big Government: The Programme Approach*, London: Sage Publications.

Rose, R. (ed.) (1985), *Public Employment in Western Nations*, Cambridge: Cambridge University Press.

Weber, M. (1976, 5th edition), *Wirtschaft und Gesellschaft: Grundrisse der Verstehenden Soziologie*, Tuebingen: J.Mohr

Wise, L (1996), Internal labour markets, in A.J.G.M. Bekke, J.L. Perry and Th.A.J. Toonen (eds.), *Civil Service Systems in Comparative Perspective*, Blookington: Indiana University Press.

2.   The British Civil Service System

Geoffrey K. Fry

INTRODUCTION

The United Kingdom of Great Britain covers an area of 241 600 square kilometres and it presently has an estimated population of 58 040 000 people. It is a constitutional monarchy with a bicameral parliament. The head of state is the hereditary monarch, and all acts of parliament are made in his or her name. The House of Commons, which is the lower house of parliament currently comprises 659 members elected directly on a constituency basis at intervals of not more than a five years. The House of Lords, which is the upper house, comprises (around 90 elected) hereditary peers, nominated life peers, senior judges and bishops, which together number approximately 650 members. Legislation requires the approval of both houses of parliament before enactment. The government is normally formed by the political party which has majority support in the House of Commons, and most ministers are drawn from that body, though some may be peers. The twenty or so most senior ministers comprise the cabinet (East 1996). The career civil service operates within this political context and takes its character from it.

After ceasing to be prime minister in 1990, Margaret Thatcher made the usual tribute to 'the sheer professionalism of the British civil service, which allows governments to come and go with a minimum of dislocation and a maximum of efficiency [which was] something other countries with different systems have every cause to envy' (Thatcher 1993). Yet, during the period of the Thatcher Conservative governments of 1979–90, the British career civil service was subjected to an order of radical change unknown before in peacetime, and this approach also characterised Mrs Thatcher's successor (Fry 1995).

Clement Attlee, who had been at the head of the Labour governments of 1945–51, the first one of which would rank with those of Mrs Thatcher as a strong government, recalled in 1954 that, nine years before:

When I succeeded Mr Churchill as prime minister and returned to the conference at Potsdam, I took with me precisely the same team of civil servants, including even the principal private secretary, as had served my predecessor. This occasioned a lively surprise among our American friends who were accustomed to the American system whereby the leading official advisers of the president and of the members of his cabinet are usually politically of his and their own political colour. The incident brought out very forcibly the very special position of the British civil service, a position which has developed during the past hundred years as the result of the Northcote – Trevelyan reforms. I do not think that this remarkable attribute of impartiality in the British civil service is sufficiently widely known nor adequately recognises for what it is – one of the strongest bulwarks of democracy. (Attlee 1954).

Certainly, socialist writers such as Harold Laski had not anticipated this (Laski 1933; Laski 1938). As Attlee remarked, it seemed with Laski in mind, 'there were certainly some people in the Labour Party who doubted whether the civil servants would give fair play to a socialist government, but all doubts disappeared with experience' (Attlee 1954). Laski himself appeared to be unrepentant (Laski 1951), and it could be said that the British political climate had been transformed since his predictions by World War II, which had dramatically changed perceptions of what was politically possible in terms of taxation and public expenditure, and hence, in part, what role the state could play in the economy and in social provision.

Economic liberalism and the policies which followed from its observance were pushed aside, largely by the ideas of the renegade liberals, J.M. Keynes, with his demand theory of national economic management, and Sir William Beveridge, with his plan for the Welfare State. The public corporations which were to run the nationalised industries were organised along the lines favoured by Labour's Herbert Morrison, but the model was the Central Electricity Board established by the Conservative government of Stanley Baldwin in the 1920s. The Keynesian or Managed Economy Welfare State was as much the creation of the all-party Wartime Coalition government of 1940–45 as it was of the Labour governments of 1945–51. So, aside from sometimes bitterly disputed detail, and sloganising of the type that Winston Churchill at one time engaged in about the evils of bureaucracy, domestic British politics at least were conducted on a largely consensual basis, irrespective of whether the Conservative Party or the Labour Party was in office or not, from the first Keynesian Budget in 1941 to the collapse of Keynesianism in 1976, after which economic liberalism returned as the orthodoxy (Fry 1979).

Towards the end of the first decade after World War II when the Keynesian order still seemed readily compatible with an internationally successful economy, and Britain still ranked as a great power, the centenary of the Northcote-Trevelyan Report of 1954 took place. The conventional wisdom was that the Victorian reformers had created a remarkable instrument for good government in the British civil service (Wheare 1954; Griffith 1954), and, understandably, Sir Edward Bridges, the then head of the civil service, certainly thought so (Bridges 1954).

Like Laski before him, the Fabian socialist academic expert on public administration, W.A. Robson, took a different line. 'The British civil service continues ... to be the best in the world,' Robson wrote, much like everybody else, but he also chose to list just about every critical comment made about that service in the past twenty years, plainly concurring with many of them. The contemporary Crichel Down Affair, which was seen at the time as being solely the result of maladministration by officials, was cited by Robson as illustrating the civil service's failings (Robson 1954). Viewed later, the Crichel Down case seemed a more complex matter than this, both as regards the actual behaviour of the officials (Nicolson 1986), and in relation to the current working of the constitutional convention of ministerial responsibility, the principle around which not only the policy work of the higher civil service was organised, but also that of central government departments as a whole (Fry 1969). British arrangements may well have been best for that country, but after the Crichel Down Affair, this proposition had at least to be argued for, and in relation to means of dealing with maladministration in the civil service, there were reformers who became interested in copying the French *Conseil d'État*, or the Scandinavian Ombudsman system.

Admiration for the latter eventually led to the establishment of the office of Parliamentary Commissioner for Administration in 1966, the work of whom was an incursion into the doctrine of ministerial responsibility (Fry 1970). Specifically Swedish arrangements for organising the work of central government departments, which structurally separated out policy and management work, attracted interest. So did the technocratic nature of the French Higher Service, believed to have been shown to good effect during the unsuccessful negotiations for Britain to enter what was then the European Common Market. Britain's diminished international position and relatively declining economy invited a form of reappraisal, but the emphasis that both Labour and Conservative governments placed on institutional reform in the 1960s and the first part of the 1970s was ridiculous, given that, without changing the ambitious nature of the ends pursued in, notably, economic and social policy, there were bound to be at best very limited benefits from reorganising the machinery of administration and its practices, and losses in efficiency could not be ruled out (Fry 1981).

Thus, prioritising public expenditure in the manner recommended by the Plowden Report on its control (Plowden Report 1961) was sensible in principle, and in presentation more sophisticated than traditional treasury control, but, in practice, in the Keynesian context, the arrangements acted to safeguard spending programmes, leading to the reintroduction of cash limits in 1976 to restore a form of order. The Plowden Report also argued that, given the scale of resources being handled by government departments, the civil service needed to professionalise its management systems and behaviour and, under the aegis of the treasury, the service began to do so.

The Fulton Report on the home civil service (Fulton Report 1968) also emphasised managerialism as part of a reform programme that was otherwise similar to that proposed by Laski and Robson in the past. Quite why the Fulton Report was regarded as radical was a mystery even at the time (Fry 1969), and a sceptical verdict was confirmed by closer study of the Fulton Committee's work (Fry 1993). The service effectively chose what changes it would implement. Further than this, the Fulton Committee did not seriously challenge the continuance of a large-scale career civil service organised along broadly familiar lines. The Thatcher governments eventually did challenge this having, from the outset, never disguised their preference for private sector forms of organisation as well as private sector solutions to public policy questions, and after several years of casting around for ways to do so, from the Next Steps Report of 1988 onwards, the Conservatives promoted a radical order of change in the civil service (Fry 1995).

Against this dramatic and historically uncharacteristic background, the development and present organisation of the British civil service will be examined. There will be three main themes. One will be the preferred role for the state in contemporary society, which acts as a determinant of the functions of the civil service. Another theme will be the place of the civil service in the British constitution, being non-political in the party sense. A third main theme will be the career civil service as such.

THE DEVELOPMENT OF THE CIVIL SERVICE SYSTEM

Administrative change commonly tends to be slow and especially so, it may be broadly assumed, in countries which are characterised by political stability as is the case with Britain, like England before it. The scale of recent changes in Britain, though, invites consideration of the earlier development of the machinery of government and of the civil service, not least interpretations of it, such as those by Geoffrey Elton and others who have followed his example, which have detected 'revolutionary' periods of change at various times.

There had been three administrative revolutions in English history, according to Elton. The Anglo-Norman creation of a centralised feudal state governed by the king in his household was one such revolution. The second was the Tudor administrative revolution of the 1530s, which Elton himself wrote about at length, and which some of his critics believed Elton invented. Elton believed that a revolution took place when an administration relying on the household was replaced by one based exclusively on bureaucratic departments and officers of state. The principle then adopted was not in turn discarded until what Elton called 'the much greater administrative revolution of the nineteenth century, which not only destroyed survivals of the medieval system allowed to continue a meaningless existence for some three hundred years, but also created an administration based on departments responsible to parliament in which the Crown for the first time ceased to hold the ultimate control.' Elton stated that 'medieval government was government by the king in person and through his immediate entourage.' Early modern government was independent of the household, bureaucratically organised in national departments, but responsible to the Crown.

In present day government, the bureaucratic departments have ceased to be responsible to the Crown and have instead become responsible to the House of Commons. Elton emphasised that these changes were reflected in the civil service, 'The medieval household system was served by men recruited from church and household; the middle period used clients of ministers, trained in their service and promoted by and through them; this second method of supply lasted until it was replaced by the modern civil service with its examinations.' (Elton 1953).

The Elton interpretation dealt with what might be called the development of the civil service within the constitution and in relation to it, and only indirectly with the changing role of the state itself for the performance of which, of course, the efficiency of the machinery of administration was crucial. The Tudor state, for instance, recognised a range of responsibilities in the economy and in social provision, but whether it had the means to translate intention into consistent action may be doubted. Indeed, the supposed Mercantilist state of the sixteenth, seventeenth, and eighteenth centuries which Adam Smith denounced in *The Wealth of Nations* for its pervasive regulation of the economy seems to have existed in his mind rather than in reality, since there was not the bureaucratic organisation to pursue such a coherent set of policies (Fry 1979). Smith's admirer, Edmund Burke, and Smith's fellow economic liberal, Jeremy Bentham led the way with the Economical Reform Movement of the 1780s, which began the rationalisation of the machinery of British central government, partly to assist parliament's control over public expenditure and to push the Crown to one side, and partly to regularise staffing, which, at the time, was based on patronage appointments and the use of contractors. The conditions of service of officials were gradually changed, so that salaries replaced fees, and there was provision for pensions.

By the mid-1850s, what had been a collection of largely separate offices had been brought at least into a working relationship with the Treasury, which, according to its then head, Sir Charles Trevelyan, meant that this department was 'the chief office of the government'. Of the Treasury, Trevelyan wrote, 'two-thirds of the civil establishments are directly subordinate to it, and the expenditure of the remaining third is under its superintendence. No estimate can be laid before parliament, no new appointment can be created, and no alteration can be made in any civil or military allowances, without its sanction. The whole public service is, therefore, either directly or indirectly subjected to the influence of this office' (Cohen 1941; Chester 1981). The presence of Trevelyan himself, as well as stars such as Sir Edwin Chadwick, Sir John Simon, and Sir Rowland Hill suggested that the unflattering picture of the unreformed civil service that Trevelyan and Sir Stafford Northcote presented in 1854 in their famous report on the organisation of the permanent civil service was an exaggerated one (Fry 1969).

For most of the nineteenth century, the prevailing ideology in Britain was the form of economic liberalism advocated by Adam Smith and his fellow classical economists, who favoured *laissez-faire* in principle, while not proposing that it should be universally practised. As their preferred role for the state was unambitious, it might be believed that, like the economy, the classical economists would wish to leave the civil service to its fate, aside, inevitably, from resentment at the waste of resources involved or thought to be. As a classical economist, Jeremy Bentham, followed by others, preached Utilitarianism, with the implication that if there had to be a civil service it must be an efficient one (Fry 1979). Ironically, a reformed civil service made it prospectively a more effective instrument of government, thus making greater recourse to statism practicable. The tendency, though, to write about 'the reforms of 1854' in relation the Northcote-Trevelyan Report (Bridges 1954) was misleading because the reform programme it advanced could not be said to have been fully implemented much before 1920, if indeed, in some respects, it ever was.

Northcote and Trevelyan wanted to see created a largely self-sufficient career civil service that would train its own administrators so that they could, on merit, hold the highest positions in the service, instead of, as at the time, having often to fill them from outside its ranks. They advocated a more unified service, with its work subjected to a more satisfactory division between intellectual and mechanical duties, with its direct entrants recruited by open competitive examinations, and not by patronage, and with promotion within the service being on the basis of merit in place of seniority. Though it was not their prime objective, Northcote and Trevelyan had designed a service that could be realistically seen as being politically anonymous, since civil servants received their initial appointments independently of ministers, and, indeed, the convention of ministerial responsibility was only universally accepted after the Northcote-Trevelyan reforms came to be slowly implemented (Fry 1969).

The establishment of the Civil Service Commission in 1855 to hold entry examinations marked the beginning of the reform process. At first, there were only limited competitions among nominees. The Superannuation Act of 1859 made it necessary for officials to hold a certificate from the commission in order to be eligible for a civil service pension. The civil service order in council of 1870 introduced open competitive entry examinations for those departments whose ministers agreed, which, at that stage, did not include the Home Office and the Foreign Office (Chester 1981). It was only in 1914, when the MacDonnell Royal Commission was reviewing the civil service, that all departments came into line, although in the case of the Foreign Office this was only partially so.

World War I, like World War II, opened up the service to other entrants, and after it, as after World War II, special arrangements for ex-Armed Forces recruitment displaced open competition for a time. The civil service never was composed solely of those recruited by open competition. Similarly, promotion by merit was an important principle to state, but no large organisation was going to entirely exclude seniority as a factor in advancement, especially in relation to the more routine jobs; and the division of labour between intellectual and mechanical work never really closely reflected the structure of the civil service.

The eventual development of the first division or administrative class, an elite of generalist administrators, would seem to correspond to the intellectual element although, of course, the civil service always employed lawyers and other specialists, latterly in large numbers. The rest of the civil service was not simply mechanical, and classified as, say, second division clerks. The structure was always more elaborate than this, and always included special departmental classes. After the World War I, the Treasury, together with the staff association representatives on the then recently created Whitley system of joint consultation, established the familiar administrative class – executive class – clerical class structure on the generalist side of the service, but there were always numerous departmental classes too.

After World War II, further official committees reorganised the various groups of specialists, and it was then, for example, that the scientific civil service was established. Though, as noted before, Treasury control of expenditure, and, because of that, control of the numbers employed, provided a form of centralisation, and the expansion of the state's role, notably in social provision, eroded some barriers, the overall structure of the civil service was markedly departmentalised until 1914. World War I eroded some more barriers and in 1919, the permanent secretary to the Treasury was made head of the civil service, with powers relating to promotions at the very highest levels across the range of departments, including the staff of the Foreign Office.

The behaviour of Sir Warren Fisher as head of the civil service between the wars proved controversial, and, although the powers were retained by his successors at the head of the Treasury until 1968 as regards the leading posts in the home civil service, the Eden and Bevin reforms of 1943–45 made the Foreign Service, later Diplomatic Service, a separate entity. The period between 1919 and 1943 was thus the only period when Britain could be said to have had a unified civil service (Fry 1969).

Northcote and Trevelyan had designed a career civil service to serve a regulatory state of the kind tolerated by the classical economists. T.H. Green turned liberalism in the direction of a purposive role for the state in social provision, as did Alfred Marshall in his writings as one of the neo-classical economists. The civil service proved well able to implement the Liberal social reforms of the Campbell-Bannerman and Asquith governments of 1905–15 and, indeed, the introduction of national health insurance, in particular, had demonstrated the service's adaptability. The economic and social order thus created, the social service state, under which economic liberalism still prevailed, was superseded by the Keynesian welfare state during World War II and immediately afterwards, and the career civil service had a part not only in the transition, but also, of course, in running the new arrangements.

For all the praise heaped upon the civil service by Attlee, it remained the case that public corporations were created to run the nationalised industries with separate staff of their own. The government department model was not trusted. The functions of many departments had moved a long way from being little more than expanded offices of ministers, and many officials were involved in a range of functions that seemed not only too wide for traditional political control to be applied, but also in some areas of public policy too ambitious in scope. The Treasury, together with its conventional roles, had responsibility for macro-economic management, which under the Keynesian dispensation, had the objectives of increasing real incomes, the attainment of price stability, the maintenance of full employment, and the continual expansion of the social services, all of them to be realised perennially (Fry 1979).

Not surprisingly, the Treasury 'failed', and opprobrium was heaped upon it by critics. What was said to be needed was a reformed civil service, and the Fulton Committee was set up to construct one. The Fulton Report of 1968 made three main proposals. The first was that a unified grading structure should be established from top to bottom of the home civil service. Unified grading was only introduced for the highest posts in the service. Elsewhere, classes were abolished or merged (which was the fate of the Administrative – Executive – Clerical structure) and called groups. This was simply a change in nomenclature. The second main proposal in the Fulton Report was that a civil service college should be established. This was done by expanding and re-naming an existing training centre. The third main proposal was that the role of central management of the home civil service should be given to a civil service department and thus removed from the Treasury. This was done.

The staff doing the work remained much the same, and the Treasury retained control of the relevant public expenditure. So, there was duplication (Fulton Report 1968; Fry 1993). The role which the Treasury performed that needed to be changed was, of course, that of Keynesian economic management, and the economic crisis of 1976 brought this about, leading to the election in 1979 of the Thatcher Conservative government with an economic liberal programme.

Inevitably in only the broadest terms, the Raadschelders and Rutgers model holds for the British civil service up to 1979, but less so after that as the Thatcher governments strove to change the service and, from 1988, to change it in a radical direction. Those governments set about cutting the number of officials, initially freezing recruitment, and 'de-privileging' the service, most notably by refusing to continue with the service's system of pay determination. The heavily unionised service fought back with a long strike in 1981, and once Mrs Thatcher had won, the Civil Service Department was abolished, with its functions being divided between the Cabinet Office and the Treasury. The Conservative government did not seem to know what to do with their victory, although, from 1982 onwards, the Financial Management Initiative was used to introduce private sector management practices into a career civil service that remained essentially much the same (Fry 1985).

The Next Steps Report of 1988 provided a radical answer. An adapted form of the Swedish central government arrangements was proposed which would lead to the establishment of small policy ministries, with the remaining functions allocated to separate agencies, and with, prospectively, the career civil service being limited to a central core (Next Steps Report 1988). As far as the setting up of agencies was concerned, the Next Steps programme was implemented at a great pace by the Thatcher government and its Conservative successors. As for the civil service itself, those governments wanted it to be much smaller and to be more like the private sector whenever practicable, and for its work to be assigned to that sector whenever possible, a policy of privatisation that the Conservative governments pursued with vigour (Fry 1995).

THE INTERNAL LABOUR MARKET

The classic definition of what constitutes the British civil service is that provided by the Tomlin Royal Commission of 1929–31 which stated that it comprised 'servants of the Crown, other than holders of political or judicial offices, who are employed in a civil capacity and whose remuneration is paid wholly and directly out of moneys voted by parliament' (Tomlin Report 1931). A less clumsy definition is that of the present writer which states that 'the civil service is that body of men and women who work directly for ministers held to account in parliament' (Fry 1985).

On 1 April 1995, there were 516 893 permanent civil servants of whom 474 876 were non-industrial staff, and 42 017 were industrial staff. In addition, there were 18 244 casual staff. The distinction between non-industrial and industrial civil servants, in general terms, is the same which exists in the private sector between white and blue collar workers. The largest employer of industrial staff is the Ministry of Defence, which employs about 87 per cent of the total. Civil servants constitute about 2 per cent of the working population in employment, and about 10 per cent of all public sector employees. There are many community services such as health, education, local government, personal social services, defence, and policing which are largely provided by other public servants, though civil servants are often involved in the formulation of policy for such services.

Many civil servants are engaged in providing services to the public such as staffing job centres, paying pensions and benefits, issuing driving licences, among other roles. Others provide policy advice, including economic and statistical advice, and internal departmental services and service-wide support functions. Increasingly, the operational functions are being undertaken by semi-autonomous Next Steps executive agencies within the civil service, while some self-contained support functions, formerly undertaken in-house, are now purchased from the private sector (Office of Public Service 1995). Unless otherwise stated, all references to the civil service in subsequent discussion will be to the home civil service and its dominant non-industrial element.

When the Fulton Committee proposed a unified grading structure from the top to the bottom of the home civil service, it was seeking to impose an even more centralised structure than already existed. There had always been departmental classes, and the main body of officials at the Board of Inland Revenue and the Board of Customs and Excise, for example, were always organised on a separate basis. Otherwise, on the generalist side of the service, all related to the famous administrative – executive – clerical classes structure, which was treated as the core. Indeed, in the inter-war period, they were referred to as the Treasury Classes. The salary scales were standardised for the various grades in the hierarchy, and it was a straightforward matter to multiply the numbers by the pay rates and thus to compute the cost of the service, especially as there were only 163 000 civil servants even in 1939. With the exception of the lawyers, members of the various groups of specialists tended to have inferior salaries and prospects compared with their generalist colleagues. That the rationalisation of the generalist classes took place after World War I, but that of the specialist groups was delayed until after World War II was indicative of their relative status within the civil service, as well as, of course, the increased range and complexity of the work of the service (Fry 1969).

The higher civil service of the inter-war period, meaning that of the assistant secretary grade and above and their equivalents, had very largely comprised generalist administrators, together with some specialists, mainly lawyers. By the time that the Priestley Royal Commission of 1953–55 reviewed the service, the proportion of generalist administrators at assistant secretary and above and their equivalents was about one-third, though they still dominated the very highest posts, promotions to which were still decided by the head of the civil service (from 1956, head of the home civil service), if in a more formalised manner than under Fisher. The Priestley Commission also found a civil service in which there continued to be opportunities for promotion between classes and also within them, on the basis in the latter instance particularly of qualifying for a promotion field decided by seniority.

Once a brief probationary period had been served, established civil servants, though not the minority with unestablished or temporary status, had a job for life, if they so wished, rewarded at the end of their careers with a non-contributory pension. Although security of tenure on this scale was absent from the private sector, the Priestley Report of 1955 granted the civil service the right to pay scales based on 'fair comparisons' with salary levels in that sector on the basis of investigation conducted by the service itself (Priestley Report 1955). The government was excluded from the operation of the Priestley machinery until its findings were known, and since the size of the service had more or less tripled since 1939, ministers were often unable to meet the costs, thus frustrating expectations on the part of the civil servants and promoting discontent in the service's heavily unionised ranks (Fry 1974).

The Fulton Committee unthinkingly endorsed the Priestley 'fair comparison' formula and its envisaged unified grading arrangements were meant to be a universalised pay system cutting across a structure based on occupational groups which was to replace the class system. The latter change seemed to have only emotional value, but it was made once that particular recommendation had been approved by the machinery of the Whitley system of joint consultation, which was the same committee that ruled out across-the-board unified grading. Only the highest grades were placed in the open structure and, in the case of the generalists, the remainder of the administrative–executive–clerical structure formed the administration group. On a similar basis, a science group was formed, and a professional and technology group, among other mergers. If there was a serious rationale behind the Fulton Committee's proposals, it had been to depose the administrative class, and thus to change the dominant culture of the higher civil service from that of the generalist administrator to that of the technocrat. One way to have done this would have been to make the civil service college into an Anglicised version of the Parisian *ENA.*, but the service's staff associations, soon to be unions, wanted egalitarianism not elitism, as, indeed, inconsistently, so had the Fulton Committee with its emphasis on promotion from below.

About 90 per cent of the post-entry training given by the service was provided at departmental level. As for direct entry recruitment, except for the leading administrative, executive, and specialist posts, which remained the remit of the Civil Service Commission, this had also become primarily a departmental responsibility. In terms of status, the Fulton Committee removed the distinction between established and unestablished civil servants, thus enabling all civil servants to have rights in relation the non-contributory pension scheme. Legislation in 1972 granted index linked pensions to the civil service, meaning that they were inflation proof (Fry 1985).

The home civil service that the Thatcher government inherited in 1979 had many of the characteristics of being a pay and promotion system with the needs of the work seeming at times to be treated as a subordinate consideration. For many years, the government had no coherent strategy for change, beyond that provided by hostility. The relevant official inquiry frustrated the government's attempt to remove the right to index-linked pensions from the service, but, after crushing opposition from the unions, the government did replace the Priestley pay arrangements, substituting for it a more market based system along the lines recommended by the Megaw Committee in 1982. Though a small measure of performance pay was introduced, the post-Megaw system was essentially an-across-the board one. This meant that the terms and conditions of civil servants, and, hence, the costs of employing them, remained largely standardised, thus rendering the Financial Management Initiative of 1982, designed the introduce managerialism on the private sector model, with cost centres and so on, ineffectual.

Further, the government extended unified grading, so that by 1986 it embraced not just

- Grade 1 (permanent secretary),
- Grade 1A (second permanent secretary),
- Grade 2 (deputy secretary), and
- Grade 3 (under secretary), but also
- Grade 4 (executive directing bands),
- Grade 5 (assistant secretary),
- Grade 6 (senior principal), and
- Grade 7 (principal)

and, of course, their corresponding professional and scientific grades, forming the open structure. At the other end of the service, it was decided to rename the clerical officer and clerical assistant grades and to call them administrative officer and administrative assistant respectively. Except to confuse future historians of the British civil service there was no useful purpose served by this change, which was accompanied by yet another across-the-board pay settlement. Pay 'spine' arrangements, with which performance pay was integrated, and which marginally departed from traditional salary hierarchies, were introduced for scientists and professionals in 1987 and elsewhere afterwards. None of this, though, added up to the radical change that Mrs Thatcher was looking for (Fry 1995).

This would also have been the case with the Next Steps Programme launched in 1988, if it had not led to more than the separating out of policy ministries from executive agencies. As it was, when the government announced in 1994 that it was creating a senior civil service comprising staff at grade 5 level and above, and obviously to be based in the policy ministries (White Paper 1994), radical critics argued that the top of the civil service had escaped real change, although, in fact, the Treasury, the heartland of the civil service, was made a particular target for staff cuts, and the proposed pay improvements were compensation for the removal of security of tenure. The Fast Stream form of direct entry of generalist administrators straight from university, the present-day successor to the examination system begun in 1870, still persisted, even though the Civil Service Commission itself was actually broken up into agencies in 1991 – the office of the Civil Service Commissioners, and the recruitment and assessment services agency (Fry 1995), the latter body being privatised in 1996, a possible fate for all agencies. No less than 67 per cent of civil servants had been placed in executive agencies. The majority of chief executives of such agencies were placed on fixed-term contracts, and no less than 33 of the first 113 such executives had been recruited from outside the civil service. A framework document was published for each agency, setting out its aims and objectives, relationship with ministers and parliament, and the regime under which it was to work. Corporate and business plans were to be made. Performance targets for the agencies were published, and each agency published an annual report and accounts relating to these targets (Office of Public Service 1995). More importantly, with effect from April 1996, all departments and agencies were given delegated powers to decide the pay and grading of all civil servants below the senior civil service. As the main body of the civil service also had its work subject to market testing with the possibility of it being transferred to the private sector, most civil servants had experienced radical change since 1988.

REPRESENTATIVENESS

From 1870 onwards, if only in broad terms, open competition had been the main principle upon which direct entry recruitment to the civil service was conducted, and until the 1950s, for most of that service this meant success had to be obtained in examinations held by the Civil Service Commission at the centre, and also at interviews. This was certainly the case with the famous administrative–executive–clerical structure, until the attainment of particular educational qualifications entitled candidates to compete in the latter two categories, with appointments dependent on success in interviews.

The administrative entry eventually became that of the Fast Stream, essentially being a method of recruiting a small number of generalist administrators by means of centrally conducted tests and interviews, with the successful more or less being guaranteed a direct route to the higher posts. There always has been promotion from below, and transfers across from the specialist groups, in both cases, in principle, on the basis of merit. So, neither the senior civil service, as it is now called, nor its predecessors, ever did solely consist of the equivalent of the Fast Stream, but, of course, those recruited on the fast track naturally attracted most attention.

Once reformed, and once governments became involved in social engineering, the civil service was used at times as an example to the rest of society. Thus, from 1919 onwards, the civil service became one of the few organisations to adopt the Whitley system of joint consultation, which provided it with a form of representativeness, in the narrow sense that the staff associations, later unions, were involved in the service's management. This involvement still left the associations, later unions, free to complain, depending on whom they were representing, that there were, for example, too few scientists, or engineers, or former middle rank executives, or clerks at or near the top of the service, and some outside critics were sympathetic.

After both world wars, entry to the service was dominated by former members of the armed forces, for whom special competitions were held. After World War I, the conventional forms of open competition were only reintroduced for the administrative class in 1925, and only introduced for the executive class in 1928 and the clerical class in 1927. After World War II, normal competitions resumed in 1948. In 1922, a special competition for women was held which led to three of them entering the administrative class. In future, women were able to compete for posts on the same basis as men, although not in the case of the Foreign Office and Diplomatic Service until 1946 (Reader 1981). For many years afterwards, it was only the exceptional writer (for example Kelsall 1955) who was concerned about low representation of women in senior posts.

The British obsession with social class dominated discussion of representativeness until recently. The classic study of the inter-war higher civil service showed that the Diplomatic Service was overwhelmingly elitist in terms of social origins, private schooling, and Oxford and Cambridge higher education, and the higher civil service was much the same except that the leading officials were more likely to be drawn from the upper middle class than the upper class (Dale 1941). Open competitive examinations only lead to careers to be open to talent if the competitors were relatively socially privileged to start with, and there were also those who believed that the addition of an interview to the examination after World War I added another social filtering process, which was certainly the case with the Diplomatic Service until the Eden–Bevin reforms of the 1940s (Kelsall 1955).

The system of university scholarships that followed the Education Act of 1944 eventually did open up more opportunities for those with lower middle class and working class origins, although, as critics pointed out, there remained plenty of scope for social prejudice in the extended interview system of recruitment from 1948 onwards, alongside the traditional examination system until 1969 and then as the sole means of direct entry recruitment of generalist administrators. The Fabian socialist critics of the civil service seemed to want it to be socially democratic in composition, but the civil service commissioners, and the departments and agencies when most recruitment passed to them, had to select people on the basis of those made available by the existing educational system, not an idealised one.

Both major studies of British permanent secretaries (Theakston and Fry 1989; Barberis 1996) recognised the persistence of social elitism, but in the former case suggested that, whatever administrators' origins, the actual working environment tended to encourage conformities. There always was promotion from below in the civil service, which made the attention given to direct entry recruitment disproportionate, and there always were those whose careers took them from at or near the bottom of the service to at or near the top, or actually the top in the case of Sir Horace Wilson, the head of the civil service between 1939 and 1942, although, inevitably, in general, the higher level of entrant tended to progress relatively faster than others.

The issue of social class has become less important in discussion of the civil service, possibly because of changes in the structure of the labour force, and also because the disadvantages of the residual working class seem to have become even more dispiriting than before. Whatever the reasons, other groups have come to attract more attention under the heading of equal opportunities. In support of this, three programmes of action were introduced: for women (introduced in 1992), for people of ethnic minority origin (1990), and for disabled people (1994). There is regular monitoring. This showed that in 1995 the number of registered disabled people in the service represented 1.6 per cent of those employed, which compared well with other employers. The number of civil servants of ethnic minority origin represented 5.4 per cent of those employed, which compared with a benchmark figure of 4.8 per cent for the economically active population. They are well represented in the junior grade levels, with lower but slowly increasing representation at more senior levels. Women represent 51 per cent of the total number of civil servants, about 69 per cent of employees at the most junior levels, and 9 per cent of staff in the top four grades of the service. The pattern of a lower representation of women at senior levels is changing, with, for example, 21 per cent of staff at grade 7 level in 1995 compared with 8 per cent in 1985 (Office of Public Service).

POLITICISATION

Britain has a long tradition of a career civil service, with political appointments being made only to a small number of specific and normally temporary posts, and that practice has only been widespread since 1964, when the incoming Labour government of Harold Wilson created several posts for political advisers, apparently because of a belief that the leading permanent officials would otherwise frustrate the Labour Party's plans. Since then, Conservative as well as Labour governments have used political advisers as well as career civil servants in policymaking, but the latter are more numerous and predominate. Britain does not have changes of political regime, because in modern times it has always been a constitutional monarchy with a system of representative government. So, the most that normally happens is that the Labour Party defeats the Conservative Party, or vice versa, at a general election and inherits the same civil service as its predecessor worked with, bringing in a small number of people of its own. Thus, the British civil service is a classical Weberian one in the sense that the presumption would be that it would faithfully carry out the preferred policies of the government of the day irrespective of that government's political complexion.

It is also a civil service which would have an independence based on the continuity that resulted from a career commitment on the part of the overwhelming majority of civil servants. Though the highest ranking civil servants are precluded from participating in national party politics, this is not the case with the broad mass of the service. Those of whatever rank who were elected to parliament would be expected to leave the service with no right to return. The divide between party politicians and the career service is a clear one. It is a fact that the three prime ministers before Mrs Thatcher had all been civil servants in earlier career. Harold Wilson had been a wartime civil servant. Edward Heath had been a civil servant briefly in the immediate post-war period. Both Wilson and Heath resigned upon entering party politics. James Callaghan, who had been an inland revenue clerk, had moved into staff association work long before going into politics. These men may well have belonged to an exceptional generation. No twentieth century prime minister before Wilson had a civil service background, and indeed, the professionalisation of politics in Britain has come to increasingly mean that ministers have as little experience of outside worlds as many of their civil service advisers.

The notion advanced by some commentators, and some civil servants, and the latter's unions, that Mrs Thatcher undermined the non-political nature of the civil service had no substance to it. Essentially, the civil service had benefited in terms of numbers, career prospects, and rewards from the expansive bureaucratic structure associated with the Keynesian Welfare State, and, hence, its self-interest was bound up with that economic and social order. As an economic liberal, Mrs Thatcher was committed to a different form of economic policy and to attempting to rationalise the welfare state.

The imposition of political will on the part of an elected government could hardly be said to represent politicisation of the civil service, because, to the extent that the vested interest of the service was tied up with a particular economic and social dispensation, it was politicised already, although this allegiance was not necessarily party political, since all parties had been previously committed to that order. The allegation that Mrs Thatcher abused her powers as prime minister by promoting the senior civil servants who were her favourites or ideological allies had no foundation. All prime ministers since 1920 had the powers to make such senior appointments on the advice of the head of the civil service. Most had left it to Sir Warren Fisher and his successors to make these advancements. Mrs Thatcher intervened more than her predecessors not to promote economic liberals, who were anyway unlikely to be numerous in a Keynesian dominated generation serving in a career public bureaucracy, but to try to change the culture among the higher reaches of the civil service in the direction of a more purposive approach to public policy, and it was those she detected as having such qualities that she tended to choose from among the candidates presented to her (Fry 1995).

PUBLIC OPINION

> In the popular conception, the typical civil servant is a tea drinking file passing incompetent, with more respect for precedent than for human problems. He wears pin striped trousers and a black jacket, and is pedantic and inhuman in ordinary intercourse; indeed he prefers to deal with the rest of humanity by letter, or at best by telephone. His short term thoughts are on the clock and his expenses sheet, while his long term concerns are his pension and his annual leave. So wrote a former senior civil servant in 1961, having also observed that when the British civil service was praised for being 'second to none', this was 'usually the prelude to a sermon on some fresh bureaucratic iniquity' (Walker 1961).

The British career civil service has been heavily praised by prime ministers and by other ministers often retrospectively, and also by other commentators, but it has never experienced a shortage of critics. The advocates of extensive state activity such as the Fabian socialists plainly need a large-scale civil service to do the work, but most of their writings have emphasised the service's supposed failings and the need for improvements. The economic liberals have the virtue of consistency, if little more than this, in preferring the private sector to run things, asserting that banks and insurance companies, for instance, are more efficient than the civil service. To the extent that a popular view can be identified, the hostility to the civil service of the kind that economic liberalism promotes would seem to be representative, with the public wanting the services that the state provides while being resentful of paying the necessary taxation. The politically informed may well be aware of the high quality of the senior civil service, but the ordinary voters more usually come into contact with the clerks and at times of, say, unemployment or sickness, and such experiences may provide one reason for such popular antipathy as exists towards a civil service that still seems remarkably efficient.

CONCLUDING REMARKS

Change in the British civil service has tended to be insular in style during its history, primarily because until relatively recently Britain was a great power and thought in terms of leading by example, not least in the case of what was then her Commonwealth and empire. Britain's position in the world has been changed considerably in the last forty years or so, not merely by the loss of empire, and membership of what is now called the European Union, but mainly because of relative economic decline, which was only arrested by the Thatcher governments. During the period of the Keynesian welfare state there was interest in the French technocratic tradition, but this waned with the change to a less ambitious economic and social order, and there has been little interest in emulating what tends to be seen as the ponderous bureaucracy of the European Commission. For no obvious reason, interest in Swedish central government organisation survived. It does seem that in the British debate about civil service reform, foreign examples tend to be used to justify already held positions. It would be familiar for the domestic debate about the civil service taking place outside its ranks to be led by adherents of the Fabian socialist tradition on one side of the political divide, and those of the economic liberal tradition on the other. In the past, the civil service itself generated its own reforms, and often decided which external proposals for change should be adopted. The Thatcher governments and their Conservative successors imposed change on the civil service in a manner without peacetime precedent.

In examining civil service reform, it seems best to distinguish between what is currently called the senior civil service and the broad mass of the service. At senior civil service level, Britain can be said to have historically observed a governance tradition. The leading civil servants have been involved in policymaking, and submitting material to ministers for presentation to parliament, and their training has been largely one of experience in dealing with these kinds of work in a particular political setting. In other words, the leading civil servants have been a type of permanent politician.

The Thatcher governments wanted to change the ethos of the senior civil service and to make it more managerialist in style. Attempts to introduce a more managerial outlook into the service dated back to the Plowden Report on the Control of Public Expenditure of 1961, but the senior civil service did not seem to take much notice, partly because this change of role was uncongenial and also because a succession of inept governments, both Conservative and Labour, seemed heavily dependent upon the leading civil servants for policy advice. The Thatcher governments had no need of such advice, knowing what their political direction was to be, and they treated what is now to be called the senior civil service as an adversary, and the running costs of the civil service as a whole seemed to be perceived as an area that should be, first, quantified, and, secondly, reduced. Savings also followed from a programme of cuts in numbers of staff, and through the mechanism of the Financial Management Initiative, the creation of cost centres as a means of allocating financial responsibility and of emphasising the need to contain spending.

As has been said before, the crucial breakthrough was the Next Steps Report of 1988, which not only divided up government departments by hiving off their main managerial activities to agencies, but also emphasised the dividing up of the civil service itself with the result that there was less uniformity in conditions of service and security of tenure, thus furthering managerial discretion and control. A form of New Public Management thus emerged. The *Competing for Quality* White Paper of 1991 also promoted efforts to transfer more civil service work to the private sector, following exercises on comparative costs known as market testing. Some of the devolved agencies have been privatised, much as arsenals and dockyards were earlier. The order of change has been such that to call it reform may underestimate its scale and importance (Fry 1995).

When the present writer's book, *Statesmen in Disguise* was published in 1969, it contained a history of the British civil service, and particularly of the then leading class within it, and related that history to the changing role of the state over the previous century and more. In the context of the Keynesian welfare state, it seemed evident that the civil service was in need of radical reform, and that the Fulton Report of 1968 did not provide the relevant programme (Fry 1969). The Fulton proposals were largely implemented, but, except in terms of formal classification, they essentially left the career civil service intact (Fry 1981). The collapse of the Keynesian element within the existing economic and social order was bound to lead to questioning about what the role of the state should be (Fry 1979), and hence, about the role of the civil service too.

Embracing economic liberalism, the Thatcher governments wished to reduce the scale of state activity, and not merely to cut the size of the civil service but also to change its culture so that it more closely resembled that of private sector management. The scale of change that followed was radical by, say, Fulton standards, but the career civil service survived the first part of the

Thatcher era broadly intact (Fry 1985). This could not be said for the period after the Next Steps Report of 1988. For its implementation led not only to radical change in the structure of government departments as a consequence of agentification, but also in the civil service itself, which has come to have 3000 recruitment points, pay and grading devolved from the centre for most officials, and the differentiation of tenure arrangements to the detriment of the career concept. In addition, privatisation initiatives have made inroads into what was or had become traditional civil service work. While, in the long run, it could not be ruled out that these changes might be reversed or undermined, at the time of the Civil Service White Paper of 1994, it did seem that the broad mass of the civil service had experienced change of an order that it was not an exaggeration to describe as revolutionary, even if, critics believed, what was now called the Senior civil service had survived relatively intact, an interpretation that experience might or might not validate (Fry 1995).

In a country like Britain there is always the temptation to regard developments in the civil service as self-generated, and this was especially the case in those recent years in which Margaret Thatcher was prime minister, providing dynamic political leadership where, previously, there was more usually soporific 'moderation', and appearing to be guided by an ideology – economic liberalism – instead of the more common pragmatism. The consistency in the behaviour of the Thatcher governments tended to be exaggerated by friend and foe alike. Neither those governments nor their Conservative successors, for example, achieved their objective of radically reducing, in real terms, the scale of public expenditure, and, hence, taxation.

Establishing New Public Management in the civil service may or may not be of value in promoting efficiency in that service, but it could only be a secondary objective. The civil service was not the reason why the British economy had been in relative decline for a hundred years, if not more, and changing its arrangements did not explain why that decline was arrested during the Thatcher era. Nevertheless, for the civil service itself, the changes were important, even, since 1988, dramatic, and changes undermining of unity. Two reflections follow from this activity, the first of which is that if, in their promotion, bureaucracy was the perceived enemy, closer involvement with the European Union, and, hence, the European Commission only served to sustain its influence. The other is that as the recent changes in the organisation of British central government departments owe something to the example provided by the Swedish system, plainly comparative study of different civil service systems is more than an intellectual exercise.

BIBLIOGRAPHY

Attlee, C.R. (1954), 'Civil servants, ministers, parliament and the public', *Political Quarterly,* (October–December): 308–15.

Barberis, P. (1996), *The Elite of the Elite: Permanent Secretaries in the British Higher Civil Service,* Aldershot: Dartmouth.

Bridges, Sir E.E. (1954), 'The reforms of 1854 in retrospect', *Political Quarterly,* (October–December): 316–23.

Chester, Sir D.N. (1981), *The English Administrative System 1780–1870,* Oxford: Clarendon Press.

Cohen, E.W. (1941), *The Growth of the British Civil Service 1780–1939,* London: Allen & Unwin.

Dale, H.E. (1941), *The Higher Civil Service of Great Britain,* London: Oxford University Press.

East, R. (ed.) (1996), *Keesing's Record of World Events 1996,* Cambridge: Catermill.

Elton, G.R. (1953), *The Tudor Revolution in Government: Administrative Changes in the Reign of Henry VIII,* Cambridge: Cambridge University Press.

Fry, G.K. (1969), *Statesmen in Disguise: The Changing Role of the Administrative Class of the British Home Civil Service 1853–1966,* London: Macmillan.

Fry, G.K. (1970), 'The Sachsenhausen concentration camp case and the convention of ministerial responsibility', *Public Law,* (Winter): 336–57.

Fry, G.K. (1974), 'civil service salaries in the post–Priestley era 1956–1972', *Public Administration,* (Autumn): 319–33.

Fry, G.K. (1979), *The Growth of Government: The Development of Ideas about the Role of the State and the Machinery and Functions of Government in Britain since 1780,* London: Cass.

Fry, G.K. (1981), *The Administrative 'Revolution' in Whitehall: A Study of the Politics of Administrative Change in British Central Government since the 1950s,* London: Croom Helm.

Fry, G.K. (1985), *The Changing Civil Service,* London: Allen & Unwin.

Fry, G.K. (1993), *Reforming The Civil Service: The Fulton Committee on the British Home Civil Service 1966–1968,* Edinburgh: Edinburgh University Press.

Fry, G.K. (1995), *Policy and Management in the British Civil Service,* Hemel Hempstead: Prentice Hall/ Harvester Wheatsheaf.

Fulton Report (1968), *The Civil Service: The Report of the Committee 1966–1968, Cmd. 3638,* London: HMSO.

Griffith, L.W. (1954), *The British Civil Service 1854–1954,* London: HMSO.

Kelsall, R.K. (1955), *Higher Civil Servants in Britain: From 1870 to the Present Day,* London: Routledge & Kegan Paul.

Laski, H.J. (1933), *Democracy in Crisis,* London: Allen & Unwin.

Laski, H.J. (1938), *Parliamentary Government in England,* London: Allen & Unwin.

Laski, H.J. (1951), *Reflections on the Constitution,* Manchester: Manchester University Press.

Next Steps Report (1988), *Improving Management in Government: The Next Steps,* London: HMSO.

Nicolson, I.F. (1986), *The Mystery of Crichel Down,* Oxford: Oxford University Press.

Office of Public Service (1995), *Civil Service Statistics 1995,* London: HMSO.

Plowden Report (1961), *Control of Public Expenditure, Cmd. 1432,* London: HMSO.

Priestley Report (1955), *Report of the Royal Commission on the Civil Service 1953–1955, Cmnd. 9613,* London: HMSO.

Reader, K.M. (1981), 'The Civil Service Commission 1855–1975', in *Civil Service Studies 5,* London: Civil Service Department.

Robson, W.A. (1954), 'The Civil service and its critics', *Political Quarterly,* (October–December): 299–307.

Sisson, C.H. (1959), *The Spirit of British Administration*, London: Faber & Faber.

Thatcher, M. (1993), *The Downing Street Years*, London: Harper-Collins.

Theakston, K., and G.K. Fry (1989), 'Britain's administrative elite: permanent secretaries 1900–86', *Public Administration,* (Summer): 129–47.

Tomlin Report (1931), *Report of the Royal Commission on the Civil Service 1929–1931, Cmd. 3909,* London: HMSO.

Walker, N. (1961), *Morale in the Civil Service*, Edinburgh: Edinburgh University Press.

Wheare, K.C. (1954), *The Civil Service in the Constitution*, London: Athlone Press.

White Paper (1994), *The Civil Service: Continuity and Change, Cmd. 2627*, London: HMSO.

APPENDIX 2A.1

Table 2A.1 The size of the British national civil service

Non-industrial civil service	474 876
Industrial civil service	42 017
Total	516 893

Note: These figures emanate from material in Office of Public Service 1995. They refer to the numbers in the civil service as at 1 April 1995.

Table 2A.2 The development of the size of the national civil service

1902	50 000
1910	55 000
1920	161 000
1930	111 000
1939	163 000
1950	433 000
1960	380 000
1970	493 000
1980	547 000
1990	495 000
1995	458 000

Note: These statistics, which relate to the non-industrial civil service only, were sent to the author by the Office of Public Service. The figures for 1900 and for 1940 are not available.

Table 2A.3 Entry level salaries for civil service positions (expressed in US$)

Grade 7 (Principal and corresponding scientific and professional grades, the lowest rank in the open structure)	$ 37 066
Scientific officer	$ 25 161
Technology officer	$ 25 161
Executive officer	$ 16 812
Administrative officer (i.e. clerk)	$ 13 167
Typist	$ 10 871

Note: These figures emanate from material in Office of Public Service 1995. They relate only to national salary scales in the non-industrial civil service in departments which do not have delegated pay arrangements.

Table 2A.4 Representativeness of the national civil service

Grade level	Women Numbers	%	Ethnic minorities Numbers	%
1	2	5.3	Nil	nil
2	10	8.1	Nil	nil
3	46	9.8	1	0.2
4	28	7.2	Nil	nil
5	388	13.2	55	2.2
6	672	12.7	114	2.6
7	3 237	17.8	318	2.0
SEO	3 369	13.9	383	1.8
HEO	17 357	21.6	1 530	2.4
EO	56 298	45.9	4 105	3.9
AO	119 267	69.0	10 458	7.1
AA	65 130	71.5	5 576	7.4
Other	591		7	
Total	266 395	51.1	22 547	5.2

Source: author.

3.   The Irish Civil Service System

Michelle Millar and David McKevitt

INTRODUCTION

This chapter deals with the civil service system in the Irish Republic. As a country which received its independence from Britain in 1922, the Irish civil service is modelled on the Westminster–Whitehall model of government.

The island of Ireland lies off the north-west coast of the continent of Europe. According to the 1996 census, the population of the Republic of Ireland is 3.62 million. Ireland's location and proximity to her nearest neighbour, Britain, have to a large extent shaped Irish history in the last 800 years. As an island to the west of continental Europe, Ireland – which has been inhabited for about 7000 years – has experienced a number of incursions and invasions. Independence from Britain was achieved in 1922, and the constitution of 1937 (*Bunreacht na hEireann*) and the Republic of Ireland Act 1948, severed Ireland's last formal links with Britain.

Ireland is a parliamentary democracy. Its law is based on common law and legislation enacted by the parliament under the constitution. Since Ireland's accession to the European Community in 1973, regulations of the European Union also have the force of law in Ireland. The president is elected every seven years by the people as the head of state. The parliamentary system is bicameral, the Houses of the Oireachtas are respectively known as Dail Eireann (House of Representatives) whose members are directly elected and the Seanad (Senate) where a mix of vocational and list system and political nominations are used. Executive power is exercised by or on the authority of the government which is accountable to the Dail. The head of the government is the Taoiseach.

THE DEVELOPMENT OF THE CIVIL SERVICE SYSTEM

The seventeenth century was a watershed in Irish history and it marked the beginning of a pre-modern administration which was founded on the English colonisation of Ireland. Historically, and in keeping with other European countries in the late feudal period, Ireland was ruled by local dynasties whose remit was restricted to specific geographic areas of the country. The Irish code of law – Brehon Law – was part of the native administrative framework covering land, personal rights and inheritance. The system of administration was centred on the household of Irish dynasties and there was no national or indeed regional system of administration, except for the English administrative complex centred in Dublin.

The flight of Ulster aristocracy in 1609 to Europe, following on the defeat of the native Irish at the Battle of Kinsale in 1603, presaged the beginning of the decline of the old gaelic order. The Irish Rebellion of 1640, the plantation of Ulster in the early 1600s and the Cromwellian conquest of the late 1640s and 1650s signalled the final subjugation of the Gaelic administrative tradition. While the administrative – as opposed to military influence – remit of the English did not have a nationwide coverage, the settlement by English and Scottish settlers did help build the legal and administrative complex of English jurisdiction.

During the eighteenth century, the Lord Lieutenant as the representative of the British Crown in Ireland was the head of the national administration. He was assisted by the chief secretary, whose small bureau contained three important components of the public administration; civil, military and yeomanry. By the end of that century there were twenty-two departments in Ireland, the size of which varied considerably, encompassing some 4 700 civil servants. The heads of departments obtained their positions through patronage and loyalty and were usually active politicians, demonstrating the absence of a clear cut division between politicians and higher civil servants in the Irish administrative system (McDowell 1964: 2–4).

In the 1700s, the employment conditions and opportunities for Irish civil servants were comparable to those in Britain. Recruitment by patronage was widespread and dispensed by the lord lieutenant and heads of departments as the spoils of office. The remuneration of eighteenth century civil servants was erratic (both interdepartmentally and intradepartmentally). In a considerable number of the departments, some of the employees were paid by fees, and thus their salaries fluctuated. The spoils system was viewed by many aspirant office holders as attractive particularly in the Revenue Commission and the Courts, as remuneration was performance-based, hence enticing civil servants to work harder. Sinecures and pluralities were common and eschewed rates of remuneration. Many of those individuals holding sinecures had been appointed to high offices in Dublin but did not want to leave the

London circuit to join Dublin society. They engaged a deputy to conduct their duties in Ireland, paying them a small portion of their income. Pluralities were to a large extent the domain of the lower offices. Remuneration was erratic, however, and McDowell deduces that 'the working occupants of government offices in Dublin ... had rarely less than £50 a year and shared amongst them over 300 posts with incomes ranging from £200 to £1000' (McDowell 1964: 11). Promotion was gained by seniority for the most part; however, many of the Lord Lieutenant's supporters were often rewarded senior posts in the administration having been previously outside the service. In 1784, members of the Irish House of Commons argued that promotion should be based on merit and seniority, and higher offices should be open to those persons who had worked in the lower grades. The recommendation was quickly subverted by placing an individual destined for higher office in a lower one, thus purporting that they had been promoted internally (McDowell 1964: 6).

Politically, the 1800s were a turbulent time, as the Irish were no nearer to accepting British rule. An escalation of social crisis and the contemporary mood of revolution and republicanism in other European countries, ensured that discontent became manifest in Irish society. Events reached a crisis in the breakout of rebellion in Dublin during May of 1798, and spread throughout the island. The 1798 Rising was probably the most concentrated event of violence in Irish history and the English deemed a tighter control over Ireland necessary. Hence, the enactment of the Act of the Union 1800, which abolished the Irish House of Commons, albeit that it brought little change to the system of administration in Ireland.

The government of Ireland and its administration was far from integrated with that of Britain, and Ireland was treated as a 'special' case compared to Britain's other colonies. For example, education and the police were administered on a national scale unlike England where it had a local structure. The allocation of government functions and the administrative structure in nineteenth century Ireland allowed a measure of decentralisation not seen in the United Kingdom. The centralisation of administrative powers persists to the present day despite the European Union policy of subsidiarity. Ireland like the United Kingdom, has one of the most centralised administrations in the European Union. After the Act of the Union, Ireland was an integral part of the United Kingdom and while some Irish departments were merged with their British counterparts, others were not. Simultaneously in Britain, reform and reorganisation of the administration was occurring in an attempt to eradicate inefficiency and corruption.

Early reform efforts began during 1815–21, three commissions were established to investigate the mechanics of the Irish administrative system. The published findings resulted in considerable reforms and by the 1830s many reforms had been implemented. For the first time, a superannuation[1] scheme was established, payment by fees had been abolished, sinecures were almost obsolete, administrative processes had become transparent and salaries reflected the work which was transacted (McDowell 1964: 22–3). Hence, by the 1830s, changes were gradually introduced in the Irish public administration yet the substantive issues of grading and remuneration remained to be resolved. The year 1855 was a watershed in Irish administrative history with the arrival of the Civil Service Commission, established to conduct qualifying tests for those seeking employment in the service. By 1871, open competitive entrance examination was the accepted mode of entry to the civil service.

These changes were in keeping with the recommendations of the Northcote-Trevelyan Report 1854, implemented in mainland Britain. With regard to the grading structure, there was a consensus that there should be sections in the service where the duties of the civil servants differed. Thus in 1871, two modes of recruitment were announced; Regulation I and Regulation II. The differences between the two were not clarified until 1875, by the Civil Service Inquiry Commission as; those entering under the former were 'expected to be drawn from the best class of university men and were intended to join the superior class in those offices with high social and educational acquirements.' Regulation II candidates were to be 'persons of less mature age and less extended acquirements', (cited in McDowell, 1964: 25).

While transitional problems emerged, by the end of the nineteenth century, the allocation of duties amongst the grades was established. There existed a sizeable civil service with more than 27 000 employees spread over 29 Irish departments and 11 'imperial' departments. At this stage the methods of recruitment and grading corresponded to the system in existence in mainland Britain. However, the notion that the best method of recruitment was personal knowledge of the candidate prevailed in Dublin as it did in London, with success appearing to a large extent to depend on the whims of those personalities in powerful positions.

By the beginning of the twentieth century signs of political turbulence remained in Ireland. Nationalists had been demanding Home Rule in the House of Commons since the 1880s and they succeeded in having the necessary legislation passed in 1914. The Bill proposed the establishment of a bicameral parliament in Dublin which would legislate in areas of domestic affairs. The Protestant majority in Ulster rejected the Bill, and a separatist struggle began in 1916 with the Easter Rising by the Irish Republican Brotherhood and ending with the partition of Ireland by the Government of Ireland Act 1920. The 1920 Act, broadly replicated the 1914 Bill; however, it provided for parallel institutions in Dublin to govern the 26 counties now known as the Irish Free State, and Belfast, to govern those six counties of Ulster with a Protestant majority. While the legislation was welcomed in the North this was not the case in the south. Nationalist military opposition began and resulted in the Anglo-Irish Treaty of 1922, which established the 26 counties as a Commonwealth state with a parliamentary oath of allegiance to the king of England; partition was however, to remain.

The Civil Service in the Irish Free State

From an administrative perspective, the civil service structure in the new state experienced minimal change with the retention of the Westminster (Whitehall) model of government which, in light of the long struggle for independence from Britain, could be viewed as almost paradoxical. The administrative infrastructure developed by the British served the new state well. In 1922, 98.9 per cent been recruited under the old regime. The fact that such a large corps of civil servants could adapt to working in an entirely different state is explained by what McBride termed as the 'greening' of the Irish civil service, a consequence of the development of open recruitment practices for the lower grades of the civil service in the 1870s and a discriminative policy of promoting and appointing civil servants of a nationalist persuasion (McBride 1991: 304–12). With regard to the structure of the public administration, the formal organisation was established by the Ministers and Secretaries Act of 1924, which to date is the fundamental statute governing Irish administration. Strategic change to the civil service management was introduced by the Public Service Management Act 1997. The 1924 act had two important features: it provided the legal basis for the structure and organisation of the central administration by defining the extent of ministerial responsibility; and it established the departments of state and distributed public activities amongst them (Chubb 1982: 248).

The contemporary conditions of employment of civil servants are rooted in the reforming measures introduced under British Rule in the late 1800s. The current organisational structure came into being with the introduction of the Civil Service Regulations Act 1956. With regard to recruitment, the Civil Service Commission Act of 1956 establishes that the vast majority of civil servants must be appointed by the Civil Service Commissioners. Methods of promotion were recently overhauled in 1984 with regard to the higher posts. Since then appointments to assistant secretary posts are made by the government based on the report from the Top Level Appointments Committee. However, promotion for the majority of civil servants is in principle merit-based and authorised by the minister in charge of the department.

THE INTERNAL LABOUR MARKET

The Irish civil service comprises 27 000 of the Irish labour force of 1.6 million. In the life of the Irish state, civil servants have enjoyed relatively secure and well-paid posts in comparison to an economy with fluctuating unemployment and a population in which approximately one-third of its citizens are living below the poverty line.

The contemporary job definition and classification system of the Irish civil service has its roots in the British development of civil servant categories and functions of in the late 1800s. In broad terms, the service may be divided into two sub-systems, the clerical, executive and administrative grades, and those generally referred to as the technical and professional grades (see Appendix Table 3A.1). While efforts have been made to abolish the general service/professional divide, the dual structure still persists albeit with some movement from the latter structure to the former. In addition to those two classes, there exists departmental grades which are specific to a few departments, such as Foreign Affairs, Agriculture and the office of the comptroller and auditor general, third secretaries, counsellors, ambassadors and taxation officers. The Devlin Report of 1969, encapsulates the position concisely as:

> the civil service consists of, first of all, of a central corps of general service officers who are recruited to perform the general duties of departments from the routine clerical operations to the highest policy advisor and managerial work. These officers are recruited at varying educational levels. ...The emphasis is on a general education and every recruit can if he obtains the necessary educational qualifications and experience aspire to the highest positions in the civil service. ... There are in addition, two groups of specialist classes. The first group consists of those officers who like general service officers are recruited with a general educational qualification, but are assigned to work specific to a department. The second group are those who are recruited to the civil service for the performance of specialised work with a qualification related to the work to be performed. If the qualification is of university degree standard, they are called professional officers, if it is lower they are called technical officers. (Public Services Organisation Review Group 1969: pars. 7.4.4–7.4.6.).

Like many of its European counterparts, the Irish civil service is characterised as having both a rigid and narrow classification system. These characteristics are inherent due to the dual structure of the service, that is the general and technical grades, creating a situation in which clear access to the higher echelons for the technical grades is not the norm. Furthermore, there is no legal definition of a grade; servants are appointed to what are called 'positions' in the service. Dooney and O'Toole explain that positions which require broadly the same level of qualifications and with comparable levels of work, responsibility, pay and conditions of service, are grouped by the Department of Finance into grades. Thus, those in the various general service grades are expected to be able to perform efficiently any work assigned to them (1992: 110–11). In fact, the primary purpose of the grading structure appears to be for administrative ease in determining the terms of remuneration.

With regard to the tenure of Irish civil servants, it has been said that it would be easier to sack Jesus Christ than it would a civil servant. Paradoxically, an Irish civil servant's tenure is legally one of the most insecure in the world. However, in reality the opposite is true. The Civil Service Regulations Act 1956, states that every established civil servant shall hold office at the will and pleasure of the government (S. 5). The legislation does not, however, specify reasons or grounds for the dismissal of civil servants. Hence, employment in the Irish civil service is viewed by many observers as a job for life, with dismissal reserved for 'grave misconduct'.

Promotion is for all intents and purposes treated similarly to recruitment, as it is regarded an appointment. The majority of civil servants are selected for appointment by the Civil Service Commission, operating under the Civil Service Commissioners Act 1956. The Commission comprises of the *Ceann Comhairle* of the Dail (Speaker of the House) the secretary to the government, and an assistant secretary in the Department of Finance. The act identifies two distinct appointment categories in the civil service; an established and unestablished post. Section 13 of the 1956 Act requires that appointments to permanent positions must be made by the government or following the holding of a competition by the Civil Service Commission. The method of appointment of an unestablished civil servant is as that for established posts; however, their appointment can be terminated by the minister which they serve. The form of competitions vary but for the most part would include a written, oral or practical examination or an interview. Legally, the minister in charge of each department is the employer of all the staff within his department, and as the names of those selected by the Commission are submitted to the minister for approval, the minister in theory appoints his civil servants. However, alternative names are not provided, thus, those persons recommended by the Commission are appointed.

Until recently, the unofficial ethos regarding promotion in the Irish civil service was one of seniority as opposed to merit. With the belief that one must have served one's time before enjoying the fruits of promotion, this invariably had its detrimental effects with the loss of some young ambitious civil servants. Promotion is usually progressive from grade-to-grade and it would be most unusual for a civil servant to skip a grade. In principle, officers seeking promotion should be selected on merit, thus the head of the department must certify that the officer up for promotion is not only qualified but the best qualified of all those officers eligible for the post. It is at the discretion of the head of the department as to which civil servants are regarded as most deserving of a promotion, subject to the approval of the minister. Thus until recently in practice, if not in law, civil servants were not appointed to the general service but to a department. However, interdepartmental promotions are now occurring for one in three vacancies at assistant principal and principal officer level.

Since 1984, a new system has been operating for appointments in the higher posts in the civil service. The Top Level Appointments Committee (TLAC) was established in 1984, to accommodate interdepartmental competition for assistant secretary posts and secretary, including non-general service grades. The committee comprises of approximately five senior civil servants and one member from the non-public sector. It initially suggested one name to the minister of the department in which a vacancy existed to, with regard to the person they deemed suitable for the position. This was slightly modified in 1987, in that in the case of secretary, three names are put forward and the minister has a choice which name is communicated to government. The objective of the TLAC is to promote interdepartmental mobility and to end the dual structure of professional and non-professional career structures (Murray, 1990: 108). Secretary appointments are made for a seven-year period and this was seen as an integral part of the new system. However, as yet a decision has not been made about the conditions of service for those secretaries whose seven-year term has ended prior to reaching retirement age. To date two such civil servants have gone on to subsequent posts in the private sector. Civil service secretaries have also been appointed to other departments prior to the end of their seven-year term, thus circumventing the seven-year convention.

With regard to training and staff development, the position is ambiguous. There is no formal policy or legislation in this area. Up until recently staff training was the responsibility of each individual civil servant and it was up to them to present themselves for the training courses on offer. The remit of staff training is the responsibility of each individual department, usually coordinated by the appointed training officer. A unit known as the Centre for Management and Organisation Development (CMOD) was established to coordinate the training of civil servants at the level of higher executive officer and upwards. CMOD offers a variety of courses, all nominations for training have to come via the training officer in the individual's department and courses are available for middle and senior level civil servants. The Centre also provides facilitative support to departments with regard to training and offers a structure to coordinate networks for the senior and middle management grades (Department of Finance, 1996).

The report 'Delivering better government' (Report of the Coordinating Group of Secretaries 1996), under the Strategic Management Initiative (SMI), stresses the importance of staff development and training and attempts to redress its current low status. Thus, the report reintroduces the notion of an annual staff appraisal, conducted by the civil servants' superiors. One of the important elements of the appraisal is to be the stocktaking of the training completed by individuals and the recommendation for participation by them in particular courses. One of the other noteworthy developments contained within the SMI with regard to training, is the tripling of the amount allocated in each department's budget for training, increasing it from 0.75 per cent of the departmental budget to 3 per cent. Current figures were not available regarding the number of civil servants involved in external educational or training courses. However, the numbers are claimed to be low. In 1992, of the 27 000 civil servants in Ireland, 1400 were receiving financial aid for the third-level course that they were registered on and 300 were on educational career breaks (Hussey 1995: 86). On the positive side, in most cases full fees are reimbursed to those civil servants involved in external education. Hussey a former cabinet minister, states that 'it is unusual for a candidate for a post of principal officer to present himself or herself without at least one degree to his or her name' (ibid.: 87). Thus, while a second-level education is the basic requirement for entry to the civil service, the majority of civil servants who enjoy career mobility have a third-level education, mainly earned during their working years.

The superannuation and payment schemes offered to Irish civil servants is regarded as generous by many private sector workers. The current schemes have their origins in the nineteenth century, prior to the publication of the Northcote-Trevelyan Report in 1854. The majority of civil servants have pay scales which provide for a number of increments or age-related pay points. There are lengthy increment scales for the basic recruitment grades and medium-length increment scales for both the lower and higher level grades, while secretaries have flat salaries (Dooney and O'Toole 1992: 121). 'The system of incremental scales derives in the main from a presumption that a person's effectiveness in a new job is at lowest when he enters it and that he should be rewarded year by year as his responsibilities increase and he is able to more effectively discharge the full duties of his post' (Dooney 1976: 77). The system of increments attempts to invoke an incentive to work harder, and prior to the granting of an increment the secretary must certify that the civil servant has done his work satisfactorily. Under the Civil Service Regulations Act 1956, the Minister for Finance has the power to fix the rates of pay of the civil service, however, the ultimate power rests with the government.

The superannuation scheme is governed by various pieces of legislation. The Superannuation Act 1834, is the primary piece of legislation and its most recent amendment is the Pensions (Increases) Act 1964. The scheme provides for the payment to established civil servants of a pension and tax-free lump sum at or after the age of 60 in return for pension contributions towards the cost of the scheme. In most cases the pension paid is 1/80th of the pay on the last day of reckonable service for each year of service up to a maximum of one-half of salary. The lump sum is calculated as 3/80th of pay for each year's service up to a maximum of one and a half times pay. A pension is vested after five years' service and death gratuities and short service gratuities are also provided under the scheme (Hughes 1988: 1). These benefits are generous and the percentage of civil servants who are covered for retirement benefits by the civil service superannuation scheme is almost 100 per cent as membership is mandatory. The main criticism of the scheme relates to its cost to the Exchequer and the notional contributions paid by the civil servants.

With regard to rewards in the civil service, there are very few in Ireland, as the basic salary is viewed as the sole reward and the increments the only form of performance-related pay. The legislation dealing with rewards is old and concise. Civil servants are bound by the Corruption Acts, 1889–1916. These provide penalties for corrupt acceptance of gifts or other rewards or inducement for doing or not doing some act or for showing favour or disfavour with regard to the business of the department. The abuse of official information for private gain is also regarded a corrupt practice.

REPRESENTATIVENESS

Ireland is a relatively homogenous society, 88 per cent of the population of 3.62 million are Catholics, the vast majority of the people speak English as their mother tongue. Net immigration in Ireland was 141 000 during 1992–5. However, most of this movement into Ireland was the return of Irish citizens with their families who had joined the path of mass emigration in 1980s. By European standards, Ireland has a young population with 45 per cent of the citizenry under the age of 25. In addition, there has been a significant increase in the proportion of students participating in both second- and third-level education. Society in Ireland is not as rigidly stratified into classes as that of Britain. In 1993, 12.5 per cent of the labour force were engaged in agriculture and almost 21 per cent of the labour force were unemployed. Urban expansion has been rapid since modernisation in the 1960s, with almost one-third of the population living in the greater Dublin area.

Thus, if the Irish civil service is to be representative of the Irish population, it would be relatively homogenous, as ethnicity is not as widespread in Ireland as in other Western democracies, and Ireland is a monoglot country. However, issues such as educational and geographical backgrounds are important, as is the representation of women in the Irish civil service. Unfortunately a lack of response from the Civil Service Commission, in furnishing the authors with current data and the absence of academic interest in the area, has resulted in many answers to important questions regarding representation left unanswered.

We would argue that the concept of representation which dominates the Irish civil service is one of equal opportunity. This can be seen from the fact that the recruitment of Irish civil servants is based on ability and is impartial and rests upon functional and standardised recruitment criteria. As much of the recruitment is carried out on the basis of success in second-level education final examinations, that is the leaving certificate, and success in the entry examination set by the Commission, this would imply that the recruitment system promotes equal opportunity. In recent years the completion rates to the end of the secondary school cycle have increased to 77 per cent of the relevant age cohort. Hence, in theory it would seem plausible that a large proportion of the Irish population are at present qualified to apply for membership to the civil service at the basic entry level, if we isolate success in the entry examination for the purpose of this argument. Thus, this general education facility is one of the main criticisms against a move towards a more graduate-only recruitment within the Irish civil service as a significant proportion of the population would not have the chance to be represented.

This was not always the case however; during the 1950s through to the early 1970s, employment in the civil service was seen as a lucrative and secure career by many school leavers for those who wished to partake in further education, but were financially unable to do so. The service provided employment and the opportunity to engage in third-level education outside of their working hours. This form of representation has attracted criticism by many academics for two reasons. The first from a class perspective, secondary education in Ireland was not free until 1967, thus very few children from low income families were provided with the opportunity to partake in second-level education. There were however, secondary schools run by religious orders, which provided education quite cheaply, so that children of low salaried parents and farmers could attend school. Chubb argues that success at the civil service examinations was more prized than a university scholarship, for it opened up the prospect of immediate self-sufficiency and a good career (1982: 265). The second criticism is that because of the dominance of religiously organised education, in the 1950s up until the 1970s, the civil service was said to have an outlook and tradition crafted by the Christian brothers. O'Mathuna, a civil servant, claimed that in the 1960s that no less than three-quarters of the administrative, executive and clerical grades had been educated by the brothers (cited in Chubb: 119). Lee, a twentieth century historian, critiques the effect of this schooling on Irish civil servants which dominated the service well into the 1960s. Recruits for the first forty years of the state were, claims Lee, 'the victims of the general intellectual constipation of the wider society during these decades. The educational system reflected this ethos as it generally interpreted its mission as a duty to drill derivatives into pupils, and to discourage innovative thinking as virtual insubordination' (1985: 4).

To some extent, the existence of the Top Level Appointment Committee system has failed to remove this dominant culture of Christian brothers-educated, relatively middle class men, at least in the higher civil service. With regard to the age profile and the urban/rural origins of senior civil servants, the average age of departmental secretaries in the civil service has fallen to the mid-40s in the 1990s as compared to the late-50s in the 1980s. However, there are indications of a rural male, middle-aged preponderance in the Irish civil service. In 1997, of the 15 departmental secretaries, six were educated in the same Christian brothers school.

'No organisation can exclude 50 per cent of its talent and prosper in the modern world' (de Buitleir 1991: 3). The Irish constitution enshrines the family as the nucleus of the state and in its fundamental rights states, 'The state shall, therefore, endeavour to ensure that mothers shall not be obliged by economic necessity to engage in labour to the neglect of their duties in the home' (Art. 41.2.2 of *Bunreacht na hEireann*).

In keeping with this Catholic driven ethos, the Civil Service Regulation Act of 1956, provided for the retirement of women in the civil service on marriage under S. 10 of the Act. Upon Ireland's accession to the EEC in 1973, this section was deemed to be in direct conflict with the Treaty of Rome and the equal opportunity legislation of the Community. Thus, in April 1973, what was known as the 'Marriage Bar' in the Irish civil service was lifted. Twenty-three years later the effects of the Bar are still evident. At present there is one female departmental secretary, Ms Margaret Hayes in the Department of Tourism and Trade, and five female assistant secretaries, appointments only made within the last few years. Table 3.1. below highlights the dominance of women in the lower spectrum of the civil service grades. This trend could be said to be illustrative of women's positions in most Irish organisations.

Table 3.1   Number of male and female employees in the Irish general civil service grades (1995)

Grade	Male	Female
Secretary	24	1
Assistant secretary	84	5
Principal officer	292	43
Assistant principal	754	226
Higher executive officer	1 206	697
Administrative officer	66	17
Executive officer	1 183	1 220
Staff officer	257	772
Clerical officer	927	3 526
Clerical assistant	847	3 837
Total	5 640	10 344

Source: Adapted from 'Delivering Better government' 1996, p. 48.

POLITICISATION

Another central characteristic of the Irish civil service inherited from British Rule is the neutrality or political impartiality of the civil servants. Political impartiality ensures that the civil servants serve and are loyal to the government of the day. Ridley, commenting on Britain, described this phenomenon as a chameleon-like ability to identify with successive governments of quite different political complexions (Ridley 1983). Thus, the classical Weberian civil service system dominates with regard to the politicisation of the civil service stemming from the changes introduced by the Northcote-Trevelyan Report of 1854, in an attempt to eradicate patronage and nepotism. To a large extent, this impartiality is accepted as the norm and remains unquestioned in Ireland, by the citizenry and politicians alike, with only slight modifications being made since the inception of this rule. In summary, Ireland accepted the tradition of civil servants' political impartiality it inherited from Britain without question.

With regard to the interdependencies between the political and administrative systems, while the minister of the department officially employs his department's civil servants, they do so on the recommendation and nomination of individuals by the Civil Service Commission. Political affiliation or support is extraneous to the procedure. It is required of any successful candidate appointed to the civil or public service, if he or she is a member of a political party, that such membership be relinquished on appointment. Furthermore, a civil servant who declares himself a candidate for a local, national or European election must retire from the service regardless of the election outcome. Since the 1960s the civil service associations battled against this tradition. In 1974, the government introduced a modification to this rule, regarding political activity, by permitting clerical staff, analogous grades in the technical area and industrial workers to engage in politics. The modification did however, expressly forbid civil servants from standing for election regardless of their grade. Civil servants involved in the framing of policy documents and proposals remain completely barred from political activities, this includes those servants found in the administrative, middle and higher management grades in the general service. The government of the day introduced this modifying measure by attempting to balance two arguments; that in a democratic society it is desirable that as many citizens as possible should play an active part in the public affairs of the community, balanced by the notion that the public interest demands that confidence be maintained in the political impartiality of civil servants.

Dooney and O'Toole assert that those civil servants barred from partaking in politics are content with this position; 'they rarely discuss party politics, and the vast majority of civil servants do not know how their colleagues vote at elections. They tend to be very critical of the occasional colleague who may be seen to be overtly political' (1992: 121). From both the ministers' and civil servants' point of view, there are longstanding arguments for the eradication of this tradition and its consequences.

From the civil servants; viewpoint, in accordance with *Bunreacht na hEireann*, it is the natural right of every citizen over the age of 21 to stand for election to the *Dail* (Art. 16.1 (1) of *Bunreacht na hEireann*). Thus the enforced political impartiality of Irish civil servants is in direct conflict with their rights protected by the constitution. The argument is heightened by the fact that civil servants are in a unique position with regard to their intimate knowledge of the government's administrative machinery and would theoretically, because of this experience, be well qualified for service in *Dail Eireann*. The current practice in Ireland is in direct contrast to other countries where civil servants are positively encouraged to become politically active. In addition, in an economy where the post of a civil servant is deemed as being one of the more secure and well-pensioned modes of employment, there has been only one civil servant throughout the history of the state, who has been willing to gamble this security for an indeterminate life in Irish politics and she failed to be elected in her first attempt in the 1997 elections.

With regard to the ministerial view, much of the argument pertains to the legal position of the minister and what is commonly referred to as 'ministerial responsibility'. The Ministers and Secretaries Act of 1924, establishes the concept of the minister as being the 'corporate sole' of the department by stating, 'Each of the ministers, heads of the respective departments of state ... shall be a corporation sole under his style or name aforesaid ... and shall have perpetual succession and an official seal, and may sue and be sued under his style or name aforesaid.'

In essence, the Act provides that the minister is the department and is ultimately accountable and responsible for the actions of the civil servants within his department to the parliament and, by extension to the citizenry of the state. Given the size of the civil service in 1924 and its expansion to 32 000 at present, including the defence forces, the act while deemed reasonable at the time of its inception, today is an administrative if not legal fiction. The concept of ministerial responsibility is unrealistic for contemporary ministers with a hectic schedule to execute. Departmental affairs amount to a small proportion of a minister's working hours, the vast amount of his time encompasses attendance in the Dail, European Union council meetings, ministerial related public appearances, constituency relations and Oireachtas Committees. In the words of a former Taoiseach and minister 'the idea that they have much time to spare to manage their department is illusory to the point of being absurd' (Fitzgerald 1996).

In reality, the higher civil servants within a department are the de facto management of the department, yet the minister carries legal responsibility. Hence, the pivotal point of this argument is should the minister then be in a position to not only know the political colour of the higher civil servants but have a true choice regarding the appointment of the department's higher civil servants. This would ensure that the department's policy will be both formulated and implemented in accordance with the governing party's philosophy. In theory the minister formulates the policy and the civil servants implement that policy, in fact the minister acts on the advice of his senior civil servants when deciding on policy proposals. This argument can be linked to the lack of formal accountability of Irish civil servants. The civil servants themselves are not happy with the current practices stemming from the Ministers and Secretaries Act of 1924. In a survey of the members of the Association of Higher Civil Servants in May 1990, 80 per cent felt that initiative went unrewarded in the civil service, 83 per cent said that management grades were not encouraged to be innovative or take risks and 93 per cent said morale was bad in the civil service (Hussey 1995: 85).

In recent years, the politicians have been taking matters into their own hands and have incrementally introduced a buffer zone within the politics/administration structures. Ministerial advisors and programme managers have recently entered the policymaking arena in Ireland, presenting themselves as neither politicians nor civil servants. Irish ministers have always had their own private offices, separate from the civil service. In more recent years, beginning in the 1950s, there has been an expansion in the ministers' private offices, not to accommodate sinecures or pay-backs, but to coordinate the tasks of the ministers' internal and external departmental affairs.

Ministerial advisers are usually recruited by the minister personally from outside the ranks of the civil service and are viewed as an alternative source of advice to the minister on issues ranging from economic and social affairs to political issues. These advisers are usually appointed for the duration of the minister's term of office, returning to their previous employment when the government leaves office (Costello 1986: 25). It is said that the complexity of contemporary government and the demands on a minister's time have necessitated the development of these advisers. As far as can be ascertained the first such adviser to be appointed was Mr Riche Ryan a young solicitor, appointed by James Everret, Minister for Justice, in the government of 1954–7. The next appointment was not until 1970, when Dr Martin O'Donoghue became personal adviser to the then Taoiseach, Mr Jack Lynch. In the government of 1973-7, the appointments were gaining ground when five such appointments were made. The role of ministerial adviser has recently been defined in the Public Management Act 1997. Section 11 of the Act provides for the appointment of one or more 'special adviser' to each minister or minister of state. The act defines the role of the adviser as, 'to assist the minister ... by providing advice, monitoring, facilitating and securing the achievement of government objectives that relate to the department ... and performing such other functions as may be directed by the minister'. The Act also stipulates that the special adviser be accountable to the minister and that his term of office shall cease on the day on which the minister ceases to hold office. This shows that Ireland is losing its status as a an example of a true Wilsonian politics/administration dichotomy and moving towards the French *cabinet du ministre* system of politico-administrative relations.

Programme managers are a more recent development in the minister's office. In 1993, the new Fianna Fail and Labour coalition government appointed a group of programme managers to assist ministers with their work on the implementation of the *Programme for a Partnership Government*. What was interesting about these posts was that Fianna Fail appointed civil servants to them, while Labour, wary of returning to government with Fianna Fail and after an absence from government for six years, appointed outsiders. These appointments were in line with the new government's decision that ministers could now appoint to their office, a special adviser and a pro- gramme manager in addition to the established positions in the office.

In Ireland, the impartiality of civil servants towards politics and its activi- ties, is seen as the lesser of two evils. In the words of Richard Rose regarding British administrative practices, 'administrative practice ... works on the assumption ... that people of ability, of power and influence, in the higher civil service can feel no sense of impropriety, futility, dishonesty or disloy- alty, either to the state or to their party (if they have one) or to their con- sciences, by working as hard as they can to execute the policy of one party and defend it against the opposition, and then reverse the role completely when the opposition becomes the government' (cited in Murray 1990: 65).

PUBLIC OPINION

In Ireland, civil servants are viewed as an important component of the politi- cal machinery but separate from politicians. While the perception held by the public of the civil service can be linked to the view of the politicians, particu- larly with regard to the state of the economy and the standard of living, we would argue that the political impartiality of Irish civil servants and the absence of political involvement in both the recruitment and the promotion of civil servants, separates them from the government in the eyes of the public. Minimal research has been conducted concerning public opinion towards civil servants while there are frequently published opinion polls concerning the popularity of political parties in the national newspapers. In this section we have utilised the European values systems study and the annual report of the Ombudsman on the working premise that most official public complaints against the civil service are dealt with by the Ombudsman.

The European values system study was conducted in 1984 and the Euro- pean values study of 1990. The first study was published under the title 'Irish

Values and Attitudes' by Fogarty, Ryan and Lee. The confidence level regarding the civil service is depicted in Table 3.2.

Table 3.2   Confidence in the Irish civil service

	Percentage of each group				
	Catholic	Protestant	No religion	Atheist	Weekly church attender
Great deal	14	10	0	0	15
Quite a lot	41	32	18	21	44
Not very much/none	44	59	82	80	39

Source: Murray, C.H. (1992), 90.

Without dissecting the differences between Catholics and the other groups regarding confidence levels, it is notable that by and large, the pattern is the same for the other institutions (listed below) and answers beyond this lie far beyond the scope of this chapter. What we can derive from this survey, given the dominance of Catholics in the Irish population, about 88 per cent, the figures relating to them, if taken as a proxy for those applicable to the state as a whole, it could be stated that 55 per cent of the population had a great deal or quite a lot of confidence in the civil service, yet 44 per cent – almost half – had either no confidence or not very much confidence in the civil service. By utilising a similar approach for the other institutions the confidence factors list as follows (Murray 1992: 90–1):

- the police   87
- the church   79
- the armed forces   76
- the education system   67
- the legal system   58
- the civil service   55
- the parliament   53
- the major companies   50
- the press   45
- the trade unions   38

Thus, the most that we can deduce from these figures is that the civil service ranks somewhere in the middle of a public spectrum of confidence in national institutions. The 1990 study by Hardiman and Whelan compares Irish confidence levels against the European average. As highlighted in Table 3.3

below, Ireland is comparable to other democratic countries with regard to confidence in national institutions. However, three-fifths of Irish people compared with two-fifths in Europe overall, express confidence in the civil service.

Table 3.3   Confidence in Irish public institutions

	Ireland 1990 (%)	EU 1990 (%)	Ireland 1981 (%)
The police	85	65	86
The army	61	51	77
The civil service	59	39	56
The parliament	51	43	53
The legal system	47	51	58
The trade unions	43	34	37
The press	36	35	44

Source: Hardiman and Whelan (1994).

Many observers might be startled at the high level of confidence in national institutions, given that much of the population allege to be disillusioned with politics and politicians in Ireland. Hardiman and Whelan provide an explanation, 'what is elicited here is the overall level of confidence people have that the institution in question will function in a fair and efficient manner' (1994: 103–104). We would argue the premise that the very nature of political impartiality of the Irish civil service segregates it from the politicians in the opinion of the citizenry.

The introduction of the Office of the Ombudsman was a late development in the Irish system of public administration. The Office of the Ombudsman Act 1980, provided for the establishment of the office and entitles the holder to investigate any administrative action taken by or on behalf of a department of state or other specific persons or bodies which appear to have had an adverse effect. If complaints are to be taken as a proxy for negative public opinion towards the civil service, then the Ombudsman's reports may help in highlighting important indicators. If we consider the complaints received by the Ombudsman in 1995 and the breakdown of complaints in Tables 3.4 and 3.5, we can observe that half the complaints received at the office concerned the civil service.

The Ombudsman reported that complaints fell into one of the following categories; unfair discrimination, proportionality, an absence of openness and transparency, with regard to the provision of information a lack of generosity with adequate advice, abuse of discretionary powers (Annual Report of the

Ombudsman 1995, 1996: 9-26). Thus, while the complaints are individual in nature they appear to fit into common areas of concern.

Table 3.4   Complaints handled by the Ombudsman in 1995

Complaints	Numbers
Received in 1995	2 879
Outside jurisdiction	629
Total within jurisdiction	2 250
Carried forward from 1994	809
Total for 1995	3 059

Table 3.5   Breakdown of complaints within jurisdiction of the Ombudsman handled in 1995

Body	Numbers	
Civil service	1 428	
Social welfare		704
Agriculture, food and forestry		293
Revenue commissioners		157
Education		107
Environment		46
Other civil service departments		121
Local authorities	775	
Health boards	418	
Telecom eireann	358	
An post	80	
Total	3 059	

Source: Office of the Ombudsman 1996, p.4.

To summarise we can consider the importance of politics in everyday life in Ireland. The European Values Study of 1990, outlined in Table 3.6 below, shows that it is clear that politics ranks well below other involvement in the pecking order of what is important in Irish people's lives.

This ranking is not unique to Ireland, as can be seen from the table other Europeans are only slightly more interested in politics and likely to consider it important. The figures discussed here feature data from 1990. However, one must consider recent controversial events in Irish politics, which might influence the public confidence levels of both the government and the civil service. Since 1990, there have been a number of cases involving both the civil service and politicians revealed to the citizenry by the media. Beginning with the report of the Beef Tribunal held in 1992, which investigated alleged malpractice in Beef Exports to Iraq by the granting of large sums of export credit insurance by the government to two beef exporting companies. This tribunal resulted in 33 million pounds sterling in legal costs and circa 100 million pounds sterling in fines for irregularities to be paid to the European Commission. Monetary damage aside the tribunal did irreparable damage to civil servants and politicians alike and a conflict of evidence between the two sides erupted during the trial (see O'Toole 1995).

Table 3.6   *Importance in life of different areas: Ireland and Europe compared*

	Percentage considering each one important	
	Ireland 1990	European average
Family	99	97
Work	91	88
Friends	94	90
Religion	84	49
Leisure time	81	84
Politics	28	35

Source: Hardiman and Whelan 1994, p.105.

In late 1994, controversy broke over the handling of the Fr Brendan Smyth extradition file by the office of the attorney general, which eventually culminated in the resignation of one of the senior civil servants involved in the case. In 1994, two senior planning officials in An Bord Pleanala (the National Planning Board) were dismissed on charges of corruption and bribery. In 1996, a tribunal of inquiry investigated the infection of Anti-D blood supplies with hepatitis C, processed by the Irish Blood Transfusion Board, and claims that politicians and senior civil servants had known about the problem for quite a while, which resulted in the infection of one mother of six having died as a result of a contaminated transfusion. These events encompass civil servants and politicians and have caused public outrage.

With regard to political culture, Ireland is clearly a plural one. Another main characteristic is the dominance of coalition governments in recent years. Since the 1970s, there has been a combination of one of the two main political parties: Fianna Fail and Fine Gael, in partnership with the smaller parties: Labour, Progressive Democrats, Democratic Left.

CONCLUDING REMARKS

The development of the Irish civil service, and in general its system of public administration and management, represents a history of continuity that owes much to its colonial inheritance from the United Kingdom. The centralisation of decision-making in Dublin, the ongoing emphasis on policy creation rather than management of service delivery and the underdevelopment of flexible labour markets (in particular mobility between the public and private sector) distinguish Ireland from its European Union partners. The strengths of the Irish system, its representativeness, cohesion, lack of politicisation, have hitherto protected the civil service from public criticism. As we discussed in the last section, however, with recent examples of maladministration there is now a growing political and public awareness that the very strengths of the civil service structure and systems may well result in defects such as a lack of responsiveness, opaque frameworks of accountability and a general sense that civil servants owe their first allegiance to politicians rather than to the public at large. What are the prospects, then, for administrative change and renewal in the Irish civil service that will allow it to enjoy high public esteem and become more citizen-orientated rather than simply a defender of majoritarian political values?

We have already referred to the Public Sector Management Act of 1997 which seeks to clarify managerial responsibility at the executive level within the civil service, establish a formal strategy process at departmental level and to open up civil service decision-making to the external scrutiny of Dail committees. The adequacy and scope of the strategy process has been reviewed elsewhere (McKevitt and Keogan 1997); the impetus behind the administrative reforms are a mixture of political and civil service consensus that the current system lacks responsiveness to the citizen-client, is too focused on policy to the detriment of operational efficiency and that personal accountability should be strengthened. There are other legislative provisions such as the Freedom of Information Act 1997, Ethics in Public Office Act 1995, Comptroller and Auditor General (Amendment) Act 1993, which together place specific new responsibilities on the civil service; these legislative enactments represent a potentially formidable array of additional responsibilities on civil servants. There are also proposals to extend the scope of the Ombudsman to cover all bodies which receive at least 50 per cent of their funding from the Exchequer as well as specific changes to the Civil Service Regulation Act 1956 that governs appointments and conditions of employment of civil servants.

The array of legislative and administrative change proposed and enacted for the civil service is unprecedented in the history of Irish administrative structures. While some of these changes relate to specific Irish conditions and circumstances, some of the changes represented a general OECD-wide political concern with the effectiveness of public management systems in general (McKevitt 1996). It will take time to monitor and appraise the effectiveness of the change programme as it is clearly and deliberately designed to be a coherent set of administrative reform proposals (*Delivering Better Government* 1996). It is likely that a programme of change on the scale envisaged will take many years to be realised. It is also likely that a deliberate strategy on such a scale will not be fully realised, indeed we could speculate that the change programme is seeking transformational change when a more incremental, emergent strategy, may be appropriate. The reform programme, underpinned by legislation, is to be welcomed given the almost glacial rate of change in the last 50 years. We need, however, to be aware that the objective of public service is support of the citizen and not simply the fashioning of 'modern' administrative structures. The Irish modernisation would do well to remember these traditional objectives of civil service action.

NOTE

1. 'Superannuation' is an old British term for an old-age or retirement pension. The superannuation scheme of the civil service refers to its pension scheme. The scheme provides for the pavement of a pension and tax-free lump sum to civil servants and is based on the number of years service hence 'annuation'.

BIBLIOGRAPHY

Buitleir, D. de (1991), 'Reflections on management in the public service', *Seirbhis Phobli,* **2** (12).

Chapman, R. and J. Greenway (1990), *The Dynamics of Administrative Reform*, London: Croom Helm.

Chubb, B. (1982), *The Government and Politics of Ireland*, Harlow: Longman.

Co-ordinating group of secretaries (1996), *Delivering Better Government*, Dublin: SMI.

Costello, D. (1986), 'Ministerial private offices in the Irish civil service', *Seirbhis Phobli,* **4** (7): 22–7.

Department of Finance (1996), *Human Resource Development Services: 1996 Programme*, Dublin: Stationery Office.

Department of the Public Service (1985), *White Paper: 'Serving the Country Better'*, Dublin: Stationery Office.

Dooney, S. (1976), *The Irish Civil Service*, Dublin: IPA.

Dooney, S. and J.O.'Toole (1992), *The Government of Ireland*, Dublin: Gill & Macmillan.

Fitzgerald, G. (1996), 'Civil Service must cease hiding behind dated idea', *Irish Times,* (11 November): 14.

Foster, R.F. (1988), *Modern Ireland: 1600–1972*, London: Penguin.

Hardiman, N. and C.T. Whelan (1994), 'Politics and democratic values', in C.T. Whelan (ed.), *Values and Social Change in Ireland*, Dublin: Gill & Macmillan, 100-35.

Hughes, G. (1988), *The Irish Civil Service Superannuation Scheme*, Dublin: Economic and Social Research Institute.

Hussey, G. (1995), *Ireland: The Anatomy of a Changing State*, London: Penguin.

Lee, J.J. (1985), 'A third division team?', *Seirbhis Phobli,* 1 (6).

McBride, L.W. (1991), *The Greening of Dublin Castle: The Transformation of Bureaucratic and Judicial Personnel in Ireland 1892–1922*, USA: Catholic University Press.

McDowell, R.B. (1964), *The Irish Administration 1801–1914*, London: Routledge & Kegan Paul.

McKevitt, D. (1988), *Managing Core Public Services*, Oxford: Blackwell.

McKevitt, D. (1996), 'Strategic management in the Irish civil service: Prometheus rebound or the phoenix redux', *Administration,* 4 (43): 34–50.

McKevitt, D. and J. Keogan (1997), 'Making sense of strategy statements: a user's guide', *Administration*, 3 (45).

McKevitt, D. and A. Lawton (1996), 'The manager, the citizen, the politician and performance measures', *Public Money and Management,* 3 (16): 49–55.

Millar, M. and T. Verheijen (1998), 'Reforming public policy processes and ensuring accountability: Ireland in a comparative perspective', *International Review of Administrative Sciences,* 1, 97-118.

Millar, M. et al. (1998), 'Public management reform in Ireland', in D. Coombes and T. Verheijen (eds), *Public Management Reform*, London: Edward Elgar.

MSc Strategic Management Class of 1993/94 (1994), *Strategic Management in the Irish Civil Service: A Review Drawing on Experience in New Zealand and Australia*, Dublin: Trinity College Dublin.

Murray, C. H. (1988), 'The top level appointments Committee', *Seirbhis Phoibli,* 1 (9): 10–7.

Murray, C. H. (1990), *The Civil Service Observed*, Dublin: IPA.

Murray, C.H. (1992), *The Civil Service Observed*, Dublin: IPA.

OECD (1990), *Public Management Developments in OECD Countries*, Paris: OECD.

Office of the Ombudsman (1996), *Annual Report of the Ombudsman 1995*, Dublin: Stationery Office.

O'Toole, F. (1995), *Meanwhile Back at the Ranch, the Politics of Irish Beef,* London: Vintage.

Public Services Organisation Review Group (1969*), Report of the Public Services Organisation Review Group*, Dublin: Stationery Office.

Ridley, F.F. (1983), 'The British civil service and politics: principles in question and traditions in Flux', *Parliamentary Affairs,* 1 (36).

Stapleton, J. (1991), 'Civil service reform 1969-87', *Administration,* 4 (39).

Whelan, C.T. (ed.) (1994), *Values and Social Attitudes in Ireland*, Dublin: Gill & Macmillan.

APPENDIX 3A

Figure 3A.1   The grade structure of the Irish civil service

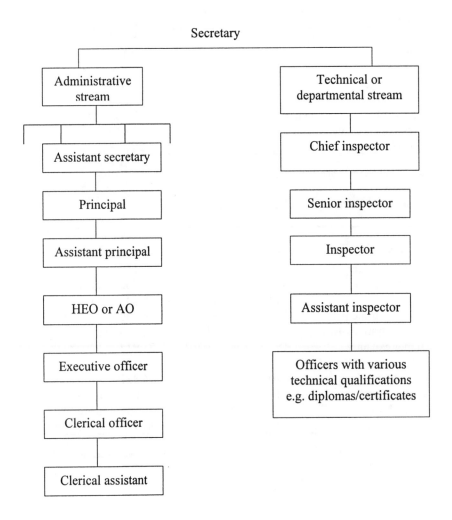

Minister

Secretary

Administrative stream

Technical or departmental stream

Assistant secretary

Chief inspector

Principal

Senior inspector

Assistant principal

Inspector

HEO or AO

Assistant inspector

Executive officer

Officers with various technical qualifications e.g. diplomas/certificates

Clerical officer

Clerical assistant

Civil Service Systems in Western Europe

Table 3A.2.1   Size of the national civil service in July 1996

Non-industrial civil servants	29 832
Industrial civil servants	1 791

Table 3A.2.2   Breakdown of civil servants by grade, 1996

Grade	Number
Administrative and executive	8 753
Clerical	10 134
Typing	1 804
Professional	2 870
Inspectorate	1 540
Supervisory and maintenance	2 865
Messenger, cleaner	1 416
Total	29 382

Source: Institute of Public Administration Yearbook 1997.

Table 3A.3 Salaries of Irish civil servants, 1995/96

Position	Salary £ p.a.			Salary $ p.a.		
Secretary	75 047			127 580		
Deputy secretary	60 037			102 063		
Assistant secretary	44 472	to	51 143	75 602	to	86 943
Principal	34 850	to	40 783	59 245	to	69 331
Assistant principal	26 118	to	30 969	44 400	to	52 647
Administrative officer	13 794	to	22 703	23 450	to	38 595
Higher executive officer	18 772	to	22 703	31 912	to	38 595
Executive officer	9 610	to	18 772	16 337	to	31 912
Staff officer	14 642	to	18 237	24 891	to	31 003
Clerical officer	8 140	to	14 590	13 837	to	24 802
Clerical assistant	8 070	to	11 990	13 720	to	20 380

Source: Adapted from the Department of Finance (1996), State Directory 1996/97, Dublin: Stationery Office.
Note: US $1.7 = 1.00 Irish punt.

4. The Development and Current Features of the German Civil Service System

Klaus H. Goetz

INTRODUCTION

The historical development of the German civil service is inextricably tied to the evolution of the German state, both as an empirical reality and a legitimising idea. In the twentieth century alone, German statehood underwent four fundamental transformations: from Empire to Republic in 1918; from democracy to dictatorship in 1933; from Nazi rule to Allied occupation, followed by the creation of the democratic Federal Republic under the aegis of the Western Allies and the Socialist German Democratic Republic under Soviet control in 1949; and from division to unification in 1990. Below the level of regime change, statehood during the twentieth century was also transformed more gradually. The single most important force of change was the rise of the *Leistungsstaat*, which took the form of a progressive extension of the scope of state activity, most notably in the provision of social welfare and education. An immediate consequence of the evolution of the *Leistungsstaat* was the steady growth in the absolute size of the civil service. Yet, while the civil service was extended well beyond the traditional confines of *Eingriffsverwaltung*, with its focus on the exercise of sovereign state authority (*hoheitliche Aufgaben*), it also gradually lost its erstwhile dominance in public sector employment.

If expansion is at the heart of a quantitative account of the German state for much of the twentieth century, this trend has begun to change perceptively over the last two decades or so; public sector employment growth initially slowed down but then quickened again (see Tables 4.1 and 4.2).

Table 4.1   Development of public personnel in the Federal Republic prior to Unification (in 000s)[a]

Year	Total	Direct public administration						
		Federation, Länder, local government				Special Purpose local adm.	b.Federal railways	c.abs: Federal post serv.
		Total	Fed.	Länder	local authorities			
		Total						
02/09/50	2199.8	1337.2	63.3	739.9	574.0	0.0	528.8	293.8
02/10/55	2510.2	1647.6	116.9	881.9	648.8	0.0	503.4	359.2
02/10/60	3006.3	2083.9	363.5	1006.6	713.8	19.7	495.7	407.0
02/10/65	3396.7	2481.0	499.3	1152.5	829.2	22.8	462.4	430.5
02/10/70	3692.2	2798.1	543.7	1334.3	920.1	27.2	409.2	457.6
30/06/80	4430.5	3547.0	567.0	1823.4	1156.7	40.2	341.5	501.8
30/06/89	4607.2	3767.3	579.3	1911.5	1276.5	50.6	257.8	531.4
		Officials, judges, soldiers						
02/09/50	788.5	466.5	32.1	329.0	105.4	0.0	188.6	133.4
02/10/55	1052.2	638.5	64.8	449.1	124.6	0.0	224.9	188.8
02/10/60	1320.8	858.8	223.6	519.5	115.7	1.0	241.1	219.9
02/10/65	1506.2	1021.2	297.6	593.2	130.4	1.0	239.4	244.6
02/10/70	1641.7	1169.4	327.9	702.0	139.5	1.0	219.4	251.9
30/06/80	1972.4	1489.8	348.6	999.9	141.3	2.0	188.4	292.2
30/06/89	2053.0	1584.1	363.5	1061.7	158.9	2.3	148.8	317.7
		Salaried employees						
02/09/50	547.9	481.4	14.1	254.9	212.4	0.0	2.2	64.3
02/10/55	563.6	515.8	27.3	252.5	236.0	0.0	2.2	45.6
02/10/60	699.8	640.1	67.9	300.5	271.7	8.4	2.1	49.2
02/10/65	871.7	805.1	94.5	370.4	340.2	9.7	7.2	49.7
02/10/70	1041.1	954.8	102.4	446.7	405.7	12.4	9.2	64.7
30/06/80	1401.9	1321.6	103.1	623.1	595.4	22.4	8.7	49.3
30/06/89	1534.4	1444.9	103.5	650.4	691.1	30.5	6.2	52.8
		Workers						
02/09/50	863.4	429.3	17.1	156.0	256.2	0.0	338.0	96.1
02/10/55	894.1	493.3	24.8	180.3	288.2	0.0	276.0	124.8
02/10/60	985.7	585.0	72.0	186.6	326.4	10.3	252.5	137.9
02/10/65	1018.8	654.7	107.2	188.9	358.6	12.1	215.8	136.2
02/10/70	1009.4	673.9	113.4	185.6	374.9	13.8	180.6	141.0
30/06/80	1056.2	735.7	115.3	200.4	420.0	15.8	144.4	160.2
30/06/89	1019.8	738.2	112.4	199.4	426.5	17.8	102.8	160.9

Notes: a. Data partially estimated, 1950 and 1955 not including the Saarland.
      b. Since 1994, Federal Railways Fund.
      c. Since 1995, removed from public service as a result of privatisation.
Source: Statistisches Bundesamt (1998) Personal des öffentlichen Dienstes 1997, 179.

Table 4.2   Development of public personnel since Unification (in 000s)

Year	Total	Direct public administration					Spec.purp. local adm.	Fed. railw./east a.Germ. railw.	b.abs: Fed. Post serv.	Indirect public adm.
		Total	Federation, Länder, local govern.							
			Total	Fed.	Länder	Local auth.				
				Total						
30/06/91	6737.8	6412.6	5219.8	652.0	2572.0	1995.9	55.5	473.8	663.5	325.1
30/06/92	6657.2	6305.0	5171.2	624.7	2531.3	2015.2	58.3	433.9	641.5	352.2
30/06/93	6502.6	6114.8	4997.7	602.9	2510.7	1884.1	62.7	417.7	636.8	387.9
30/06/94	6094.3	5666.3	4866.0	577.6	2482.0	1806.4	66.9	128.5	605.0	428.0
30/06/95	5371.0	4921.1	4735.4	546.3	2453.4	1735.6	65.9	119.8		449.9
30/06/96	5276.5	4813.9	4634.5	533.2	2429.9	1671.5	67.8	111.6		462.6
30/06/97	5163.8	4713.3	4543.6	526.4	2401.9	1615.2	68.2	101.6		450.5
				Officials and Judges						
30/06/91	1843.5	1811.7	1355.8	115.3	1072.4	168.0	2.5	138.7	314.7	31.8
30/06/92	1900.2	1866.7	1422.2	124.3	1126.0	172.0	2.5	132.5	309.4	33.5
30/06/93	1945.6	1903.4	1466.0	131.6	1160.7	173.6	2.7	128.0	306.8	42.2
30/06/94	1972.1	1928.9	1510.4	132.5	1201.3	176.6	2.7	122.2	293.6	43.2
30/06/95	1701.1	1653.9	1537.4	134.1	1227.1	176.2	2.7	113.7		47.3
30/06/96	1711.6	1662.4	1555.5	135.0	1244.4	176.1	2.7	104.2		49.2
30/06/97	1718.4	1668.0	1570.7	134.6	1258.8	177.4	2.6	94.6		50.4
				Professional and Temporary Soldiers						
30/06/91	257.3	257.3	257.3	257.3						
30/06/92	245.8	245.8	245.8	245.8						
30/06/93	230.9	230.9	230.9	230.9						
30/06/94	212.7	212.7	212.7	212.7						
30/06/95	194.3	194.3	194.3	194.3						
30/06/96	190.8	190.8	190.8	190.8						
30/06/97	191.8	191.8	191.8	191.8						
				Salaried Employees						
30/06/91	3010.7	2738.4	2515.4	142.4	1205.3	1167.7	34.6	81.6	106.8	272.3
30/06/92	2999.2	2701.6	2439.9	132.1	1122.3	1185.5	36.5	128.8	96.3	297.6
30/06/93	2918.7	2595.2	2346.5	126.0	1084.0	1136.5	38.4	115.3	95.1	323.5
30/06/94	2735.6	2402.2	2272.6	125.1	1061.8	1085.8	40.5	0.6	88.4	333.4
30/06/95	2585.8	2235.7	2194.7	119.1	1025.9	1049.8	40.3	0.7		350.1
30/06/96	2536.9	2176.8	2132.6	113.7	998.8	1020.2	41.8	2.4		360.1
30/06/97	2472.8	2122.0	2077.3	110.3	968.1	998.8	42.4	2.4		350.8
				Workers						
30/06/91	1626.4	1605.3	1091.3	137.0	294.2	660.2	18.5	253.5	242.0	21.0
30/06/92	1512.0	1490.9	1063.2	122.5	283.1	657.7	19.3	172.6	235.8	21.1
30/06/93	1407.4	1385.3	954.3	114.3	266.0	574.0	21.6	174.5	234.9	22.2
30/06/94	1174.1	1122.6	870.2	107.3	218.9	544.1	23.7	5.7	223.0	51.5
30/06/95	889.7	837.2	808.9	98.8	200.5	509.6	22.9	5.4		52.5

Table 4.2   Continued

Year	Total	Direct public administration					Spec.purp. local adm.	Fed. railw./east a.Germ. railw.	b.abs: Fed. Post serv.	Indirect public adm.
		Total	Federation, , Länder, local govern.							
			Total	Fed.	Länder	Local auth.				
30/06/96	837.2	783.9	755.7	93.7	186.8	475.2	23.3	5.0		53.3
30/06/97	780.9	731.6	703.8	89.7	175.1	439.0	23.2	4.6		49.3

Notes: a. Since 1994, Federal Railways Fund.
   b. Since 1995, removed from public service as a result of privatisation.
Source: Statistisches Bundesamt (1998) Personal des öffentlichen Dienstes 1997, 129.

The international discussion of public sector change during the 1980s and 1990s revolved around a political agenda that sought to 'push back the frontiers of the state', most notably through privatisation, coupled with internal reforms aimed at greater economic efficiency (Wright 1994). Until the early 1990s, the Federal Republic seemed less affected by retrenchment and economisation than many of its European neighbours (Benz and Goetz 1996). On the contrary, unification was accompanied by a massive expansion of public sector employment by some 40 per cent in 1990/91. Moreover, the predominant model of post-communist institution-building in the new German Länder followed a logic of West–East 'institutional transfer' (Lehmbruch, 1993), in which the principles of West German political, administrative and economic organisation were 'exported' to the East, usually with minimal formal modifications. This included the decision, laid down in the Unification Treaty, to (re)introduce the institution of the civil service in the territory of the former GDR, where the status distinction between officials and ordinary public personnel had long been abolished (Goetz 1993).

But while unification initially appeared to reaffirm the validity of (West) German administrative traditions, including the civil service, the massive pressures on public finances at all levels – Federal, Land, and local – that ensued soon began to put the search for greater efficiency in the public sector and a reduction in its size back onto the political agenda. As the precepts of the New Public Management (NPM) received increasingly vocal support among German politicians and scholars of public administration, defenders of the traditional public bureaucracy model found themselves on the defensive. In the context of this debate, the constitutionally-safeguarded 'traditional principles of the civil service' (*hergebrachten Grundsätze des Berufsbeamtentums*) also came under renewed attack. Demands for the wholesale abolition of the civil service, or at least its restriction to core tasks, became increasingly frequent during the 1990s. At the same time, the number of civil servants[1] in the Western part of the country declined, while several of the new Länder were reluctant to follow the guidance of the Unification Treaty and sought to keep civil service appointments to a minimum, preferring ordinary employment contracts instead.

It is, then, possible to speak of a dual challenge facing the German civil service at the beginning of the new century. First, the civil service is contracting. Second, and perhaps more important, politicians from all major parties are increasingly critical of the traditional principles of the civil service. The principles include, in particular:

- all administrative tasks that regularly involve the exercise of 'sovereign authority' (*hoheitliche Aufgaben*) must, as a rule, be entrusted to officials rather than ordinary public employees (*Funktionsvorbehalt*) (for a discussion of the historical evolution of this principle see Leitges 1998);
- an emphasis on formal educational qualifications, professionalism, seniority, and political neutrality;
- officials are recruited to one of the four main civil service categories (basic, intermediate, executive, and higher services). In accordance with the career principle (*Laufbahnprinzip*), they usually enter the service at the lowest level in their respective category;
- life-long tenure (*Lebenszeitprinzip*);
- full-time service;
- no right to strike;
- a special commitment of civil servants to the state, which finds its complement in the special responsibility of the state *vis-à-vis* its officials and their dependants (*gegenseitige Treuepflicht*).

The insistent questioning of the continued need for a civil service that is organised with reference to these 'traditional principles' is part of, and symptomatic for, the erosion of the basic ideational foundations on which the public bureaucracy state and the professional civil service have rested. Briefly, these basic assumptions can be characterised with reference to three interlinked ideas. First, the state is imbued with internal sovereignty (*Hoheitlichkeit*) *vis-à-vis* its citizens and has a monopoly over the means of legitimate coercion. Sovereign state tasks that involve the exercise of the state's coercive powers must regularly only be carried out by civil servants. Second, at the institutional level, the civil service acts as the promoter and guarantor of the public good (*Gemeinwohlverpflichtung*). Third, at the individual level, the 'traditional principles' of the civil service are safeguards that allow officials to be able act as guardians of the public good in the exercise of sovereign state tasks by helping to ensure impartiality, objectivity and regularity.

These intertwined ideas are at the heart of a dual conception of bureaucratic legitimacy that balances democratic accountability with the positive recognition of bureaucratic autonomy (see, for example, Dreier 1991; 1992; Jestaedt 1993). In German constitutional doctrine, the civil service is expected to act to some degree as a counterweight to the changeable and volatile political executive. In one of its early judgements, the Federal Constitutional Court clearly emphasised this role. Thus, it noted that the Constitution regards the 'civil service as an institution, which ... should secure a stable administration and thereby constitute a balancing factor (*ausgleichenden Faktor*) *vis-à-vis* the political forces that shape the life of the state' (*Entscheidungen des Bundesverfassungsgerichts*, V. 7, p. 162; my translation, KHG). A degree of autonomy from the transitory wishes of political decision makers is, therefore, necessary, if the civil service is to make its distinctive contribution to the constitutional order.

To some, the very language used to describe the legitimating bases of the civil service will appear quaint and outmoded. Certainly, it is difficult to mount an effective defence of the civil service at a time when the notions of the sovereign state, the public good and public bureaucracy seem themselves to have become obsolete. For example, it is often argued that the internal sovereignty of the state, such as it was, has long been eroded to an extent where any attempt to conceptualise state-society relations in hierarchical terms is profoundly misguided, as state authority gives way to the 'network state' (Lehmbruch 1997). The sovereign state evolves into the 'co-operative state' that relies on negotiation, bargaining and persuasion, rather than command and control, to achieve its objectives (Benz 1996). This co-operative mode of state action, it is suggested, is not just the preserve of *Leistungsverwaltung*, but is also increasingly common in the field of *Eingriffsverwaltung*, which had traditionally been associated with an authoritative mode of administrative intervention.

There is no lack of gloom-and-doom scenarios that invoke the perils to the civil service. Its former centrality in state employment has been undermined; its traditional principles are in decay; and, most critically, its specific contribution to democratic governance, and, thus, its very *raison d'être*, is in doubt. Before we fully subscribe to such a scenario, it is, however, necessary to distinguish between the institutional and the individual level in the analysis of the civil service. The developments briefly hinted at so far may well weaken the centrality, identity and coherence of the civil service as an institution; but it is much less clear how they influence the individual civil servant, especially when it comes to officials who operate at the interface between politics and administration (Goetz 1999b). For example, the top ministerial bureaucracy in Germany has, thus far, remained the almost exclusive reserve of civil servants, whose terms of employment have not been altered significantly. Unlike many of their Western European counterparts, Federal top civil servants have not yet been subject to contractualisation and fixed-term appointments (Page and Wright, 1999). It is also worth noting that privatisation has opened up new fields of activities for (former) officials outside the established realms of the higher civil service. In the wake of the privatisation of the Federal post, telecommunications and railway services, many former high-ranking officials from the Ministries of Post and Telecommunications and Ministry of Transport have switched sides and found lucrative employment in the privatised and liberalised former public monopoly sector. These remarks are not intended to suggest that individual officials are unaffected by the challenges to the institution of the civil service; but what can be described as a systemic crisis may well offer new opportunities for certain categories of officials.

THE DEVELOPMENT OF THE CIVIL SERVICE

As was noted at the outset, the historical evolution of the German state and of its critical reflection provides the single most important point of reference for understanding continuity and change in the civil service. The key empirical and ideational dimensions of state development may briefly be indicated through a series of qualifications that describe Germany as a *Nationalstaat* – nation state; *Rechtsstaat* – state based on the rule of law; *Bundesstaat* – federal state; *Sozialstaat* – social and welfare state; *demokratischer Parteienstaat* – democratic party state; and *europäisierter Staat* – Europeanised state. What is of interest in the present context are the implications of these characterisations for public administration, in general, and the civil service, in particular.

The German nation-state was a product of unification in the 1860s and early 1870s under the leadership of Prussia. This nation-state took the form of what would today be characterised as an asymmetric federation, in which the individual constituent units enjoyed differential rights and prerogatives and in which Prussia outweighed any of the other states in political power and influence. Yet, although Prussia was the driving force behind unification and dominated the Empire, the creation of the unified state 'from above' could build on a fully-fledged and culturally defined 'national identity'. It is often argued that social, economic and political modernisation in Germany was encouraged, guided and controlled by the state; it is this modernising role which is crucial to the oft-invoked portrayal of Germany as a state-centred society (Dyson 1980). To the extent that the analysis of a state-led modernisation is correct, the civil service can be understood as a modernising agent. It is not surprising, therefore, that classical German bureaucratic theory should stress the link between the professionalisation of the civil service and economic and social progress. Crucially, however, modernisation under Prussian hegemony did not mean state-led nation building, for the emergence of a German nation with a sense of identity preceded political unification rather than being its product.

The congruence of nation and state was achieved through a federal political construct. Since the 1870s, the degree of centralisation in the German polity has varied as has, of course, the nature of the federal system. But, with the exceptions of the Nazi period and of 'democratic centralism' in the GDR, decentralisation has been a key constitutive principle of political and administrative organisation in German history. As regards the Federal Republic, the consequences of the federal principle for the civil service have been numerous and far-reaching, but two deserve highlighting. First, there is no national civil service. Rather, the civil services of the Federation, the individual Länder and local governments have retained their institutional independence and personnel management practices are diverse. Second, the majority of civil servants are employed by the Länder and local government rather than by the centre.

The preponderance at the Land level is, in part, explained by the constitutional presumption is favour of decentral administration, whereby Federal legislation is to be implemented by the Länder. Perhaps more important, policing and public education are very manpower-intensive Land tasks, which account for a high proportion of overall public sector employment (see Derlien and Peters, 1998). In fact, as one German commentator has recently argued 'If, in the medium and longer-term, it were possible to exclude teachers from the civil service, this would undoubtedly constitute a decisive success for fundamental critics of the civil service ... In terms of numbers, the civil service would become a marginal factor, negligible in public discussion, if in future teachers were no longer to be appointed civil servants' (Manssen 1999: 253; my translation, KHG).

The concept of the *Rechtsstaat* was central to German political thinking even before the achievement of German unity in the 1870s (Böckenförde, 1991), but its chief tenets – the supremacy of law, full state liability for illegal public actions, comprehensive rights of appeal against administrative acts (Johnson 1983: 15) – were only fully and effectively realised in the Federal Republic. Importantly, it was only in post-war Germany that the *Rechtsstaat* idea became infused with a natural rights context. At least three major consequences flow from the requirement of a public administration under the rule of law. First, officials operate within a tightly knit network of public and administrative law. Their discretion is, accordingly, restricted. Second, the density of legal regulation helps to guard against the unrestrained instrumentalisation of officials by political principals. As such, the *Rechtsstaat* provides an institutional defence for administrative autonomy (Merten 1999b). Third, civil service law itself, as a specialised branch of administrative law, is highly developed.

Like the notion of the *Rechtsstaat*, the social state preceded the advent of democracy; in fact, it could be argued that, in some respects, the growth of welfare state legislation was used as a substitute for popular participation in the political process that was withheld during the Empire. There are, of course, many important differences between the incipient welfare state that emerged under Wilhelmine rule and the post-war *Sozialstaat*; but both are based on the recognition of the positive role of the state in welfare provision and impose obligations on the state for the effective realisation of social rights. If the origins of the welfare state antecede democracy, its massive expansion during the second half of the twentieth century is a familiar story throughout Western Europe. The rise of the social state went hand in hand with the expansion of the civil service. As a result, the typical civil servant is, by now, more likely to work in the field of *Leistungsverwaltung* (notably education) rather than *Eingriffsverwaltung*. The latter provided the initial context and justification for the 'traditional principles' of the civil service; but the expansion of the *Leistungsstaat* has very much loosened the idea-tional link between the civil service and hierarchical-authoritative administration.

The discussion of the nation-state, the state based on the rule of law, and the social state helps to highlight the pre-democratic inheritance of the civil service, although these qualifications of statehood have themselves undergone a partial democratic redefiniton. By contrast, the democratic party state and the Europeanised state are, in essence, constitutional developments of the post-war period. The pivotal position that political parties have come to occupy in the Federal Republic contrasts sharply with earlier periods in German history. Whereas during the Empire and the Weimar Republic, party politics and the national interest were widely considered to be antagonistic, political parties since 1949 have come to assume such a central role in the political life of the country as to give currency the description of Germany as a party state.

As Dyson (1982) has pointed out, the concept of the party state has been used both in a legitimating and in a pejorative sense; but whether the Federal Republic is more appropriately classified as a democratic party state or a strong party democracy is a definitional, rather than an empirical, question (Padgett 1993). Certainly, the positive recognition of political parties in the Basic Law and supportive rulings by the Federal Constitutional Court have bolstered the privileged position of political parties in the political process; so has their strong governmental orientation in a centripetal party system with a comparatively low degree of ideological confrontation. The Christian Democratic parties (i.e. the CDU and its Bavarian counterpart, the CSU), the Social Democratic Party, the small liberal Free Democrats, and, more recently, the Greens have, therefore, gradually developed into what Katz and Mair (1995) label 'cartel parties' that maintain a symbiotic relationship with the state, if they have not, in effect, metamorphosed into state institutions themselves. Critics of the democratic party state often point to its allegedly corrosive effect on the party-political neutrality of the civil service and highlight the dangers of party politicisation of the personnel system, in particular within the ministerial bureaucracy (see below).

For students of public administration, European integration provides a welcome addition to the already long list of challenges to what Guy Peters has called the 'old-time religion' of traditional public administration (Peters 1996). As Page and Wouters have noted (1995: 185) 'Almost all discussions of administrative change in Europe in the wake of the development of closer European integration are couched in terms of a potential'; yet few scholars seem deterred by their sceptical conclusion that 'there is no strong reason to believe that (...) "Europeanization" necessarily brings with it any substantial change in the national administrative structure of member states' (ibid.: 203). To the extent that the impact of European integration has been studied empirically, the findings are certainly not clear-cut (for a review of the comparative literature see Goetz 2000). But two immediate consequences of the integration process are evident and uncontested. First, the quintessentially national institution of the civil service, historically tied to the nation-state, has had to be opened up to non-nationals from other EU countries (although there remains, for the time being, a protected national core). Second, individual civil servants, in particular senior officials working in the Federal and Länder ministerial administrations, have experienced a growing 'delimitation' of their scope of activity and are now regularly operating within transnational networks (Wessels and Rometsch 1996), with potentially far-reaching consequences for traditional national administrative culture.

The six qualifications of German statehood introduced here provide important reference points for a consideration of the historical evolution of the German civil service, but they do not easily lend themselves to a straightforward chronological narrative. The discontinuities and repeated fundamental reorientations that have characterised the evolution of German statehood since the middle of the nineteenth century have necessarily left their mark on the civil service. It is not possible here to do justice to the complexity of this historical development (see instead, Hattenhauer 1993). But it is worth highlighting that, with the brief exception of the Weimar Republic from 1919 to 1933, the German civil service operated, until the middle of the twentieth century, in a non-democratic context, and only came to terms with the imperatives of public administration under a democratic rule of law after the foundation of the Federal Republic.

The most serious threat to the civil service as an institution was posed by the Nazi dictatorship, not because it sought to abolish the civil service outright, but because it compromised its fundamental ethical principles. Thus, on the basis of the perversely entitled Law for the Restoration of the Professional Civil Service of April 1933, the civil service was purged of real or imagined political opponents and 'Jews' (I use quotation marks here, because it was Nazi legislation that decided who, in the eyes of the authorities, was to be considered Jewish). From August 1934, civil servants were required to swear a personal oath 'to be loyal and obedient to Adolf Hitler, leader of the German Reich and people'. The instrumentalisation of the civil service by the Nazi party also found its expression in the German Civil Service Law of 1937, which defined the civil servant as 'the executor of the will of the state based on the National Socialist German Workers' Party'. 'By this development, the civil service was cut off from its traditions, its integration into the first German republic, which had not yet been successfully completed, was interrupted, and the historical continuity of the civil service, which had survived the revolution of 1918 and might have offered a bridge between monarchy and republic, was destroyed' (Wiese 1972: 27; my translation, KHG).

If, nonetheless, the civil service was quickly restored after World War II in the Western occupied zones, this was in part a consequence of the interests of civil servants to maintain their status, and in part a reflection of the Allies' decision to leave the basic legal and organisational framework of public administration intact, while trying to remove those officials who had been most closely identified with the Nazi regime. The restoration of the civil service was actively supported by most of the Land governments that were quickly formed in the Western zones. Thus, 'The aim to use the work of the whole state apparatus as effectively as possible at a time of contingency dominated. Where they existed, reform ideas appeared modest, compared to previous and later ideas' (Püttner 1987: 1126; my translation, KHG). The Basic Law of 1949, with its explicit safeguards for the 'traditional principles' of the civil service, then completed its restoration (Barner 1997).

THE INTERNAL LABOUR MARKET

The condition of the civil service labour market in Germany constitutes something of a paradox. On the one hand, the operation of the internal labour market is governed by a comprehensive, dense and uniform hierarchy of legal norms, comprising constitutional, statutory and non-statutory regulations. The hierarchy of civil service legislation establishes a country-wide framework that secures a high degree of standardisation regarding key aspects of the internal labour market, including job definition, deployment rules, job security and membership, and reward structures and wage rules. Yet, despite the emphasis on detailed legal regulation of the civil service, personnel management practices vary greatly not just between the Federation and the Länder and amongst the latter, but also from authority to authority, as can be seen, in particular, at the Federal ministerial level.

The constitution lies at the heart of civil service law. Article 33 of the Basic Law specifies the principles of access to public office, defines the duties of civil servants, and safeguards the 'traditional principles of the civil service'. Article 33 (4) states that 'The exercise of sovereign authority on a regular basis shall, as a rule, be entrusted to members of the public service who stand in a relationship of service and loyalty defined by public law'. Paragraph 5 stipulates that 'The law governing the public service shall be regulated with due regard to the traditional principles of the professional civil service'. The civil service is, thus, an integral part of the constitutional order created by the Basic Law. Below the level of constitutional regulation, Federal statutory law establishes common parameters, in particular through the Federal Civil Service Framework Law (*Beamtenrechtsrahmengesetz – BRRG*) and the Federal Remuneration Law (*Bundesbesoldungsgesetz*). Despite its characterisation as a 'framework law' under Article 75 of the Basic Law, the BRRG does, in fact, go far beyond establishing broad guidelines for legal relations of persons in the civil service; rather, its stipulates in very considerable detail the internal organisation of the service. As a consequence, the civil service laws adopted by the individual Länder, although, in principle, intended to allow for regional diversity, largely replicate the provisions of the BRRG. Similarly, the Federal Remuneration Law, adopted under the Federation's concurrent legislative powers, establishes a common pay structure for all civil servants, whether they are employed by the Federation, any of the sixteen Länder or local authorities. The same holds for the Federal Civil Service Pension Law (*Bundesversorgungsgesetz*). Finally, relevant decrees and guidelines adopted at Federal and Land levels tend to be 'harmonised', i.e. standardised, even where legal scope for diversity exists, a practice that reflects the preference for close intergovernmental co-ordination and substantive agreement in Germany's federal system.

The main features of the internal civil service labour market (see Table 4.3) can briefly be summarised as follows:

- There is no national civil service. Instead the services of the Federation, the individual Länder and local governments are legally separate. This implies, *inter alia*, that the geographical mobility of officials is restricted, as there is no legal obligation on the part of one *Dienstherr* (literally: service master) to accept an official originally employed by another.
- The civil service is divided into four career categories (*Laufbahngruppen*), including the basic (*einfacher Dienst*), intermediate (*mittlerer Dienst*), executive (*gehobener Dienst*) and higher services (*höherer Dienst*).

Table 4.3   Full-time public personnel in Germany as of 1 June 1997

Status and Category (T = Total; W = Women)		Total	Direct public administration							Indirect public administration
			Total	Federation, Länder, local government				Special purpose local adm.	Federal Railways Fund	
				Total	Federation	länder	Local authorities			
Officials, judges and soldiers	T	1679322	1632934	1537705	321407	1053084	163214	2481	92748	46388
	W	411553	395702	391000	23530	325428	42042	324	4378	15851
Higher service	T	358139	352224	350836	30860	294872	25104	628	760	5915
	W	72903	71920	71848	2578	66391	2879	44	30	983
Executive service	T	690887	655218	639549	63277	493400	82872	1221	14448	35669
	W	240289	226593	225699	7651	194421	23627	141	753	13696
Intermediate service	T	574424	569934	496012	185524	255922	54566	593	73329	4490
	W	96579	95418	91712	12114	64115	15483	131	3575	1161
Basic service	T	55872	55558	51308	41746	8890	672	39	4211	314
	W	1782	1771	1743	1189	501	53	8	20	11
Salaried employees	T	1824880	1529041	1495000	92479	685704	716817	31858	2183	295839
	W	1110025	934605	916385	50667	421481	444237	16568	1652	175420
Higher service	T	207183	186373	182501	5670	125853	50978	3752	120	20810
	W	66197	61310	60457	1418	44156	14883	787	66	4887
Executive service	T	514956	421331	412720	15982	221291	175447	7888	723	93625
	W	261346	219745	216801	5335	128166	83300	2468	476	41601

Table 4.3   Continued

Status and Category (T = Total; W = Women)		Total	Direct public administration							Indirect public administration
			Total	Federation, Länder, local government				Special purpose local adm.	Federal Railways Fund	
				Total	Federation	länder	Local authorities			
Intermediate Service	T	1058468	881548	861029	68485	323488	469056	19194	1325	176920
	W	754430	627476	613715	42374	240110	331231	12664	1097	126954
Basic Service	T	44273	39789	38750	2342	15072	21336	1024	15	4484
	W	28052	26074	25412	1540	9049	14823	649	13	1978
Workers	T	580628	543625	522083	85618	143034	293431	17027	4515	37003
	W	113988	105643	103136	12525	32267	58344	2234	273	8345
Total	T	4084830	3705600	3554788	499504		1173462	51366	99446	379230
	W	1635566	1435950	1410521	86722	779176	544623	19126	6303	199616

Source: Statistisches Bundesamt (1998) Personal des öffentlichen Dienstes 1997, p. 29.

- An official is recruited into one of those four categories, typically at the entry level (*Laufbahnprinzip*). Subsequent transfer to a higher category is rare. Educational qualifications are paramount in determining access to a career category. For the higher service, a university degree is required. Exemptions are only granted in exceptional circumstances.
- Decisions on recruitment and promotion must be based on an individual's ability (*Befähigung*), suitability (*Eignung*) and performance (*Leistung*). The first refers, in particular, to a candidate's relevant professional qualifications, the second to 'personal, intellectual, (and) character traits' (Kunig 1999: 673; my translation, KHG), the last to professional experience. All three criteria are 'indeterminate legal expressions' (ibid.), and, as such, require interpretation and the exercise of judgement.
- Officials are, in principle, appointed for life (there are some very limited exceptions to this rule). In the majority of cases, appointment for life is preceded by a period of appointment on probation, which may vary in length.
- Remuneration and pensions are governed by Federal law that applies uniformly throughout the Federal Republic. They are based on the 'alimentation principle' (*Alimentationsprinzip*), according to which remuneration and pensions must ensure that both the official and his family are provided with a livelihood appropriate to the rank, importance and responsibility of the civil servant's office (*amtsangemessener Unterhalt*) (Merten 1999a). The traditional justification of the alimentation principle has been that it enables the official to devote himself fully to the public service and secures his economic independence (Lecheler 1996: 737f.).
- Remuneration consists of several components. For the Federal civil service, this regularly includes the basic salary, determined by pay grade and, for officials on the A grade scale, 'service age' (principally dependent on age, age at entry, and length of service); a family supplement (for married officials and officials with children); a general supplement (only for officials on grade A5 to A13); an annual special bonus paid in December; and an annual holiday payment (see Statistisches Bundesamt 1998a). To these may be added a variety of extra payments or *Zulagen*, for example for officials who are temporarily forced to live away from home or carry out particularly dangerous tasks. Although such *Zulagen* are frequently criticised in public discussions for their lack of transparency, there is, in fact, very little discretion involved in their award and the sums involved are typically small in relation to officials' basic pay. It is important to stress that they do not amount to discretionary shadow payments, as they exist in some other European civil services, especially at the level of top officials.
- Uniformity of pay means that remuneration plays little or not role in the competition for staff between the Federal, Länder and local authorities.

Until very recently, civil service law also did not allow for performance-related pay, although the civil service reform law of 1997 has made possible the introduction of performance-related pay elements for certain posts (see below).

If German civil service law has traditionally constituted a decisive element of integration in an administrative system that is functionally and territorially highly differentiated, its unifying power must not be overestimated, especially as regards personnel management. Decisions on recruitment, personnel deployment, promotion and in-service training are very much decentralised, and there are few institutions in place that would help to secure a common approach to public sector personnel management. As Johnson (1983: 180) has pointed out: 'Each of the three main tiers of government recruits its own personnel, and within them the separate units and agencies are largely responsible for meeting their personnel needs independently. Each local authority and each Land recruits its own personnel, and in the Federal Government there is no such thing as a public service commission responsible for securing staff for the whole federal administration. The departments are autonomous in the appointment of staff, though technically it is the President who confirms entry into the permanent federal civil service ... Most of the subordinate agencies coming under the supervision of federal departments also enjoy some independence in the selection of personnel, though not in fixing the level of staffing' (Johnson 1983: 180).

The fierce resistance of the Federal ministries against any encroachment on their *Personalhoheit* – i.e. 'sovereignty' in personnel matters – has, until now, defeated any attempt to develop a co-ordinated Federal personnel policy. In 1987, a report on personnel and organisation in the Federal ministries by the Federal Commissioner for Administrative Efficiency was severely critical of the unsystematic and haphazard way in which officials for the higher civil service were recruited (Präsident des Bundesrechnungshof 1987). More than a decade later, little has changed, although some ministries, such as the Ministry of Labour, have sought to develop more transparent recruitment procedures.

What applies to the recruitment of members of the higher civil service also holds, *mutatis mutandis*, for deployment, promotion and training (Goetz 1999b). As the 1997 report of the (Federal) Commission on the 'Lean State' has argued, the Federal administration is still a long way away from making the shift from personnel *administration* to active personnel *management* (Sachverständigenrat 'Schlanker Staat' 1997: 132ff.). For example, there is no equivalent to the British model of 'fast-tracking' younger officials of outstanding potential through a carefully planned process of postings in different departments. Career planning is largely down to the individual official, and while there are recognised routes to advancement – notably through work in the Chancellery and the political support units in the ministries that are connected directly to the political executive – chance, luck and connections play a large part in getting to the top. For instance, although it is, in principle, good practice for younger officials to gain work experience in different divisions within their ministry, personnel sections can find it difficult to obtain agreement from powerful heads of division, who are keen to hold on to promising officials. Similarly, in-service training is very much dependent on the insistence of individual members of staff; again, superiors in pressurised sections and divisions might be unsympathetic to such requests from key personnel. To complete the picture, it is worth recalling that decisions of promotion above a certain level – usually that of *Referatsleiter* (head of section) – will typically involve both the administrative state secretary (a political civil servant) and the minister. The intensity of the latter's involvement may vary considerably, but it is widely held that during the 1990s, close engagement by ministers in personnel policy became more common.

REPRESENTATIVENESS

The decentralised nature of the recruitment system helps to account for the diverse composition of the civil service. As Renate Mayntz observed some time ago in relation to the Federal ministerial higher civil service, there is a 'lack of cohesion and homogeneity among civil servants as a group' (Mayntz 1984: 202). Accordingly, both their willingness and ability to act collectively are narrowly restricted: 'the higher civil service, instead of sharing and jointly promoting the collective interest of any particular social class or group, reflects the full range of diverse and often conflicting interests that are organisationally represented in the departments and departmental divisions of the Federal bureaucracy' (ibid.: 203).

What applies to top echelons of the Federal civil service also seems to hold for the civil service élite of the country as a whole. In this context, the findings of the 1995 élite study carried out at the University of Potsdam are of particular importance (Bürklin et al. 1997). This study covered 4587 individuals occupying élite positions in politics, public administration, business, finance, business associations, trade unions, professional associations, the judiciary, academe, the mass media, cultural life, churches, environmental and new social movements, and the military. As regards public administration, the study's sample included a total of 683 positions, including 25 administrative state secretaries, 135 heads of division and 220 heads of subdivisions in the Federal ministries; 60 heads, deputy heads and divisional heads in other Federal authorities; 154 state secretaries in Land ministries; 47 heads of important Land authorities; 32 heads of meso-level decentralised Land authorities; and 10 German members of the EU administration.

The Potsdam study allows insights into the recruitment, composition, outlook and coherence of the administrative élite and the extent to which it is integrated or separated from other social élites. Although it is not possible here to do justice to the sophisticated and detailed analysis of the study, a few key findings deserve highlighting. Like much of the German élite, top officials are primarily recruited from amongst the lower and higher services classes (defined by the profession of the father). The social recruitment profile of the administrative elite is not markedly dissimilar from that of the other sectoral élites. Fifty-two per cent are Protestant, 31 per cent Catholic and 16 per cent have no confession; the respective percentages for the country's élite as a whole are 45, 27 and 28. Given the strong emphasis on formal educational attainment, it is not surprising that the overwhelming majority of top administrators possess one or several university qualifications (37 per cent have passed the state examinations (*Staatsexamen*), 26 per cent have obtained the state examination and a PhD, and 18 per cent are trained academics). In terms of subjects studied, law dominates (57 per cent), but the *Juristenmonopol*, i.e. the monopoly of lawyers in the senior civil service, has clearly been broken.

The élite study underlines that a career in the civil service benefits from professional experience gained elsewhere. Thus, only 47 per cent of top officials took their first job in public administration; the majority started their career in another sector, e.g. in academe, the judiciary or in the political sphere. This explains why today's top officials first entered public administration at the relatively high average age of 34. Civil servants may not just gain outside experience prior to entering the civil service, but also in mid-career, e.g. by leaving public administration on a temporary basis to work for the parliamentary parties (Goetz 1997). This type of 'interrupted' civil servant (Bürklin et al. 1997: 172) accounts for some 14 per cent of all top officials. It is not surprising, therefore, that the administrative élite has a much more varied pattern of professional experiences than the notion of the 'career civil service' might suggest. Of the Federal ministerial administrative élite, only 22 per cent had not previously been employed elsewhere; 17 per cent had worked for more than one administration; 7 per cent in politics and administration; 9 per cent in politics, administration and elsewhere; 16 per cent in the judiciary and administration; 8 per cent in the judiciary, administration and elsewhere; 13 per cent in academe and administration; 4 per cent in education and administration; and 4 per cent in business and administration.

The findings of the Potsdam study and earlier work by Mayntz and Derlien (1989) underline the pluralism of the German senior civil service, which is encouraged and reinforced by a decentralised personnel management system. The autonomy enjoyed by individual authorities in recruitment and decisions on promotion favour a plural composition of the higher civil service; and the comparative weakness of institutional devices for fostering a common civil service *esprit de corps* militates against the emergence of an internally cohesive administrative élite able to act in defence of its own collective interests.

Against this background, it becomes apparent why, in recent decades, issues of representativeness have, on the whole, played little role in political and academic discussions of the higher civil service. This sanguine outlook is all the more remarkable given the sensitivity to issues of representativeness during earlier periods of German history. Thus, discrimination on confessional grounds – especially against Catholics in the Prussian bureaucracy was an expression of the strong religious cleavage in German society during the Wilhelmine Empire. The virtual exclusion of Jews and people of Jewish descent from the higher echelons of the Reich bureaucracy also attested to a personnel system in which 'any effort towards confessional parity was lacking' (Morsey 1997b: 17; my translation, KHG). The brief experience of the Weimar Republic could do little to alter this picture dramatically, but, instead, highlighted the dangers of a 'state within the state', distinct not just in terms of social and confessional background, but in large part also distant, if not actively hostile, towards Weimar's democratic constitution. It was only to be expected, therefore, that in the early years of the creation of a Federal ministerial administration, the issue of the confessional background of higher civil servants should have given rise to political controversy (Morsey 1997a). Yet, these concerns quickly faded away, probably not least since the main party of government, the CSU/CSU, consciously tried to give itself a cross-confessional appeal.

The one aspect of representativeness to attract major attention over the last two decades has been gender (see Table 4.4). Although the percentage of women in the civil service has gradually increased, not least because of their stronghold in primary and secondary education, there has been a widespread perception that, in the civil service as a whole, women are underrepresented and their career chances limited. In response, at both Federal and Länder levels, special laws have been adopted to further the advancement of women in public administration. In most major authorities, the position of *Frauenbeautragte* or *Gleichstellungsbeauftragte* – women's or equal opportunities' commissioner – has been created, charged with ensuring that the interests of female staff are fully taken into account in public personnel management.

Yet, although progress has been made towards increasing the career opportunities for women in the public sector, there continue to exist very marked dissimilarities in career patterns. Based on 1992 data, a recent analysis of Derlien and Peters (1998) underlines that 'In Germany, only 20 per cent of the full-time civil servants are female; women dominate in the group with employee status (64 per cent) ... female employment is characteristic of Land (48 per cent) and local government employment (60 per cent).

Table 4.4   Full-time and part-time officials working for supreme federal authorities – as of 30 June 1998

	BPr+BprA	BT+BR BK+BKA BPA	AA	BMI	BMJ	BMF	BMWi	BML	BMA	BMV	BMBau	BMVg	BMG	BMU	BMFSFJ	BVerfG	BRH	BMZ	BMBF	Total
All officials and judges	60	1 035 380	1 549	820	368	1 360	1 022	558	491	610	261	1 374	303	421	248	90	450	329	582	12 311
of whom women	16	245 58	360	128	97	288	215	99	97	43	55	169	77	76	93	33	73	75	97	2 394
Members of the higher civil service	27	289 194	592	337	183	571	508	282	270	349	147	479	169	256	102	28	144	175	327	5 429
of whom – women	3	74 26	94	50	48	113	85	45	47	28	28	47	48	42	37	7	15	37	50	924

Notes:

BPr and BprA: Federal President and Federal President's Office

BK, BKA and BPA: Federal Chancellor, Federal Chancellery, and Federal Press Office

BMI: Federal Ministry of the Interior

BMF: Federal Ministry of Finance

BML: Federal Ministry of Agriculture

BMV: Federal Ministry for Transport

BMVg: Federal Ministry for Defence

BMU: Federal Ministry for the Environment

BverfG: Federal Constitutional Court

BMZ: Federal Ministry for Economic Co-operation

BT and BR: Bundestag and Bundesrat

AA: Foreign Office

BMJ: Federal Ministry of Justice

BMWi: Federal Ministry of Economics

BMA: Federal Ministry of Labour

BmBau: Federal Ministry for Construction

BMG: Federal Ministry for Health

BMFSFJ: Federal Ministry for Women, Senior Citizens, Family and Youth

BRH: Federal Audit Office

BMBF: Federal Ministry for Education and Research

Source: Bundestagsdrucksache 14/2678 (14.02.2000) Verwendung von Beamtinnen und Beamten bei den obersten Bundesbehörden (Nachfrage).

Women, in 1992, were underrepresented among the federal administrative-personnel ... at the state and local levels of government women are particularly over-represented in education and health care service delivery, rather than in management positions' (Derlien and Peters 1998: 63). More recent figures indicate that since then, the representation of women has somewhat improved, in particular if one also includes part-time officials (who are overwhelmingly female). Thus, by 1997, 9.4 per cent of all members of the Federal higher civil service were female. Of those 7815 higher Federal officials classed by the Federal Statistical Office to work for the 'Political Executive and in Central Administration', 920 (or 11.8 per cent) were female (*Statistisches Bundesamt* 1998b). But in the top echelons, female representation is still lower than these already very modest averages suggest.

POLITICISATION

It has long been part of the received wisdom about public administration in the Federal Republic that party-political considerations feature prominently in personnel policy. Attention has centred on the top echelons of the Federal ministerial bureaucracy, where data on officials' party membership, turnover of civil servants following a change of government, and much anecdotal evidence suggest that party-political sympathy with the government of the day is a relevant factor in decisions on recruitment and promotion to senior positions. In the eyes of some, however, the phenomenon of the *Parteibuch-bürokratie*, i.e. the 'party book bureaucracy' (Dyson 1977a; 1997b) goes much further. Thus, it is frequently suggested that party politicisation is not just evident at the top end of the ministerial bureaucracy, but extends equally to its lower reaches, the non-ministerial administration, the Länder level and also local government (for reviews of the German literature see Auf dem Hövel 1996; Lorig 1994). One of the most fervent and vocal critics of this phenomenon, von Arnim, has suggested that 'Whoever does not possess the right party-book may in fact be prevented from access to, and a career in, the public service' (von Arnim 1997: 227; my translation, KHG). Moreover, partisan personnel policy is said to encompass the judiciary, the public media, the public enterprise sector and a broad range of para-public institutions (ibid.: 226ff). According to von Arnim and others, party-book administration is amongst the most visible and invidious manifestations of the 'party state' (*Parteienstaat*). The state, it is suggested, has become the prey of the political parties in an 'exploitative system' in which all political parties participate, camouflaged by a 'cartel of silence, an omertà of the political class' (ibid.: 229; my translation, KHG).

Whereas criticism of partisanship in personnel policy is widespread, reliable empirical data are scarce. As Derlien noted at the beginning of the

1980s, it was typical of charges of party politicisation and party patronage that 'no data or no representative data were provided' to substantiate them (Derlien 1984: 689; my translation, KHG). A more recent survey on the subject noted that complaints about the comprehensive politicisation of public administration 'lack any empirical basis' (Auf dem Hövel 1996: 92; my translation, KHG). To the extent that relevant empirical information has been collected, it is largely confined to the higher ranks of the Federal ministerial bureaucracy. Thus, Derlien and Mayntz (Derlien 1984; 1988; Mayntz and Derlien 1989) have been able to show that there has been a growing tendency for senior Federal ministerial officials to be members of the governing parties. The importance of party membership is also supported by the findings of the 1995 Potsdam élite study. 70 per cent of Germany's administrative élite are members of a political party (amongst sectoral élites, this share is only surpassed by the political élite itself and senior trade unionists). As regards senior Federal ministerial officials, in 1995, 57 per cent of all administrative state secretaries, 46 per cent of all heads of division and 35 per cent of all heads of subdivision were members of the CDU/CSU (Bürklin et al. 1997: 116). To this figures one would need to add supporters of the Free Democratic Party, who are likely to have been concentrated in ministries that had long been under the control of the Liberals, notably the Ministries of Foreign Affairs, Economics and Justice. Partisan identification with the governing parties increased, the more senior the position in the bureaucratic hierarchy. It is consistent with this picture that following the change of government at the end of 1998, the majority of top officials were sent into temporary retirement within the first few weeks after the Schröder government took office. There was also an extensive reshuffle of administrative personnel further down the hierarchy, in particular in key political co-ordination units such as the Chancellery.

Party does matter, then, at least in the top civil service. But in what ways does it matter? While party-political patronage sometimes plays a role, for the most part patronage does not account adequately for the importance of partisan orientations at the top of the bureaucratic hierarchy. Instead, it is important to recognise the relevance of 'political craft' in the Federal policy-making system and to understand the link between political craft and partisan identification (Goetz 1997). Even in countries where, unlike in Germany, one finds a strong emphasis on establishing clear functional boundaries between politicians and officials, it is usually acknowledged that administrative-technical expertise alone is insufficient to secure an official's promotion beyond junior ranks. For senior officials in the German ministerial bureaucracy, political craft is an indispensable prerequisite for performing their role successfully. This implies, in particular, the ability to assess the likely political implications of policy proposals; to anticipate and, where necessary, influence the reactions of other actors in the policymaking process, notably other ministries, parliament, subnational governments and organised interests; and to design processes that maximise the chances for the realisation of the political leadership's substantive objectives.

Germany is, of course, by no means exceptional in placing a premium on the political skills of senior civil servants. In the Federal Republic, however, political craft is especially important because of the institutional fragmentation of the policymaking system and the intricate interplay between formal and informal processes (Benz and Goetz 1996). The Federal policy process is characterised by the strong unmediated influence of political parties, the close involvement of members of parliament in the early stages of policy initiation and development, and the integration of the Länder in the executive decision process. Since the degree of executive autonomy is low, it is vital for senior officials to be able to draw on personal networks of information and communication that extend beyond their own ministry and the Federal core executive into the parliamentary parties, Länder administrations and also the institutions of interest representation. Under the conditions of party democracy, partisan orientation will necessarily be of critical importance in structuring such inter-institutional networks. Consequently, central elements of political craft are highly susceptible to alterations in political conditions and decisive actor constellations. Thus, officials who learnt the art of political administration under the government of Chancellor Kohl have necessarily found it difficult to work equally effectively under the new SPD-led government, since both the political skills they had acquired and the networks in which they previously operated reflected specific political circumstances. Political craft is a necessary skill of senior officials, but one that is highly sensitive to the volatility of political circumstances.

REFORM

Many observers of the German public sector in general, and the civil service, in particular, have tended to highlight major obstacles to comprehensive reform as a key feature of administrative policy in the Federal Republic. The civil service, it is argued, enjoys an effective institutional guarantee through Article 33 (4) and (5) of the Basic Law, which could only be altered by a two-thirds majority in both the Bundestag and the Bundesrat. Such a majority requires an (informal) 'grand coalition' between the Christian Democratic and Social Democratic parties and between the Federation and the Länder. The civil service is largely regulated through Federal statutory legislation, which, again needs both Bundestag and Bundesrat consent. Even where changes to the status of civil servants are envisaged, they must respect the entrenched rights and legitimate expectations of current civil servants and their dependants, if they are not to fall foul to challenges before administrative and constitutional courts.

Not only is the civil service institutionally deeply embedded; an effective coalition for change is also difficult to put together. A national civil service does not exist; responsibility for managing the civil service is institutionally dispersed; and civil service trade unions are strong. Moreover, it is often argued, both the majority of German executive politicians and members of parliament, whose political will is critical in promoting reform, are themselves deeply immersed in the traditional civil service culture. Thus, during the thirteenth Federal legislative session (1994-1998), civil servants accounted for 34.1 per cent of all members of the Bundestag, and another 10.7 per cent of parliamentarians had a professional background as public employees (Hess 1995). These figures were in line with long-term trends. Against this background, it does not seem difficult to explain the failure of repeated political initiatives in the post-war period to modernise the civil service let alone create a *einheitliches Dienstrecht*, i.e. a common legal framework for all public sector staff that would do away with the distinction between officials, employees and workers.

An analysis along such lines certainly goes some way towards explaining the trajectory of civil service development in the post-war period; but it is in danger of overplaying stability and resistance to change. In the first instance, it is worth noting the amendments to the Federal civil service laws that were adopted in 1997 and came into force in July 1998 (for a brief overview see Maiwald 1999; Köpp 1999; the legislative process is documented in Claus 1999). The reform law did not meet the more radical demands for the wholesale abolition of the civil service or the formal redefinition of its traditional principles. Such demands had been voiced by some Länder and Federal politicians, mostly from the Social Democratic and Green parties, but also found the support of some Christian Democrats. The package did, however, contain a series of notable changes to the traditional status of civil servants, which, in the eyes of critics, came dangerously close to undermining essential civil service features. In particular, the reform has facilitated the secondment and transfer of officials to another *Dienstherr* even against their will; has extended officials' opportunities to work on a part-time basis; allows for the adoption of Länder legislation that may require newly-appointed civil servants to work part-time (this appears to call into question the 'traditional principle' of regular full-time service; for a differentiated discussion see Siedentopf 1997); has tightened the conditions under which civil servants can take early retirement; and has placed greater emphasis on individual performance, for example through extending both one-off and permanent performance-related bonus payments for officials on the A grade scale (Göser and Schlatmann 1998; for a discussion of some of chief implementation problems see Bönders 1999).

For the most part, the 1997/98 reform was not directly aimed at senior officials. It did, however, also contain potentially significant innovations for this category of officials, by introducing new provisions relating to senior executive positions (*Amt mit leitender Position*) (for details see Bayer 1999). In the Federal civil service, this category is taken to include, in particular, heads of divisions and subdivisions, and heads of other non-ministerial Federal authorities on the B scale. Such positions are now to be filled on a probationary basis; only if the probationary period is discharged successfully, will the official be appointed to the position for life. Otherwise, he will have to return to his previous post. Proposals that would have transformed Federal senior posts into fixed-term appointments did not find a majority. But the Federal Government was forced to concede to the Länder the right to allow fixed-term appointments to senior posts in their own administrations.

The rhetoric surrounding the reform law chimes with the suggestion that administrative development in Germany is increasingly influenced by the international reform agenda associated with the New Public Management (see recently, e.g., Budäus and Finger 1999; Pitschas 1999; and, with a focus on the Federal administration, König and Füchtner 1999, all with further references). If we restrict ourselves to the Federal level, the recent modernisation discussion has, indeed, been dominated by a concern with the 'economisation and managerialisation of state and public administration' (König and Füchtner 1999: 11; my translation, KHG). At least from the mid-1990s, the Kohl government came to proclaim its support for a remodelling of public authorities in the image of 'service enterprises' (*Dienstleistungsunternehmen*). Although this rhetoric left the organisation of the Federal ministerial administration largely unaffected, the professed commitment to a 'lean state' (see Sachverständigenrat 1997) helped to justify staff cutbacks in both the ministerial and the non-ministerial administration (for an official summary of the results of the Kohl government's reform measures see Lenkungsausschuß 1998).

The new Federal Government of the Social Democrats and the Greens, which came into office in late 1998, has professed its intention to give a new political orientation to the modernisation of state and public administration. In its programme 'Modern State – Modern Administration', adopted by the Cabinet on 1 December 1999 (Bundesregierung 1999), the Federal Government rejected the previous concept of the 'lean state', since 'it was too restricted to the reduction of public tasks and, thus, only offered a negative definition of objectives' (ibid.: 1; my translation, KHG). Borrowing heavily from the international discussion on the 'enabling state', the new guiding conception of public sector modernisation is to be the 'activating state' that takes account of the new 'division of responsibilities between state and society' (ibid.: 2; my translation, KHG). The activating state is 'not so much a decision-maker and producer, but rather the moderator and activator of societal developments, which it cannot and should not determine alone' (ibid.; my translation, KHG). The Federal Government, it is noted, has a particular responsibility for creating the legal framework 'for a citizen oriented and co-operative state with an efficient public administration' (ibid.; my translation, KHG).

As regards the civil service, two main projects initiated by the new Federal Government in pursuance of its strategy of the activating state deserve highlighting. First, the Federal Government has announced its intention to seek a further reform of civil service legislation. The main objectives are to increase flexibility in remuneration, strengthen the performance principle in decisions on pay and promotions, and, put somewhat cryptically, to 'to optimise leadership functions' (ibid.: 10; my translation, KHG). Second, all Federal ministries have been asked to develop 'personnel development plans', on the basis of which career development plans for individual officials are to be developed. Both projects are to be completed by 2001.

It is too early to say what the effect, if any, of these longer-term reform plans on the Federal higher civil service will be. By contrast, the consequences of the move of to Berlin and the partial transfer of ministerial personnel from Bonn to the new capital have immediate and far-reaching consequences. It leads to an organisational division in the Federal ministerial administration, as each ministry now has two sites, one in Bonn and one in Berlin. Overall, about two-thirds of ministerial staff remain in Bonn, while approximately 8500 officials and ordinary employees work in Berlin (for details see Bundestagsdrucksache 14/1601; Goetz 1999b). With the seat of the Chancellor, the Government, the Parliament and the Bundesrat in Berlin, it is very likely that there will rapidly evolve an informal status differentiation between ministerial officials who are close to the political decisions-makers and those who work in the 'back offices' on the Rhine. Given the close involvement of executive politicians in decisions on senior appointments and promotion, proximity to the seat of power is especially important.

CONCLUDING REMARKS

Political reform initiatives provide a significant challenge to the adaptive capacity of the civil service as an institution, as does the partial transfer of the ministerial bureaucracy from Bonn to Berlin to individual officials. The effects of these developments must be considered in the context of a broader and deeper transformation of the classical public bureaucracy state. This transformation is not driven by a coherent and comprehensive reform design, but rather proceeds through the accretion of piecemeal and gradual change. It is propelled not so much by an identifiable reformist coalition than by a complex set of actors with partly contradictory aims, priorities and preferences. And while it involves, in part, changes in administrative law, legislation provides, at best a partial guide to the changing reality of German public administration. It is because of these features of administrative transformation that reform-centred accounts are in danger of underestimating the depth of change that German public administration is undergoing.

Very briefly, this transformation can be described as a decline of the public bureaucracy state, notably under the influence of Euroepanisation and post-modernisation (for a fuller discussion see Benz and Goetz 1996; Goetz 1999a). As part of this development, sovereign-hierarchical modes of administrative action lose their centrality; the boundaries between public and private law become increasingly porous; territory declines as a key principle of administrative organisation; and entrepreneurial and market rationalities increasingly complement (or even replace) the classical bureaucratic rationality. At the same time, the forces of integration that have helped to bind together a functionally, hierarchically, territorially and organisationally highly differentiated public administration become weaker. In particular, the growing reliance on institutions established under private law for the fulfilment of public tasks (including, increasingly, tasks involving the exercise of legitimate coercion) weakens the integrative potential of public law. Administrative culture becomes increasingly pluralised and, perhaps, polarised, especially as a consequence of the advancement of management values that challenge the traditional bureaucratic rationality. Moreover, inter-institutional co-operation and co-ordination, always at a premium in Germany's decentralised political system, are partly remoulded in the form of contract-based market-type exchanges.

Within such a context, the civil service, whose rise has been so closely tied to the emergence and consolidation of the internally and externally sovereign nation-state, must appear increasingly obsolete. Traditional justifications for the existence of a civil service that is distinguished by its functions, organisational principles, its special bond of loyalty to the state, and a legitimation grounded in its special role as a guardian and guarantor of the public good, are more and more difficult to reconcile with the reality of modern governance. If not its formal abolition, than at least an internal hollowing out of the civil service seems inevitable.

Yet, there is an alternative future. Although the longer-term survival of the institution of the civil service can certainly not be taken for granted, neither must its resilience and adaptability be underestimated. The civil service, with its pre-democratic inheritance, not only survived democratisation, but flourished in the democratic Federal Republic; despite its origins in the *Eingriffsstaat*, it adapted successfully to the extension of the social welfare state. Historical precedence holds a promise, therefore, that the civil service may also be capable of coming to terms with the shift from national government to internationalised governance. As the preceding discussion should have made clear, the German civil service is not a monolith, and nor are German officials a separate caste insulated from the society in which they live and work. This diversity and plurality of the civil service offer perhaps the best promise for its long-term future.

NOTES

1   In the following, the terms 'civil servant(s)' and 'official(s)' are used interchangeably.

BIBLIOGRAPHY

Arnim, H.H. von (1997), *Fetter Bauch regiert nicht gern. Die politische Klasse – selbstbezogen und abgehoben*, Munich: Kindler.

Auf dem Hövel, J. (1996), 'Politisierung der öffentlichen Verwaltung durch Parteien? Ursachenforschung und normative Debatte', in *Zeitschrift für Parlamentsfragen*, 27 (1): 82–95.

Barner, C. (1997), 'Remaking German democracy in the 1950s: was the civil service an asset or a liability', *German Politics*, 6 (3): 16–53.

Bayer, D. (1999), 'Ämter mit leitender Funktion', *Die Personalvertretung*, 42 (8): 338–56.

Benz, A. (1996), 'Beyond the public - private divide: institutional reform and cooperative policy Making', in A. Benz and K.H. Goetz (eds), *A New German Public Sector? Reform, Adaptation and Stability*, Dartmouth: Aldershot: 165–87.

Benz, A. and K.H. Goetz, (1996), 'The German public sector: national priorities and the international reform agenda', in A. Benz and K.H. Goetz (eds), *A New German Public Sector? Reform, Adaptation and Stability,* Dartmouth: Aldershot: 1–26.

Böckenförde, E.W. (1991), 'The origin and development of the concept of the Rechtsstaat', in A. Benz and K.H. Goetz (eds), *State, Society and Liberty: Studies in Political Theory and Constitutional Law,* Oxford: Berg.

Bönders, T. (1999), 'Neue Leistungselemente in der Besoldung – Anreiz oder Flop?', *Zeitschrift für Beamtenrecht*, 47 (1): 11–21.

Budäus, D. and S. Finger (1999), 'Stand und Perspektiven der Verwaltungsreform in Deutschland', *Die Verwaltung*, 32 (3): 313–43.

Bundesregierung (1999), Moderner Staat – Moderne Verwaltung. Cabinet Decision of 1 December 1999 (http://www.staat-modern.de/programm/index.htm).

Bundestagsdrucksache 14/1601 (13.09.99) Bilanz der Maßnahmen zum Umzug der Bundesregierung nach Berlin und der Ausgleichsleistungen für die Region Bonn.

Bürklin, W. et al .(1997), *Eliten in Deutschland: Rekrutierung und Integration* Opladen: Leske & Budrich.

Claus, A. (1999), 'Die Beamtenrechtsgesetzgebung des 13. Bundestages von 1994 bis 1998', *Zeitschrift für Beamtenrecht*, 47 (2): 37–52.

Derlien, H-U. (1984),'Einstweiliger Ruhestand politischer Beamter des Bundes 1949–1984', *Die Öffentliche Verwaltung*, 37 (17): 689–99.

Derlien, H-U. (1988), 'Repercussions of government change on the career civil service in West Germany', *Governance*, 1 (1): 50–78.

Derlien, H-U. and B.G. Peters (1998), *Who Works for Government and What Do They Do?* Bamberg: Universität Bamberg, Verwaltungswissenschaftliche Beiträge 32.

Dreier, H. (1991), *Hierarchische Verwaltung im demokratischen Staat,* Tübingen: Mohr.

Dreier, H. (1992), 'Zur 'Eigenständigkeit der Verwaltung', i*Die Verwaltung,* 25 (2): 137–56.

Dyson, K. (1977a), *Party, State and Bureaucracy in Western Germany,* Beverly Hills, Ca: Sage.

Dyson, K. (1977b), 'The West German 'party Book' administration: an evaluation', *Public Administration Bulletin,* **25**: 3–25.

Dyson, K. (1980), *The State Tradition in Europe,* Oxford: Robertson.

Dyson, K. (1982), 'Party government and party state', in H. Döring and G. Smith (eds), *Party Government and Political Culture in Western Germany,* Basingstoke: Macmillan: 77–100.

Goetz, K.H. (1993), 'Rebuilding public administration in the new German Länder: transfer and differentiation', *West European Politics,* **16** (4): 447–69.

Goetz, K.H. (1997), 'Acquiring political craft: training grounds for top officials in the German core executive', *Public Administration,* **75** (4): 753–75.

Goetz, K.H. (1999a), 'Between autonomy and subordination: bureaucratic legitimacy and administrative change in Germany', in L. Rouban (ed.), *Citizens and the New Governance: Beyond Public Management,* Amsterdam: IOS Press: 157–74.

Goetz, K.H. (1999b), 'Senior officials in the German Federal administration: institutional change and positional differentiation', in E. C. Page and V. Wright (eds), *Bureaucratic Elites in Western European Countries: A Comparative Analysis of Top Officials,* Oxford: Oxford University Press: 147–77.

Goetz, K.H. (2000), 'European integration and national public administrations', *West European Politics,* **23** (4).

Göser, H. and A. Schlatmann (1998), 'Neue Leistungsbezahlungselemente in der deutschen Beamtenversorgung', *Verwaltung und Fortbildung,* **26** (2): 133–43.

Hattenhauer, H. (1993), *Geschichte des deutschen Beamtentums,* Cologne: Carl Heymanns Verlag, 2nd enlarged ed.

Hess, A. (1995), 'Sozialstruktur des 13. Deutschen Bundestages: Berufliche und fachliche Entwicklungslinien', *Zeitschrift für Parlamentsfragen* **26** (4): 567–85.

Jestaedt, M. (1993), *Demokratieprinzip und Kondominalverwaltung,* Berlin: Duncker & Humblot.

Johnson, N. (1983), *State and Government in the Federal Republic of Germany: The Executive at Work,* Oxford: Pergamon, 2nd ed. .

Katz, R. and P. Mair (1995), 'Changing models of party organization and party democracy: the emergence of the cartel party', *Party Politics,* **1** (91): 5–27.

König, K. and N. Füchtner (1999), 'Schlanker Staat zwischen Bonn und Berlin', *Verwaltungs-Archiv,* **90** (1): 1–20.

Köpp, K. (1999), 'Öffentliches Dienstrecht', in U. Steiner (ed.) *Besonderes Verwaltungsrecht,* Heidelberg: C. F. Müller Verlag, 6th revised ed.: 381–483.

Kunig, P. (1999), 'Das Recht des öffentlichen Dienstes', E. Schmidt-Aßmann (ed.), *Besonderes Verwaltungsrecht* Berlin: de Gruyter, 11th ed.: 627–725.

Lecheler, H. (1996), 'Der öffentliche Dienst', in J. Isensee and P. Kirchhof (eds), *Handbuch des Staatsrechts der Bundesrepublik* Deutschland, vol III, Heidelberg: C. F. Müller Verlag, 2nd amended ed.: 717–73.

Lehmbruch, G. (1993), 'Institutionentransfer. Zur politischen Logik der Verwaltungsintegration in Deutschland', in W. Seibel et al.(eds), *Verwaltungsreform und Verwaltungspolitik im Prozeß der deutschen Einigung,* Baden-Baden: Nomos Verlagsgesellschaft: 41–66.

Lehmbruch, G. (1997), 'From state authority to network state: the German state in developmental perspective', in M. Muramatsu and F. Naschold (eds), *State and Administration in Japan and Germany,* Berlin: de Gruyter: 39–62.

Leitges, K. (1998), *Die Entwicklung des Hoheitsbegriffes in Art. 33 Abs. 4 des Grundgesetzes,* Frankfurt a.M.: Peter Lang.

Lenkungsausschuß Verwaltungsorganisation (1998), 'Schlanker Staat': Bilanz und Ausblick.

Zweiter Bericht zum Aktionsprogramm zur weiteren Steigerung von Effektivität und Wirtschaftlichkeit in der Bundesverwaltung. Cabinet Decision of 17 June 1998, Bonn: Bundesministerium des Innern.

Lorig, W. H. (1994), 'Parteipolitik und öffentlicher Dienst: Personalrekrutierung und Personalpatronage in der öffentlichen Verwaltung', *Zeitschrift für Parlamentsfragen*, 25 (1): 94–107.

Maiwald, J. (1999), 'Geschichte des Beamtenrechts', in J. Maiwald (ed.), *Beamtenrecht des Bundes und der Länder*, (Stand: October 1999) Heidelberg: R. v. Decker.

Manssen, G. (1999), 'Der Funktionsvorbehalt des Art. 33 Abs. 4 GG', *Zeitschrift für Beamtenrecht*, 47 (8): 253–7.

Mayntz, R. (1984), 'German Federal bureaucrats: a functional elite between politics and administration', in E. Suleiman (ed.), *Bureaucrats and Policy Making: A Comparative Analysis*, New York: Holmes & Meier: 174–205.

Mayntz, R. and H.-U. Derlien (1989), 'Party patronage and politicization of the West German administrative elite 1970–1987 - toward hybridization', *Governance*, 2 (4): 384–404.

Merten, D. (1999a), 'Aktuelle Probleme des Beamtenversorgungsrechts', *Neue Zeitschrift für Verwaltungsrecht*, 18 (8): 809–20.

Merten, D. (1999b), 'Das Berufsbeamtentum als Element deutscher Rechtsstaatlichkeit', *Zeitschrift für Beamtenrecht*, 47 (1): 1–11.

Morsey, R. (1997a), 'Personal- und Beamtenpolitik im Übergang von der Bizonen- zur Bundesverwaltung (1947–1950). Kontinuität oder Neubeginn? in *Von Windthorst zu Adenauer*, Paderborn: Ferdinand Schöningh: 71–112.

Morsey, R. (1997b), 'Zur Beamtenpolitik des Reiches von Bismarck bis Brüning', in *Von Windthorst bis Adenauer*, Paderborn: Ferdinand Schöningh: 13–26.

Padgett, S. (1993), 'Introduction: party democracy in the new Germany', *Parties and Party Systems in the New Germany* Aldershot: Dartmouth: 1–21.

Page, E.C. and L. Wouters (1995), 'The Europeanization of national bureaucracies', in J. Pierre (ed.), *Bureaucracy in the Modern State* Cheltenham: Edward Elgar: 185–204.

Page, E.C. and V. Wright (1999), 'Conclusion: Senior Officials in Western Europe', in E.C. Page and V. Wright (eds.), *Bureaucratic Elites in Western European States: A Comparative Analysis of Top Officials*, Oxford: Oxford University Press: 266–79.

Peters, B.G. (1996), *The Future of Governing: Four Emerging Models*, Lawrence: University of Kansas Press.

Pitschas, R. (1999), 'Verwaltungsmodernisierung, Dienstrechtsreform und neues Personalmanagement', *Die Verwaltung*, 32 (1): 1–19.

Präsident des Bundesrechungshof als Bundesbeauftragter für Wirtschaftlichkeit in der Verwaltung (1987) *Personal- und Organisationsaufgaben in der Öffentlichen Verwaltung am Beispiel oberster Bundesbehörden*, Stuttgart: Kohlhammer.

Püttner, G. (1987), 'Der öffentliche Dienst', in K.G.A. Jeserich et al. (eds*)*, *Deutsche Verwaltungsgeschichte, Band 5: Die Bundesrepublik Deutschland*, Stuttgart: Deutsche Verlags-Anstalt: 1124–42.

Sachverständigenrat (1997), 'Schlanker Staat' Abschlußbericht (no publisher).

Siedentopf, H. (1997), 'Der öffentliche Dienst in Europa: Grundsätze und Gefährdungen', in R.Morsey et al. (eds), *Staat, Politik, Verwaltung in Europa. Gedächtnisschrift für Roman Schnur*, Berlin: Duncker & Humblot: 327–51.

Statistisches Bundesamt (1998a), *Dienstbezüge der Bundesbeamten*, Wiesbaden: Statistisches Bundesamt, Fachserie 16, Reihe 4.4.

Wessels, W. and D. Rometsch (1996), 'German administrative interaction and European Union: the fusion of public policies', in Y. Mény et al. (eds), *Adjusting to Europe*, London: Routledge: 73–109.

Wiese, W. (1972), *Der Staatsdienst in der Bundesrepublik Deutschland,* Neuwied: Luchterhand.
Wright, V. (1994), 'Reshaping the state: The implications for public administration', *West European Politics*, **17** (3): 102–37.

5. The Development and Current Features of the Norwegian Civil Service System

Tom Christensen

INTRODUCTION

Norway is a small Scandinavian country with five million inhabitants. It was under Danish rule for 400 years, and the subordinate country in a union with Sweden from 1814 until 1905. The 1814 constitution established a separation of powers system that was modified in 1884 with the introduction of the parliamentary principle which created a close connection between the legislative and executive powers, and between the political and administrative parts of the executive. The first parties, the Conservative and the Liberal, were established in the same period, followed by the Labour Party. The number of parties increased somewhat after changing the electoral system (1921) from a majority rule in single constituencies to a proportional system based on party lists in the counties. After World War II the Labour Party has dominated among the parties, and it has been in office for 39 of the last 53 years. In 1972, through a referendum, the Norwegian people said 'no' to joining the EEC, and the same happened again in 1994, after first applying for membership of the European Union. Norway has always had a close relationship with the other Scandinavian countries, politically, culturally and economically, and the main axis of cooperation outside Scandinavia is the Atlantic one, reflected in the membership in NATO since 1949.

The point of departure in this chapter is that the development and current features of the central civil service system in Norway can best be understood by separating and contrasting two theoretical approaches, a *structural-instrumental* perspective, based on Gulick's work (1969) and Simon's work (1957), and a *institutional-cultural* perspective, based on Selznick's (1957) works (Christensen and Peters 1999).[1]

The fundamental point of departure for a *structural-instrumental* perspective is that there could be no political order and no political system without a structural basis, that public activities are organized activities, and that the instrumental aspect is connected to the possibility for *political* or *organizational design* (Egeberg 1987; Sabine and Thorson 1968; Wolin 1960). We relate this perspective here primarily to some kind of 'public organization theory tradition', combining political and organizational theories (Allison 1971; Gulick 1969; March and Olsen 1976 and 1989; Mayntz and Scharpf 1975; Olsen 1983a; Simon 1957).

The structural-instrumental perspective emphasises that formal structure matters when it comes to decision-making behaviour in public organisations (Egeberg 1987; Gulick 1969; Weaver and Rockman 1993; Weber 1970). The formal structure constrains and channels the models of thought and actual decisions of different actors, influencing the premises of decision they attend to (March and Olsen 1976; Simon 1957). The rationality is an organisational rationality, not an individual one, connected to a 'holistic' manner of organising intended to modify the cognitive limitations of individual actors (Scott 1992).

Politicians and top civil servants can use insight from the effects of different types of formal, administrative structures and try consciously to design or redesign whole administrative systems, certain bodies or certain administrative roles, to fulfill political goals (Egeberg 1987). Such a conscious policy of administrative development could be related to political and administrative leaders scoring high on systematic, cognitive capacity, either through having a lot of experience or using special bodies to collect and handle data about administrative changes (Olsen and Peters 1996). But it is also important that they have the control and power to implement new formal structures (Dahl and Lindblom 1953). This implies focusing on the structures of access (problems and solutions) and the structures of decision (participants) respectively, or on the processes of definition and activation they constrain (March and Olsen 1976).

The operationalisation and application of such a perspective on the development and current features of the Norwegian civil service system has been done in a rather straightforward and simple way, avoiding the pitfalls that have plagued studies of structural configurations and their effects (Egeberg 1987). The organisational thinking and decision-making connected to the development of two structural dimensions will be discussed. This first one is how and to what degree the civil service is vertically or horizontally specialised (Christensen and Lægreid 1999). *Vertical specialisation* focuses on how administrative bodies are co-ordinated and controlled, including what types of co-ordination means are used and how public authority is spread among actors and levels. *Horizontal specialisation* emphasises how civil service systems have divided functions and tasks between units and positions on the same level, including types of differentiation, and how divided a system is (Gulick 1969).

The other dimension is whether the specialisation relates to specialisation internally or externally in the civil service, characterised as: *intraorganisational specialisation* focuses on specialisation inside an administrative unit, for example a ministry, either vertically or horizontally, while *interorganisational specialisation* emphasises the specialisation between different units inside a civil service system (for example between ministries and directorates/agencies). We combine these two dimensions in the description and analysis of the development and current features of the Norwegian central administration.

A *cultural-institutional perspective* stresses that the development of administrative systems first of all can be seen as some kind of slow and gradual adaptation process to internal and external conditions or pressure (Selznick 1957). This natural process of adaptation, the institutionalisation process, creates a unique combination of informal, normative values and norms, and gives the organisation a 'soul', or culture, that differentiates it from other organisations. The formal structure is through this process of institutionalisation infused with values, adding to the technical and instrumental system. One can argue that different institutional norms and values develop or create different politics and actors, and different decision-making processes, public policies, citizens and societies (March and Olsen 1989).

The process of institutionalisation emphasises the integrative aspects of political administrative systems and creates stability in a changing world. Public actors, like civil servants, are supposed to have a feeling of common history, obligations and reason; they internalise these norms and values and use them for the creation of meaning and interpretation of internal and external stimuli and changes (March and Olsen 1989; Selznick 1957).

The institutional norms and values that characterise political-administrative organisations may combine norms and values of a general character in different ways, stressing that the system must attend simultaneously to many different considerations (Egeberg 1987, 1997). Such important norms and values are 'attending to the voices of the past and future', individual rights and obligations, 'political areas of freedom' and so on, all values that have to be defended against more pragmatic and instrumental considerations. Or the institutional norms and values can be more narrowly connected to the relationship between political and administrative bodies in certain sectors, to intraorganisational factors or to different ways to enact the role as a civil servant (Christensen and Róvik 1999). This supposedly leads to variety and uniqueness.

Structural and cultural processes in the civil service can constrain each other. On the one hand, the institutional-cultural processes in the central administration can historically constrain political efforts to intentionally design and change the administrative apparatus, thereby emphasising the need for continuity and political neutrality in the civil service system (Christensen and Peters 1999). On the other hand, political changes and reforms can change the formal structures of a civil service and therefore gradually change some of the main values and norms in the administrative culture.

The main idea in this chapter is that the Norwegian political-administrative system first of all is characterised by relatively high integration, homogeneity and equality, and that this is a result of a continuing reinforcement of structural and cultural processes working together (Christensen and Peters 1999). This idea seems to differ somewhat from some research results in Norway. Lægreid and Olsen (1978) in their large study of the Norwegian civil service emphasise that it is fragmented and heterogeneous concerning structure, demography, the models of thoughts and the patters of contacts of the civil servants, and so on. Egeberg et al. (1978) talk about a political segmentation of the political administrative system, and problems with coordination. And Olsen (1983d) stresses that top civil servants are 'key players on different teams'.

But I have two counter-arguments. First, compared to most other Western countries, Norway has had and still has a relatively homogeneous and integrated political-administrative system. Second, heterogeneous structural features in this system are made possible and are based on an egalitarian and homogeneous culture and are not threatening the co-ordination and integration in the system. In the following, we emphasise the homogeneity of the system but also describe the heterogeneous features and how they are dealt with.

The chapter is structured as follows. We start by describing and analysing the structural development of the Norwegian civil service in the period 1814 to 1996, followed by an analysis of the development of the administrative culture. Then some main points are further elaborated, starting with an analysis of the relationship between political leaders and the civil service. Some main cultural features that surround the civil service are then discussed. This is followed by an analysis of the development of the personnel policies, both from a structural point of view, that is how it has been organised, and concerning the cultural norms and values that have developed. One part of this development, the recruitment and representativeness of the civil servants is then emphasised, combining an analysis of the structuring and criteria/norms of selection.

THE DEVELOPMENT OF THE CIVIL SERVICE SYSTEM

Structure and Demography

In 1814, Norway got its first constitution, based on a Montesquieu-like division of powers system and a unitary state principle, but not its independence. The status as the inferior country in a 400-year relationship with Denmark was exchanged with being, in reality, the subordinate part in a union with Sweden (lasting until 1905). During these years, Norway had no separate and independent central civil service, but had a central administration together with Denmark, based in Copenhagen, and characterised by collegiate organisational structures (Christensen and Roness 1999).

The central administrative apparatus that was built up from 1814–15 had hierarchical features.[2] At first six ministries were established, all recognisable in today's structure: Church and Education, Military Services, Police, Judiciary Affairs, Finances and Commerce, and the Interior (Maurseth 1979). This *interorganisational horizontal specialisation* at the highest level of the central administration remained moderate and almost unchanged up until the early 1900s, and the increase in the number of civil servants was not significant.

As early as the 1820s and 1830s, demands came from new professional groups, such as engineers, teachers, doctors, military personnel and theologians, to change the central administrative system. Their main demands were for creating independent administrative bodies outside the ministries to further professional competence and improve the quality of the public decisions and services.[3] In two waves, in the 1840s and 1870s, these demands achieved a breakthrough and a number of independent agencies, called the directorates were created, totalling 10 to 15 in 1884 (Christensen 1997). These units, whose organisational model imitated Sweden's, were hierarchical units placed outside of and subordinated to the ministries and as such the result of *vertical interorganisational specialisation*. The increase in the number of civil servants in these units was much higher than in the ministries in the period 1840–84 (Benum 1979). This seemed to undermine the political and administrative control of the ministries. The reason for establishing this new organisational form was, besides the demands from the professional groups, that the parliament (the Storting) from the mid-1850s tried to undermine the political power of the king, in alliance with the professional groups.

The period 1814–84 has been characterised as the 'the civil servants' state', implying that the civil servants, and thereby the jurists as a professional group, dominated the Storting, the central administration, and the courts, and shared attitudes and values (Hernes and Nergaard 1990; Seip 1963). This similarity created a potential weakening of the constitutional macro design by somewhat blurring the formal constitutional separation of powers. This feature also potentially undermined the power of the king, especially if the civil servants collaborated with other groups, as they did with political and professional groups leading up to 1884. And the processes of influence got even more complicated with the emergence of the new professional groups (like engineers) in the directorates, threatening the dominance of the jurists.

In 1884, after strong conflicts and an impeachment process, the traditional 'division of powers' principle was in fact replaced by a parliamentary principle. This principle united the political power in the parliamentary chain, and implied the dissolution of the political importance of the king in Norway. This was a breakthrough for popular rule, an expanded popular sovereignty, based on a coalition between peasants and the urban intelligentsia (Olsen 1983b). Parliamentarism brought the Storting and the Cabinet close together; they were playing much more on the same team. This meant that further development of the directorate structure was generally stopped, it was more the time to strengthen the ministries again and control the directorates (Debes 1978; Jacobsen 1964). Except for establishing the Ministry of Foreign Affairs in 1905, this did not mean a lot of new ministries in the next 50 years, but more an expansion of the ones that were there, even though the economic crisis in the 1920s made that difficult to fulfill.

Between the world wars, the directorate structure was again under discussion. The political leadership wanted to move many of the directorates into the ministries again, motivated both by wanting to increase political control and to save money (Christensen and Roness 1999). This was intended to create another directorate model, apart from the independent one (the Swedish) or the one inside the ministries (the Danish), called the Norwegian model, characterised by the directorate being independent and simultaneously a department within the ministry (Jacobsen 1964; Tønnesson 1979). The structural policy of creating such a new and mixed model was only partly successful in this period, and was pretty much abolished after World War II, meaning that the independent directorate solution again totally dominated.

The ministerial structure in Norway changed quite a lot after World War II in two phases; the first decade after the war, and from the 1970s. The first wave brought Ministries for Fisheries, Communications, Industry, Commerce, Local Affairs and Labour, Wages and Prices, and Family and Consumer Affairs (Christensen and Egeberg 1997a). This was a mixed bag of ministries, some a reflection of modernisation and new issue areas, others just a reorganisation of older ones which had grown too large. The second wave, starting in the early 1970s, showed once again how new political questions received political and organisational attention. Ministries for Environmental Affairs, Oil and Energy, Culture and Foreign Aid were established (Christensen and Roness 1999). Some of these areas in the 1980s and early

1990s were included in larger ministries in a period of rationalisation and merger. A new cabinet appointed in late 1996 reversed most of these mergers again.

Generally, the ministerial structure in the postwar period showed increased *horizontal interorganisational specialisation* for a long time, while the last decades have brought a despecialisation trend, even though there are signs of some renewed specialisation again now. In 1996 there were 16 ministries in Norway, including the Prime Minister's Office.[4]

The increase in the number of employees in the ministries was 63 per cent from 1947 to 1991. The *horizontal intraorganisational specialisation* in the ministries increased in many ways in the same period. In the 1950–95 period, there was an increase in the number of departments by 95 per cent and in the number of sections and divisions by 73 per cent, meaning that there were smaller organisational units and more leaders (Christensen and Egeberg 1997a). But from the early 1990s, we also experienced some mergers, or despecialisation, in the internal structure of the ministries. The increase in internal horizontal specialisation seems to occur in waves, that is certain types of units are politically and administratively popular in certain periods. The last decade seems to have brought more emphasis again on integrated solutions.

The postwar period in the ministries also brought a strong increase in the *vertical intraorganisational specialisation*, reflecting the need for co-ordination in expanding and complex units. Not long after World War II, new positions of under-secretaries of state and administrative heads of ministries, secretaries-general, were established, as were later positions of assistant and deputy directors-general.

Historically speaking, professional groups in Norway have achieved the solution they wanted for the directorates, an independent solution, while the political and administrative leadership has struggled to influence the development in a more integrated direction (Christensen 1997). After World War II, this historical pattern changed in two ways. First, the political and administrative leadership became the main actors in developing the structure of the directorates, while the professional groups were more in the background. Second, the political leadership changed their main point of view and created a new administrative doctrine. This doctrine simply said that the political leaders had problems of capacity, that the ministries were too large, that resources should be moved out of the ministries, especially those connected to technical and apolitical issue areas. This policy of 'hiving off', aimed at creating exactly the same solution for the directorates, an independent solution, as the one traditionally favoured by the professional groups. But the political leaders said that this solution would create increased political control, not more professional autonomy. These opposing views, the development that followed, and experiences with structures based on this doctrine, illustrates quite clearly two analytical aspects: first, any organisational structure may have both positive and negative effects concerning the fulfilment of certain aims and considerations (Gulick 1969); second, backing changes in public organisational structures often takes as a departure immediate problems with existing ones without having much of a broad insight into the possible effects of new ones (Christensen 1997).

From the time the new administrative doctrine was formulated in 1955 and for the next 15 years, there was a strong increase in the number of directorates, bringing the total number up to about 70 or 80. But from the 1970s and up until now, very few new directorates have been established. This is because of a combination of a short period of some economic stagnation, more electoral support for conservative parties and a general decentralisation trend, creating scepticism towards directorates and general expansion of the public sector.

From 1947 to 1991, the increase in the number of employees in the directorates was 214 per cent, over three times more than in the ministries (Lægreid and Rolland 1992). Today the directorates have three or four times more employees than the ministries.

The main argument for the operation of the hiving-off doctrine, and the one repeated in the New Public Management concept, is that the political leadership should make the strategic and general decisions and delegate implementation to lower levels in the apparatus (Christensen and Lægreid 1998, 1999). One problem with this, seen in the ministry–directorate relationship today, is that the political leadership still has problems of capacity, attention and control, and that the directorates handle political important issue areas nearly *as if* they were ministries. But large ministries, resulting from vertical integration, can both create even more problems of capacity and give strong professional groups direct access to the political leadership, as experienced in the health administration sector in Norway (Christensen 1994, 1997).

The postwar period has brought some significant changes in some demographic features of the civil service. We have systematic data first of all from the ministries. An important change is in the type of higher education. The relative share of law graduates is down from 70–80 per cent to about 20 per cent over the last 50 years, while new groups are coming in, like national economists in the 1950s and business economists and social scientists (mostly political scientists) in the last two decades (Christensen and Egeberg 1997a). This indicates a change from emphasis on rule-oriented knowledge to more means-end-oriented competence.

Another major change, occurring first of all in the last two decades, is the fast growing percentage of women in the central administration. One can even talk about a 'feminisation period' (Lægreid 1995a). In the period 1976–96, the share of women in the ministries increased from 11 to 43 per cent and from 22 to 38 per cent (the last decade) in the directorates. Woman are most under-represented in the leadership positions (Christensen and Egeberg 1997a).

Norway has, especially since World War II, experienced increased participation of interest groups in public decision-making processes. This mixed corporatist, or corporative pluralist system has since been a main feature of the political system in Norway (Rokkan 1966; Kvavik 1976; Olsen 1978; Christensen and Egeberg 1979, 1997b; Egeberg 1981). The impact of this mixed corporatist system on the civil service was evident early on because the civil service has always been the main point of contact with public authorities for the interest groups, even though some of them, especially employers' and employees' organisations, have always had good contacts with the cabinet and the main political parties.

This relationship is mutual in many ways (Olsen 1983d). On the one hand, the civil service, on behalf of the political leadership, has contact because the public sector needs the participation of the interest groups. Through this participation, expertise can be provided, participation rights be enacted and interdependence attended to (Christensen and Egeberg 1979, 1997b; Egeberg 1981). Participation gives more centrality to the civil service in the decision-making process.

On the other hand, interest groups can fulfil their own goals, convert private problems into public problems and solutions, and show that they are representative and responsible through such participation. But the negative side of such a participation is that their ideological purity can be threatened, they can have problems in balancing internal democracy and external effectiveness, they can be responsible for public policies that are problematic, and so on (Christensen 1983; Olsen 1983d).

During the last 20 years, partly because of a more conservative voter population, more questions have been asked about the participation of interest groups, often seen as special interests, in public policy. The last decade has, however, changed little concerning the influence of interest groups in Norwegian polities. They are still important, even though their positions are under more pressure. One indication of this is that the number of public committees, normally a stronghold for the interest groups, has been cut down (Nordby 1994). And a recent survey in the civil service shows that interest group contacts with the civil service are less frequent than before and they are perceived as less important actors (Christensen and Egeberg 1997a). Interest groups now seems to concentrate more of their contacts with the Storting partly in collaboration with professional lobby firms.

THE DEVELOPMENT OF THE POLITICAL-ADMINISTRATIVE CULTURE

In the period 1814–84, the central administration was small and very much 'belonged' to the civil servants as a social class. Even though the civil servants had great influence in the central administration, the cabinet and the Storting, and as such created homogeneity in a system characterised by opposing powers, they were in some kind of cross-pressure (Hernes and Nergaard 1990). On the one hand, they attended to the king, but on the other hand worked for a national sovereign public administration. This implied a more political role, also in relating to increasingly important actors in the Storting, like the farmers, and later the labour movement. And the influence of the administrative leaders, mostly law graduates, was also placed under pressure from professional groups that were rather successful in influencing the structural development of the central administration. Adding to this was the fact that the division of power created a somewhat heterogeneous culture. Generally, one can say that this period developed a kind of mixed administrative culture, combining common values and norms among the civil servants with constant conflicts with other actors and between institutions.

After 1884, with the establishment of the parliamentary principle in Norway, there was a strong connection between the Storting and the Cabinet, a connection that since has created homogeneity, integration and legitimacy (Hernes and Nergaard 1990). Instead of being two competing political bodies, they should now work together. The Storting should heavily influence the creation of the Cabinet, give laws and rules, decide upon spending and control the executive, while the Cabinet, besides attending to the Storting, had the power, through the central administration, to prepare and implement the policies. This way of organising the executive–legislative relationship can generally be seen as creating a relatively high degree of *political attentiveness* and *loyalty* from the civil servants (Jacobsen 1960). This means attention both to the executive and to the Storting. And such attention generally secured the legitimacy of the civil service, leaving it both with more trust and freedom in the long run. That has been especially important in relation to the Storting, which has no direct formal line of authority and no subgovernmental means of control towards the civil service, as in some other countries (Hernes and Nergaard 1990; Olsen 1983b).

The most evident indicator of how the system is working is the longlasting principle of ministerial responsibility (Hernes and Nergaard 1990; Lægreid and Roness 1996). This principle stresses that each and every member of the Cabinet has political responsibility for all the issues and decisions that take place inside their own ministry. It creates awareness towards the scrutiny of the Storting. But it also creates a close relationship between the political leaders and administrative leaders inside each ministry. The minister knows that he or she is responsible politically and is dependent upon a smooth and professional relationship with the administration to succeed towards the Storting. And the civil servants know that a close relationship to the political leaders demands loyalty and attentiveness, which will pay off in increased influence and resources without compromising on the professional premises (Christensen 1991).

Some of these characteristics of the early parliamentary period seem to be as evident today: first, there is still a close relationship between the executive and the legislative branches and between the cabinet and the central administration (Hernes and Nergaard 1990). These relationships seem to have changed little during the years, even though the parliamentary situation has changed.[5]

Second, the civil servants traditionally seemed to have balanced the political and professional considerations quite well, as well as coping with an increasing number of other considerations (Christensen 1991, 1995; Egeberg 1997; Jacobsen 1960). The balance in their role is difficult to define precisely, but the ambiguity seems to have been functional for creating stability and avoiding conflicts.

The political loyalty of Norwegian civil servants is not one-dimensional and unambiguous. Traditionally, it is balanced with premises from professional autonomy and other considerations, and it gives the civil service more of a *general feeling of direction* than specific guidelines. Over the years, because of the increased complexity of public structures and issues, and increased problems of capacity of the political leaders, civil servants have gained increased discretionary influence. This underscores that the civil service is less guided by strict rules than by more general processes of internalising political signals and administrative culture. An important point is that this process historically has been made easier by high political stability and broad political consensus among the major parties.

During the last decade, partly because of the influence from the New Public Management, there has been an increasing tendency to try to demarcate the distinction between politics and administration (Christensen and Lægreid 1998, 1999). This trend, though not closely in accordance with the historic traditions in the civil service, has had difficulties in really changing the relationship between politicians and the civil servants, and therefore has symbolic features. As part of the new market-oriented trend there have also been some tendencies, often paradoxical and controversial, to politicise the civil service, especially the ministries (Olsen 1983c). This trend has had to struggle with the cultural traditions in the civil service. It has been controversial because it is threatening the professional autonomy and discretion of the civil service as well as the open decision-making process.

Third, the role of the civil servants in Norway, especially for those in the ministries, has been one of mutual trust with the politicians, a relatively active 'political' role, not too preoccupied with the distinction between politics and administration, a role characterised more by socialisation to the administrative culture than relying on externally-imposed rules. The role has been less politically attentive in the directorates, an effect of a different formal structural position, removed more from the political leadership (Egeberg 1989). In the directorates the considerations connected to clients, lower levels of public authorities and the private sector have been relatively more important, in addition to the professional premises (Christensen and Egeberg 1997a). This reveals one problem, as seen by the political leadership, with the independent directorate model.

There are, of course, many other factors that can assist in explaining the relatively homogeneous and cooperative administrative culture and role enactment in the central administration. One is that the judicial system means next to nothing politically, both a reflection of the weak formal status of the judiciary in the constitution and the actually development on which it is based (Hernes and Nergaard 1990). Another important factor is that Norway is a small and homogeneous country as for population, it has few and not very deep crosscutting cleavages, and therefore has potentially fewer conflicts built into the administrative structures. A third factor is that for a long time, the public sector has been large, the trust in political and administrative institutions and actors has been great and the status of civil servants has been high, resulting more in consensus and a general feeling of playing on the same team than in conflicts and division.

The specialisation of the formal structure has increased substantially in this period, both vertically and horizontally, creating potential for fragmentation, administrative self-interest, subcultures and resistance against political control. But the coordination efforts, both through collegial bodies and new leadership positions, and common cultural norms and values, have had to cope with these tendencies.

Focusing on administrative reforms and its content – norms and values – can also give insight into the political-administrative culture. The reform tradition in government and civil service in Norway is more towards making smaller and pragmatic changes based on changing political signals in public reports, than on making broad and sweeping reform based on political ideology. Since World War II, there has been a growing concern for the government to develop an administrative policy that could change the administrative apparatus in a systematic way. One way to understand this policy is to look at it as changing the balance of different considerations and values (Christensen and Lægreid 1998). This set of considerations, often inconsistent and ambiguous, appears to have grown more complex over time. Main considerations have been political control, democratic participation (from internal and external actors), rationalisation, efficiency, formal rights, professional autonomy, local autonomy and consumer/client orientation (Egeberg 1997).

In the first years after World War II, great emphasis was put on internal administrative and technical problems of rationalisation (Christensen and Lægreid 1998). This period resulted in the establishment of a directorate called the Rationalisation Directorate, later the Directorate of Public Management. In the 1950s, attention was more on questions of developing proper procedures for public decision-making, including securing formal rights. This priority resulted in an Ombudsman for public administration (1962), a law defining proper procedures of casework in public administration (1967) and a law for easier access to information about public decision-making processes (1970). In the 1950s initiatives were also taken, as mentioned, to strengthen the ministries as 'political secretariats', as units more at the disposal of the political leadership, and more preoccupied with policy developing and planning.

In the 1970s, as some kind of general reflection of international trends, values of democracy were emphasised in the administrative reform work (Christensen and Lægreid 1998). This was done by creating more opportunities for employees to participate in internal processes without actually changing the political and administrative control of the processes. At the same time a decentralisation wave also occurred, with a breakthrough at the county level, and with strengthening of the local authorities on the lowest level (Fevolden 1997; Larsen 1997).

In the 1980s and early 1990s, emphasis in the public sector, as in many other countries, has been on New Public Management (Christensen and Lagræid 1999). For many years, the non-socialist parties had claimed that there was something wrong with the public sector and public bureaucracy, that is was too large, ineffective, costly and not tending to the clients. The new trend in the 1980s was that the Labour Party accepted much of this critique. This was demonstrated in the similarity of two programmes for the development of the government, called a modernisation programme and a renewal programme, made in 1985/86 and 1987, respectively, by a conservative and a labour government. These programmes talked more about market orientation, efficiency, flexibility, merit pay, consumer orientation, and so on than before. It was far more reluctant, however, than comparable programmes in other countries to comply fully with any kind of managerial public revolution (Olsen 1996). This shows that the political leadership took into consideration the traditional values in the civil service, which in many ways were not compatible with this new trend.

A survey in the ministries in 1996 shows that the New Public Management for the most part is a reform wave with implementation problems in the Norwegian civil service (Christensen and Lægreid 1998). Norway is a slow learner and a reluctant reformer when facing this strong international trend (Olsen 1996). Efforts at privatisation are largely seen as irrelevant, as is internal pricing mechanisms and contracts. Management or government by objectives is seen as the one part of the reform trend that is most relevant, not as a strict system, but more in general as attending to goals, use of resources and results. It is easier to show an increased consciousness in this regard than to show any increase in political control or actual cost efficiency.

The impression is that the main cultural norms, connected to the balance between political control and professional autonomy, to equality and universalism, to rights, to openness and scrutiny, to responsiveness, and so on, are relatively stable in this half-century period. It is interesting to note that some of the reforms come in waves that are similar to the reforms in other countries, showing that diffusion, imitation, reform fashions and myths are important (Downs and Larkey 1986; Olsen and Peters 1996).

POLITICISATION

The relationship between political leaders and civil servants can be discussed according to both a structural perspective, emphasising how it is organised, and a cultural perspective, that is what characterise the main norms and values in the interaction.

The Norwegian civil service is a combination of a classical Weberian, a professional and responsible civil service (Heady 1996). It is classical Weberian in many structural ways: civil servants are supposed to closely attend to laws and rules of a universal character, the central administrative apparatus is dominated by a hierarchical structure, civil servants are recruited based on higher professional education and knowledge and so on (Christensen 1995; Lægreid and Olsen 1978; Lægreid and Roness 1996; Olsen 1983b). But it is a 'softer' version of the Weberian model in the sense that much more weight is put on the socialisation of civil servants, internalising important values in the administrative culture and providing them with a stable and equal incentive structure, than relying on tight programming of what they do or corrections by the leaders of their handling of different decisions (Christensen 1991; Christensen and Egeberg 1997a; Christensen and Peters 1999); Lægreid and Olsen 1978).

The political loyalty the civil servants show to each and every new political leadership coming into office is relatively strong, that is they attend to and emphasise that political signals and decisions are important. Stronger political loyalty would have created problems when new political leaders take office, as well as problems of professional administrative continuity (Jacobsen 1960). Accordingly, Norway does not have any system of politically appointed civil servants, and they all stay in their jobs when there are changes in government. The political sensitivity of the civil servants could have been stronger from a political point of view, but this is not any real problem for at least one reason, that is the relatively small political differences between the leading parties, which makes continuity a good option.

Norwegian political leaders have always put great emphasis on professional expertise in public decision-making in order to secure the quality of decisions and create continuity (Christensen 1991). This generally implies a norm of partial professional autonomy. This autonomy has gradually increased over the last decades because of problems of capacity of political leaders and the development of frame laws and more administrative discretion (Christensen and Egeberg 1997a). One can of course say that more professional autonomy may encourage civil servants to attend to their own self-interests or professional, normative values. But civil servants in the central administration in Norway seem primarily to be furthering interests connected to their formal structural unit, position and tasks, and to attend to main cultural values and history (Egeberg 1978 and 1989). There is also every reason to believe that the values and norms of the civil service are in accordance with the mainstream of the political leadership.

Concerning the interdependency between the political and administrative system, political and administrative careers and roles are pretty much separated in Norway. The central politicians are generally not recruited from administrative positions, even though some under-secretaries of state have held such positions. And civil servants seldom have backgrounds from higher political positions, even though they are active in political activities outside their job (Lægreid and Olsen 1978).[6] The norm is that the civil servants' political activities cannot be closely connected to the tasks they carry out in their public positions.

Civil servants are normally the closest contact interest groups have with public authorities, thereby reflecting in the administrative structure, interests and cleavages in society (Christensen and Egeberg 1979; Lægreid and Roness 1996). This feature can potentially give the interest groups influence, create alliances with the civil servants, increase fragmentation and increase the pressure on coordination. There are many interest groups, however, with opposing interests trying to influence the civil service, and some interest groups also have close connections with the political leaders, so it is *not* obvious that corporative features are weakening the political leadership (Christensen and Egeberg 1997b).

Political leaders in Norway expect civil servants to be both simultaneously loyal and professional, a reflection and mutual reinforcement of the formal parliamentary chain and the cultural homogeneity in the system.

PUBLIC OPINION: LEGITIMACY AND TRUST

Cultural-institutional norms and values are important as a context for the legitimacy of a political administrative system. The system needs a more general support basis and more specifically support for certain institutions, actors, procedures and decisions.

General diffuse support for the system in Norway is relatively high, as measured through the confidence and trust the citizens express in their government, their institutions, their parties and fellow citizens (Miller and Listhaug 1990). Compliance to the system and obedience to laws seem to be relatively high, but also pragmatic, based on a combination of fear of consequences and commitment to the system (Listhaug and Miller 1985). Compared to other European countries the confidence in Norwegian public institutions is well above average for most types of institutions (Listhaug and Wiberg 1995). And the same tendency is evident in comparison to the USA (Miller and Listhaug 1990). The confidence in public institutions seems to be decreasing during the last decades, and this tendency appears also in Norway, and especially in the trust of the Storting and the public administration, the latter one moves down to an European average (Listhaug and Wiberg 1995). This development is not easy to explain, especially since the data on public administration are not for the central administration in particular, but for all types of public administration.

The tradition high level of confidence in Norwegian political leaders, in different political institutions and the public bureaucracy seems to create a large reservoir of legitimacy or slack for the government, perhaps a reflection of wide political agreement on a large public sector and welfare state and a relative satisfaction with how the system is controlled and public services delivered. It even seems to create trust that the public processes sometimes are relatively slow, because this means that consultations and negotiations have taken place, fulfilling a lot of different interests and ideas.

The cleavage structure in Norway is not complex and deep, thus there are potentially fewer problems for the political and administrative systems to cope with in creating and implementing public programmes than in many other systems (Christensen and Peters 1999). This may generally also explain why the level of critique towards the civil service in Norway seems to be relatively low. Another important factor explaining this low level is the relative weakness of the court system as a political actor and the lack of even a special court handling cases from the public administration. This seems to lead to a less complex and less adversarial political and administrative decision-making process, less ambiguous political signals, less conflicts and more favourable conditions for the public administration. The public apparatus is not an enemy or something you take to court, but more a 'friend', someone you rely on and trust.

Another way to explain the general high trust and positive image of the political system generally and the civil service more specifically, is to explain Norway's position according to the cultural group/grid theory of Mary Douglas (1986 and 1990).[7] Norway seems to be closest to what this theory calls an 'egalitarian type'. On the one hand, Norway scores high on group, that is the importance of collective definitions is high, either as belonging to the system as a whole or to different societal groups. On the other hand, Norway scores relatively low on grid, meaning that the behavior inside and between groups is not very much determined by strict, detailed and differentiated rules. This may seem to be a paradox since the political-administrative system is also preoccupied with Weberian features like laws, rules and procedures, but these can more be seen as 'meta-rules' (Christensen and Peters 1999). They have more of a frame character; they are not very detailed, are universal and are not much differentiated according to different groups.

In Norway the legitimacy of the government seems partly to be based on collectively-oriented procedures, not substantive criteria, due processes and individual rights, like for example in the United States (Heady 1996). It is relatively more important to follow the 'rules of the game', both of a formal and cultural character, to do 'things the right way' instead of doing 'the right things' (Christensen and Egeberg 1997a; Christensen and Peters 1999). This is, of course, not an argument for Norwegian public decision-making processes lacking goals and political administrative control.

THE INTERNAL LABOUR MARKET: THE DEVELOPMENT OF PERSONNEL POLICIES

We analyse the development of the personnel policy field in the civil service in Norway both from a structural point of view, how its structure is developing, but also from a cultural perspective, focusing on the main norms and values that emerge and develop.

Generally speaking, the field of personnel policy, as one important part of the general administrative policy field, has traditionally been divided into four parts in Norway: internal personnel administrative policy, the policy of internal participation, wage policy and the recruitment or career policy (Lægreid 1989). Historically, key aspects of personnel management functions, like personnel-administrative tasks, wage policy and internal participation, have either been connected to the Ministry of Finance, with low political prestige internally, or to a ministry for governmental administration (the last 30 years), with relatively little general political significance (Christensen and Lægreid 1998). Traditionally, personnel policy decision-making processes have been characterised by a combination of central control by the government and negotiations with the top unions in the public sector, especially the Norwegian Federation of Trade Unions, with some variety between its different fields.

The policy towards internal personnel administration has historically been centralised and co-ordinated by the government, but developed more features of negotiation over time. The focus of this policy has been a gradual institutionalisation of a very complicated law for civil servants, established in 1917, with an ever-stronger emphasis on their rights and the rule of law (Roness 1996). The higher civil servants in Norway had already received guarantees against layoff in the 1814 constitution. That right was also established, in a somewhat weaker form, for middle and lower level civil servants in 1917, and has lately been made even stronger.

Historically speaking, almost no one has lost their job in the central administration in Norway, according to the rule of 'major changes in tasks and functions'. Even in the 1920s and early 1930s, civil servants were not laid off, but the positions removed after people quit or got their retirement pension. During the last decade, there has been a conflict over cutback man-·agement in some of the communication directorates. Some directorates have been converted to organisational forms that are more loosely coupled to the political leadership, to cope with market-exposure (Christensen and Lægraid 1999; Roness 1996). The result of such new forms seems to have been a real downsizing of the workforce in some few directorates.

Wage policy in Norway has historically been loosely coupled to the personnel-administrative policy, but is now formally organised together in the Ministry of Government Administration. Traditionally, the content of this policy has been the result of negotiations between the government and the top labour organisations for civil servants. For a long time now, the main principles of the wage system have been standardisation, equality, tenure and education. In 1948, a collective wage system for the central public sector was established, but before that sectorial wage agreements existed which built on the same principles (Roness 1996).

Over the last ten years, the tightly controlled and co-ordinated wage system has loosened, but it is still attending very much to traditional values. The most important feature is that most of the top civil servants have been taken out of the traditional system and put on leadership contracts in a type of merit pay system (Lægreid 1993a, 1993b and 1995b). This system, which initially substantially raised some administrative leaders' salaries, has been controversial and implemented in a much more reluctant way than originally planned. The gap relative to salaries of leaders in the private sector seems not to have decreased through this reform (Roness 1996).

Historically, the policy towards the participation of the civil servants in 'co-determination' in the central administration has been more varied and less co-ordinated than for the other two areas. In 1974, a major agreement regulating the rights of representatives for the employees' organisations in wage negotiations was reached (Roness 1996). This was one main factor leading up to an agreement in 1980 formalising the participation rights of civil servants' unions in internal processes, showing the relationship between wage policy and participation policy. The rights of participation for the civil servants are primarily connected to a 'narrow' definition of relevance, and are differentiated according to the political importance of the issues. If the political leaders define a decision-making process as politically important, for example, concerning reorganisation or recruitment, they can decide to close the decision process, thereby giving civil servant organisations relatively minor influence (Christensen 1994).

The recruitment of civil servants has always been decentralised in the ministries and directorates, meaning that each administrative institution exercises a good deal of control over the selection process. Norway has never had any obligatory career path through certain universities, any central administrative school or centralised selection process, nor any sharp division between different types or classes of civil servants. Normally, most start on the lowest hierarchical level when they are recruited from higher education and have, in principle, equal opportunity to reach the top level of administrative leaders.

Decentralised recruitment is based on a common set of merit criteria, but the criteria open up for local adaptation and discretionary behavior (Røberg 1991). The most important factor for recruitment for a first job in the ministries is higher education, while tenure and performance are more significant as one rises in the hierarchy (Christensen and Egeberg 1997a; Lægreid 1989). In the directorates, the share of people having higher education when recruited is lower, but some of the larger ones historically have had programmes for internal education and training.

Traditionally, civil servants have had their entire career inside one ministry or directorate. This has changed somewhat the last decades, but is still the rule. If a civil servant leaves a job in a ministry, it is normally to move to another ministry. In the directorates, the exchange is more often with the private sector. Only about 10 per cent of the leadership positions in the ministries are historically filled by external applicants who are horizontally recruited, most are promoted from within (Christensen and Egeberg 1997a).

In one particular way, the wage and the recruitment policies of the last decade have been more connected than before. Traditionally, the wages in the central administration have been the same on each and every hierarchical level, and a position at a higher level has always meant leadership responsibility. This has changed with the sharp increase in the number of advisor positions (Christensen and Egeberg 1997a). This system, dividing the civil servants on each hierarchical level into two groups, those with and those without leadership responsibilities, can make it easier for the political leaders with capacity problems to control and coordinate. They relate to fewer administrative leaders and can make more flexible use of the advisors. But this system has built-in problems of authority ambiguity and conflicts over career paths and salary.

REPRESENTATIVENESS

The question of the representativeness of the civil service is related to how it organises its recruitment processes and to the main cultural norms and values in these processes. The recruitment of civil servants in Norway has historically been based on a concept of equal opportunity representativeness.

The composition of the civil servants in the central administration has never been any kind of mirror image of the population (Lægreid and Olsen 1978; Olsen 1983c; Christensen and Egeberg 1997a). In fact, it is among the least representative political and administrative bodies in Norway. Middle-aged men from higher social strata in Oslo with a law degree have traditionally been strongly overrepresented. Even though the demography of the civil servants has changed somewhat the last decades, for example concerning the share of women, the main picture of a very biased group remains. This also means that the social-economic background of the civil service, the social representative aspect of the concept of representation, has had relatively minor significance for its legitimacy.

Civil servants in the Norwegian system are first of all supposed to represent the opinions of the people, furthered through the national elections, the Storting and the executive (Olsen 1988). The political signals and decisions produced in the parliamentary channel are somewhat biased related to over-representation of certain political parties, but are probably less so than in many other political systems. The political decisions and signals are, however, often complex and ambiguous, intentionally or not, leaving the civil servants with some discretion (Christensen 1991; Christensen and Egeberg 1997a). This discretion in Norway is traditionally enacted very much according to different types of professional knowledge.

Norway has no tradition of clientele relations, but after World War II has had a political and administrative culture relatively open to the participation of interest groups in public decision-making processes. On the one hand, this can be seen as some kind of pluralistic, democratic safeguard, but also as a biased system favouring the strong interest groups which represent business and employees' organisations (Christensen and Egeberg 1997b; Egeberg et al. 1978; Olsen 1983b). The contact civil servants have with interest groups can be seen as some kind of 'withinputs', that is they further or represent certain strong private interests in decision-making processes. But civil servants can also represent groups and interests with few resources, like we see in the social and health sector, and as such they are securing some kind of institutional pluralism (Egeberg 1978).

One main societal reason for having a system of representativeness in the central administration based on the parliamentary chain, and not on social pluralism, is that Norway is small and homogeneous, with few and not very deep cross-cutting cleavages. This is again reflected in the relatively few political parties and interest groups based on religion, ethnicity, language, gender, geography, and so on.

Summing up, the representativeness of the civil service in Norway is based on three aspects working together to secure its legitimacy. First, the organisation, procedures and cultural values in the recruitment processes are common and not controversial, even though the processes are decentralised, creating a feeling of equal opportunity. Second, the civil servants are representative in the sense of being representatives for public opinions and political leaders in the numerical election channel. Third, they are representative through channelling opinions and premises from the interest groups in the corporate channel to public decision-making processes.

CONCLUDING REMARKS

A main argument in this chapter is that major trends in the development of the Norwegian service system can best be understood by combining a *structural-instrumental* and a *cultural-institutional* perspective. One major point is that the macro-constitutional design, the parliamentary principle, structurally creates a close and homogeneous relationship between the legislative and the executive branches. This again has had major impacts on the way the civil service is organised and on the development of norms and values in the administrative culture, especially the combination of political responsiveness and professional autonomy. The administrative culture which developed has also constrained the structural development of the civil service, thereby creating continuity and predictability.

Generally, the Norwegian civil service system resembles the type Heady (1996) labels 'policy responsiveness'. Characterising the Norwegian civil service with words like continuity, relative homogeneity, and equality imply many important development factors. First, the civil service system has historically been moderately structurally specialised, making it easier to coordinate. The changes in specialisation have traditionally been gradual and slow, reflecting a desire by the political leadership to attend to setting norms and values. When the process of specialisation was speeding up after World War II, emphasising both vertical and horizontal inter- and intra-organisational specialisation, it was partly planned and controlled and considerable emphasis was put on creating collegial bodies for co-ordinating the hierarchies in order to avoid fragmentation in an increasingly complex system. Even though growing administrative specialisation has created tendencies of fragmentation and civil servants attending to unit-specific tasks and values, there have been relatively few conflicts in the system, mainly because the civil servants share some common cultural norms and values in the political-administrative milieu.

The relative structural homogeneity of the system very much reflects the social homogeneity in Norwegian society and the lack of deep and crosscutting cleavages. Scoring low on social pluralism implies that the structure of the civil service is not primarily based on such factors as geography, ethnicity, religion, and so on, thereby providing fewer possibilities for conflict.

The structural integration and homogeneity in the civil service has created a strong and homogeneous administrative culture based on close attention for political decisions and also to professional considerations. This combination, which has changed relatively little over time, has fostered a high legitimacy for the civil service, towards the political leadership in the executive branch, to the Storting and to public opinion at large. It has combined democratic features with professional expertise and performance. Even though civil servants have always been a social elite in Norway, the close integration in the 'parliamentary chain' and their expertise and attention to universal procedural rules has created a high trust in the civil service. The feeling is of being players on the same team, not of adversity and conflict, even though attention also is given to substructures and subcultures.

The feature of integration and homogeneity is also related to equality in the system. Recruitment to the civil service has not been based on any bias concerning attending any special university or administrative school, quite unlike countries such as France or Japan. Even though law graduates dominated recruitment to the civil service for a long period of time, it has been open to many types of higher education, even more so after World War II. Nor has the civil service been divided into different classes of civil servants, making it potentially relatively easy to have a lifelong career for anyone, with gradual promotions to a higher level. The wage system has also been characterised by equality by securing equal pay for equal functions and tasks regulated in standardised wage systems.

During the last 20 years, some of the traditional structural features and culture of the civil service in Norway have been threatened by newer reform trends, like the New Public Management. The civil service has, however, reacted slowly to the reforms attempts, much more slowly than in comparable countries, a feature that is understandable based on our interpretation of the Norwegian civil service with its integration, continuity, homogeneity and equality (Christensen and Lægreid 1998, 1999; Lægreid and Pedersen 1996). A combination of structural and cultural reasons results in Norway being a reluctant reformer and a slow learner (Olsen 1983e; Olsen and Peters 1996).

NOTES

1. To treat central civil service systems in different countries as institutions may imply different definitions to different scholars, as reflected in the diversity of the organisation theory field. Some, like March and Olsen (1989, 1995), use a broad perspective and a key concept in their orientation is the 'logic of appropriateness', focusing on different formal and informal rules that guide actors' models of thoughts and behaviour (Christensen and Róvik 1999). Others would first of all relate to Selznick's (1949, 1957) cultural theory and its different offshoots, emphasising that public organisations gradually develop a distinct character or 'soul', that reflects the combinations of internal and external constraints. A third institutional angle is the literature connected to symbolic interactionism and theories of how myths develop and spread in systems of organisations (Meyer and Rowan 1977).
2. The recent decades' non-hierarchical structures have been more popular again in central administrative systems all over the world. This seems to exemplify that there are cyclical changes between organisational forms (Meyer and Rowan 1977).
3. Independent agencies are not in fact independent of the political leadership, which has the political responsibility for the directorates, but represent an organisational form that is relatively more independent than most others in the civil service.
4. Normally there is one minister in each ministry in Norway, and the country has no system with junior ministers, but two ministries have two ministers: foreign affairs (for foreign policy and foreign aid) and social and health affairs.
5. In 1921, when the electoral system changed, the number of parties was four, while there are currently eight major parties, seven represented in the *Storting*.
6. Over the years there has been some discussion about the top positions in the directorates, the directorships, which primarily are administrative positions. Some of these directors have in recent decades come from central political positions, primarily in the Labour Party, but they have generally been well qualified and had sectorial experience, and functioned mainly in an administrative role.
7. The following discussion is based on Christensen and Peters 1999.

BIBLIOGRAPHY

Allison, G.T. (1971), *Essence of Decision*, Boston: Little, Brown.

Benum, E. (1979), *Sentraladministrasjonens historie, Bind 2 1845–84*, Oslo: Scandinavian University Press.

Christensen, T. (1983), *Organisasjonslederskap under endrete handlingsbetingelser*, Tromsø: Scandinavian University Press.

Christensen, T. (1991), 'Bureaucratic roles: political loyalty and professional autonomy', *Scandinavian Political Studies,* 14 (4): 303–20.

Christensen, T. (1994), *Politisk styring og faglig uavhengighet: reorganisering av den sentrale helseforvaltningen*, Oslo: TANO.

Christensen, T. (1995), 'The Scandinavian state Tradition and Public Administration: The case of Norway', Paper prepared for the APSA Meeting, Chicago.

Christensen, T. (1997), 'Utviklingen av direktoratene, aktører, tenkning og organisasjonsformer', in T.Christensen and M. Egeberg (eds), *Forvaltningskunnskap*, Oslo: TANO.

Christensen, T. and M. Egeberg (1979), 'Organized group-government relations in Norway: on the structured selection of participants, problems, solutions and choice opportunities', *Scandinavian Political Studies*, **3** (2): 239–60.

Christensen, T. and M. Egeberg (1997a), 'Sentraladministrasjonen- en oversikt over trekk ved departementer og direktorater', in Christensen, T. and M. Egeberg (eds), *Forvaltnings kunnskap*, Oslo: TANO.

Christensen, T. and M. Egeberg (1997b), 'Noen trekk ved forholdet mellom organisasjonene og den offentlige forvaltningen', in T. Christensen. and M. Egeberg (eds), *Forvaltningskunnskap*, Oslo: TANO.

Christensen, T. and P. Lægreid (1998), 'Administrative Reforms Policy: the Case of Norway', *International Review of Administrative Sciences*, **64**: 457–75.

Christensen, T. and P. Lægreid (1999), 'New Public Management – are politicians losing control?' Paper presented at ECPR Joint Sessions, Mannheim.

Christensen, T. and B.G. Peters (1999), *Structure, Culture and Governance: A Comparative Analysis of Norway and the United States*, Lanham, MA: Rowman & Littlefield.

Christensen, T. and P.G. Roness (1999) (eds), 'Den historiske arven-Norge', in P. Lægreid and O.K. Pedersen (eds), *Frq opbygning til ombygning i staten,* Copenhagen: Jurist-og Økonomforbundets Forlag.

Christensen, T. and K.A. Róvik (1999), 'The Ambiguity of Appropriateness' in M. Egeberg and P. Lægreid (eds), *Organizing Political Institutions*, Oslo:Scandinavian University Press.

Dahl, R.A. and C.E. Lindblom (1953), *Politics, Economics and Welfare*, Chicago: University of Chicago Press.

Debes, J. (1978), *Statsadministrasjonen*, Oslo: NKS-forlaget.

Douglas, M. (1986), *How Institutions Think*, Syracuse NY: Syracuse University Press.

Douglas, M. (1990), 'Risk as a forensic resource', *Daedalus*, 119 (4): 1–16.

Downs, G.W. and P.D. Larkey (1986), *The Search for Government Efficiency. From Hubris to Helplessness,* Philadelphia: Temple University Press.

Egeberg, M. (1978), 'Institusjonell pluralisme som interesseartikulerende system', *Tidsskrift for samfunnsforskning*, 19: 42–54.

Egeberg, M. (1981), *Stat og organisasjoner*, Oslo: Scandinavian University Press.

Egeberg, M. (1987), 'Designing public organizations', in J. Kooiman and K.A. Eliassen (eds), *Managing Public Organizations*, London: Sage Publications.

Egeberg, M. (1989), 'Om å organisere konkurrerende beslutningsprinsipper inn i myndighetsstrukturen', in M. Egeberg (ed.), *Institusjonspolitikk og forvaltningsutvikling: bidrag til en anvendt statsvitenskap*, Oslo: TANO.

Egeberg, M. (1997), 'Verdier i statsstyre og noen organisatoriske implikasjoner', in T. Christensen and M. Egeberg (eds), *Forvaltningskunnskap*, Oslo: TANO.

Egeberg, M., J.P. Olsen and H. Sætren (1978), 'Organisasjonssamfunnet og den segmenterte stat', in J.P. Olsen (ed.), *Politisk organisering*, Bergen: Scandinavian University Press.

Fevolden, T. (1997), 'Fylkeskommunen – fra hjelpeorgan til selvstendig forvaltningsnivå', in T. Christensen and M. Egeberg (eds), *Forvaltningskunnskap*, Oslo: TANO.

Gulick, L. (1969: Reprint 1937), 'Notes on the theory of organizations, with special reference to government', in L. Gulick and L.Urwick (eds), *Papers on the Science of Administration*, New York: A.M. Kelley.

Heady, F. (1996), 'Configurations of civil service systems', in A.J.G.M. Bekke, J. Perry and Th.A.J. Toonen (eds), *Civil Service Systems in Comparative Perspective*, Bloomington & Indianapolis: Indiana University Press.

Hernes, G. and K. Nergaard (1990), *Oss i mellom: Konstitusjonelle former og uformelle kontakter Storting – Regjering*, Oslo: FAFO.

Jacobsen, K.D. (1960), 'Lojalitet, nøytralitet og faglig uavhengighet i sentraladministrasjonen', *Tidsskrift for samfunnsforskning*, 1: 231–48.

Jacobsen, K.D. (1964), *Teknisk hjelp og politisk struktur*, Oslo: Scandinavian University Press.

Kvavik, R. (1976), *Interest Groups in Norwegian Politics*, Oslo: Scandinavian University Press.

Larsen, H. (1997), 'Kommunene som forvaltnings-og selvstyreorgan', in T. Christensen and M. Egeberg (eds), *Forvaltningskunnskap*, Oslo: TANO.

Lægreid, P. (1989), 'Rekrutteringspolitikk i Sentraladministrasjonen', in *paper no. 31*, Bergen: Norwegian Research Centre in Organization and Management.

Lægreid, P. (1993a), 'Rewards for high public office: The case of Norway', in *report no. 11*, Department of Administration and Organization Theory, Bergen: University of Bergen.

Lægreid, P. (1993b), 'Salary policy reforms for high public office in Norway', in *report 9320*, Bergen: Norwegian Research Centre in Organization and Management.

Lægreid, P. (1995a), 'Feminization of the central public administration', in Karvonen, L. and P. Selle (eds), *Women in Nordic Politics: Closing the Gap*, Aldershot: Dartmouth.

Lægreid, P. (ed.) (1995b), *Lønnspolitikk i offentlig sektor*, Oslo: TANO.

Lægreid, P. and J.P. Olsen (1978), *Byråkrati og beslutninger*, Bergen: Scandinavian University Press.

Lægreid, P. and O.K. Pedersen (1996), *Integration og decentralisering, personale og forvaltning i scandinavien*, Copenhagen: Jurist–og Økonomforbundets Forlag.

Lægreid, P. and V. Rolland (1992), 'Institusjonelle rammer for forvaltningspolitikken i Norge', in *LOS-paper no. 38*, Bergen: University of Bergen.

Lægreid, P. and P. Roness (1996), 'Political parties, bureaucracies, and corporatism', in L. Svåsand and K. Strøm (eds), *Challenges to Political Parties*, Ann Arbor: University of Michigan Press.

Listhaug, O. and A.H. Miller (1985), 'Public support for tax evasion: self-interest or symbolic politics', *European Journal for Political Research*, 13: 265–82.

Listhaug, O. and M. Wiberg (1995), 'Confidence in political and private institutions', in H. D. Klingemann, and D. Fuchs (eds), *Citizens and the State: Beliefs in Government, vol. I*, Oxford: Oxford University Press.

March, J.G. and J.P. Olsen (1976), *Ambiguity and Choice in Organizations*, Oslo: Scandinavian University Press.

March, J.G. and J.P. Olsen (1989), *Rediscovering Institutions: The Organizational Basis of Politics*, New York: Free Press.

March, J.G. and J.P. Olsen (1995), *Democratic Governance*, New York: Free Press.

Maurseth, P. (1979), *Sentraladministrasjonens historie 1814–1844, Bind 1*, Oslo: Scandinavian University Press.

Mayntz R. and F. Scharpf (1975), *Policy-making in the German Federal Bureaucracy*, New York: Elsevier.

Meyer, J. and B. Rowan (1977), 'Institutionalized organizations: formal structure as myth and ceremony', *American Journal of Sociology*, 83 (September): 340–63.

Miller, A. and O. Listhaug (1990), 'Political parties and confidence in government: a comparison of Norway, Sweden and United States', *British Journal of Political Studies*, (29): 357–86.

Nordby, T. (1994), *Korporatisme på norsk 1920–1990*, Oslo: Scandinavian University Press.

Olsen, J.P. (1978), 'Folkestyre, byråkrati og korporativisme', in J.P. Olsen, (ed.), *Politik organisering*, Bergen: Scandinavian University Press.

Olsen, J.P. (1983a), *Organized Democracy*, Bergen: Scandinavian University Press.

Olsen, J.P. (1983b), 'The ups and downs of Parliament', in J.P. Olsen, *Organized Democracy*, Bergen: Scandinavian University Press.

Olsen, J.P. (1983c), 'The dilemmas of organizational integration in government', in J.P. Olsen, *Organized Democracy*, Bergen: Scandinavian University Press.

Olsen, J.P. (1983d), 'Top civil servants – key players on different teams', in J.P. Olsen, *Organized Democracy*, Bergen: Scandinavian University Press.

Olsen, J.P. (1983e), 'Still peaceful coexistence and revolution in slow motion?', in J.P. Olsen, *Organized Democracy*, Bergen: Scandinavian University Press.

Olsen, J.P. (1988), 'Representativitet og politisk organisering', in J.P. Olsen, *Statsstyre og institusjons utforming*, Bergen: Scandinavian University Press.

Olsen, J.P. (1996), 'Norway, slow learner – or another triumph of the tortoise?' (eds), in Olsen, J.P. and B.G. Peters, *Lessons from Experience*, Oslo: Scandinavian University Press.

Olsen, J.P. and B.G. Peters (1996), *Lessons from Experience*, Oslo: Scandinavian University Press.

Rokkan, S. (1966), 'Norway, numerical democracy and corporate pluralism', in R.A. Dahl (ed.), *Political Oppositions in Western Democracies*, New Haven, CT.: Yale University Press.

Rolland, V.W. (1999), 'Organisasjonsendring og forvalltningspolitikk i Norge', in P. Lægreid and O.K. Pedersen (eds), *Frq opbygning til ombygning i staten*, Copenhagen: Jurist – og Økonomforbundets Forlag.

Roness, P. (1996), 'Institusjonell orden – Norge', in P. Lægreid and O.K. Pedersen, *Integration og decentralisering: personale og forvaltning i Scandinavien*, Copenhagen: Jurist – og Økonomforbundets Forlag.

Roberg, V. (1991), 'Politikkutforming gjennom personellrekruttering?', Department of Political Science, Oslo: University of Oslo.

Sabine, G.H. and T.L. Thorson (1968), *A History of Political Theory*, London: George G. Harrap.

Scott, W.R. (1992³), *Organizations: Rational, Natural and Open Systems*, NJ, Englewood Cliffs, 3rd edn,: Prentice-Hall.

Seip, J.A. (1963), *Fra embetsmannsstat til ettpartistat og andre essays*, Oslo: Scandinavian University Press.

Selznick, P. (1949), *TVA and the Grass Roots*, New York: Harper.

Selznick, P. (1957), *Leadership in Administration*, New York: Harper & Row.

Simon, H. (1957), *Administrative Behavior*, New York: Free Press.

Tonnesson, K.D. (1979), *Sentraladministrasjoens historie, Bind 4 1914–40*, Oslo: Scandinavian University Press.

Weaver, R.K. and B.A. Rockman (1993), 'Assessing the effects of institutions', in R.K. Weaver, and B.A. Rockman (eds), *Do Institutions Matter? Government Capabilities in the United States and Abroad*, Washington DC: Brookings Institution.

Weber, M. (1970), 'Bureaucracy', in H.H. Gerth and C.W. Mills (eds), *From Max Weber*, London: Routledge and Kegan Paul.

Wolin, S.S. (1960), *Politics and Vision: Continuity and Innovation in Western Political Thought*, Boston: Little, Brown.

APPENDIX 5A

Table 5A.1 The development of the Norwegian civil service

	Number of ministeries	Number of departments	Number of divisions/ sections	Number of Employees	Number of directorates	Number of employees
1814	6			60		
1844	7		32	260	8	20
1884	7		46	370	28	190
1914	9	16	57	500	25	
1934	9	54	80	510	32	
1947	12	47	184	2 160	42	3 500
1957	14	55	212	2 010	48	4 100
1967	14	64	216	2 050	57	6 200
1977	14	81	304	2 730	65	8 500
1990	17	96	348	3 524*	73*	11 000*
1995	16	89	343	3 628	70	9 682
1997	16	93	338	–	76	–

Notes: The main sources for the table is a database at the Norwegian Research Centre in Organization and Management, University of Bergen, Lægreid and Rolland (1992); Rolland (1999). The sources are using somewhat different methods for counting the number of units, but the main development picture should be right.
*These figures are from 1991.

Table 5A.2 Entry-level salary for civil service positions (US$), 1996

Type of position	Entry-level salary
Director-general	61076*
Assistant director-general	49231
Deputy director-general	45692
Head of division	43846
Senior executive officer	34461
Executive officer	33846

Note: *This is an average for this group in a merit pay system for administrative top leaders.

Table 5A.3   Characteristics of the Norwegian civil service: structure, demography, attitudes and contacts, 1996

	Ministeries (%)	Directorates (%)
Head of division or higher hierarchical level	50	35
Formal and explicit leadership responsibilities	29	22
Coordination as main function	16	12
Working with single cases as main function	13	16
Very or relatively unambiguous rules directing their work	36	39
Political considerations and signals very important to attend to	74	32
Professional considerations very important to attend to	61	61
Own administrative unit (ministry or directorate) very important when making decisions	83	54
The Storting very important when making decisions	54	29
The Cabinet very important when making decisions	66	26
Agree that MBO has increased political control	29	21
Agree that MBO has increased cost-efficiency	31	28
Coming to ministry or directorate directly from higher education	36	30
Ten years or more tenure in own ministry or directorate	33	49
Younger than 40 years old	44	36
Women	38	43
Higher education in law	22	9
Higher education in economics (national and business)	18	10
Higher education in social sciences	18	6
Higher education in natural science/civil engineering	5	19
	($n = 1482$)	($n = 1025$)

Note: The table is based on two surveys in the central administration in Norway in 1996. All employees in the ministries, from the executive officers and above in the hierarchy, received the questionnaires, and 71.6 per cent answered. In the directorates one third of the same group received the questionnaires and 64.5 per cent answered.

6.   The National Civil Service in Belgium

Annie Hondeghem[1]

INTRODUCTION

This chapter contains a report on the Belgian 'national' civil service (CS). It is necessary, however, to put this 'national' level in context as Belgium formally became a federal state in 1993. Through a series of state reforms, the importance of the national level has decreased. This is clarified through a brief description of the historical context.

At the time of its foundation in 1830, Belgium was conceived as a unitary state. From the beginning, however, there were several differences in Belgian society that disturbed the unity, including the differences between French-speaking and Dutch-speaking people and the differences in economic conditions between Flanders (rather poor) and Wallonia (rather rich). For 150 years, a so-called pacification policy attempted to find an equilibrium for these differences. The differences remained, however, and other answers to the lines of fracture were needed if the Belgian state was to survive. Since 1970 such solutions have been sought.

The revision of the constitution in 1970 was a first fundamental step towards the conversion of Belgium into a federal state. Since then Belgium consists of three communities (the Flemish, the French and the German community) and three regions (the Flemish, the Walloon and the Brussels region). The communities are based upon the existence of language and cultural groups, while the regions are geographical areas. The regions and communities do not coincide, however, so the structure of the Belgian state is very complex. In 1970, institutions were created in order to establish the cultural autonomy of the communities and in 1980 the Flemish and Walloon regions received their own institutions. In 1988, during the third state reform, the institutions for the Brussels region, where the two communities live together, were created. More competencies were also transferred from the central government to the communities (e.g. education) and to the regions (e.g. public works). New rules were established for the financing of the different administrative levels. Finally, during the last state reform in 1993, the institutions, competencies and financing of the regions and the communities were adjusted once again. The members of the state parliaments are now elected directly, and incompatibility was installed between a mandate in the national parliament and a mandate in a state parliament. The constitution was amended to transform Belgium into a federal state.

In contrast to other federal systems like Germany and Switzerland, which are centripetal, the federal system in Belgium is centrifugal as it evolved from a unitary to a federal state (Baakman, Bouckaert, Maes 1994). This poses an important challenge and it is uncertain whether a lasting equilibrium will be achieved. There are tensions in several important policy areas on the national level (e.g. social security). The latest state reform may, therefore, be a step in the direction of still more, until perhaps the Belgian State disintegrates. An important factor here is that there are no political parties anymore that act on a national level and depend on the support of voters of the whole country.

The national civil service has been severely reduced as a consequence of the different state reforms. In 1999 the national level employed only 29 per cent of the personnel in the public sector: 20 per cent was employed in the federal government and 9 per cent in particular bodies such as army, police and justice; the regional states employed 42 per cent of the civil servants including the educational sector. Only 7 per cent of civil servants were employed in the national ministries as important functions have been transferred to autonomous public institutions.

This chapter is about civil servants in the Belgian national ministries. Many of the observations, however, also apply to other levels in the public sector because the national civil service system has for a long time served as a model for other sectors.

HISTORICAL DEVELOPMENT OF THE CIVIL SERVICE

Origin of the Belgian State

The Belgian State is relatively young. It was founded in 1830 after the revolution against and the split from the Kingdom of the Netherlands. The Belgian State is neither the construction of a dynasty, nor the result of a long historical tradition. The construction of Belgium has to be viewed as the search for a new balance in Europe after the collapse of the Austrian empire and of Napoleon's regime.

The Belgian people's scepticism and mistrust of central authority originates in their history – up until 1830, foreign kings and emperors, including the king of Spain, the emperor of Austria, the French emperor Napoleon and the king of Holland, ruled over the Belgian people. The history of the catholic Netherlands has been marked by continuous tension between the foreign authorities' process of unification and centralisation of power and the struggle of the regional institutions (e.g. the counties) for the maintenance and consolidation of privileges and autonomy. The specific characteristics of Belgium's civil service system, therefore, must not be sought in the administration of the central state, but rather in the tradition of autonomy and struggle of provinces and cities against the central power. The civil service in Belgium is not the incarnation of a strong state, but has a more humble character (Molitor 1974).

DEVELOPMENT OF THE BELGIAN ADMINISTRATION

From 1830 until 1930: Civil Servants as Public Servants

Public perceptions of the civil service in 1830 reflected partly the system in France. It assumed that the administration had its own characteristics and tasks such that civil servants could not be considered as 'normal' employees. They served the general interest of the country and received different treatment: they enjoyed privileges such as security of tenure (only *de facto*, it was not yet a legal principle), monthly salary, leave and pension rights. But there was no uniform system; each administration had its own rules.

Fear of invasion made the first governments in Belgium governments of national unity, suppressing the opposition between the Catholics and the Liberals for a period of fifteen years. In this period there was no real difference between politicians and public servants as many civil servants were elected and became members of parliament.

Debate about the position of civil servants was opened when the unity was broken and political parties campaigned for power to themselves. Parliamentary membership of civil servants caused some problems. Because of the lack of a statute, civil servants were vulnerable. Ministers determined their wages and promotions and when civil servants voted against the government in the parliament, they were often removed.

In 1848, the law on incompatibilities was passed and civil servants could no longer combine an administrative with a parliamentary mandate. This was a necessary but insufficient step towards a competent and neutral civil service. Ducpétiaux (1859), amongst others, points to many problems relating to the civil service in this period: excessive centralisation, inertia, lack of unity, lack of guarantees for civil servants, lack of dedication, omnipotence and arbitrariness of ministers, entanglement of politics and administration, nepotism.

The period between 1830 and 1930 saw the emergence of civil servants as public servants. Civil servants become servants to the state and not just to the king. This is expressed in the oath that has to be taken by every civil servant. Other elements that characterise this phase include the introduction of entrance examinations for lower staff in some ministries and the recruitment of graduates in law without exams but starting at a lower level. Other university graduates were recruited for specialised posts such as engineering.

Apart from in technical departments, all civil servants were recruited in the lower grades and proceeded to the higher posts via promotions. This system differed for example from the elitist administrative class in the UK. The Belgian civil service has remained less elitist and more open and representative than other European public services. What was emerging, however, was the specific Belgian phenomenon of political interference in the recruitment and promotion of civil servants.

From 1930 until 1980: Civil Service as Protected Service and Professional Service

During the crisis of the 1930s, the government was confronted with an overextended civil service. A special commissioner (Louis Camu) was appointed to design a better and more competent civil service. The Camu ropositions (named the Camu statute) were based on Belgian traditions, but also on aspects of the English civil service and the French school of administrative law. Camu developed a Weberian model of a neutral, apolitic and competent civil service based on an objective selection system with competitive examinations, and a career system with promotions based on either seniority for lower grades or on merit for higher grades. The rights and duties of civil servants were set down in detail in a statute established by Royal Decree (1937). The statute applied to all ministries and unified the different regulations in existence at that time. A major innovation of the Camu statute was the valorisation of university graduates into the system. From then on they were directly recruited for higher posts in the civil service. This aimed to enhance the innovation capacity of the administration.

The Belgian civil servant had now definitely become a 'public' servant and the civil service system had the characteristics of both a protected and professional service. With this reform, Belgium caught up with other countries like the UK (Northcote-Trevelyan) and France.

It soon became clear, however, that the reality differed from the legal principles of the Camu statute: political nominations and nepotism were rife, ministerial cabinets took over administrative tasks and different techniques were invented to get out of applying the statute. Promotions and nominations were divided amongst the parties in office in such a way that the merit principle was undermined. This in turn led to the demoralisation of civil servants.

Different explanations can account for this state of affairs. The detailed and bureaucratic nature of the statute caused a lack of flexibility in the system. But the situation also illustrates some specific aspects of the Belgian culture: the fact that everything is negotiable, the strivings towards a representative bureaucracy, the weakness of the central government and the distribution of power amongst dozens of economic, social and cultural interest groups in society.

From 1980 until Now: Federalisation and Modernisation

The last period is characterised by two fundamental processes, which have reshaped the civil service in Belgium drastically: the federalisation process and the modernisation process. As a result of the federalisation process, the national level has become less important. Dynamic parts of government (e.g. education, welfare, environment) have been transferred to the state level, leaving the national level with some old departments, such as finance and justice. This has certainly an impact on the innovation capacity. Things seem much more difficult to change at the national level than at the state level.

Like in other countries, the civil service has also been the object of a severe modernisation process. The fundamental rights (security of tenure and careers) of the civil service are being questioned and demands for greater flexibility are being heard. Public managers with a broad responsibility are beginning to appear.

The current wave of reforms in Belgium support both the governance tradition and the management tradition. Attention is being paid to the civil service as a mechanism for effective governability and political legitimacy and to the efficiency and economic rationality of the civil service (Ingraham 1996). The reforms are occurring at different levels (Ingraham 1996): budgetary and financial, structural, technical-procedural and relational.

On the budgetary level, the federal government has pursued a strict policy of austerity. In addition, changes were introduced in the government's financial system.

On a structural level, government is gradually withdrawing from some sectors including the public financial institutions and transport and communication. Another important structural reform deals with external and internal devolution. A major innovation here is the introduction of management contracts, replacing the traditional hierarchical steering relations by contractual ones.

As to the technical and procedural reforms, some innovations were carried out. The most important innovations with regard to personnel management are: a review of the real staff needs; the introduction of a new performance appraisal system; the simplification of careers and a review of the salary scales; and the introduction of a mandate system for top civil servants (cf. below).

Finally, relational reforms refer to measures taken to improve the responsiveness of public bureaucracies and civil servants to political officials. Apart from the mandate system, a number of other measures have been agreed upon to improve the relations between the administration and the minister, such as a reduction of the staff of the ministerial cabinets and the strengthening of the role of the board of secretaries-general.

The most important relational reforms in the civil service, however, do not concern the relations between the administration and politics, but rather the relations between the administration and the citizens. In 1992 a citizen's charter was elaborated to improve the 'client-orientation' of the civil service. This charter was an answer to the crisis in legitimacy of the government which became very clear after the elections of 1991 (cf. below).

THE CIVIL SERVICE IN FIGURES

In 1999, almost 850 000 persons were employed in the public sector in Belgium, which is about 25 per cent of the active population. Only 60 000 of them are employed in the national ministries. This is the result of a long historical process.

In 1830 the central government consisted of five ministries and there were 14 000 people employed. Throughout the nineteenth century the administration grew. In this period, Belgium followed the traditional European method of dealing with new public services by the creation of new ministries (Chapman, 1966).

By the end of the nineteenth century, the so-called quangos come into being as autonomous institutions, linked with government but at a distance. At that time these were merely commercial services for which a bureaucratically shaped ministry was not appropriate (e.g. public banks, public transport, public utilities). Later on quangos were also set up for other purposes, such as the execution of social legislation. From World War I onwards the growth of public employment was more important in the sector of the public institutions than in the ministries. Devolution and agencification thus has been a long tradition in Belgium and is not an innovation of new public management. The creation of quangos was justified in terms of the need for greater flexibility and efficiency, but they were also used for political patronage.

In 1952, the number of civil servants in the national administration had increased by 273 per cent compared with 1885, while the population growth rate was 47 per cent (Depré 1973). If the state police and the army are included the growth rate of the civil service comes to 391 per cent and if the quangos are added it rose to 1 000 per cent. It is evident that population growth in itself cannot account for the increase of the public sector. More important were changes occurring in society such as economic growth, technological evolution, political notions about the role of the state, traditions and customs and cultural factors such as the existence of two language groups, the organisation of government and the opinions about public management.

After World War II, the growth of the public sector continued. The period has been characterised by the further development of social security and the welfare state. Government became involved in all aspects of society, such as education, public health, culture, sport and the environment.

The social, cultural and sports sectors became almost completely managed outside the official public sector and interest groups involved in the politics of welfare were accommodated. This resulted in fragmentation of the public services and in a weak central authority. The government remained the financier via a complex network of subventions, but there was a loss of structure and steering. This is illustrated by the deteriorating budgetary situation. In 1981 the budget deficit amounted to 12 per cent and the total public debt to 93 per cent of the GNP. Between 1964 and 1980, the number of civil servants employed by the government increased with 340 000 (from 524 000 to 864 000) whilst those working in the ministries fell from 19 per cent to 10 per cent.

After 1980 public employment more or less stabilised. Contrary to other countries, privatisation of public employment was limited as Belgium has never had an important sector of public enterprises. Large numbers of civil servants, however, were transferred from the national level to the state level as a result of the federalisation process. Also, the quality of public employment has changed: more flexibility has been introduced, giving way to more contractual employment and part-time jobs.

INTERNAL LABOUR MARKET

Internal labour market (ILM) is defined by Wise (1996) as 'the rules pertaining to job definition or classification, deployment, job security and membership, and reward structures'. Other studies (e.g. Baron et al. 1986; Rosenbaum 1984; DiPrete, 1989) give a more strict definition of the ILM concept; they state that ILMs are characterised by: 1) job ladders; 2) few ports of entry only at the bottom of the hierarchy; 3) promotion from within, 4) firm-specific skills giving rise to skill gradients that demarcate career paths, 5) seniority-based rewards, 6) low turnover due to strong identification with the firm.

Taking into account these characteristics, one can conclude that the Belgian CS is a typical example of an ILM. The allocation of positions is strictly regulated. Rules on seniority, training, exams and merit determine the mobility between positions. Recruitment takes place in the lower grades, while vacancies in higher grades are filled through internal promotions. The seniority criterion is not only a determining factor in the allocation of positions, it is equally important for the remuneration of the civil servant. Despite the recent changes in the system, these characteristics remain valid.

In the literature on this matter (Doeringer and Piore 1971; Kanter 1977; Wise 1996), three main reasons are brought forward to explain ILM-structures. First, ILM is a means of developing and maintaining a specific expertise for the organisation; second, by offering a career perspective, an ILM has built-in incentives for loyalty and motivation; third, the recruitment at a young age and the clearly-defined career paths guarantee a better socialisation of staff. In the Belgian context another reason can account for the ILM. As clientelism and nepotism are fundamental characteristics of the Belgian political culture, the ILM offers strict rules that can lower the arbitrariness in the management of personnel. Because of the accumulation of regulations, however, the personnel system has become so rigid that a flexible human resources management is very difficult.

In what follows, the rules concerning the remuneration and the allocation of personnel are described. These rules were introduced at the time of the Camu statute in 1937 (cf. above) and have been little changed for half a century. In the 1990s, the rules were reviewed to adjust the civil service to the new structure of the State, but also to face the new challenges of a modern administration.

JOB DEFINITION AND CLASSIFICATION

The CS is divided into 'levels', 'ranks', 'grades' and 'salary scales'. The division into 'levels' is a classic phenomenon found in various Western European countries (France, Germany, etc.). This division is based, on the one hand, on the nature of the work, and on the other hand, on the existing system of education. Until recently, the civil service was divided into four levels (1, 2, 3, 4), but a fifth level was added (level 2+), to revalorise specialised functions requiring a higher education. Direct access to a level is only possible with the right educational qualifications. But, as education, certainly in the past, was an important aspect of social stratification, a correction was built in to avoid the forming of an élite. Promotion to a higher level is possible if one has some seniority in the lower level and if one succeeds in an examination.

Each level is subdivided into 'ranks' which mirror the hierarchy within the system. Before the reform, there were 28 different ranks.

Table 6.1   Evolution of the employment in the public sector in Belgium

	1953	1964	1970	1980	1989	1995	1999
Ministries[a]							
• national					77,232 (10%)	62,535 (7%)	62,771 (7%)
• regional					7,848 (1%)	26,804 (3%)	27,601 (3%)
• total	83,797 (21%)	99,198 (19%)	108,074 (17%)	88,062 (10%)	85,080 (11%)	89,339 (10%)	90,372 (11%)
Public institutions							
• national					166,098 (21%)	149,575 (17%)	105,607 (13%)
• regional					13,634 (2%)	47,888 (5%)	51,757 (6%)
• total	131,341 (33%)	126,292 (24%)	115,969 (19%)	198,402 (23%)	179,732 (22%)	197,463 (22%)	157,364 (19%)
Particular bodies[b]	85,830 (21.5%)[b,c]	199,806 (38%)	272,684 (44%)	392,336 (45%)	352,965 (44%)	358,780 (40%)	349,559 (41%)
Local government	97,200 (24.5%)	98,010 (19%)	120,299 (19%)	184,643 (21%)	188,556 (23%)	244,729 (27%)[d]	244,729 (29%)[d]
Legislature	1,000 (0.2%)	1,000 (0.2%)	969 (0.1%)	1,232 (0.1%)	1,773 (0.2%)	2,282 (0.2%)	2,815 (0.3%)
TOTAL	398,168 (100%)	524,306 (100%)	617,995 (100%)	864,675 (100%)	808,106 (100%)	892,593 (100%)	844,839 (100%)

Notes:
(a) inclusive personnel of scientific institutions
(b) army, police force, justice, teachers
(c) exclusive teachers of free schools (approximately 80.000)
(d) data of 1994

This is now reduced to 13 ranks, following a general trend to decrease the hierarchy. Essentially, every level has two ranks: a starting rank and a promotion rank.

Every rank consists of a number of 'grades'. The grades give an idea of the function of the civil servant. As in other countries (Germany, Great Britain, etc.), there is a close link between the grade and the function. However, with increased specialisation, the number of grades had increased markedly and this raised problems in respect of the mobility of civil servants. The reform, therefore, drastically reduced the number of grades. At the same time an operation was started to introduce job descriptions, which are not statutorily formalised, but used as an instrument of modern human resources management.

Every grade is linked with a number of 'salary scales'. In the past every grade had only one salary scale, but this has been modified so that a civil servant can now pass through several salary scales even when remaining in the same grade. These so-called 'financial' careers were created to compensate for the reduced chances of promotion, due to the decrease of the number of ranks.

JOB SECURITY RULES AND MEMBERSHIP

In principle, civil servants in Belgium are appointed statutorily and their rights and duties are fixed unilaterally by the government. The statute of civil servants has several advantages, including security of tenure, social benefits (e.g. a state pension), and the prospect of a career.

The principle of statutory nomination is firmly anchored in the Belgian administration and is strongly supported by the unions. As soon as measures are introduced with a possible impact on the statute, the unions are able to mobilise the civil servants. Support for the statute of civil servants follows three different lines of argument, including the need for a stable administration, the protection of civil servants from political arbitrariness, and the attractiveness of the civil service. Research has shown that the security of tenure and the state pension are two main reasons for entrance into office of many civil servants (Hondeghem, 1990).

In reality, however, there are a lot of non-statutory personnel in the civil service. In the federal ministries 21 per cent of the civil servants have a contract, whilst this rises to 35 per cent in the public institutions. This can be explained partly by the rigidities of the statute. Temporary or contractual personnel are recruited to provide flexibility. Another explanation lies in the social role of the government: by employing temporary staff, unemployment can be reduced. Also, the impulse towards political nominations is an explanation: while politicisation is difficult with statutory nominations, it is a lot easier with temporary or contractual personnel (cf. below).

So, although the statutory nomination is anchored in the ideology and system of the civil service, the reality is different. This has many disadvantages for personnel management: statutory and contractual personnel have different rights and duties although they do the same work, leading to an intrinsic injustice in the organisation. The contractual personnel have no career perspective within the civil service and so they are either seeking to regularise their situation by getting statutorily nominated or looking for work in the private sector. The turnover of contractual personnel is therefore very high.

Instead of holding on to the ideology of the statutory nomination, it seems more appropriate to evolve gradually towards convergence of the labour relations in the public and the private sector. However, it will be some time before such reforms are adopted not least because of opposition from the unions.

DEPLOYMENT RULES

Considering the ideology of the civil service in Belgium, it is clear that a great deal of importance is attached to the career of the civil servant. Until recently, the career was mostly perceived as a hierarchical process in which advancement was equal to a promotion. But with the movement towards flatter organisational structures (cf. above), a financial career has been added to the hierarchical career enabling civil servants to move to a higher salary scale but in the same grade.

The career of a civil servant depends formally on four factors or criteria. The first important criterion is seniority. To be considered for promotion, the civil servant must have a minimum of seniority. As a result of these seniority requirements, moving up fast on the career ladder is almost impossible. Research has shown that careers are proceeding very slowly (Hondeghem, 1990). Top civil servants are on average 55 years old; it takes more than 25 years of service before one is appointed to a middle management or top position.

Apart from being a minimum requirement, seniority is also a decision criterion, certainly in the lower levels. If a choice needs to be made out of different candidates, the one with the highest seniority will be chosen. Whether this tradition will be kept in future, is uncertain. It is possible that other criteria, like performance appraisal, will play a more important role in nominations than seniority.

A second criterion in the career system is the taking of examinations. Those who want to move up to a higher level have to pass an examination.

Promotions within the same level can also be made dependent on an examination.

A third criterion is the performance appraisal of the civil servant. In principle, promotions are awarded to civil servants with the best reviews. Until recently, however, performance appraisals were mere formalities. Whether the new system will change this is still unsure.

The last criterion is the advice of the Board of Directors, which consists of the top civil servants in a department. They have to advise on all promotions in level 1. Until recently, this advice was often ignored by the minister as the political affiliation of the candidate was decisive (cf. below). With the depoliticisation of the nomination policy, however, the Board of Directors has become more important. In their advice, attention is given to the profile of the vacancy and the merits of the candidate.

An important innovation in the deployment rules since the reform is the introduction of a mandate system for top civil servants, which means a new career system, replacing permanent by temporary nominations of five or six years. This new system must be situated in the trend to enhance responsibility and accountability of top civil servants and has already been applied to the autonomous public enterprises (Depré and Hondeghem 1996).

The federal government decided in 1994 that the mandate system would be introduced for all top civil servants in the national ministries and public institutions, covering 250 to 300 posts. Only civil servants who had proven their management competencies would be selected for a mandate. Principal and practical arguments, however, have hindered the implementation of this decision. There was indeed a lot of resistance. First, it would mean a fundamental change in the traditional relation between ministers and top civil servants. The minister would have more freedom to nominate the top civil servants, but many top civil servants feared that their evaluation would be on political grounds instead of achievement and results. Second, the introduction of the mandate system could only be realised if it was accompanied by an important financial compensation as top civil servants would have to take more risks, which is a problem considering the state's budget. Finally, there remained a number of technical difficulties, e.g. concerning the selection, the training and the career of the mandated official.

The idea of a mandate system, however, has never been abandoned, and is one of the key aspects of the modernisation plan of the government (cf. below).

REWARD STRUCTURES

Basic Components

In the remuneration of civil servants, there are three components: the salary, social benefits, and allowances and premiums.

The grade is the basis of the civil servant's salary and each grade has salary scales. This salary scale comprises a minimum salary, salary steps or increases according to seniority, and a maximum salary. The salary scales are fixed by Royal Decree, after negotiations with the unions. Account is taken, on the one hand, of the rank of the grade and, on the other hand, of the importance of the function normally corresponding to the grade. Although the system is based on an implicit scheme of job evaluation this system has never been made explicit, causing most salary scales to evolve as a result of tradition and negotiations with the unions.

For more than 20 years, the salary scales of the national ministries were fixed by the Royal Decree of 1973. During the recent reform of the career system, all salary scales were reviewed. The underlying idea was to revalorise the civil service and to reassess the relation between salary scales. However, there have been no spectacular changes. The budget possibilities on the national level for increases in salary are indeed very limited because of the total public debt.

Salary negotiations are not conducted from a strategic personnel vision, as advocated in modern HRM nor is there extensive preparation prior to the negotiations. Budget possibilities are the main, if not the only, consideration taken into account in the negotiations. Under pressure of the unions, changes in the structure and the system of remuneration tend to be applied linearly.

In addition to a salary, a civil servant receives a number of social benefits: child allowance, a premium at the end of the year, pension and holiday money. The pension is fairly high: 70 per cent of the salary of the last five years before retirement. This amount is linked to the index and to the evolution of the salaries of the civil servants in service. The pension is perceived as a deferred salary and justifies to some extent the relatively lower wages in the public sector. The cost of the state pension is becoming a big problem with the ageing of the population. Since the state pension is a charge on the current budget, this puts great financial pressures on it. In some public organisations the pension costs take up more than half of all personnel expenses. The unions strongly defend the state pension as an important achievement and will resist any attempt to reduce it. Serious social tensions seem to be unavoidable.

A third component of a civil servant's remuneration are allowances and premiums. Departments use a wide range of them, e.g. allowances for training, driving, exceptional performances, travel costs, clothing, office costs, degree bonuses and linguistic premiums. An explanation for this diversity lies in the fact that ministries can decide which allowances to award, in contradiction to the fixed salary scales which apply to all the ministries. Sometimes allowances were used to correct the rigid salary scales and to overcome difficulties in attracting technical staff. Such allowances are quickly regarded as earned rights, even if the basis of justification disappears. In contrast with the Flemish administration, management premiums for top civil servants did not exist in the national ministries until now.

THE SALARY SPAN

The gross salary span for the total civil service is around 4. This means that a secretary-general earns four times as much as a lower official. A comparison with data of 1960 and 1983, shows that the total salary span has decreased: it was 6 in 1960 and 5 in 1983 (Depré and Hondeghem 1987). The salary span is higher in the higher levels than in the lower levels. Civil servants in the higher levels are thus financially more advantaged by a career than in the lower levels. When account is taken of deductions from the gross salary, including pension, health insurance, tax on income, the salary span is much lower (approximately 2.5).

As important as the salary span within a ministry, is the difference in salary among public services. Several public services pay significantly more than the federal ministries, including some cities and communities, public financial institutions and autonomous public enterprises (Van Hooland, 1992).

Since the federalisation of Belgium there is also a salary span between the public service on the national and on the regional level. In comparison with the salary scales of the national government, the salary scales for similar functions in the Flemish community for example, are more favourable. In addition to this, moving up in the financial career does not depend on the existence of a vacancy, so the career prospects are more favourable as well. Moreover, the middle and top managers can receive a management premium from 0 to 20 per cent on top of their normal salary.

Besides the salary span in the public sector, there also exists a salary span between the public and the private sector. Traditionally, the wages in the public sector are lower than in the private sector. Three factors are often advanced to justify this difference: the favourable working conditions in the public sector (for example flexible hours, leave possibilities), the state pension and the security of tenure. Because of this, one has to be cautious when comparing salaries. The following conclusions drawn from the study by Dejaeghere and Van Hooland (1992) were that first, qualified workmen are paid significantly less in the public sector than in the private sector; second, the difference in salary is usually bigger at the start than at the end of the career; third, the salaries in the public sector are more formally linked with the level of education than in the private sector; and last, managers are paid significantly less in the public sector.

The conclusion from all this is that the salary policy on the national level is relatively unfavourable. On the one hand, there are few market stimuli to pay competitive salaries and on the other hand, there is the immense public debt that does not allow for a substantial raise in salaries. This is likely to have a negative impact on the attractiveness of the civil service on the national level in comparison with other levels.

REPRESENTATIVENESS

There are two fundamentally contradictory doctrines on representativeness in the Belgian civil service.

The official one is the principle of equal chances and merit. Every Belgian must have an equal chance to apply for a vacancy in the administration and selection is made on the grounds of merit with the best candidate selected. This principle is ensured by organising competitive examinations.

In the official doctrine, representativeness is mainly realised via the composition of the parliament and the government. The parliament is a reflection of the population because of the election system of proportional representation, and the parliament forms the basis for the composition of the government. In accordance with the bureaucratic model of Weber, the administration is considered a neutral and impartial instrument in the hands of the legitimate political power. The doctrine intends this instrument to be loyal towards those who are politically responsible and in that way responsive towards the population.

In practice, however, there is another concept of representativeness that is dominating in the Belgian administration, namely mirror-image representativeness. This principle asserts that the different social groups in society have to be represented proportionally in the administration.

In the Belgian administration, a balance is sought on three levels: language, religion and politics. These three dimensions originate from the three fundamental lines of fracture in the Belgian society. The language factor reflects the existence of two communities: the Flemish and the French community. The religion factor reflects the conflict between Catholics and non-Catholics. Although Catholics are in the majority, there was always a concern to protect philosophical minorities against Catholic dominance. Finally, the politics factor refers to different ideological tendencies between three major political families: the Christian-democrats, the liberals and the socialists.

In Belgian society these lines of fracture are coincident. Flanders is Flemish-speaking, is predominantly Catholic and Christian-democrat whilst Wallonia is French-speaking, rather liberal (non-Catholic) and with a dominance of the socialists. This causes the Belgian State to be very fragile. In the last decades, some conflicts nearly resulted in the disintegration of Belgium. Separatism or a division of Belgium into two areas (Flanders and Wallonia) is therefore not out of the question.

Up to now, a pacification policy has prevented the break-up of Belgium. This policy aims at keeping an equilibrium between the different groups in the population: every group gets what they are proportionally entitled to have. It has been successful so far, but at the expense of a lot of political energy. Moreover, a high price has been paid: the public debt is partly due to this policy. But the government has always succeeded in solving the conflicts in a non-violent way, which cannot be said for other states with similar lines of fracture.

Representativeness in the administration is part of this pacification policy. In contrast to the thesis of Van der Meer and Roborgh (1996) that mirror-image representativeness can be explained solely in terms of the aspiration towards legitimacy and responsiveness of the administration, it can also be seen as the means of ensuring a balance of power and the preservation of the Belgian State.

Consequently one can only speak of a 'passive' and not of an 'active' representativeness. Whilst civil servants can be classified in a particular category (according to language, political party and religion), this representativeness is being forced onto them from the political system. Once nominated, they mostly resume their independence.

The representativeness of the civil servants in the national administration will be analysed in terms of three dimensions: social origin and education, language and sex (Depré and Hondeghem 1991). Representativeness according to political affiliation is dealt with in the section on politicisation.

Representativeness According to Social Origin and Education

Because of the traditional privacy aspect, little is known about the social origin of civil servants in Belgium. The few studies point towards the Belgian administration, more specifically the senior civil servants, as being neither élitist, nor the product of a particular social class. Most civil servants are in the middle layers of the society and the degree of auto-recruitment is high. This recruitment pattern can be explained by the fact that the Belgian administration is not at the centre of power in Belgium (cf. below). Therefore, it has limited attraction for the upper class.

Education is closely linked with social origin. Despite the democratisation of university education, university students are still largely drawn from the higher social classes. Since the introduction of the Camu statute in 1937, direct access to level 1 is only possible with a university degree. However, in contrast to other countries, advancement of civil servants without a university degree has always been a matter of concern. For a long period, this internal recruitment from lower levels was more important than external recruitment (Hondeghem 1987).

In the 1980s half the civil servants in level 1 had a university or equivalent degree and in most ministries 75 per cent of the level 1 civil servants had been to university. Law (33 per cent), economics (23 per cent) and applied sciences (17 per cent) were the most common degrees although the kind of degree depended strongly on the specialisation of the ministry. This confirms that Belgium has always attached importance to the expertise of its administration, as opposed to other countries, such as the UK with its preference for generalists.

Representativeness According to Language

The representativeness in the administration according to language has a long history and symbolises an important social struggle. For centuries, the élite in Belgium, including the Flemish part, spoke French which became the official language when Belgium was declared independent in 1830. Gradually, however, as a result of fierce political struggle, the Flemish people have obtained their rights as citizens and as civil servants.

From 1932 on, the principle of homogeneity in language has prevailed, which means that the official language in Flanders is Dutch, in the Walloon part of Belgium it is French, and Brussels is bilingual. The civil servants who work at the central administration in Brussels are divided in a Dutch and a French language group. Most of the administrations have adopted the rule that posts must be equally divided between the two groups. Since 1966, this rule has been obligatory for senior civil servants.

The relations between the French and Dutch-speaking civil servants at this moment can be described as a situation of 'armed peace'. The parity-rule was introduced to stabilise the power relations between the two groups, although this is not in line with the demographic reality as the Flemish people make up 58 per cent of the population. The French people hold tenaciously to this parity rule, which they consider as a protection of their minority status. The Flemish people in contrast, are aware of their preponderance, not only on a demographic, but also on an economic and political level.

Economically, the relation between Flanders and Wallonia has been completely reversed. In the nineteenth and early twentieth century, Wallonia was the prosperous region, due to its flourishing heavy industry, but since the 1970s Flanders has become the leading economic force in Belgium. In Wallonia economic decline has resulted in a depressed region that depends heavily on the prosperous Flemish part of the country. Also on a political level Flanders is more important. The office of Prime Minister for example, has been occupied by a Flemish person for over two decades.

The conflict between the two regions clearly exceeds the language difference. In essence, it is a conflict about economic resources and political power and this has to be kept in mind when discussing representativeness in the administration according to language.

Representativeness According to Sex

The representation of women in the administration is similar to the general position of women in the labour market. The number of women in the ministries has increased since the 1970s: 19 per cent of civil servants were women in 1970 and 46 per cent in 1999. Since 42 per cent of the working population are women, it is clear that the central administration is representative of the society. However, there are substantial differences between the ministries. Women are a majority in some ministries (e.g. Employment, Social Affairs, Health and Environment), but under-represented in others (e.g. Justice, Traffic and Infrastructure, Agriculture). These differences can be explained by the growth period of the ministry, but also by the nature of the work and the required qualifications. Like in other economic sectors, there is still a strong horizontal segregation of labour between men and women in the public sector.

This horizontal segregation is also expressed in differences in status. Men hold more statutory nominations, while women are employed as contractual personnel. Core functions are mostly occupied by men, whilst female civil servants are concentrated in peripheral functions.

Apart from horizontal segregation, there is also a strong vertical segregation. The higher the level in the hierarchy, the less women are found. In 1999, women held 28 per cent of level 1 posts but only 12 per cent of top management positions. The fact that women did not enter universities on a large scale until the 1970s can account in part for the under-representation of women in level 1. Today they make up 50 per cent of university students and so their occupation of posts in level 1 is likely to increase. Whether this will be the case for top functions in the administration is less certain. The mobility of women into top positions is very difficult in all sectors of society. Some factors, including the traditional role model, prejudices against women assuming top functions, and the lesser participation of women in informal and political networks, impede women from getting promoted.

Since the 1980s there has been a policy of affirmative action to improve the position of women in the administration. This policy is partly due to stimuli on this matter emanating from the European Union. In 1987, a state secretary/minister was appointed and since 1991 affirmative actions are obligatory for the public sector. So far, the results of this policy, however, are limited. In contrast to other forms of representativeness (language, politics), sexual representativeness emanates from external pressures (the European Union, the women's movement) and not from within the political system itself. That explains why political support is limited and the active implementation of the policy is more difficult.

POLITICISATION

The politicisation of the civil service has always been a matter of discussion in Belgium, mainly because of the phenomenon of political nominations. This phenomenon is hard to eradicate due to a number of fundamental characteristics of the Belgian political and administrative system, such as the system of 'clientelism' and the pacification policy.

Ideal-type of the Civil Service

As early as the nineteenth century, the Weberian bureaucratic model was considered as an ideal for the relation between politicians and civil servants. Only politicians are politically responsible and required to render an account of their policies to the citizens. They rely on loyal and neutral civil servants to carry out their policies.

According to the principles of the Camu statute, a loyal and neutral civil service can best be realised through the application of the merit principle in nominations. Recruitment is based on competitive examinations executed by an independent institution, the 'Vast Wervingssecretariaat' (now SELOR). Promotions in turn are depoliticised by introducing criteria such as seniority, examinations, performance appraisal or the advice of the Board of Directors (cf. above).

The reality, however, is that political criteria have always played a substantial role in recruiting and promoting civil servants (cf. below). The ideal model, however, is still adhered to. Research, which investigated the civil servants' perception of the career system (Depré 1973; Hondeghem 1990), confirms that. According to civil servants, promotions should be made on the grounds of their general and specific capacities and their merit. This, however, contrasts with their perception of reality where relations with political groups and unions are perceived as being the most important factor in promotions. So there is a great difference between the perception of the actual situation and the ideal type of administration.

Aspects of Politicisation

In the discussion on politicisation, it is important to start from a good definition. Politicisation can be defined as the interaction between the political and
the administrative system. In an earlier publication (Hondeghem 1994), we
identified three different aspects of politicisation: the civil servant's political
attitude and his/her political activities; the civil servant's role; and political
nominations.

Although there is a correlation between these dimensions of politicisation,
it is important to distinguish between them. The occurrence of one dimension
does not necessarily imply the presence of another dimension although they
may overlap. Moreover, the causes and the appreciation of the different
forms of politicisation can differ a lot. Political sensitivity of civil servants at
times of policy formulation is regarded as positive, while political nominations are generally considered as negative. These three dimensions are examined below.

Political Attitude and Political Activities of the Civil Servant

The attitudes of civil servants towards politics in Belgium are generally
rather negative. Research has shown a high degree of political alienation
amongst top civil servants (Dierickx and Majersdorf 1993). They dislike the
political aspects of their job and they feel superior to the politicians morally
as well as in terms of expertise. On the other hand, Belgian civil servants
participate widely in political activities. Many are members of a political
party and/or of the union linked with a party. The same study reveals that
about three-quarters of top civil servants in the ministries are members of a
political party although only 40 per cent are politically active. In contrast to
other countries there are few limits on the political activities of civil servants
in Belgium. Civil servants can assume a political mandate if this is at another
administrative level.

Role Conception and Execution

The second dimension of politicisation refers to the division of tasks between
politicians and civil servants or the functional politicisation of the civil service (Derlien and Mayntz 1989). Using the typology developed by Aberbach
et al. (1981) four types of relations between politicians and civil servants can
be distinguished: the civil servant as a neutral executor, an adviser, a media-
tor between different interest groups, and a decision maker. As the civil
servant passes from the first towards the fourth type, his role becomes more
politicised because he is more involved in the weighting of values and interests.

Until recently, the first type was most representative of the relations between civil servants and politicians. Policy formulation and mediation between interest groups was monopolised by the ministerial cabinets (cf. below). This deprived position of the administration in the policy process in Belgium is in sharp contrast with the situation in other countries (for example the UK, the Netherlands, Germany, France).

Recently, however, this situation has been reversed due to the decreasing legitimacy of the political system. Ministerial cabinets have become smaller, so that politicians are forced to call upon the administration. There is also a change of culture which supports the idea that the administration should be more involved in the development of policies

Political Nominations

A third dimension of politicisation refers to the use of political criteria when recruiting, promoting or dismissing civil servants.

In the national departments, the recruitment of civil servants is in principle depoliticised since comparative examinations are the main decision-factor in recruitment. In the past, however, this principle has often been bypassed through the recruitment of temporary civil servants and through the system of first nominations in a new service, ignoring the general statutory regulations.

In the case of promotions, political nominations mostly occurred at level 1. Until recently, deliberations between the political parties were decisive for promotions. These deliberations occurred in informal commissions. This tradition started off in the 1960s as a means of dividing nominations evenly amongst the political parties. At first, the deliberations in the commission were very informal, but gradually they were institutionalised and evolved into a mechanical system of positioning. Every nomination had a certain value, depending on the place in the hierarchy. The nominations were divided according to quota that reflected the strength of the political parties in parliament. These quota, as well as the rules of the deliberations, were fixed in a protocol between the parties of the majority. In the beginning, the deliberations only concerned top functions, but gradually it was expanded until by the 1980s every promotion in level 1 was deliberated upon.

Because of this practice, the nomination policy of the federal ministries gained a bad reputation. During the Martens VIII government (1988) therefore, an important change was agreed upon. Whenever a Board of Directors was unanimous over a particular promotion, the commission would follow their advice. This resulted in more unanimity at the level of the Board of Directors and thus in a shift of power over promotions back to the ministry. According to recent data, the government follows the administration's proposals in 85 per cent of cases. This is an important step in the direction of depoliticisation. Recent changes in the statute of civil servants support this trend (e.g. the introduction of a new performance appraisal system).

Explanations for the Politicisation Phenomenon

Explanations are different depending on the dimension of politicisation. The political alienation of the Belgian civil servants can be explained from three points of view. First, Belgian civil servants have always had a technocratic character (Dierickx and Majersdorf 1993). They view themselves in the first place as 'servants of the State' and as 'experts' and only in the last place as 'servants of a political program'. Second, civil servants occupy a rather isolated position in the policy process. Politicians have limited expectations of civil servants and this creates a self-fulfilling prophecy. Politicians and civil servants mind their own affairs, resulting in a strong mutual alienation. Last, political nominations are a cause of political alienation. To be a member or an activist of a political party is often more important than capacity or performance. This results in aversion towards politics and in a general demoralisation of civil servants. This also explains the apparent contradiction between the political alienation of civil servants and their high degree of political activity. Civil servants are politically active out of necessity rather than out of political conviction. Belgian civil servants are thus in a schizophrenic situation: they despise politics, but they need it.

The restricted role perception and executive activities of Belgian civil servants can be explained by the central position of the ministerial cabinets in the decision-making process. Ministerial cabinets have always existed, but their size, structure and function have evolved in the last century (Van Hassel 1988). Nowadays, each minister has an average of 60 people working in his cabinet. These people are either civil servants from the administration (about 50 per cent), or members from the minister's political party, or people with specific expertise.

The ministerial cabinet performs a number of functions: it takes care of the personal secretariat of the minister and the relations with the media; it supports the minister in the policy process; it meets the claims of interest groups; and it plays an important role in the case work of the minister. Therefore ministerial cabinets have some positive effects. They strengthen the position of the minister in regard to the civil service, thus increasing democratic control over the administration. They also provide for innovation in the policy process.

Ministerial cabinets, however, also have negative effects. They often have evolved into parallel administrations, reducing the civil service to a merely executing organ. By drawing (capable) civil servants from the administration, the cabinets have weakened it. Finally, cabinets have played a major role in political nominations which they co-ordinate and from which they profit (Hondeghem 1990).

Because of these dysfunctions, there is a trend for reducing the extent of the ministerial cabinet. The cabinet has to perform its essential function, which is political support to the minister, but at the same time, the administration has to be revalorised in the policy process.

PUBLIC OPINION

Studies

As to the public opinion in Belgium towards the civil service, some studies can illustrate the situation.

In 1990 a poll was held investigating the power hierarchy as perceived by the public (Dewachter and Das 1991). The respondents were asked to rank 15 positions on a scale indicating their influence on politics. The result was that top civil servants occupied only the ninth place. They were preceded by other positions, which, according to the formal rules of the constitution, have no influence on political decision making: the presidents of the political parties, the leaders of employees' and employers' organisations and journalists. In the same period a similar study was held involving the Belgian élite as respondents. They were asked to rank the same positions according to their actual influence on the decision making (Dewachter and Das 1991). The élite placed top civil service almost at the bottom of the hierarchy. A similar study in 1967, produced the same results.

Public opinion surveys, dealing with public confidence in the administration, were carried out by the Interuniversity Centre for Political Opinion Research (ISPO).[2] In 1995, following degrees of confidence in the administration were found: very much confidence (0.5 per cent), much confidence (13 per cent), neither much nor little confidence (50.5 per cent), little confidence (28 per cent), very little confidence (5 per cent) and don't now (3 per cent). It appeared from the study that there was a significant correlation between the degree of confidence and sex (women had less confidence in the administration) and age (some age groups had more confidence than others).

A public opinion poll concerning the functioning of the political-administrative system in 1996 showed a rather alarming result (*La Libre Belgique*, 26 December 1996). 64 per cent of the citizens believed that the democracy in Belgium was in danger. Some 83 per cent thought the institutions, function 'very bad', 'bad' or 'rather bad' and 77 per cent of the citizens had no confidence in the politicians to solve the problems. Although the mistrust towards the institutions and the political world was general for the whole of Belgium, the results were more negative in the Walloon part where the poor social-economic situation and recent scandals were important factors. When interpreting these results, one needs to know that the poll was held at the time when the political agenda in Belgium had been dominated for a period of four months by the tragic disappearance and murder of several young girls, thought to be connected to a network of criminals involved in paedophilia and child pornography (the so-called Dutroux case). It appeared that the police as well as the judiciary force had blundered. It led to a protest march which mobilised 300 000 citizens asking for urgent reforms.

More recent public opinion polls, however, have not shown a significant amelioration of public confidence in government.

EVALUATION

The studies indicate that the public's image of the political institutions in general and of the civil service in particular is not very positive. This image has deteriorated seriously in recent years. Explanations for this loss of public confidence are manifold.

One explanation is that Belgian citizens have always mistrusted authority especially central authority due to frequent occupations by foreign powers. Another explanation lies in the Belgian culture of clientelism. Citizens view the state and its institutions as a series of services rather than as a collective authority that guides the society. Their perception of political decision making is rather negative as they see decisions more the result of compromises, of a game of giving and taking, than the result of a rational process. The experiences with nepotism and patronage also have a negative impact on public opinion. Last, government may have waited too long to meet the concrete expectations and complaints of the citizens. The government has been preoccupied with its own political agenda of reform of the State. The price for its slowness in attending to the political and social problems in society is the loss of legitimacy.

The first signal to this loss of legitimacy came with the elections of 1991, which were a turning point for the political system in Belgium. The date of 24 November 1991 is still referred to as 'black Sunday'. The traditional parties lost ground to extremist right wing and anti-politic parties which obtained 11 per cent of the vote whilst 7 per cent of the voting-papers were blank or invalid (note: voting is still obligatory in Belgium). Many citizens believed that the politicians ignored their real day-to-day problems such as unemployment, criminality, immigrants, etc. Citizens turned away from the traditional parties and voted for parties which offered simplistic solutions to their problems.

As a reaction to this signal, the government developed in 1992 a 'contract with the citizen', which is a political programme that approaches all sorts of societal problems. Suddenly there was more money for poverty policies, for renovations of towns and for social housing. Measures were taken to deal more rapidly with criminality. The access of the citizens to the public service was improved through a citizen's charter, which emphasised three important principles: transparency, physical and psychological accessibility of public services, and legal protection of the citizen. The charter is currently being implemented.

CONCLUDING REMARKS

This chapter has been on the national civil service in Belgium, more exactly on the civil servants in the national ministries. It is important to stress that this sector only represents 7 per cent of the public employment in Belgium. Although the national civil service system has for a long time served as a model for other sectors, the analyses and conclusions cannot be transferred as such to other sectors.

The national civil service manifests itself as a modest administration: its prestige is limited and its position in the political decision-making process is marginal. The administration is the product of the Belgian political culture with compromises, equilibriums and clientelism as main features.

The most striking thing is the gap between the formal and the real system. Formally, civil servants are loyal and politically neutral and are nominated on the basis of merit and capacity. In reality, however, there is a constant aspiration towards a representative administration which mirrors the main socio-logical and ideological forces within Belgian society.

The national civil service has been object of drastic reforms in recent years. These reforms deal with two important challenges. First they respond to the lack of legitimacy of the political-administrative system, which has become very clear since the elections of 1991. In order to enhance legitimacy, a citizen's charter has been developed. Secondly, they support an evolution towards an efficient, effective and economic administration. This is neccessary because of the enormous public debt at the national level. This evolution, however, is often hindered by the excessive regulations concerning the statute of the civil servants. These regulations are in turn the result of a fundamental mistrust of the civil servants against the political system.

On the national level, the existence of two different cultures (the Flemish and the Walloon community) is also hindering the reforms. Whether a solution for these tensions will in the future still be found in a Belgian context remains an open question. The differences between the two parts of Belgium are growing, which may lead to a further desintegration of the Belgian state. The national civil service is the victim of this desintegration. Dynamic parts of government have been transferred to the state level, leaving the national level with some old departments. Without legacy from the past and without serious budget problems, the new institutions on the state level (e.g. the Flemish administration) have the opportunity to prove themselves. Reforms seem to be much easier at the state level than at the national level. In contrast with the past the national level has become a follower rather than a triggering force. This might have a negative impact on the attractiveness of the national civil service.

EPILOGUE

This book will appear in a period of enormous change for the national civil service in Belgium. After the elections of June 1999, a new government was installed with far-reaching ambitions concerning the modernisation of the administration. The minister responsible for the civil service has proven his competencies as a change agent already in the Flemish administration, where he was for almost ten years responsible for the civil service.

In the meantime, the outline of the modernisation process was written down in the so-called Copernicus plan, named after the man who discovered that the earth is turning around the sun and not vice versa. If the Copernicus plan is approved and implemented, the national civil service in Belgium will go through a similar revolution. Following proposals are part of the plan:

- The structure of the federal departments and institutions will be reshaped, following the division between core departments and executive agencies;
- Job definition and classification, deployment rules and reward structures will be based upon principles of competence management;
- Ministerial cabinets will be reduced drastically; they will be replaced by a departmental board, responsible for policy development; this board will be chaired by the minister and will be composed of internal as well as external experts; policy divisions will be set up in each department, consisting of temporary personnel;
- The mandate system will be introduced for top functions in the administration; in contrast with former proposals (cf. supra) it will also be possible to recruit outsiders for these functions; public managers will have a performance contract, separate from the contract of the organisation;
- Ministers will be able to chose the head of a department out of a group of top managers who have been selected by the federal selection agency (SELOR).

As the Copernicus plan still has to be made operational, it was impossible to take these changes into account in this study.

The Copernicus plan has the ambition to modernise the civil service in Belgium and to link up with international developments. The challenge is enormous. As is apparent from this chapter, due to institutional factors, the national civil service in Belgium has considerable arrears comparing with other administrations, nationally as well as internationally. Resistance to change is inevitable. But for the first time in a long while, there is hope again...

NOTES

1 The author would like to thank the following individuals for their contribution to this article: Prof. dr. Roger Depré (Public Management Centre, K.U. Leuven) for his intellectual and moral support and Dries Van Hamme (Public Management Centre, K.U. Leuven) and Sylvia Horton (University of Portsmouth) for their help in translating the text into English.
2 The data were made available by the ISPO–Interuniversity Centre for Political Opinion Research (K.U.Leuven)- sponsored by the Federal Services for Technical, Cultural and Scientific Affairs. The data were originally collected by Jaak Billiet, Marc Swyngedouw, Ann Carton and Roeland Beerten. Neither the original collectors of the data not the Centre bears any responsibility for the analysis or interpretations presented here.

BIBLIOGRAPHY

Aberbach, J.D. (1981), R.D. Putnam and B.A. Rockman, *Bureaucrats and Politicians in Western democracies*, Cambridge: Cambridge, MA: Harvard University.
Baakman, N.A.A., G. Bouckaert and R. Maes (1994), 'Besturen in Vlaanderen en Nederland', *Bestuurskunde*, V.3, N.6, 235–45.
Baron, J.N., A. Davis-Blake and W.T. Bielby (1986), 'The structure of opportunity: how promotion ladders vary within and among organisations', *Administrative Science Quarterly*, **31**, (2), 248–73.
Bekke, A.J.G.M., J.L. Perry and Th.A.J. Toonen (eds) (1996), *Civil Service Systems in Comparative Perspective*, Bloomington and Indianapolis: Indiana University Press.
Bouckaert, G., A. Hondeghem and R. Maes (eds) (1994), *De overheidsmanager*, Leuven: V.C.O.B.
Chapman, B. (1966), *The Profession of Government*, London: Unwin.
Dejaeghere, P. (1992), 'Wegwijs in ambtenarenlonen', *Tijdschrift voor bestuurswetenschappen en publiek recht*, **47**, N.7, 476–91.
Depré, R. (1973), *De Topambtenaren van de Ministeries in België*, Leuven: V.C.O.B.
Depré, R. and A. Hondeghem (1987), 'Recruitment, career and training of higher civil servants in Belgium', in *The HigherCcivil Service in Belgium and in the Industrialised Countries: Recruitment, Career, and Training*, Brussels: I.I.A.S.
Depré, R. and A. Hondeghem (1991), 'Rapport sur la représentativité de l'administration en Belgique', in V. Wright, (ed..), *La Représentativité de l'administration publique*, Brussels: I.I.A.S., 93–126.

Depré, R. and A. Hondeghem (1996), 'Belgium', in J. Barlow, D. Farnham, A. Hondeghem and S. Horton, (eds), *The New Public Managers in Europe, Public Servants in Transition*, London: Macmillan, 79–99.

Derlien, H.-U. and R. Mayntz (1989), 'Party patronage and politicisation of the West German administrative elite 1970–1987, towards hybridisation', *Governance*, **2**, (4): 387–404.

Dewachter, W. and E. Das (1991), *Politiek in België, Geprofileerde machtsverhoudingen*, Leuven: Acco.

Dierickx, G. and P. Majersdorf (1993), *De politieke cultuur van ambtenaren en politici in België*, Bruges: Vanden Broele.

DiPrete, T.A. (1989), *The Bureaucratic Labour Market: The Case of the Federal Civil Service*, New York: Plenum Books.

Doeringer, P.D. and M.J. Piore (1971), *Internal Labour Markets and Manpower Analysis*, Lexington: Heath Lexington Books.

Ducpétiaux, E. (1859), *Etude sur la réforme administrative*, Brussels.

Hondeghem, A. (1987), 'Vingt-cinq ans de recrutements d'universitaires par le Secrétariat Permanent de Recrutement', *Res Publica*, **29**(2): 231–58.

Hondeghem, A. (1990), *De Loopbaan van de Ambtenaar, tussen Droom en Werkelijkheid*, Leuven: VCOB.

Hondeghem, A. (1994), 'De politisering van de ambtenarij', in A.H. Berg et al, *Strategie en beleid in de publieke sector*, Alphen aan den Rijn: Samsom, B3130–1–B3130–26.

Hondeghem, A., 'De politieke en ambtelijke component in het openbaar bestuur', in R. Maes and K. Jochmans (eds), *Inleiding tot de Bestuurskunde, deel 2*, Brussels: STOHO, 44-72.

Hondeghem, A. and M. Robbroeckx (1986), *Tewerkstelling van universitairen in de openbare sector*, Brussels: VLIR.

Hondeghem, A. and H. Weggemans, (1994), 'Personeelsbeleid in Vlaanderen en Nederland: van divergentie naar convergentie', *Bestuurskunde*, **3**(6): 253–62.

Ingraham, P.W. (1996), 'The reform agenda for national civil service systems: external stress and internal strains', in A.J.G.M. Bekke, J.L. Perry and Th.A.J. Toonen (eds), *Civil Service Systems in Comparative Perspectives*, Bloomington: Indiana University Press, 247–67.

Kanter, R.M. (1977), *Men and Women of the Corporation*, New York: Basic Books.

Meer, F.M. van der and L.J. Roborgh (1996), 'Civil servants and representativeness', in A.J.G.M. Bekke, J.L. Perry and Th.A.J. Toonen (eds), *Civil Service Systems in Comparative Perspective*, Bloomington: Indiana University Press, 119–33.

Molitor, A. (1974), *L'Administration de la Belgique*, Institut belge de sciences politiques, Brussels: CRISP.

Rosenbaum, J.E. (1984), *Career Mobility in a Corporate Hierarchy*, Orlando, FA: Academic Press.

Van Hassel, H. (1988), 'Het kabinetssyndroom in historisch perspectief', *Gemeentekrediet van België*, **42**(166): 11–36.

Van Hooland, B. (1992), 'De wedden en lonen van onze ambtenaren', *De gemeente*, **67**(11): 503–11.

Wise, L.R. (1996), 'Internal labor markets', in A.J.G.M. Bekke, J.L. Perry and Th.A.J. Toonen (eds), *Civil Service Systems in Comparative Perspective*, Bloomington: Indiana University Press, 100–18.

7. The Development and Current Features of the Dutch Civil Service System

**Frits M. van der Meer and
Gerrit S.A. Dijkstra**[1]

INTRODUCTION

The Netherlands are strategically located in the Northwest of Europe. To a large extent, the development of Dutch state and society has been influenced by its powerful neighbours, in particular the United Kingdom, France and Germany. And yet the Netherlands has an identity of its own characterised by the decentralised unitary state. Although the Netherlands is a unitary state in principle, (subnational) governments and societal groups have been provided (or left) ample autonomy to participate in public affairs. The deep political, religious and societal cleavages are held responsible for this decentralised system of governance. The high level of 'tolerance' rightly or wrongly ascribed to Dutch society can in fact be understood as an institutionalised method for securing a peaceful cohabitation between different groups in society. The cohabitation enshrined in the decentralised unitary state involves a basic agreement on the rules of the game governing the Dutch polity. The pivotal nature of these (constitutional) rules explains what has been called the institutional conservative nature of Dutch politics and government (Andeweg 1989). Evolution, not revolution, is the key for understanding the development of the Dutch state and society. Analysing the development and nature of the Dutch civil service system likewise demands emphasising its interdependence with the wider societal and political administrative contexts.

The evolution of the Dutch civil service system will provide a starting point for our analysis. Its characteristics, peculiarities and problems are shaped by the development of Dutch state and society. Attention will also be directed to the Dutch civil service as a system of personnel. The definition of civil servants is not a mere 'legal and technical' question. Regulations and policies in this area are a reflection of basic ideas concerning the position of the civil service within the wider context of the Dutch polity. Having defined civil servants in the Dutch context, we will have a look at the numbers. First, the changing size of government employment in general and the staff of central government departments will be studied. In relation to this, the functional distribution according to major policy field in central government will be examined. The hierarchal division between lower, middle and higher civil servants will be a second theme. How do civil servants get to their functional and hierarchical positions? This involves a scrutiny of the methods of recruitment and career patterns. Both the empirical and policy dimension form part of our discussion.

Civil servants are not only part of a government organisation, but they also are 'attached' to society (Peters 1996). First, the social composition of the civil service will be examined. Both the demographic as well as the political composition of the national civil service will be reviewed. Issues involved in demographic civil service representativeness include the gender division, age structure, religious, social, educational and the ethnic background of civil servants. In our discussion of politicisation, we refer both to the politicisation of recruitment and behaviour. After our discussion of representativeness and politicisation, public opinion about the civil service is addressed.

THE DEVELOPMENT OF THE CIVIL SERVICE SYSTEM: STATE, POLITICS AND THE CIVIL SERVICE

From Autocracy to the Development of the Decentralised Unitary State: 1815–70

The foundations of the present Dutch state were laid in 1813 after the defeat of Napoleon by the allied forces. The French occupation left a fairly centralised state that was supported by a central administrative apparatus. These instruments were at the disposal of the new king, William I. At first, little resistance was voiced against the personal (autocratic) rule of the king. Large segments in society were all too happy to refrain from further democratic experiments since the memory of the last years of the French Era (the annexation to France) was not an altogether happy one. Both the elite and the general public were content to be subjected to a relative subordinate position. William's personal rule was tempered by what was seen at that time as his 'good intentions'. This positive attitude primarily applied to society in the Protestant-dominated north of the country. In the southern Catholic parts, presentday Belgium, resentment grew as a result of having a Protestant king who was assisted by the northern Dutch-speaking administration. His autocratic rule was considered particularly objectionable to the French-speaking Belgian elite who was more liberal minded.

This internal tension finally resulted in a separation between the present-day states of the Netherlands and Belgium, formalised in 1839. After the Belgian Revolt (to use the Dutch point of view), the old constitution had to be adapted to the new situation. Opinion was voiced by increasing segments of the elite that this revision should be more substantial and not restrict itself to a mere technical exercise. Even in the Netherlands, liberalism gradually took hold. Although fundamental changes did not enter the constitution of 1840, this revision denoted the move to a more fundamental change in 1848. Being impressed by the revolutionary spirit of the day, King William II turned 'in one night from a conservative into a liberal'. Under the liberal leader Thorbecke, the foundation for a new model of state was laid – the features of which still determine modern Dutch government. A new constitution laid the foundation for ministerial responsibility (and from the 1860s on, parliamentary sovereignty), provincial, municipal acts and so on. Centralism was modified by granting more autonomy to local governments. This resulted in the creation what is now called the decentralised unitary state.

From an administrative point of view, the abolition of the General Secretariate in 1840 has been a crucial step in political administrative development. The general secretary had been a crucial instrument for the king in maintaining a grip on the administration. With the termination of the General Secretariate, a vital instrument for interdepartmental coordination ceased to exist. Increasing ministerial autonomy in relation to the king meant an increase in executive fragmentation since there was no mature party system. Ever since, efforts have been made to accommodate the need for political coordination. But basically each minister remained individually responsible to parliament. The executive became essentially fragmented. Cohesion had to be found in non-structural dimensions such as the sense of political purpose of a cabinet and its relation toward parliament.

With regard to the bureaucracy, in the greater part of the nineteenth century, civil servants were recruited by the political and bureaucratic office-holders from wider family, political and business circles (Van der Meer and Raadschelders 1998b; Randeraad 1994; Van Braam 1957). Patronage was therefore still an important method of recruitment. The elitist nature of the civil service was reinforced by comparatively low salaries and poor labour conditions. For instance, the salaries were kept at the same level between 1828 and 1864 (Van IJsselmuiden 1988). The low salaries were supposedly compensated by the high esteem of holding public office. As the lower civil servants in particular could not supplement their income by private means, public employment implied a 'dignified' poverty (Randeraad 1994). These conditions led to an aristocratisation of the higher civil service in the early parts of the nineteenth century (Van IJsselmuiden 1988). The weak position of civil servants was augmented by the fact that during the greater part of the nineteenth century, the legal position of civil servants was not protected by a special status (Van IJsselmuiden 1988). Gradually, having to attract skilled personnel, some provisions were issued starting with pensions and widow assistance schemes later in the century. Only with great effort and pressure from within the civil service and with assistance from legal experts, was a Civil Servant Act (CSA) adopted in 1929.

From a 'Night-watch' State to a 'Welfare State': 1870–Present

The constitutional system created in 1848 still provides the context for the modern Dutch system of government. The actual direction of Dutch society and government since 1870 has been shaped by the process of industrialisation, its social aftermath, and the development of a 'modern' party system.

The social consequences of the industrialisation process compelled government to act on negative side-effects. Likewise economic development forced central and local government to take action on physical and social-economic infrastructure. This change in attitude has been a gradual process. The dominant laissez-faire attitude of the ruling liberal coalitions was subjected to a slow process of erosion. The laissez-faire attitude was also undermined by a change in the political landscape. The dominance of liberal parties gradually gave way to the emergence of new parties. First the confessional parties came into being due to a process of social and economic emancipation of certain Protestant denominations and Roman Catholics. The influence of orthodox Protestants and Catholics had been comparatively limited because of their relatively weak economic position. The emancipation was realised by promoting social organisation along religious lines. Within the Dutch state, parallel states came into being and the foundation of the pillarised society was laid.

Somewhat comparable to the confessional parties was the emergence of a labour movement at the end of the century. Although their direct influence on the central government should not be overestimated in this particular period, trade unions and a labour party were formed as a reaction to the existing social-economic conditions. The confessional parties and the labour party can be seen as the political manifestation of segments in society uneasy about the consequences of the liberal rule. Although the confessional parties were certainly not 'revolutionary', they were more open to societal intervention than the old liberals. Social intervention should, in their opinion, involve government facilitating groups in society to organise themselves in all areas from education to the economy. Based on these developments, the public sector expanded. Between 1870 and the end of World War I, new government departments were created, that is Public Works, Agriculture, Education and Labour (Van der Meer and Raadschelders 1998b). The powerful position of the confessional parties after the turn of the century gave a stimulus to the creation of non-governmental structures which were often financed from public means.

World War I and the economic crisis of the 1930s led to a further expansion of government intervention. The effects of World War I on administration were short-lived since many of the crises agencies were dismantled; direct government intervention in the economy decreased. Nevertheless the level of government activity remained higher than before the outbreak of war (Van der Meer and Roborgh 1993). The economic crisis which hit the Netherlands in the 1930s reinforced government intervention. New tasks led to new government organisations and departments using new styles of administrative technology. Although some politicians and senior civil servants thought that the increased role of government would only be for the duration of the crisis, the outbreak of World War II proved this notion to be mistaken. After this war government expanded rapidly in terms of tasks, personnel and scope of intervention in society. Some direct necessities had to be met. The reconstruction of Dutch economy and society was the first formidable task. Furthermore the recollection of the social hardships of World War II and the economic depression of the 1930s did inspire social legislation which led to the creation and development of the welfare state. New government departments were created. The structure of government departments became more complicated as the subdivisions within these departments increased.

The increasing complexities of administration exposed an old weakness in the administrative system: the lack of intra- and interdepartmental coordination. One state committee after another produced reports to formulate ideas and proposals to tackle this problem. Before World War II the creation of a Prime Minister's Office was suggested (Van IJsselmuiden 1988). A Ministry of General Affairs was created in 1937 to be headed by the prime minister. The ministry was however short-lived and abolished again before the outbreak of World War II. The coalition nature of government as an expression of the societal and political fragmentation of society inhibited the establishment of a (strong) central political direction (Van der Meer and Raadschelders 1998b). Nevertheless since 1945 some additional measures to reinforce structures have been taken. The council of ministers was strengthened in 1983 giving it a constitutional basis. Subcommittees to the council were introduced and coordinating ministers were appointed. On the administrative side, interdepartmental committees were established. Yet, in spite of all these measures the unifying elements are weak relative to the centrifugal powers mentioned above. Although there is a collective cabinet responsibility for general government policy, ministers are still responsible for their own policy area. This restrains the possibilities of ministers implementing their coordinating tasks.

With the changes in the size, organisation and task structure of Dutch government, new demands were made concerning the required level of expertise of civil servants. New complicated tasks demanded a well-trained and better educated workforce. A first indicator is the rise in the number of higher officials with a university degree over the years. Furthermore new demands on the civil service were made as their position in the policymaking process became less reactive and more proactive. Although one has to be careful to read too much into this change, the monopoly of legal trainees has gradually disappeared, making way for the inclusion of economists and social scientists in the civil service. Another important change is the attention paid to maintaining the standards of the professional qualities of civil servants in terms of knowledge, skills and attitude. From the 1980s onwards increasing attention has been paid to devising management development programmes.

As the development of human resources became a vital topic in administration, substantial energy has been placed in the organisation of personnel administration (after 1945). A centralised approach was initially tried, and a central personnel office was created at the Home Office. It failed in 1958 because the interdepartmental balance of power didn't agree with such a centralised approach. An additional argument against centralising human resource management has to do with the demand for a more flexible personnel management. In order to enable line managers to pursue integral management, many personnel issues have been decentralised. Although a (weak) interdepartmental coordinating system was installed, day-to-day personnel management affairs remained with the individual ministries. Since the 1990s, some changes have been made in this decentralised human resource management system; these will be highlighted in the next section.

The development of a mature central government bureaucracy also had important consequences for the legal status of civil servants. From the turn of the century onward, the legal position of civil servants has been increasingly formalised: a depersonalisation of appointment, appraisal and career decisions. In this respect one can also speak of a bureaucratisation of personnel policy (Van der Meer and Raadschelders 1998b). For all ranks, formal requirements (particularly in the form of diplomas) became crucial for qualifying for an administrative position. The formalisation of the legal position of civil servants culminated in the Civil Servant Act of 1929 (CSA 1929) (Van IJsselmuiden 1988; Randeraad 1994; Van der Meer and Raadschelders 1998b). Recent policy will once again alter the special legal position of civil servants. The status of public law is under discussion. A harmonisation to the legal status as it exists within the private sector on topics of labour conditions, relations and social security is the objective. It is argued that special legal protection is less essential nowadays since private labour law provides ample safeguards. A formalisation has taken place in the private sector as well. At the same time, civil servants can acquire a more equal position with government in labour negotiations.

THE INTERNAL LABOUR MARKET

Civil Servants and the System of Personnel Management

In the fundamental rights written down in the constitution, one provision relates to the nature of the appointment to the civil service. Article 3 states, 'all Dutchmen are eligible to be appointed on an equal footing to the public service'. The public nature of government employment is symbolised by this article. The open character is seen as fundamental right. Later we will return to this particular article because it is the legal foundation for the equal treatment policy in the public sector. Article 109 of the constitution furthermore requires the drafting of civil service legislation, 'The law regulates the legal position of civil servants. Rules are drafted relating to their protection at work and their work participation'. To effectuate this Article 109, the CSA 1929 is in operation. The CSA 1929 will be used as a starting point for our civil servant definition. The CSA 1929 states, 'a civil servant in the meaning of this act is he or she who is appointed to be employed in the public service'. All agencies and (public) enterprises administered by the state and public authorities belong to the public service. The CSA 1929 only provides a very general outline for regulating the legal position of civil servants regardless of the level of government.[2] According to Article 125 of the CSA 1929 each government has to issue its own (detailed) regulation. Besides central government each province, municipality, water board and so on has to issue such provisions.

For instance the General Civil Service Regulations (ARAR) is issued for personnel working at central government departments. The ARAR contains provisions on a wide range of topics such as selection and recruitment, dismissal, resignation, working hours, leave, holidays, employee participation and disciplinary measures. In the Civil Servants Pay Decree (BBRA), salaries, holiday pay and allowances are fixed. Besides the ARAR for government departments, separate regulations have been issued for the judiciary (based on the law on legal organisation), for military defence personnel (AMAR), and for the civilian defence personnel (BARD). These systems are roughly the same in content as the ARAR. To make things even more complicated, independent (public) agencies have their own regulations.

Besides this regulatory power, decisions on personnel management and policy on recruitment and promotion of staff are situated in each government separately. The same decentralisation applies to the system of wage settlements. Before the early 1990s the system of labour negotiation was highly centralised. The outcome of central government negotiations determined local government negotiations. Competition between governments was considered unacceptable. The centralised approach has been abandoned in order to allow different governments (and government sectors) to develop an approach more appropriate to their own needs. The sectors are central government departments, the military, the judiciary, police, municipalities, provinces, water boards and education.

As has already been mentioned, staffing decisions are (often) handed to separate organisational units. At the central government level, these powers are decentralised to the various departments an departmental units. There are some formal and informal interdepartmental co-ordination bodies. The minister of the interior has political co-ordinating tasks. Because of his limited powers, his main task is to encourage interdepartmental co-operation and policy renewal.

We have presented the legal definition of civil servants. Before 1971 many different categories of government personnel were distinguished. For instance manual workers had their own pay system, as had the white collar workers who were also called civil servants in a restricted sense. This last category consisted of officials involved in policymaking and execution in whatever capacity from the secretary-general to the most humble clerk. Before the turn of the century, they were the only ones who were really considered civil servants. The other categories were seen as 'support staff'. Nowadays both the secretary-general and the blue collar worker are regarded as a civil servant in terms of their legal position. From a political and administrative science perspective, those individuals active in core activities are still pre-eminently considered civil servants. Nowadays few blue collar workers are left in central government due to processes of contracting out, decentralisation and privatisation (Van der Meer and Roborgh 1993).

The Changing Size and Functional Distribution of the Civil Service

Having defined civil servants, we turn to the actual size of the civil service. Before we address changes in government personnel and focus our analysis on the central government, we present the distribution of personnel over the different levels and sectors of government (see Table 7.1). The figures relate to the situation as of 31 December 1996.

Municipalities, (public) education and central government departments are the largest (civilian) government employers. Private education is not considered a part of government in a narrow sense. Health care and social securities institutions are a vital part of what has been called the 'parastate' (Hood and Schuppert 1988). Sub-national government combined (excluding police and public education) amounts to around 40 per cent of all personnel. Excluded from Table 7.1 are personnel working for independent public agencies and those enterprises and foundations respectively owned and controlled by government but not possessing a public law status. Examples are, for instance, (regional) bus services, rail roads and public utilities. All these exclusions lead to the conclusion that large sections of the public sector lay outside government.

Table 7.1   Dutch (civilian) government personnel according to government and government sector (1996)

Sector of government	Absolute number	Percentage of total of civilian (public) employees
Central government	105 656	21.3
Defense (total)	76 886	
Civilian personnel	22 632	4.6
Military personnel	53 921	
Enlisted men	333	
Police	45 220	9.1
(Former municipal and state police)		
Judiciary	2 179	0.4
Municipalities	175 192	35.2
Provinces	12 801	2.6
Water boards	8 734	1.8
Joint provisions	19 082	3.8
Public education	105 613	21.2
Total civilian personnel	497 109	100.0
Private education	233 611	
Grand total	784 974	

Source: Ministerie van Binnenlandse Zaken, 1997a

For a dynamic analysis of the size of government employment, the changes in the civil service employment from 1899 to the present will be reviewed. Personnel working in public education institutions are excluded from the figures in Table 7.2. Additional information on the size of public education can be found in the annotation to Table 7.2. Since statutory public enterprises have been privatised from the 1970s onwards, their inclusion can distort the long-term trend. The privatisation of the postal and telecommunication services in 1989, for instance, resulted in a decrease of about 100 000 individuals in the figures. Both the figures including and excluding (central) government statutory enterprises are presented.

Table 7.2   Number of government personnel,. 1899–1996[3]

	Including			Excluding		
	Central government enterprises					
Year	abs.[a]	i[b] =	i =	abs.	i =	i =
		1899	1950		1899	1950
1899	52 700	100.0		43 500	100.0	
1909	75 300	142.9				
1920	173 300	328.8		125 400	288.3	
1930	184 700	350.5		132 500	304.6	
1938	180 500	342.5		–	–	
1950	332 200	630.4	100.0	236 700	544.1	100.0
1960	364 800	692.2	109.8	263 300	605.3	111.2
1968	380 300	721.6	114.5	310 200	713.1	131.1
1975	454 900	863.2	136.9	369 500	849.4	156.1
1980	532 400	1010.2	160.3	429 600	987.6	181.5
1985	559 300	1061.3	168.4	448 900		189.6
1990	424 500	805.5	127.8	424 400	975.6	179.3
1994	398 900	756.9	120.0	398 900	916.3	168.3
1996	391 500	742.9	117.9	391 500	900.0	165.4

Note: abs = absolute, i = index.
Source: Van der Meer and Roborgh 1993; Ministerie van Binnenlandse Zaken, 1990–97a.

It is often remarked that the Dutch civil service has dramatically increased in size since the end of World War II and that the number only dropped after the middle of the 1980s. Looking at the data, this expansion and contraction is evident. By pinpointing this growth solely to this particular post-war period, the rapid growth rate manifest from 1900 to 1950 is underestimated. The rate of growth in this particular period is equally vigorous. The early 1900s constitute a turning point. Evidence suggests that around the middle of the nineteenth century, the number of government personnel was limited and the pace of change was quite modest (Van Braam 1957, Brasz 1960, Randeraad 1994). Nevertheless contemporaries complained otherwise. The 'lift off' at the turn of the century can be explained by more active government involvement in society. This is also the period in which public enterprises were established and began to evolve. The state mines, the public utilities at the local level, and the nationalisation of the railroads are but few examples.

An additional conclusion is that the number of government personnel did not change gradually; different stages can be distinguished. Three periods of very strong growth alternated with periods of relative stability or even decline. The periods around both World Wars witnessed vast increases of personnel. The third period of growth occurred around the 1970s. The explanation can be found in the fact that crises in society served as a catalyst for growth. Political and administrative changes speeded up. The cutbacks in government staff starting from the middle of the 1980s are primarily the result of the privatisation of central government enterprises. Nowadays, no (major) statutory public enterprises are left at the central level. Even so, looking at the data, excluding staff of these enterprises, a decrease in personnel can still be found. A first explanation is that municipal enterprises and services (that is public utilities and hospitals) have not been omitted. In the past decade these services have also been 'privatised' to a large extent. Some doubt can be expressed whether this reduction is a substantive and not a cosmetic one. Many of these services are still attached to government by financial and legal (property) links. A second explanation is situated in what can be called hiving off government agencies and the creation of so-called independent public agencies. This procedure has become standard since the beginning of the 1980s. An illustration of the effects can be found in the cutbacks in central government staff (Table 7.3).

Before discussing these figures, a preliminary remark is necessary concerning the composition of central government personnel. In Table 7.3 civilian military personnel are included. In 1992 due to the 'sectoralisation' of labour relations, a separate military sector including civilian staff (those working at the Ministry of Defence) has been created. These civilians are still included in Table 7.3 to make a valid comparison.

Table 7.3   Number of central government personnel, 1899–1996

Year	abs.	i=1899	i=1950
1899	13 500	100.0	
1920	32 500	240.7	
1930	32 300	239.3	
1942	55 700	412.6	
1950	87 400	647.4	100.0
1970	115 100	852.6	131.7
1980	143 900	1 065.9	164.6
1985	151 000	1118.5	172.8
1993	142 400	1054.8	162.9
1994	135 400	1003.0	154.9
1996	128 300	950.3	146.8

Source: Van der Meer and Roborgh 1993; Ministerie van Binnenlandse Zaken, 1990–97a.

The development of central government personnel is more or less in accordance with the general picture of government personnel, excluding central government enterprises. But as is often said, between the truth and a truth is a world of difference. In the last 10 years, the number of individuals working for central government departments has fallen by around 20 000. But the decrease of at least 10 000 individuals since 1991 can be explained by hiving off labour exchanges, property registration and a Ministry of Education service responsible for student grants (*informatiseringsbank*). These institutions do not show up in the general figures because they are not viewed as belonging to one of the earlier sectors. A number of these organisations still have a public law status and in the case of many others, government still has important powers in terms of appointment rights and finances. Although a certain decline in the size of central government staff is perhaps likely to have occurred, the necessary questions marks have to be placed on the actual size of the decline of central governmental personnel. The same also applies to the decline of the municipal workforce. What is certainly true is that the 1980s were a watershed in the sense that the expansion of central government has been halted.

Thus far we have employed the CSA 1929 definition. In Table 7.4 we have used a sociological (and administrative) definition: the white collar worker, or in other words, that official involved in a certain stage of the policymaking and/or implementation process. The extent of white collar workers in government on the total work force is used as an indicator for bureaucratisation (B).

Table 7.4   Number of administrative personnel at the central government level, 1960–94

Year	abs.	i=1960	B	i=1960
1960	72 500	100.0	74.1	100.0
1970	88 000	121.4	76.5	103.2
1988	127 000	175.2	86.4	116.6
1994	124 000	171.0	87.1	117.5

Source: Van der Meer and Roborgh 1993, authors for 1994.

What can be learned from Table 7.4 is that since the 1960s, a process of bureaucratisation (in Weberian terminology: *Verambtlichung*) of civil service personnel took place. Research shows that this phenomenon happened in a similar manner in central and sub-national governments (Van der Meer and Roborgh 1993). This process of bureaucratisation has first been caused by a higher growth rate of those sectors where civil servants (as distinguished from lower auxiliary personnel) are employed. Even in the public utility services, the civil service component grew.

In what areas are these central government officials working? In Table
7.5, the functional distribution of central government staff is compared to the
situation in 1960 and 1988. The following policy areas are general administration, infrastructure, public works, welfare and health, education, the
economy and defence.

*Table 7.5   Functional division of central government officials over the
policy areas general administration. Economic affairs including
taxation, Welfare Culture and Health and Defence from the
period 1960–96*

Year Sector	1960	%	1988	%	1993	%	1996	%
1. General	9 312	9.7	24 768	16.9	29 405	20.6	32 292	25.2
Adminis- tration	100.0	100.0	266.0	174.2	315.8	212.3	346.8	259.8
2. Economic	32 903	34.3	53 053	36.1	50 843	35.7	46 349	36.1
Affairs (incl. tax office)	100.0	100.0	161.2	105.2	154.5	104.1	140.9	105.2
3. Infrastructure	14 742	15.4	24 764	16.9	22 517	15.8	17 282	13.5
	100.0	100.0	168.0	109.7	153.1	102.6	117.2	87.7
4. Welfare	8 523	8.9	17 963	12.2	14 127	9.9	9733	7.6
Culture and Health	100.0	100.0	210.8	137.1	165.8	111.2	114.2	85.4
5. Defence	30 313	31.6	26 404	18.0	25 537	17.9	22 632	17.6
	100.0	100.0	87.1	57.0	84.2	56.6	74.7	55.7
6. Total index	95 793		146 952		142 429		128 288	
	100.0		100.0		100.0		100.0	

Source: Van der Meer and Roborgh 1993; Ministerie van Binnenlandse Zaken, 1997a.

Looking at the functional distribution, we see that defence has endured the
most job losses while general administration experienced the fastest growth.
Notably, the justice department and its (prison and correctional) services are
responsible. This rapid increase is emphasised by the equally strong expansion of judicial and police personnel. With this last exception, personnel
growth occurred particularly in those units involved in policy preparation and
in internal management affairs. The emphasis in government tasks has focused more clearly on planning, ordering and steering tasks. As a result,
public employment is concentrated in the ministerial secretariats at the central level. These ministerial secretariats are the 'core units' in the department.
Around 40 000 civil servants are at work in them. Most implementation
offices (for example the tax agency) have experienced much lower growth
rates. Since 1988, a decline in this area is evident. Due to an intensified next
steps approach, some of the organisations involved in service provision have

been privatised or (even more significantly) restructured into independent public agencies.

To summarise, what remains is for the most part a higher civil service consisting of top civil servants and persons contribution to policymaking. With the expressed preference for 'a next steps approach', executive services are kept 'at a distance'. Gradually, these services disappear from government. The civil service is thus increasingly the domain of those employed by the ministerial secretariats at the central level. Since these are considered to be political in nature, they will remain within core government, while other units/agencies/services are made more independent or even privatised. This phenomenon can be labelled as 'government going underground'.

The Hierarchical Divisions

The changing functional composition of the civil service has profound implications for the hierarchical distribution. Changes in the hierarchical distribution over the last twenty years will be our focus. Ever from the beginning of a civil service in the present Dutch state, a differentiation has been made between higher, middle and lower personnel. Originally, until the revision of the BBRA in 1984, a rank system was in operation which could be used as the foundation for the demarcation. Some names such as secretary-general, director-general, councillor (*raadadviseur*), and the director still survive but only as a 'job description'. Since the rank system has been abolished, we have to go to the grading system which is to be found in the BBRA (and ARAR).

This grading system is based on a system of functional and salary hierarchy. In the standard system, grades rank from 1 (the lowest) to 18 (the highest). Furthermore there is a so-called Annex A. Civil servants whose functions are mentioned in this annex are paid a fixed salary. Directors-general, secretaries-general and other officers with comparable positions are some examples of the individuals involved. In (government) publications, their grade is sometimes referred as grade 19. Political officeholders are also paid a fixed salary (referred to as grades 20/21) of the Act on the Legal Position of Ministers and Under-Ministers. The scale structure forms the basic part of system of payment. In addition to their salary, staff (may) receive special benefits such as holiday pay and child support. Furthermore, due to recent emphasis on making the pay structure more flexible, performance-related bonuses and allowances for attracting personnel with desirable and 'scarce' qualities have been introduced. These merit-related payments are nevertheless (still) relatively insignificant compared to the standardised payment structure.

The foundation of this pay structure is to be found in a job comparison system. This pay structure is based on a system of job (or function) classification. Nowadays, central government uses an automated system of job comparison called *Functie Waarderings Systeem* (FuWaSys: Function Assessment System). To establish the importance of a particular position, six so-called 'levels of expertise and workload' are used. Each function level is subdivided in a number of (overlapping) grades. These function levels are placed in a ranking order from one reserved for mainly unskilled work and six for top civil servants. The weight of a function is decided by criteria such as the required level of education, responsibility, independence and the risk involved. By comparing a new to an already classified job ('normative' function), this new function is located in one of the six groups and a particular grade.

Civil servants in functions groups I and II are considered here to form the category 'low'. This category includes grades 1 up to and including grade 6. The category 'middle' refers to function level III (grades 7, 8 and 9) and finally higher civil servants belong to the function groups IV, V, VI and the Annex A or grades 10 and higher in the salary system.[4] Since even this group of higher civil servants is quite large, a further demarcation is made. Group VI and the individuals mentioned in Annex A are viewed as the top civil servants.

Civil servants from function group V are appointed to the general service of the state. With the exception of the foreign office, top civil servants (from grade 17) are part of the Senior Public Service (*algemene bestuursdienst*, ABD). We return to the function of the ABD and the reasons of its creation in a later section. Civil servants in grades 1 to 14 are appointed by the minister of a particular department by ministerial decree. Civil servants in grades 15, 16, 17 and 18 (level VI) are appointed by royal decree on the recommendation of the minister. From the level of director-general on, (Annex A) appointments are made by the Council of Ministers.

The percentage of lower civil servants has fallen dramatically (see Table 7.6). What these figures do not reveal is that particularly the lowest grades (1,2 and 3) have been cut away. At the of end 1995, 3.9 per cent of all civil servants (excluding civilian military personnel) belonged to group I. The comparable percentage for 1976 was 25.5 per cent. In these grades (1,2 and 3), less complicated and manual tasks are performed. Excluding civilian defence personnel, the percentage in the category 'low' only amounts to 33.5 per cent. The explanation is to be found in the effects of processes of contracting out and privatisation. The middle and especially the higher grades have witnessed substantial increases. In absolute terms, the number of civil servants in grade 10 and higher has risen up to the present time. It should be added that the absolute top did not demonstrate the same rate of growth (Van der Meer and Raadschelders 1999). The number of top civil servants decreased in number from 496 in 1987 to 458 in 1994.

The changes in the hierarchical composition of central government bureaucracy can best be understood by pointing to the concept as propounded
by the minister of home affairs, that central government should decrease in
size and improve in quality. As previously mentioned, central government
concentrates on (strategic) policymaking and planning while the majority of
executive tasks should either be carried out in local government, independent
public authorities or contracted out to the private sector. The effect is that
lower skilled functions in particular have disappeared.

Table 7.6   *Hierarchical division of central government civil service*
              (including civilian military personnel), 1976–94

Year	I/II		III–		IV		I–VIA	
	Low		Middle		High		All	
	abs.	index	abs.	index	abs.	index	abs.	index
1976	87 675	100	30 815	100	16 630	100	135 120	100
1980	91 089	103.9	35 344	114.7	20 050	120.6	146 483	108.4
1990	70 904	80.9	46 416	150.6	31 161	187.4	148 481	109.9
1994	61 904	70.6	45 800	256.7	34 726	208.8	142 430	105.4

Year	I/II		III		IV	
	Low		Middle		High	
	abs.	index	abs.	index	Abs.	index
1976	64.9	100	22.8	100	12.3	100.0
1980	62.2	95.8	24.1	105.7	13.7	111.4
1990	58.4	90.0	26.0	114.0	15.6	126.8
1994	43.5	67.0	32.2	141.2	24.4	198.4

Source: Van der Meer and Roborgh 1993; Ministerie van Binnenlandse Zaken, 1995a.

Mobility and Recruitment

How do civil servants acquire their position, how are they recruited and what
can be said about the mobility of civil servants working in central government? Mobility implies change. That change can consist of switching jobs or
functions or attaining a different grade. All those changes presuppose recruitment and selection. Until recently most individuals were recruited for a
particular function instead of a career. Of course there were and are exceptions to this rule. A career oriented recruitment system can be found, for
instance, in the judiciary, police, military, foreign service and also to a certain extent the tax office. After finishing their pre-entry education and following recruitment, those selected will get an (extensive) post-entry
education. Examples are police and military academies and the training pro-

grammes for the judiciary and the foreign services. Nevertheless these career systems are the exceptions to the rule. It goes without saying that also in a function oriented recruitment system officials pursue careers. The course of these careers is however not formalised at the moment of entry into the public service.

Civil servants are stimulated to develop their careers but since each department is considered an individual employer, civil servants are required to quit one job before accepting another. This portrayal has to be adjusted since in recent years, higher civil servants (from grade 10) have been employed in the general service of the state. The ABD for top civil servants is another departure from the old practice. The basic idea behind these reforms is that it can assist (interdepartmental) mobility. Advancing mobility has been a central policy aim since the beginning of the 1980s for defeating 'compartmentalisation' within the civil service.

We will first examine the degree of mobility at present. We start with the level of vertical mobility. In Table 7.7, the average time spent in public service is recorded before these officials made their most recent promotion to a particular scale. Additionally the number of years in their present grade and finally their average age on promotion is presented. The different grades have been combined to the categories low, middle and high as defined earlier. Since some grades are densely populated, a subdivision has been made according to function groups I to VI and the Annex A. The average age on promotion in 1995 was around 37. This general figure disguises many differences according to hierarchical level as can be learned from the material presented in Table 7.7.

As obvious, a person's age at the time of the last promotion increases as he/she rises in the hierarchy. The only exception are officials in function group I. The climbing age suggests a certain level of transgression between function groups. This is particularly true for the higher function groups. The same conclusion can be drawn from the figures relating to the years in office before promotion. The average number of years after promotion in their new grade is relatively short, namely around four years. However the possibilities for lower civil servants to reach higher grades should not be overestimated. The education requirements inhibits such careers. Table 7.8 presents data on how long (in 1995) civil servants have been employed by their present employer (department) and the total duration of years spent in government service.

Government employment is more or less lifetime employment. Although there is certainly interdepartmental mobility, the degree is fairly limited as has already been indicated by Van der Meer and Roborgh (1993). At present, interdepartmental mobility has remained low (see Table 7.9). The relatively high 1995 figure is distorted by the transfer of a directorate-general (Culture) from the Health and Welfare to the Ministry of Education.

Table 7.7   *Average years before and after the latest promotion and the average age on promotion up to 1995*

Category	Years before promotion	Years after promotion	Average age on promotion
Low 1	5.4	6.9	35.7
Low 2	7.2	4.2	34.0
Total	7.1	4.4	34.1
Middle	13.4	3.5	37.3
High 1	10.5	3.5	37.5
High 2	10.4	4.1	39.4
High 3	13.1	5.0	44.2
Annex a	16.0	4.0	48.0
High total	10.7	3.7	37.8
Total	11.0	4.0	37

Source: Ministerie van Binnenlandse Zaken, 1996b.

Table 7.8   *Number of years personnel employed by the current employer and total years in government, 1995*

	Current employee	%	Total years in government	%
−1	5 936	5.6	4 574	4.2
1–5	19 993	18.8	15 253	14.3
5–10	19 011	17.8	15 604	14.6
10–15	19 119	17.9	18 333	17.2
15–20	17 164	16.1	19 367	18.2
20–25	12 586	11.8	15 422	14.5
25–	12 732	12.0	17 988	16.9

Source: Ministerie van Binnenlandse Zaken, 1996b.

Personnel policies have long since been directed to increasing interdepartmental mobility. Those policies directed primarily at higher civil servants proved to be largely ineffectual. Since the early 1990s new initiatives have been taken to address these shortcomings. First new trainee programmes have been established for beginning (higher) civil servants coming from university. Besides having extensive management development and (interdepartmental) training components, it also includes interdepartmental mobility. The most important initiative has been the introduction of the ABD which became operational in 1995. Officials will have to change positions and departments after a period of four years. A special directorate-general has been created at the Ministry of the Interior under the dual supervision of the minister of that department and the prime minister. The function of that directorate-general is to operate as a personnel service to the ABD. This task is supplemented by management development activities. The improvement of (intra) mobility of civil servants up to grade 16 is the responsibility of the individual ministries. The government programme of the Kok II cabinet (1998) envisaged extending the scope of the ABD to civil servants in grade 16 and in a later phase, grade 15.

In order to assess the need for an ABD, we have to look at the level of mobility displayed by the target groups. We limit ourselves to secretaries-general and directors-general. Van der Meer and Raadschelders have indicated that the average age of secretaries-general and directors-general at the moment of their appointment was respectively averaged 48.3 and 44.1 years. Their average age in 1996 was (respectively) 51.6 and 48.3 years. The present secretaries-general and directors-general have been therefore respectively 3.3 and 4.2 years in office (Van der Meer and Raadschelders 1999) The great majority of these present officials have had a long (departmental) career before arriving at their positions.

Table 7.9   The level of interdepartmental mobility and new entries, 1991–95

Year	Interdepartmental mobility	New entries
1991	460	11 736
1992	429	9 823
1993	291	7 275
1994	413	6 907
1995	639	6 567

Note: Of the 6.567 who entered central government in 1995, somewhat less than 80 per cent had central government as its first employer (5.254). Half of the entries went to the justice department.
Source: Ministerie van Binnenlandse Zaken, 1996b.

Table 7.10   Secretaries-general and Directors-general in office in 1996 according to the year in which they were recruited to their post

Period	Secretaries-General (%)	Directors-Geneneral (%)
1980–1985	–	8.7
1985–1990	7.7	13.0
1990–1994	46.2	41.3
1994–1996	46.2	37.0
	100	100

Source: Van der Meer and Raadschelders 1999.

Most present secretaries-general and directors-general have been recruited from 1990 onwards. In 1977, Rosenthal and Van Schendelen concluded that 70 per cent of top civil servants were appointed in the last 5.5 years (Rosenthal and Van Schendelen 1977) In 1996, 74 per cent of directors-general and 85 per cent of secretaries-general were appointed in a comparable time period. It could be presumed that an ABD, at least for these officials, is not altogether necessary. But this conclusion may be premature. We must first take a look at the degree of interdepartmental mobility.

Table 7.11   Recruits from the government in general (I), government departments (II), their own department (III) compared to the Rosenthal findings (percentage of total)

	I	II	III
Secretaries-general	92	85	54
Adj. secretaries-general	86	86	64
Directors-general	91	91	63
Total	90	89	61
Rosenthal 1961	87	78	71
Rosenthal 1971	86	83	82
Rosenthal 1981	86	83	75

Source: Van der Meer and Raadschelders (1999).

Few top civil servants are recruited from the private sector (See Table 7.11). Even those who are have often had previous experience in government. Furthermore few top civil servants were ever employed in the private sector. More top civil servants are leaving government to go to the private sector than vice versa. Most top civil servants are recruited from central government. In this respect, little has changed from the day of the Rosenthal research. In recent years, interdepartmental mobility among these top civil servants has increased. This is a notable departure from the past. The ABD may already have had an effect but further changes can be expected. Some doubts to this effect can be expressed, but they will be discussed in our conclusion.

POLITICISATION

Politicisation remains a difficult topic. The underlying notion is that there is a difference between the world of politics and bureaucracy and that the line of demarcation is becoming increasingly blurred. The classical politics–administration dichotomy is becoming increasingly outdated. Although the words increasingly blurred have been used, little is actually known of political administrative relations in the past. Normative (in Europe, mainly legal-oriented) theory pertaining to a politics administration dichotomy may be considered to be an empirically verified fact. Administrative historical research sheds some doubt on this 'truth' (Van der Meer and Raadschelders 1998a). Some question marks therefore need to be placed on the 'dynamic' part of the politicisation concept. Furthermore, the level of politicisation depends on the definition of the role and position of politics and bureaucracy in the policymaking process. Two topics are singled out in discussions on politicisation of the civil service: politicisation of recruitment and politicisation of behaviour.

Politicisation of recruitment implies that the traditional 'bureaucratic' recruitment and selection procedure are permeated by political criteria. Those political criteria can involve civil servants being sensitive to political process, having similar ideas on policy as the political officeholder or the extension of the realm of political patronage. Political criteria are opposite to bureaucratic (merit) criteria. It is common to distinguish four methods of politicisation of recruitment:

1. spoils system
2. cabinet ministériel
3. appointment of (permanent top) civil servants on political (party) grounds
4. appointment of political advisors

If we define the civil service as being composed of permanent officials, then only the third method could be considered politicisation. The other 'methods' would imply a limitation of the scope of bureaucracy by non-permanent political officials.

A spoils system and the cabinet ministériel are alien to Dutch government. The institute of political advisor is known, but numbers are small. Political advisors mainly operate as (political) public relation and liaison officers.

There is much speculation over the actual level of political party nominations to the permanent civil service, but scant clear-cut information is available. The political recruitment-theme is mainly a recurring pastime of certain national dailies and a few selected political and administrative scientists. Newspapers are, in effect, one of the most important sources on the political party background of the senior civil servants. Perhaps quite naturally, the people involved remain silent. Officially the practice of such politically motivated nominations is strongly denied. Merit and suitability are said to be the deciding factors in selecting a candidate. What merit consists of and what suitability actually signifies are altogether different questions.

Since hard evidence on political party patronage is lacking, political party membership of top level civil servants are often taken as an indicator. It goes without saying that this evidence is rather weak because it provides no information on the actual recruitment and selection procedure. Nevertheless in Table 7.12 the political affiliation of secretaries-general in 1996 is compared to 1994. In 1996 most secretaries-general were members of a political party compared to 5 per cent of the total Dutch population. That this information is available is a break with the past. Only two decades ago civil servants were quite hesitant to provide information about their political preference let alone membership of a political party (Van der Meer and Raadschelders 1999). Comparing 1996 to 1988, a remarkable drop in 'Christian-Democratic' secretaries-general and a corresponding rise in Labour Party secretaries-general can be seen. It is tempting to explain these changes by the change in government in 1994. For the first time in modern Dutch history, a cabinet (Kok I) was formed without the Christian Democrats but including Labour, and the Liberal Parties. The fact that particularly the Orthodox Liberals have been 'under-represented' goes against this simple explanation. Since 1996 this trend has been reinforced. The three latest secretary-general appointees are all members of the Labour Party. No secretary-general is affiliated to the Orthodox Liberals.

De Vries and Rosenthal concluded from a survey under civil servants below the top level that almost half of the top civil servants in 1995 were members of a political party. Their survey also included the directors-general and directors. Some 22 per cent of top civil servants were members of the Labour Party (PVDA). Membership in the other main political parties was significantly lower: the Social Liberal Party (D66) (7 per cent), the Orthodox Liberal Party (VVD) (7 per cent) and the Christian Democratic Party (9 per cent).

Since earlier research among higher civil servants (level 10 onwards) indicated considerably lower political party membership, it can be concluded that as one climbs higher in the hierarchy, party membership increases. Looking at political party membership, one can hypothesise that self-selecting tendencies are currently at work. This would explain the high proportion of secretaries-general being members of the Labour Party. If one accepts this explanation it also suggests that before 1996, some real political appointments have taken place based on the number of Christian Democrats.

We can contrast the information on the party membership of top civil servants with the voting behaviour of senior civil servants. In Table 7.13, figures on the political preferences of senior civil servants in 1988 (13 and higher) are compared to top civil servants (17 and higher) in 1995. For better comparison, the figures of the parliamentary election in 1994 in general and the 'higher' educated voters are presented.

Table 7.12 Political affiliation of secretaries-general, 1996

	1988		1996	
	abs.	%	abs.	%
PVDA (Socialist, Labour)	1	7.7	5	38.5
CDA (Christian Democrats)	9	69.2	3	23.1
VVD (Orthodox Liberals)	2	7.7	1	7.7
D66 (Social Liberals)	1	15.4	2	15.4
Green party	–	–	1	7.7
None	–	–	1	7.7
Total	13	100	13	100.1

Source: Van der Meer and Raadschelders 1999.

Table 7.13 Political preference of civil servants in 1988 compared to top civil servants in 1995

	I	II	III	IV	V
PVDA	31.9	22	37.9	24	27
CDA	27.5	30.7	15.4	22.2	23
VVD	18.3	27.1	25.8	20	20
D66	13.3	17.2	17.5	15.5	17
Others	9.0	3.0	3.3	18.4	13
Total	100	100	99.9	100	100

Notes: (I = All civil servants in 1988, II= High (V&VI) in 1988, III= Top civil servants 1995, IV= General election results 1994 and V= Academic population 1994.
Source: Van der Meer and Raadschelders 1999.

The main difference between the 1988 and 1995 survey with respect to the higher civil servants is the discrepancy between the Labour Party and the CDA. In the 1994 elections the CDA suffered a severe defeat. The discrepancy between the major political parties is much narrower when examining the voting behaviour than by looking at the division in the party membership. It is often argued that Christian Democratic and Liberal top civil servants have a more 'classical' (closed) attitude to politics than civil servants with a leaning to the left. Accepting the evidence from the voting behaviour, it becomes less obvious that self-selecting tendencies can explain the predominance of top positions being filled by civil servants who are members of the Labour Party.

Earlier we mentioned a change in the organisation of the top civil service by the introduction of the ABD. Prior to the ABD top level civil servants starting from the rank of director-general were appointed by the Council of Ministers. Although this council still has the final say, an extensive and formalised recruitment procedure favouring internal candidates has been added. It has been suggested that the ABD could limit the possibility of political nominations. Nevertheless many recent top level appointments have been made taking 'outsiders' who are not a part of the ABD target group.

A second perspective on politicisation is derived from examining political behaviour of civil servants. Politics can be defined in a narrow (political party) way and a more extensive way (the power to influence policymaking). The political behaviour of the civil servants can contain a multitude of meanings.

1. Civil servants can be sensitive to societal demands and aware of the democratic and political nature of their job.
2. Furthermore it can include the perception that the (top) civil service constitutes an important factor on the political scene in its own right.
3. Finally, apart from the political power of bureaucracy, civil servants can operate as (party) politicians serving and promoting their own ideas and interests.

Politicisation of behaviour can and does pertain in essence to all strata of the civil service. Although discussions on civil servants are important, political actors are mainly concentrated in the role of higher civil servants, the other dimensions are equally important to, for instance, 'street level bureaucrats' and to those civil servants active in areas of policy implementation with discretionary powers (Van der Meer and Raadschelders 1999).

Particularly among higher civil servants the importance of democratic and political sensitivity has increased. It is often remarked that the politicisation of behaviour has increased. Before going into this issue, we should emphasis that this has less to do with political party behaviour while doing the job. There are of course (some) civil servants who have a high party political profile, e.g. central civil servants elected to municipal and provincial boards or advising on party strategy. Although the actual functioning in their job and their party activities are separated, problems of perception of role confusion can arise. Nevertheless, top civil servants normally do not and cannot act in a (party) political way. The workings of the political system restricts the possibility of party manoeuvering by top level civil servants. The explanation for this limitation is to be found in the necessity of coalition-forming in Dutch politics. Because of changing coalitions, a particular government department regularly changes party hands. At the same time, ministers and under-ministers are often of a different party background. Striking a 'fair deal' between parties and installing 'political guard dogs' in sensitive departments are reasons for allowing this political heterogeneity.

Furthermore since appointments at the top level positions are subject to collective cabinet decisions, a particular minister is not autonomous in deciding on top level appointments. Of course, he/she has an important say. This means that in a department, political party congruence between minister, under-minister and the top civil service is more an exception than the rule. In fact many top civil servants have a different party background than the minister at the moment of appointment. There is, however, a tendency to appoint individuals with a party background belonging to one of the coalition parties. Recent appointments show that there is no ratio according to the sharing of posts. Most current secretaries-general have a different political colour than the minister. Since their political colour is known, it limits (even if desired by the civil servants) the tendency to behave in a political (party) way.

More important with respect to the politicisation of behaviour is a certain mutual understanding of policy problems. Recently individuals with a high profile on issues have been appointed: persons well known for their ideas on issues. In this sense top level civil servants have become more politicised. They are behaving in a political way since they are promoting ideas. Party background therefore appears to be less important than congruency in policy ideas. This is the concept of the public entrepreneur. We should warn that this species of civil servants in its pure form is fairly rare. But civil servants in general have moved more to this particular form of behaviour. Although public entrepreneurship is encouraged in a practical sense, it sometimes collides with the neutrality doctrine.

REPRESENTATIVENESS

Admission to the civil service is considered a fundamental right. Attention has been drawn to Article 3 of the constitution. Equal opportunities policies of central and local governments are directed toward increasing the inclusion of under-represented groups. But in reality, is there such an open admission? Put differently, do equal opportunities really exist? Taking equal opportunities for granted for the moment, does the composition of the civil service mirror that of society? These questions are relevant since the civil service increasingly consists of white collar workers. This fact is, in some ways, at odds with the pursuit of a more representative civil service as will be made clear below. The themes we will address with regard to this issue are the gender division, age structure, religious, educational and ethnic background of civil servants.

Gender

The position of women in the civil service has improved considerably in the course of years. Of all personnel employed in 1995 in the central government, 28.9 per cent were female. The figures for central government displays abrupt percentage changes. The steep increase in the first half of the century is particularly striking. The increased percentage reflects changing attitudes toward women being active in a paid job after their marriage. For a long time, female civil servants were compulsory dismissed after their marriage. Furthermore, the level of education enjoyed by women has increased over the years. The gap between men and women with respect to educational standards has virtually disappeared in recent years.

Table 7.14   *The number of women in central government: 1899–1995 including civilian military personnel*

Year	Central
1899	1.3
1950	17.0
1980	19.7
1990	27.4
1995	28.9

Source: Van der Meer and Roborgh 1993 Ministerie van Binnenlandse Zaken, 1996a.

In comparison to the total labour force, the relative share of women in government is still lower. Nevertheless the share of females employed in (comparable organisations in the service sector) banks and insurance companies is equally low. When comparing these figures with the labour force in industry, however, the situation in government appears far more positive. Most females are employed in the lower echelons of the civil service. Among the higher civil servants, women are still seriously under-represented. In 1995, 19 per cent of the higher positions were occupied by women. The number of women in the highest level (VI) has increased more rapidly than in the other higher grades. Perhaps their number in 1976 was so low (8 women compared to a total 656) that the increase appears distorted.

The gender distribution in the Netherlands is unfavourable in comparison to other countries. In recent years, a certain shift has occurred from lower to higher levels in the civil service. Although mobility with respect to the number of scales is higher among women than men, the net result with respect to the number of women in the higher levels remains limited. Enough qualified women are available in the labour market. The minimal degree of external recruitment due to the cutbacks in the past prohibits a more balanced division of higher civil service positions.

Age

The 1995 age distribution within the civil service reveals a substantial increase in average age (see Table 7.15). The departure of senior employees by means of early retirement should lead to a relative lower average age, but a combination of a high intake of new personnel in the 1970s with limited hiring in the 1980s resulted in a peak in the 35–50 age category. The government workforce is ageing at a more rapid rate than the total labour force.

Table 7.15   Age groups of central government personnel: 1976, 1980, 1984, 1988 and 1995 (%)

Age	1976	1980	1984	1988	1995
<=19	2.8	2.0	0.8	0.3	0.0
20–29	28.3	27.9	28.3	25.5	12.5
30–39	19.7	26.5	32.0	34.3	37.0
40–49	19.4	17.0	18.4	24.7	34.5
50=>	29.7	26.5	20.5	15.1	15.9
Total	100	100	100	100	100

Source: Ministerie van Binnenlandse Zaken, 1976–96a.

The lower civil servants are relatively young. A decrease in the number of lower civil servants means ipso facto that the percentage of younger people employed in the civil service has decreased considerably and will continue to do so at a faster rate in the future. This problem has been acknowledged by government. Initiatives to stimulate internal and external mobility have been undertaken. The problem, however, remains that the general labour market situation is unfavourable for older personnel while possibilities for hiring younger personnel are limited due to financial restraints.

Education

The average educational level has substantially increased in the past 40 years, and among higher civil servants, the monopoly of individuals with a law degree has been eroded. In municipalities especially, the percentage of economists and social scientists has increased among the higher (academically) educated personnel.

Table 7.16   *Pre-entry educational background of all civil servants and higher civil servants working for central government in 1988*

	All	High
Primary education	2.8	0.7
Primary/middle level education	41.1	12.7
Middle level education	30.7	19.0
High professional schools	13.8	24.4
University education	11.0	42.7
Other	0.6	0.4

Source: Van der Meer and Roborgh 1993.

Upon appointment, 11 per cent of central government employees have completed an academic degree (see Table 7.16). As can be seen from Table 7.17, the largest group of academics are the social scientists followed by those with a law degree. Next in importance are the technical scientists and economists. In 1930 and 1947, the share of individuals with a law degree in the policy and administrative services of government was 75 per cent and 56 per cent respectively. The share of lawyers has continued to decline since then. This can be attributed to changes in the nature of government intervention and the rise of the social sciences as academic disciplines. The generalist lawyer has given way to the technical specialist. According to Van Braam (1957), the expansion of research, documentation and public relation tasks, as well as the problems concerning reconstruction and planning have also contributed to increased demand for specialists in economics, sociography, statistics and technical matters.

Table 7.17   *Master's degrees of civil servants: 1988 (%)*

Law	29.4
Mathematics and natural sciences	1.4
Technical sciences	18.7
Economics	12.0
Social sciences	30.0
Medicine	1.4
Literature	5.9
Other	1.2
Total	100

Source: Van der Meer and Roborgh 1993.

While the 'generalist' legal-trainee of earlier times has vanished as a result of competition with other groups of academics, the specialised jurist still maintains a monopoly given the increased degree of regulation of government activity. We assume that lawyers still maintain their quantitative share, but have lost ground in a relative sense to other disciplines. Absolute and relative bureaucratisation has led to a higher demand for experts. This, in turn, decreases possibilities for realising a bureaucracy that reflects society.

Ethnicity

Significant increases in the participation of ethnic minorities occurred around 1995 thanks to ambitious planning. In the 1980s, relatively low education and (young) age were important factors in the failure to boost the percentage of civil servants from non-Dutch minority groups. The total share of minorities is 3.5 per cent according to the Act on the Improvement of Equal Labour Shares for Foreign Minorities (WBEAA). An actual reflection of Dutch society would result in 3.8 per cent employment of non-Dutch minorities. Moreover, non-Dutch minorities are particularly to be found in the lower grades.

Religion

While the number of Catholics in the civil service was highly under-represented in 1951 and they remain under-represented today, the gap has become smaller (see Table 7.18). With respect to the Orthodox Protestant (*Gereformeerd*), a slight under-representation in 1951 was transformed in 1988 into an over-representation in central government. In 1951, secularisation in the civil service was more manifest than in society, and an even greater difference is evident in 1988. This secular trend is especially apparent among higher civil servants in central government. When comparing the religious affiliation of civil servants with the total labour force, Catholic, Reformed Protestant and other groups are under-represented, and Orthodox Protestant and non-affiliated are over-represented. In comparison to the 1951 data, we can conclude that the share of Catholics has increased slightly. The share of Reformed Protestant civil servants decreased according to their decreasing share in the general population. Among central government personnel, the share of Catholics drops as the function level increases. The Reformed Protestants are relatively strongly represented in the middle-level positions, and the share of Reformed Protestants appears to grow as the function level becomes higher. Relatively speaking, the degree of secularisation at the higher level is substantial. Thus, considerable differences in religious affiliation within the civil service of central government exist.

This is especially the case when one varies the function level. An explanation for the composition of the current religious map of the Dutch civil service is to be found in the recruitment base to the civil service. Although somewhat less than in the past, most civil servants at the central government are recruited from the west of the country. An important explanation is that the seat of government (The Hague) is located in the western part of the country. The western part is more deconfessionalised and traditionally more Protestant than for instance the predominantly Catholic southern provinces. Furthermore the deconfessionalisation has been particularly strong among that part of the population with a higher education.

Table 7.18   Religious affiliation of the population and of civil servants (%)

	Roman Catholic	Reformed Protestant	Orthodox Protestant	Other	None	Total
Population (1947)	38.4	31.0	9.7	3.7	17.1	100
Civil service (1951)	26.0	38.0	9.0	7.0	20.0	100
Population (1987)	36.0	18.7	8.0	5.6	32.1	100
Civil service (1988)	27.8	15.9	7.8	4.0	44.6	100
Central government (1988)	27.7	16.7	8.7	3.4	43.5	100

Source: Van der Meer and Roborgh 1993.

Bureaucratisation and Representativeness

Does the Dutch civil service now differ fundamentally from the immediate post-World War II-period, or is there a clear continuity with the past? Although the civil service still does not reflect Dutch society, it has become more representative in a variety of ways. There is a higher degree of demographic representativeness, and the political and religious composition of the civil service increasingly reflects that of society. Whether this is the result of conscious policy or changes in the educational structure of the Dutch population remains to be answered. Still, there is no question of the Dutch civil service being a representative bureaucracy for the civil service as a whole, and certainly not for the higher echelons. This raises the question of whether changes in the type of tasks the civil service performs do not ultimately lead to changes in the level of representativeness.

Earlier attention has been drawn to the changing composition of the public service. Government personnel have increasingly become synonymous with civil servants in a limited (white collar staff) sense. In central government, lower and middle level jobs have been axed due to cutbacks and hiving off executive agencies. Analysis shows that for the remaining civil servants, mostly involved in policymaking, higher educational qualifications are mandatory. This reduction in staff decreases the recruitment of the young (given the length of education) and non-Dutch minorities (as a result of educational disadvantages). Given current educational trends, at some point women will lessen the distance once the gates to civil service jobs open again, but in the short term, their position is far from a mirror image of society and even of the population with a higher education. Relatively speaking, a potential effect of this tendency towards concentration on policymaking in central government departments is a less representative civil service.

This result in the conclusion that given this continuing bureaucratisation and concentration on policymaking of the civil service at central government, increased representativeness will be elusive as long as:

1. the education levels of the relevant minority groups fail to meet the requirements for particular governmental positions;
2. the actual restrictive recruitment policy is structurally continued resulting in serious deficiencies in the demographic composition of the civil service;
3. those in policymaking positions are concentrated in the west of the country and especially in The Hague (with respect to central government and concerning the political and religious composition).

PUBLIC OPINION

Public opinion about civil servants is an important topic to examine for two reasons. By looking into public attitude towards the civil service, the legitimacy of civil servants' action can be appraised. Furthermore, public opinion of civil servants provides an indicator for assessing civil service performance. Both elements are supposedly intertwined. One can hypothesise that support for civil service action depends on the nature of public opinion towards the civil service. This affects the effectiveness and efficiency of civil servants, performance. The most important aspect of public opinion in this regard is the assessment of civil service reliability. This section focuses on this particular aspect.

Data on the opinions of citizens about civil servants at the central government level are very scarce. There is however some material on the opinion of citizens towards local civil servants. This research concentrates more specifically on the citizens satisfaction on the quality of local public service delivery. Tops et al. (1991), have mentioned that citizens are remarkably satisfied with actual performance. In the seven municipalities included in their research, 85 to 90 per cent of the citizens who were in contact with one of the municipal departments were highly satisfied with the level of service delivery. Nevertheless general opinion of local government is strongly negative. The feelings of the respondents towards local politics and local bureaucracy in general were very negative. About 70 per cent of all the respondents had little to moderate confidence in local bureaucracy. There is therefore a distinct gap between general opinion on and actual experience with local government bureaucracy. Tops et al. (1991: 21) therefore raises the question whether the average citizen knows that the service he is satisfied with is delivered by the same local bureaucracy he has little confidence in.

The same question has been raised in American research (Goodsell 1985). General opinion on municipal government has been unfavourable when compared to the general opinion towards the private sector (Goodsell 1985: 18). Other research in the United States leads to the same conclusions (Goodsell 1985: 18). Goodsell (1985: 23) states: 'This led analysts to conclude that generalised attitudes towards bureaucracy are based not so much on concrete experiences as the cumulative impact of the mass media and the accepted beliefs in the culture.' This conclusion still fails to explain the discrepancy between public opinions toward bureaucracy in general on the one hand and service delivery on the other. To provide a preliminary explanation, in the following section we will provide a secondary analysis of a NIPO data-set on Dutch public opinions on the reliability and the functioning of Dutch civil servants.

In his dissertation, Van Braam (1957) states: 'Neither in our country nor elsewhere have civil servants ever been popular.' In the Dutch popular and (sometimes) administrative literature ample examples of stereotypes about civil servants can be found. They are considered 'lazy', 'unreliable, 'bureaucratic', 'inflexible' and 'too powerful', and all at the same time. Although contradictory, these stereotypes are virtually predominant in Dutch public opinion towards their national civil servants. Almost every day we are confronted with newspaper articles revealing serious mistakes made by the public sector. They bungle peacekeeping operations in Bosnia, they misuse powers in criminal investigations and so on. More recently politicians have joined the chorus.

The question can be raised whether public opinion on the functioning of civil servants is as critical as Van Braam (1988) tends to suggest. In Table 7.19 an overview is presented on the trustworthiness of different occupational groups.

Table 7.19   Public perception of the type of people who, in general, speak the truth

	Yes (%)	No (%)
TV-newsreaders	89	11
Professors	88	12
Doctors	86	14
Teachers	85	15
Judges	84	16
Public researchers	84	16
Scientists	81	19
Police	76	24
Man in the street	68	32
Priests, vicars	66	34
Civil servants	52	48
Union leaders	50	50
Journalists	39	61
Ministers	35	65
Politicians	30	70
Businessmen	23	77

Source: NIPO 1996, *n*=883.

Many respondents are convinced that civil servants generally express the truth. Nevertheless a substantial minority think that civil servants are not reliable in this respect. At the same time, a clear majority of the respondents think that politicians (and ministers) in general are not to be trusted. A striking feature is that the assessment of the reliability of specific categories of civil servants is more positive than that of the general categories. The average opinion of policemen (civil servants), scientists, professors and teachers (most of them being civil servants) is much more favourable than the opinion of the broad category of civil servants. The same observation is valid for journalists and politicians. For instance TV anchor men and women are viewed in a more positive light (89 per cent) than journalists in general. Likewise ministers are held in a more favourable light than politicians in general. An explanation for these difference is that concrete encounters or experiences with civil servants can counter existing stereotypes.

Income levels influence the opinion of civil servants. Of the respondents with a high income, 70 per cent state that civil servants are trustworthy. There are no outstanding variations according to differences in political preference. The only exception relates to the extremes on the political spectrum. On the basis of this material one can conclude that income is a more powerful explanation than political preferences.

In addition to the trustworthiness of civil servants, we have looked at the appraisal of civil service performance. Only a small minority of the respondents believe that civil servants frequently fail to carry out their tasks in a correct manner (21.3 per cent). Further evidence shows that only 27.9 per cent of all respondents state that they have ever been personally treated by government and the civil servants in an unjust manner. Although a small minority believes that civil servants frequently fail to carry out their tasks in a correct way, 57.2 per cent of all respondents still presume that this might be sometimes the case. There is a relation between previous personal experience of biased treatment and a negative view on the impartiality in which civil servants perform their tasks. More striking is that 15 per cent of the respondents who have never been treated in an unfair manner by civil servants declare that civil servants frequently carry out their tasks in an unfair way.

Little research has been done on Dutch public opinion towards civil servants. Secondary analyses of the NIPO database give us an initial idea of one aspect of the public opinion of civil servants, namely the perception of civil service reliability. The relative high public opinion pertaining to the degree in which civil servants are considered reliable is at odds with the stereotypes described earlier. The analysis also shows that more specific questions towards the groups involved lead to a more positive answer and vice versa. The more a respondent is forced by the preciseness of the question to consider their own direct experiences with civil servants, the more positive (or less negative) the answer will be. The question of where these stereotypes originate remains. The explanation might be found in the (lack of) visibility and openness of the public sector. Another explanation could perhaps be found in the impact of negative measures like taxation taken by the government and its civil servants on citizens. Payments to and benefits from the public sector are rarely linked in the perception of the average citizen.

CONCLUDING REMARKS

The Transformation of the Civil Service System

Our historical analysis has shown that between 1813 and the constitutional reform of 1848, central government civil servants were directly responsible to the king. The civil service was, in Heady's terms, ruler responsive. To describe this relation in the Dutch case as traditional would be mistaken since centralisation of political executive power was really novel to the Netherlands. Since 1848 civil servants have basically been accountable to their minister. The reason is to be found in the fragmentation of political authority after 1840. That fragmentation has been gradually mitigated by a weak cabinet structure and the creation of a number of coordinating mechanisms. The creation of, for instance, the office of prime minister in 1937, the formalisation of the position of the Council of Ministers and the creation of ministerial (coordinating) committees after World War II changed this situation in a very gradual way. Nevertheless, departmental 'compartmentalisation' is still a dominant feature in central government. The political and cultural heterogeneity demands a coalition style government. Since single party dominance of the political system never occurred, a party grip on the civil service has not developed.

The structural fragmentation of politics and government acquires a deeper meaning by looking into the socio-economic context. A noted feature of the evolution of Dutch society and politics in recent days has been a gradual shift from a pillarised neo-corporatist (albeit with some pluralistic elements) to a more mixed pluralised/ neo-corporatist way of decision-making. The latter method in the social-economic policy field is now described as the 'polder model'.

From the latter part of the nineteenth century, the pillarised system provided the necessary cohesion in what has been earlier called a fragmented society. The machinery of state was utilised for working out compromises between sections in society. Those compromises pertained to facilitating the relevant sections in society in order to organise their interests according to their own fashion. Pillarisation was supported by the creation of (modern) political parties as instruments to be used by the groups involved. This political power was used to organise interests with public power groups on a wide range of topics such as social security, health care education and so. When the social democrats gained force after the turn of the century they were adopted into the pillarised system. Few groups were left without a pillar.

This system has had important implications for the functioning of government and the civil service in particular. Politics and government were the meeting ground for the political leaders of these pillars. Although politics was highly ideologically based, a smooth system of cooperation in coalition government was imperative, government was therefore the marketplace for exchanging ideas between the groups and their parties involved; giving each party its due. The possibilities for realising short-term successes were mitigated by the need for longer-term stable relations. Part of the execution of policy was left to para-governmental organisations run by the respective pillars. This is one of the reasons for the resulting size of the Dutch civil service compared to many other European countries (Van der Meer and Roborgh 1993). The border line between government in a narrow meaning and organised society was very small, government played a secondary role in influencing socioeconomic developments. It was more an instrument at the disposal of key players within the pillars. It is difficult to ascertain how much civil servants were actively involved as government was part of the pillarised society. The dominance of the pillars and the highly ideological based political parties diminished the room for manoeuvre for high ranking civil servants. Of course as servants to the minister, they were part of the system, but even then they were considered a neutral instrument to be used to foster consensus by way of their (administrative) techniques.

The deconfessionalisation and the individualisation of society beginning in the 1960s eroded the existing pillars. Strangely enough the 'pillarised' mode of public service delivery has not disappeared completely. Freed from its ideological content, but often keeping the original labels, it has been used by 'professionals' working in these institutions to perform their tasks in a semi-autonomous fashion. One could say that many neo-corporatist structures have been depillarised.

For government, the process of depillarisation led at first to a politicisation of societal relations. This politicisation was short-lived. Under the influence of the economic crisis of the 1980s and the arrival of a new managerial approach, politics became less ideologically driven and more technocratic. As grand political ideas and schemes faded, politics became more dependent upon top civil servants for generating ideas. The fusion of political and administrative roles is not indicative of a politicisation (in terms of behaviour) of senior civil servants but much more the 'bureaucratisation' of politics. Political issues were (are) ideologically neutralised by formulating them as technical (administrative) problems. As a result of this bureaucratisation of politics, civil servants have increasingly strengthened their position in the political arena. This was reinforced by necessity of interest group management. In the old pillarised system, different interests were often merged in one pillar. The shift to societal pluralism implied a desegregation of those interests and the articulation of new interests in the various policy areas. That task of interest group management fell to a large extent to the civil service thus increasing their power in the policymaking process.

With regard to the personnel management of the civil service system, as a response to the demands for a professional civil service after 1945, personnel administration has become increasingly institutionalised. When the centralised interdepartmental approach failed, a decentralised option was pursued. Departmental units were created to assist human resource policy and decisions. At the interdepartmental level, the Ministry of the Interior was given a coordinating task which proved to be quite difficult since the coordination task was/is not supplemented by the necessary powers. With the exception of top civil servants, the daily running of personnel management remains with the individual ministers. The case against a centralisation of personnel management was reinforced in the 1980s under the influence of new (public) management thinking. Centralisation is seen to inhibit flexible personnel management. Powers of personnel management have to a certain extent been decentralised to the higher line managers within a particular department since the 1980s. From this point of view the system of personnel management in central government is fragmented. This corresponds with the level of fragmentation of the political system.

The senior public service or ABD has been hailed a prime example of a initiative to overcome civil service fragmentation. The ABD came into operation in 1995. The ABD for the top grades in the civil service is not only a top civil service labour exchange, but it is believed that by increasing interdepartmental mobility, a shared sense of mission of top civil servants in central government can be created. This could be a way to combat 'compartmentalisation' in the service and interdepartmental co-operation could be enhanced. The idea sounds attractive, but will it be effective? Some questions can be raised. The success depends on active, enduring political support. In the past initiatives have been launched but they proved short-lived. The (lack of) co-ordinating powers of Minister of the Interior does not inspire confidence. A point in favour of the present initiative is the fact that the directorate-general responsible for the ABD is also attached to the prime ministers office. His warm support is a first requirement to combat centrifugal powers. As remarked by Van der Meer and Raadschelders, the ABD seeks to establish a unified administrative structure, based on recruitment and mobility, for the top civil servants, while at the same time these top officials will have to operate in a fragmented political system (Van der Meer and Raadschelders 1999). Furthermore, the ABD will reinforce the closed nature of the (top) civil service. External recruitment becomes even more difficult. Is this desirable? The idea of a top administrative class has been alien to Dutch political and administrative thinking. Finally, although political nominations are often criticised they are part of reality. Due to its structure, the ABD will put barriers to the degree of politicisation. One must wait to see if and how these pressures are dealt with.

NOTES

1. The authors want to thank Jos Raadschelders and Renk Roborgh for their contribution to, respectively, the sections on politicisation and representativeness.
2. The main part of the act related to administrative legal procedures. After the integration of the administrative courts into the general legal system (administrative chambers have been created in the district courts), all these articles have been withdrawn. This numbers about 120. Of the important articles only the general provisions (articles 1 and 2), and the articles 125 and 126 remain.
3. When public education is included the following figures can be given:

Civilian employment in the Netherlands 1950–94

Year	abs.	i–1950
1950	362	100
1960	402	111.0
1970	467	129.0
1980	633	174.9
1988	635	175.5
1994	520	143.6

4. These levels are overlapping. Grade 10 for instance belongs to level IV and V. In practice level IV comprises grades 10, 11, 12; V consists of 13, 14 and VI contains grades 15, 16, 17 and 18. In this case, from a legal point of view, all civil servants grade 10 onward are appointed in the general service of the state.

BIBLIOGRAPHY

Andeweg, R.B. (1989), 'Institutional conservatism in the Netherlands', *Western European Politics,* **12** (1): 42–60.

Bekke, A.J.G.M., J.L. Perry and Th. A.J. Toonen (eds) (1996), *Civil Service Systems in Comparative Perspective,* Bloomington/Indiana: Indiana University Press.

Boels, H. (1993), *Binnenlandse Zaken: Onstaan en ontwikkeling van een departement in de Bataafse tijd 1795–1806,* Den Haag: SDU.

Braam, A. van (1957), *Ambtenaren en Bureaukratie in Nederland,* Zeist: De Haan.

Braam, A. van (1988), *Wat weten we eigenlijk van de ambtenaren?,* Leiden: Rijksuniversiteit Leiden.

Brasz, H.A. (1960), *Veranderingen in het Nederlandse communalisme: De gemeentebesturen als element in het Nederlandse stelsel van sociale beheersing,* Assen: Van Gorkum & Comp N.V.

Centraal Bureau voor de Statistiek (1948), *Jaarcijfers voor Nederland 1943–1946,* The Hague: CBS.

Centraal Bureau voor de Statistiek (1952), *Statistiek van het personeel in overheidsdienst naar de toestand op 1 januari 1950,* The Hague: CBS.

Centraal Bureau voor de Statistiek (1987), *Enquête Nederlandse beroepsbevolking,* The Hague: CBS.

Centrum voor arbeidsverhoudingen overheidspersoneel (1992), 'Leeftijdsbewust personeelsbeleid bij de Rijksoverheid', in *Publicatiereeks Overheid en Arbeid,* The Hague: Centrum voor Arbeidsverhoudingen Overheidspersoneel.

Daalder, H. (1990), *Politiek en historie: Opstellen over de Nederlandse politiek en vergelijkende politieke wetenschap,* Amsterdam: Bakker.

Daalder, H. (1993), *Van oude en nieuwe regenten Of: Politiek als beroep,* Leiden: Rijksuniversiteit Leiden.

Goodsell, Ch.T. (1985), *The Case for Bureaucracy: A Public Administration Polemic,* Chatham/New Jersey Chatham House Publishers.

Holthoon, F.L. van (1988), 'De geschiedenis van het publiek domein in Nederland sinds 1815', in A.M.J. Kreukels and J.B.D. Simonis (eds), *Publiek domein: De veranderende balans tussen staat en samenleving,* Meppel/Amsterdam: Boom.

Hood, C. and G.F. Schuppert (eds) (1988), *Delivering Public Services in Western Nations: Sharing Western European Experience of Paragovernment Organization*, London: Sage.

Hoogerwerf, A. (1986), *Vanaf de top gezien: Visies van de politieke elite*, Amsterdam: Sythoff.

Hoogerwerf, A. (1986), 'Naar een representatieve bureaucratie', *Namens, tijdschrift over vertegenwoordiging en democratisch bestuur*, **8** (1): 418–22.

IJsselmuiden, P.G. van (1988), *De geschiedenis van het ministerie van Binnenlandse Zaken en het ontstaan van de moderne overheidsbureaucratie 1813–1940*, Kampen: Kok.

IVA (1992), *Mobiliteit van rijksoverheidspersoneel: Een onderzoek in opdracht van het ministerie van Binnenlandse Zaken*, The Hague.

Meer, F.M. van der (1995), 'Crises and administrative innovation in the Netherlands', *Jahrbuch für Verwaltungsgeschichte*, **7**: 187–201.

Meer, F.M. van der and J.C.N. Raadschelders (1995), 'Between Restauration and consolidation: the Napoleonic model of Administration in the Netherlands 1795–1990', in B. Wunder, *The Napoleonic Model of Government*, Brussels: Bruylant.

Meer, F.M. van der and J.C.N. Raadschelders (eds) (1998a), *Administering the Summit*, Brussels: Bruylant.

Meer, F.M. van der and J.C.N. Raadschelders (1998b), 'Administering the summit in the Netherlands', in F.M. van der Meer and J.C.N. Raadschelders (eds), *Administering the Summit*, Brussels: Bruylant.

Meer, F.M. van der and J.C.N. Raadschelders (1999), The senior civil service in the Netherlands: A Quest for unity in E.C Page and V. Vught, *Bureaucratic elites in Western European States*, Oxford: Oxford Unversity Press.

Meer, F.M. van der and L.J. Roborgh (1988), 'Changing patterns in local and central government employment: an adaptation to a post-industrial society 1945–1985', in L.J. Roborgh, R.R. Stough and Th.A.J. Toonen (eds), *Public Infrastructure Redefined*, Leiden/Bloomington/ Rotterdam: Indiana University Press.

Meer, F.M. van der and L.J. Roborgh (1993), *Ambtenaren in Nederland*, Alphen aan de Rijn: Samsom HD Tjeenk Willink.

Meer, F.M. van der and L.J. Roborgh (1996), 'Representatieve bureaucratie: De ambtenaar tussen mens en ambt', in A.H. Berg, et al (eds), *Strategie en Beleid in de publieke sector*, Alphen aan de Rijn: Samsom HD Tjeenk Willink.

Meer, F.M. van der and R. Roborgh (1996), 'Civil servants and representativeness', in A.J.G.M. Bekke, J.L. Perry and Th. A.J. Toonen, *Civil Service Systems in Comparative Perspective*, Bloomington/Indiana: Indiana University Press, 119–37.

Meer, F.M. van der and R. Roborgh (1996), 'Civil servants and representativeness', in A.J.G.M. Bekke, J.L. Perry and Th. A.J. Toonen, *Civil Service Systems in Comparative Perspective*, Bloomington/Indiana: Indiana University Press, 119–37.

Meer, F.M. van der, J.C.N. Raadschelders, L.J. Roborgh and Th.A.J. Toonen (1991), 'Representative bureaucracy in the Netherlands in an historical perspective', in V. Wright, (ed.), *The Representativity of Public Administration*, Brussels: IIAS.

Ministerie van Binnenlandse Zaken (various years'), *Kerngegevens bezoldiging overheidspersoneel*, The Hague.

Ministerie van Binnenlandse Zaken (1984), *Rangen en schalen bij de overheid*, The Hague: Ministerie van Binnenlandse Zaken.

Ministerie van Binnenlandse Zaken (1986), *Mobiliteit en loopbaanbegeleiding bij de rijksoverheid: Een onderzoek onder rijksambtenaren in de periode 1981–1983*, The Hague: Ministerie van Binnenlandse Zaken.

Ministerie van Binnenlandse Zaken (1988), *Overheid en arbeidsmarkt*, The Hague: Ministerie van Binnenlandse Zaken.

Ministerie van Binnenlandse Zaken (1990), *Werkgelegenheid voor minderheden bij de rijksoverheid: Tweede projectperiode 1991–1995*, The Hague : Ministerie van Binnenlandse Zaken.

Ministerie van Binnenlandse Zaken (1994–7[b]), *Mensen en Management in de Rijksdienst*, The Hague: SDU.

Ministerie van Binnenlandse Zaken (1996), *Benoeming beloning en ontslag van top functionarissen in de (semi-) publieke sector*, The Hague : Ministerie van Binnenlandse Zaken.

Morgan, E. Ph. and J.L. Perry (1988), 'Re-orienting the comparative study of civil service systems', *Review of Public Personnel Administration*, **3** (8).

NIPO (Dutch Market Research Institute), database NIPOVAR, 1992, 1993, 1994, 1996.

North, D. (1988), *Institutions: Institutional Change and Economic Performance*, Cambridge: Cambridge University Press.

Peters, B.G. (1988), *Comparing Public Bureaucracies*, Tuscaloosa: University of Alabama Press.

Peters, B.G. (1996), 'Theory and methodology', in A.J.G.M. Bekke, J.L. Perry and Th.A.J. Toonen (eds), *Civil Service Systems in Comparative Perspective*, Bloomington/Indiana: Indiana University Press.

Raadschelders, J.C.N. (1998), *Handbook of Administrative History*, New Brunswick, NJ: Transaction.

Raadschelders, J.C.N. and M.R. Rutgers (1996), 'A History of civil service systems', in A.J.G.M. Bekke J.L. Perry and Th.A.J. Toonen (eds), *Civil Service Systems in Comparative Perspective*, Bloomington/Indiana: Indiana University Press.

Randeraad, N. (1994), 'Civil servants in Nederland (1815–1915)', *Bijdragen en Mededelingen over de Geschiedenis van Nederland*, **2** (109): 209–36.

Roborgh, L.J. and U. Rosenthal (1989), 'Van rechts naar links: De politieke voorkeuren van rijksambtenaren', *Namens, tijdschrift over vertegenwoordiging en democratisch bestuur*, **4** (6): 12–17.

Rose, R. (1984), *Understanding Big Government: The Programme Approach*, London/Beverly Hills/New Delhi: Sage.

Rose, R. et al. (eds) (1985), *Public Employment in Western Nations*, Cambridge: Cambridge University Press.

Rosenthal, U. (1979), 'De secretaris-generaal: Politisering of verambtelijking?', *Acta Politica:* 343–77.

Rosenthal, U. (1983), 'De mandarijnen van de rijksdienst: Modieuze stellingen en harde feiten over de Nederlandse topambtenarij', *Bestuurswetenschappen*, **5**: 302–15.

Rosenthal, U. and M.P.C.M. van Schendelen (1977), 'Ambtelijke top in Nederland', *Bestuurswetenschappen*, **6**: 383–401.

Rosenthal, U. and J. de Vries (1995), 'Series of newspaper articles reporting on a questionnaire among top civil servants', in *NRC-Handelsblad, 30 September, 6, 13, 20, and 27 October*.

Top, P.W. et al (1991), Lokale democratie en gemeentelijke vernieuwing, Delft, Eburon.

Wright, V. (ed.) (1991), *The Representativity of Public Administration*, Brussels: IIAS.

8. The Development and Current Features of the French Civil Service System

Marie-Christine Meininger

INTRODUCTION

Constitutional and Administrative Background

From the Revolution until now, France has experienced all types of constitutions: monarchist, republican, authoritarian (or Bonapartist), assembly regime, and so on. But the continuity of the administrative system since the Revolution and moreover, since the *Ancien Régime*, is remarkable and illustrates the continuity of the French administrative model.

Nevertheless, the past two decades appear to signal some major changes. Whether those changes will significantly alter this system remains to be seen; there is some evidence that French governance, while adapting to external and internal pressures, has preserved its specific features (Meininger 1999). The constitution of the Fifth Republic is of a parliamentary regime with a strong executive branch. It is based on sovereignty of parliament, direct election of the president by universal suffrage and the duality of the executive. Other innovations of the Fifth Republic are the practice of referenda, the introduction of a constitutional court and rationalisation of parliamentary government. The institutions of the Fifth Republic were created by General de Gaulle and developed in an unprecedented economic and social context. Since 1958, they have proved their longevity and ability to adapt to changing political circumstances (Meny 1998).

Despite the importance of the presidency, the most distinctive feature of the constitution is the division of the executive power between the president and the government headed by the prime minister. The president makes appointments to civil and military posts of the state: counsellors of state, prefects, heads of central government departments, etc. are appointed by the

Council of Ministers (constitution Art. 13); the prime minister is in charge of the government and appoints other civil and military posts (constitution Art. 21).

It is impossible to understand the characteristics of French governance without stressing that is built on a strong state tradition (Röhr 1995). The centrality of the state (*État* is always capitalised) is an important feature of the French administrative system. It goes with an ancient Jacobin tradition, the expansion of state intervention in the economy through a large public sector, the absence of an intermediate corps, the existence of administrative courts and the development of administrative law. Contrary to generally accepted ideas, there is no Napoleonic model of administration. It is a myth which suits the French because it affords an explanation of the administrative tradition.

It is a fact that many features of our administrative system date back to the Consular administration, which borrowed some characteristics of the *Ancien Régime* (for example the predilection for secrecy and administrative uniformity). Napoleon simply preserved what the *Ancien Régime* and the revolution had invented and which might be helpful to him in the exercise of his authority. The consulate generalised a civil service noteworthy for the establishment of a hierarchy of positions and pay, strict discipline based on a set of rules, and standardisation of work methods, added to a set of coherent structures.

The existence of about four millions civil servants, subject a special statute, and an elitist system for recruiting high level officials who share a 'sense of public service' (*sens du service public*) are an important feature of the French system. Until the end of the 1970s, secrecy, anonymity and imbalance have characterised their relations with the public.

The concept of *service public* is an essential component of the legal system and of the administrative culture. The notion of public service describes a wide variety of missions ranging from state regalia to industrial and commercial public services – sometimes but not always steered directly by public authorities – and ruled by a legal system expressing a certain values and representations (Meininger 1998). It demarcates the sphere of public management and constitutes the application of a specific legal system, the foundations of which were laid at the beginning of this century by Léon Duguit. In subordinating the action of public authorities to the ends being pursued and to the notion of service, the theory of public service fulfills a function of legitimisation of public action through several major principles: continuity, equality, adaptability and impartiality or neutrality. Therefore, the 'sense of public service' expresses the belief in the role of state and the adherence to those values and to public service ethics.

The traditional model of administration (Braibant, 1998), inherited from the *Ancien Régime*, French revolution and Napoleon, is national, unitary and centralised. It can be characterised by:

- a uniform structure throughout the country;
- organisation, operation, rules and budget decided by the nation's authorities (parliament, government and courts);
- geographical concentration in Paris;[1]
- concentration of power within the ministerial departments; and
- imbalance between the state and the local government.

Furthermore, the legal nature of the French model must be emphasised. French administration is governed by the rule of law. While the civil and criminal law were put into codes by Napoleon, the limitation of arbitrary action and the protection of citizen's rights *vis-à-vis* public authorities were progressively established by the Council of State (statutes and regulations played a secondary role). As a result, the duality of law corresponds to the duality of courts system.[2] Through jurisprudence, the Council of State has developed a body of principles in order to establish a set of privileges and constraints suited to administration's needs while providing for the protection of the rights and legitimate interests of individuals. For example, until the statute of 1945, the civil servant's main guarantees (right of defence and so on) were jurisprudential principles.

Recent reforms have partially altered this traditional model (Braibant 1998). It has become:

- more complex (especially regarding administrative structures);
- more international, as a result of the increasing importance of European law;
- more decentred (a neologism made of *decentralisation and déconcentration*);[3]
- more transparent and participatory; and
- to a certain extent, more managerial.

Nevertheless, the adaptation of traditional institutions to these changes is remarkable. For example, the prefect whose main function was to be a representative of authority charged with the implementation of national law, has transformed into a negotiator, seeking compromise between competing local interests and enforcing European law and policies (Meininger 1999).

THE FRENCH CIVIL SERVICE SYSTEM: A FIRST CHARACTERISATION

The civil service has held an extremely important position in France, not only in terms of staff numbers, but also in the role granted to it by the public powers. It still plays a very important role in extremely diversified fields affecting the life of the country.

It should be stressed that the French civil service is among the most powerful in the world. High-ranking civil servants enjoy a social prestige comparable to that of federal judges in the United States (Röhr 1995). The prestige of the high civil service is due to a large extent to the key role of the *grand corps de l'Etat*. The *grand corps* can be distinguished from the other corps: they are recruited through elitist professional schools called *grandes écoles*, they hold key positions in the central government and enjoy high internal and external mobility. Although there is some dispute about which corps merit the rank of *grand corps*, the following corps are undoubtedly on the list:

- the members of the *Conseil d'État*: the Council of State is the highest administrative court but covers a wide range of administrative activities (advises the government on draft laws and regulations);
- the members of the *Inspection des Finances* (Financial Inspectorate) and the members of the *Cour des Comptes* (Court of Audit) are in charge of financial review of public bodies (including public corporations);
- the members of the *Corps des Ponts et Chaussées* and of the *Corps des Mines* (technical corps staffed by engineers);
- in addition, the *Corps préfectoral* (prefects) and the *Corps Diplomatique* (diplomats) are often included among the *grands corps* (Kessler 1986).

The French civil service system is a unified career system, as opposed to a position system, ruled by statutes embedded in a strong tradition. Civil servants are appointed to a permanent position, in the service of a public body. Whether an employee belongs to the civil service is determined by the application of the provisions of the statute.

The present features of the civil service were drawn after World War II with the creation of the national school of administration (ENA) and the vote of the first general statute (*statut général de la fonction publique*).

For the past 50 years, the French civil service has evolved within this framework which lays down the balance between the guarantees linked with the establishment of a professionalised civil service (recruitment based on merit, neutrality, protection against political parties and so on) and the duties required by the specificity of the service of the state. It has proved its ability to adapt to the reconstruction of the country after World War II and to the growth of public services during the last three decades. Civil servants had security of tenure and a more favourable retirement system (compared to other categories of workers), in compensation for lower salaries. They enjoyed consideration and prestige. Moreover, senior officials could leave the civil service at mid-careers to hold positions at the head of public enterprises or in the private sector, which is called '*pantouflage*' (they are still allowed to do so and this practice has even evolved).

Another specific feature of French civil service is the distinction between the grade and the post (*grade* and *emploi*) which allows political appointments at senior positions. Compatible with the career principle, this system partially preserves the civil service from politisation and offers to senior officials a privileged path to a political career.

This system lasted until the 1980s without seriously being called into question. Around this time, several reforms regarding transparency (1978), administrative procedure (1983), decentralisation (1982–83) and so on, reshaped French governance making procedures and structures more democratic.

In the 1990s, civil service has faced three crises:

- a crisis of legitimacy, due to the decline of the welfare state and criticisms regarding the burden of state over society;
- a financial crisis, due to the growth of public expenses and the need to reduce the public finance deficit; and
- an identity crisis, due to the loss of consideration and powers as a consequence of decentralisation and European integration.

In response to all this, the modernisation of French administration is a recurrent issue with partial responses (Chevallier 1996a). The socialist government of Michel Rocard developed a strategy called 'public service renewal' (1989) which aimed at four objectives:

- human resources development;
- delegation of responsibilities;
- evaluation of public actions;
- adaptation of the public service to the users.

This strategy led to experimental delegations of responsibilities (settling contractual relations with autonomous units) and collective agreements with civil service trade unions regarding classifications and in-service training. It should be noted that these reforms relied on the assumption that the improvement of the conditions of service in the public sector would help administration become more efficient and provide the users with better services.

A more ambitious programme was launched by the Juppé government in July 1995 (state reform). The main principles have been confirmed by the Jospin government. This programme relies on a broad reflection about the role of the state whilst public service principles (neutrality, equal access, continuity) are reaffirmed. Although it is more focused on the needs of citizens, there is a continuity with previous reforms, at least on some aspects:

* the method: the search for a consensus through consultations as well as the experimental approach;
* the civil service: the civil service statute is preserved whilst there is an endeavour to modernise human resources management through the delegation of responsibilities, the development of a true appraisal system and so on.

The necessity to reconcile the major principles of a statutory civil service and the growing demand for new methods of management is one of the main issues of the reform process (regarding the civil service).

Another issue is the debate about the need for more stringent regulation and practice in relations between senior civil servants and politics or with business. Amongst others, the right to return to civil service after a political career or after having occupied a position in the private sector is now being questioned. But it is unlikely that such a reform will be placed on the agenda.

Nowadays, the security of tenure and a more profitable retirement scheme[4] clearly points out the civil servants as a privileged class. The recent debate about the possible extension of the legislation on the reduction of working hours from 39 to 35 per week for the civil service is even more controversial when compared to the working conditions in the public and the private sector.

THE DEVELOPMENT OF THE CIVIL SERVICE SYSTEM (HISTORICAL BACKGROUND)

From the Ancien Régime to the Republic

The civil service has developed with the growth of modern state. During the Ancien Régime, the centralisation process directed by the monarchy led to the reinforcement of administration in order to overcome rival powers (intermediate bodies, local powers and so on). The power of the absolute monarch relied on its administration. The establishment of a permanent professionalised army and the distinction between the king's property and public property are the first expressions of this evolution from a personalised to an etatist rule. The administration facilitated the assertion of monarchy, enmeshing the activities of society within codes and rules and acting as a buffer between the monolithic activity of the monarch and a stratified and corporatist society (Légendre 1968; Rouban 1988a).

But the complexity of the Ancien Régime society is reflected in the administration. The increase of hereditary posts led to the reinforcement of a patrimonial mechanism over which the monarch exercised no control. A top civil service was already emerging. French civil service at the fall of the Ancien Régime is far from being as homogeneous as the Prussian administration. Three groups can be distinguished:

- officers, having inherited their positions;
- servants commissioned for a specific task (commissioners) who could be dismissed at the discretion of the monarch; in this group, we find officials representing the king in the provinces: governors, intendants;[5]
- a third category, called '*commis*' (clerks), which prefigures the modern civil service. Being appointed, they receive a salary and some kind of allowance, and are able to enjoy a retirement pension. Nevertheless, their recruitment and career are subject to patronage and favouritism.

This diversity resulted in conflicts and divisions, especially between the nobility, holding their charges from inheritance, and those (of common birth) who represented the monarch.

During the eighteenth century, the emergence of a professionalised bureaucracy can be explained by two major reasons. First, the development of technical functions: the most striking example is the creation of the school of civil engineers in 1747 (*Ecole des Ponts et Chaussées*) the first school of administration. It illustrates the emergence of a technical role for the state, which acts more frequently like an entrepreneur, creating the infrastructure for economic activities. The second reason is the growing importance of offices (*bureaux*) in preparing the decisions taken by the secretaries of state or the general controller of finance, especially at the end of the *Ancien Régime*, as a consequence of ministerial instability and centralisation. Despite some attempts to abolish the transmission of charges by inheritance or to reduce the role of private interests, this system was not significantly altered before the Revolution.

The Revolution brought the abolition of privileges, amongst which the property of charges, and established the principle of equal access to public offices and charges, without any other distinction than those resulting from talents (Declaration of Human Rights Art. 6). After a troubled period, the need for professionalised servants leads to the appointment of many employees in the ministries (their number increases from 600 in 1789 to 6 000 in 1794).

During the Revolution, the composition of the civil service was altered. The nobles disappeared and representatives of the middle class entered the service. In spite of this, at the end of the Directoire, one-third of ministerial officials had previously served under the *Ancien Régime*, particularly in the financial administration.

The dwindling of personal allegiance, the emergence of a hierarchical structure and the development of regulations on salaries and working hours were the first signs of the transformation. During the nineteenth century, endeavours to rationalise administration – especially under the empire – were opposed by political and family influences. Thus, professionalisation had to mesh with the need to offer careers to members of specific social groups. Rationalisation was illustrated by the development of careers, and the organisation of promotions (making a career is the motivation for entering the civil service). Civil servants worked within a hierarchical structure and had some rights (to receive a salary, to be promoted, to get a pension when they retired). But personal relations and social criteria continued to prevail in appointments which remained at the discretion of the head of the state or of the ministers. Only civil engineers were recruited by a competitive exam. Upper class families controlled the access to the senior civil service and a certain income was necessary to apply for the *grands corps*. Members of the aristocracy were recruited in the prefectoral and diplomatic career while engineering schools were open to members of the middle classes.

Under the July monarchy, the persistence of patronage was grounds for discontent amongst the middle classes who complained about the lack of work in the administration. The Second Empire gave them more satisfaction. Meanwhile, the civil service provided for social promotion for the lower classes who found a way of access to the middle classes.

Another charasteristic of the monarchy of July was the high degree of confusion between administration and politics resulting from the possibility of combining a civil service post and membership in parliament. Yet, from the restoration to the Third Republic, politisation remained 'soft', compared the spoils system developed in the United States.

At the end of the nineteenth century, two factors prepared the foundation for the establishment of a professional civil service:

- The development of a public service culture was a reaction to the patronage that prevailed under the Monarchie de Juillet and the Second Empire. Especially under the Second Empire, scepticism towards politics was the norm. Professional skills and personal networks prevailed on political commitment.
- The consciousness of professional competence and the need for rationalisation, in accordance with the positivist ideology of the Third Republic,

was reinforced by the anti-parliamentarism that prevailed in the civil service.

Gradually, a new culture emerged which relied on specific values of equality and neutrality; the administrative courts has considerably contributed to the expansion of these values.

Thus the positivist ideology which founds republican values succeeds in meeting the desire of civil servants for rationality and the social aspirations of the middle-classes (Rouban 1998a). The alliance between the civil service and the republic is sealed.

Towards the Establishment of a Statute

The demand for statutory legislative protection is linked with the new awareness of professionalism and the values of public service. Despite the generalisation of competitive exams, at the beginning of the Third Republic, discretionary power still played a significant part. But in reaction to abuses, civil servants – through associations and specialised press – requested regulation for careers and disciplinary procedures.

The decisive step was the jurisprudence of the Council of State (*Conseil d'État*) at the beginning of the twentieth century, which established principles such as the civil servant's right to review his personal file in cases of disciplinary procedures, or rules regarding the regularity of promotions. These principles had tremendous influence on practices and on future legislative developments.

But the claim for a statute was still controversial amongst public employees who benefit from the protection of case law and fear being cut off from the labour sphere. The demand for the right to strike and to form trade unions remained unsatisfied until the middle of the twentieth century.

The first legislative statute, established in 1941 by the Vichy regime, is not deserving of the name (it aimed at strengthening the hierarchical powers). The end of World War II brought the first true statute (*statut général de la fonction publique*) which granted civil servants social rights under the overwhelming influence of the CGT (the trade union linked with the communist party). It should be noted that the minister in charge of the civil service was the communist Maurice Thorez, who can be considered the founding father of the statute. *The statut général de la fonction publique*, established in 1946, grants recruitment by competitive exams, the freedom of opinion, the right to unionise, the right of trade unions to take part in career management and decisions regarding the organisation of services through joint consultative commissions (*commissions paritaires*). The civil service is divided into four groups (categories A, B, C, D) depending on the level of recruitment. Although the right to strike is not mentioned, it is derived from the 1946 constitution and was recognised by the Council of State in 1950.

Since 1946, and during the Fourth Republic, this framework has undergone no major changes except at the constitutional level. The principles established in 1946 remained in force during the beginning of the Fifth Republic even though they had to be adapted to the 1958 constitution which provided for a (new) separation between matters ruled by formal legislation and matters ruled by governmental regulations (Art. 34 and Art. 37 of the constitution); consequently, a new statute had to be published by the ordinance of 1959.

In 1983–84, another statute was passed which reaffirmed the 1946 principles and extended them to local and hospital civil servants. It should be noted that this reform was launched by the socialist government, in conjunction with decentralisation. Apart from this unification of the main principles (within those principles, special legislation rules each branch of the civil service, and significant differences remain regarding recruitment and careers in local government), the 1983 statute widens civil servants' rights (for example, civil servants can obtain leave in order to attend trade union training).

THE INTERNAL LABOUR MARKET

Public Employment

Since the end of World War II to the 1990s, total employment in the public sector has grown about 150 per cent. From 1950 to 1993, the increase of the staff paid on the state budget was almost 80 per cent.[6] Yet the rate of this evolution has varied considerably, according to the period of time and to the sector. The rate of increase reached 31 per cent in the 1970s, but decreased to 4.5 per cent between 1980 and 1990. Overall, the level has remained stable since the beginning of the 1990s.

Currently, about six million workers are employed in the public sector including 1.5 million in public corporations: public transportation, electricity and gas companies, post and telephone services. The two latter services employ about 460 000 statutory civil servants who no longer belong to the state civil service. It is worth noting that in 1990 when post and telecommunications, formerly a ministerial department, were converted into autonomous agencies (telecommunications was privatised in 1996), it had been agreed that the civil servants would keep the advantage of their statute but that future recruitments would be on a contract basis.

If we limit the scope to public administration (as opposed to public enterprises), we need to consider three branches, state civil service including teachers and military forces (2 273 thousand), local civil service (1 447 thousand), hospital civil service including doctors in public hospitals, nurses, and other categories of staff (839 700).

This totals 4.5 million employees (7 per cent of the population, 13 per cent of the labour force) including public employees recruited on a contract, who represent 7.5 per cent of state employees, 13.5 per cent of local employees, and 1 per cent of hospital employees.

In 1997, state expenses incurred by the civil service (excluding public corporations, local government, health service) amounted to 673 000 million francs (38.9 per cent of the state funded budget; 8.3 per cent of GNP). This includes salaries, social contributions and allowances, pensions, subsidies to private schools for the salaries of teachers (who are not civil servants) subsidies and pensions to war veterans.

During the last decade, the proportion of state civil servants has declined compared to the local government employees. The shape of the state civil service has notably changed and redeployments have been made through creations of posts (culture, justice, interior, national education) and cutbacks (foreign affairs, development aid).

The distribution of state civil servants[7] (excluding military forces) can be presented as shown in Table 8.1.

Table 8.1   The distribution of French state civil servants

Statutory civil servants, including:	1 628 610
A (upper level)	724 292
B (middle level)	395 672
C (lower level)	508 646
Non–statutory (civil servants employed on a contract basis)	185 137
Blue collars	13 168
Total	1 826 917

Since 1990, the number of civil servants belonging to the A category has increased considerably (from less than 550 000 to 724 000), the number of B category civil servants has remained almost the same, and the number of C category employees has declined (from less than 500 000 to less than 400 000).[8] An explanation of this evolution is the modernisation of clerical work (also the increasing proportion of teachers in category A).

Actually, the distribution between ministries of statutory civil servants shows that the education department is the top public employer (928 393 civil servants). Then come the Ministry of Economy and Finance (186 029), the Ministry of the Interior (160 787), the Ministry of Public Works, Housing and Transportation (98 256), and Justice (58 947).[9]

Recruitment and Training

The civil service is divided into categories according the level of recruitment (A, B, C)[10] and more than 1 500 corps which group together civil servants who have similar training and specialisation and are expected to carry out similar tasks. This structure is an important feature of civil service.

Category A includes, of course, the *grand corps* but also *administrateurs civils*, *attachés d'administration centrale* (two corps of generalists who are expected to hold senior positions in ministerial departments or state territorial services), university professors, teachers, and so on They are required to possess at least an academic first degree. Category B includes middle positions, primary schools teachers, nurses in hospitals and so on (graduates from secondary school). Category C includes technical and clerical employees.

The members of the individual corps are equal in terms of their rights and duties, their career and job possibilities according to the provisions of the special statute that rules them (*statut particulier*).

The initial recruitment of civil servants is carried out through competitive examinations. It is based on two major principles, equality and merit (Ziller 1988) and corresponds to the legal and administrative tradition. Article 6 of the Declaration of Human Rights (dating back to 1789) stipulates that "all citizens being equal in the eyes of the law have a right to public rewards and jobs according to their capacity and without any other distinction than that of their virtues or talents". This system intends to insure impartiality in the recruitment of civil servants, and to guarantee that it is based on competence.

In a career system, individuals are recruited not only for a position or a job but for a career. During their career, civil servants climb the grades of their corps, according to length of service and merit. To be promoted to another corps, from category C to B for example, they need to pass an internal competitive exam (*infra*).

This formalised mechanism of recruitment can been criticised. First, the programmes are focused on knowledge, thus they do not enable a judgement of the professional ability of the candidates. Furthermore, these means of recruitment reflect the hierarchical tradition and the lack of flexibility of the organisation of the civil service. But these criticisms should be tempered by the importance of internal recruitment.

In the French system, public administration schools, which provide for vocational courses, play a key role in recruitment and training. Access is opened up by the competitive entry exam. Students are considered as trainee civil servants and are paid as such. The final grading determines the corps in which they will continue their career (the considerable difference between a career in a *grand corps* and a career as *administrateur civil* explains the competitiveness during schooling at the ENA).

Apart from the ENA, nearly fifty specialised schools provide A and B civil servants for initial training, for example the Taxation School, the Customs School, the Treasury School and Police Schools. Non-specialist executives of the civil service are trained within the five Regional Administrative Institutes (*Instituts Régionaux d'Administration*). *Ecole Polytechnique* and engineering schools provide training for the high-ranking technical corps.

Internal recruitment through special competitive exams is open to civil servants with a certain length of seniority (five years of service are necessary to be a candidate to internal exams opening access to category A). The ratio between external and internal candidates is determined by regulations, but the proportion of posts open to internal candidates frequently reaches 30 to 50 per cent of the vacancies. Exams are based less on academic knowledge and consider the professional experience of the candidates. Theoretically, this system allows individuals who could not afford education, to upgrade from the lowest category to the highest careers, including the *Ecole nationale d'administration*.

Overall, internal recruitment provides for almost one-third of the recruitment and remains a mean of social promotion. The selectivity of external and internal exams can be measured as shown in Table 8.2.

Table 8.2   The selectivity of external and internal exams

1996	Vacancies	Candidates	Admissions	Selectivity
External exam	43 133	634 113	40 739	15.6
Internal exam	22 638	121 924	18 355	6.6
Total	70 628	884 862	63 821	13.9

Source: Ministère de la fonction publique 1998.

The democratisation of civil service through the generalisation of internal recruitment, as a mean of promotion, was one of the main objectives of the reforms introduced after World War II, and especially of the ENA. But the system has been partially diverted from its original aim. A significant proportion of candidates taking the B and C external exams already possess degrees that would allow them to enter at the A level through the external exam. When they reach the length of service which is required, they pass the internal exam in order to be promoted. Quite often, candidates for the ENA internal exam possess the same degrees as candidates for the external exam; in most cases they were already classed in A but in a less attractive corps than those to which the ENA opens the way (frequently teachers). In addition to the initial professional training provided by the schools, continuous training has developed during the last decade. It covers two main areas: preparation for the competitive exams and advanced in-service training.

The most traditional form of in-service training is the preparation for competitive exams. Legislation and regulations recognise civil servants right to training leave and most departments provide for training programmes which allow civil servants to prepare for internal competitive exams and if they succeed, be promoted.

In 1989 the government and civil service trade unions signed an outline agreement on training which stipulated that 2 per cent of the civil service wage bill should be devoted to continuing training. The actual spending on continuing training now exceeds 4 per cent of the wage bill. A new agreement on continuing training was signed on 22 February 1996, stipulating that all civil servants must be given access to a programme of training and should have at least of three days of training per year. In practice, in-service training includes a large variety of programmes from short specialised sessions to seminars for senior managers, as those initiated in 1997 by the Civil Service Department. But the attitude of high ranking civil servants remains reluctant towards in-service training which is not compulsory, except in a few cases (external mid-career recruitment of *administrateurs civils*).

Human Resources Management and Salaries

Human resources management in the French civil service results from the provisions of the statutes (legislative provisions and regulations) tempered by practices which tend, on one hand, to introduce some flexibility (for example to facilitate mobility in loaning employees from one administration to another), but are, on the other hand, more restrictive (length of service is the most frequently, the criterion for promotion although it is not stipulated by the statutes).

Except for the higher positions where appointments result from a decree of the council of ministers, decisions regarding the careers (promotion, transfer, discipline and so on) are taken by each minister according to a procedure that gives significant influence to trade unions through joint advisory commissions where they are represented on an equal basis with representatives of the administration (*commissions administratives paritaires*). Theses commissions play a key role in day-to-day management and in setting up the lists for grade promotion (according, theoretically, to merit).

The structure of the civil service (categories and corps) determines the development of the career and the conditions of mobility. In addition to upward promotion (through internal competitive exams, professional selection or on merit), secondment procedures afford mobility opportunities from one ministry to another, and prevent the fragmentation into the corps. Furthermore, some corps are common to several departments (*admistrateurs civils*); although the civil service department is responsible for their management, the practice tends to limit the principle of interministerial mobility and most often, careers are ministerial. Finally, the members of the *grands corps* are those who enjoy the greatest mobility.

Civil servants trade unions are also involved in regular negotiations on salaries. These negotiations are tightly restricted by two types of constraints:

- the global limitation of public expenditure imposed by the economic situation[11] and the Maastricht criteria;
- the rigidity of the general pay framework.

It should be stressed that the debate on the level of salaries in the public sector and the complexity of the payment system mask the influence of corporate interests, which form a significant obstacle to the introduction of flexibility in its operation. Moreover trade unions are opposed to personalisation of salaries (performance related pay).

In 1990, the Durafour agreement which led to significant improvements for all the categories (excluding high ranking civil servants) was a compromise to introduce some flexibility without changing the basis of the system. It provided for the dissolution of the lowest category (D), whose members were upgraded to C; careers in the intermediate category (B) were made more attractive; and a special allowance (NBI) was created to reward special responsibilities or technical skills.

As in many countries the wage range in the French civil service has been progressively reduced. The highest salary at the summit of the scale (*hors échelle*) is about six times the lowest salary. But real pay is not completely reflected by the salary scale. Bonuses represent about 18 per cent of total wages and can reach 45 per cent or more for some corps or departments (technical grands corps, administrators in the Ministry of Finance).

The evolution of purchasing power and the comparison with the private sector is controversial and depends on the statistical method which is employed. Between 1982 and 1995, the increase in the salaries has been about the same in the private sector and in the state civil service (+ 0.6 per cent) (*Cahiers de la fonction publique* 1998). But averages are not meaningful for several reasons:

- the structure of employment is quite different; we already mentioned the high proportion of category A in the public sector; at the opposite in the private sector, there is a large majority of clerical workers and blue collars (63 per cent);
- civil servant pay is the result of patterns of careers, and of the negotiation power of some corps in order to obtain career improvements and/or additional allowances.

During the period 1982–92, the purchasing power of the category A officials lost 7.5 per cent; category B remained unchanged; and category C gained about 2.9 per cent. Generally, the state pays better salaries than the private sector to the lowest employees. At the top level, salaries offered by private companies may be twice to ten times as high as the salaries of directors in ministerial departments. But it seems that the average salaries of senior executives in the civil service are no lower than those of executive grades in the private sector (Rouban).

Table 8.3   Examples of salaries in the state civil service (April 1998) not including allowances and bonuses

Minimum net monthly		5 713.11 F
Maximum ('hors échelle')		34 271.17 F
Average salary		10 478.09 F
Average category A		13 017.54 F
Average category B		9 860.43 F
Average category C		7 320.97 F
Beginning and end of the career		
Administrative and technical agent	5 736.22 F	7 595.48 F
Primary school teacher	7 664.13 F	11 713.49 F
Administrateurs civils	10 272.22 F	21 962.86 F

Source: Ministère de la fonction publique 1998.

REPRESENTATIVENESS

Civil Servants as a Distinctive Social Group

Civil servants form a distinctive, relatively closed social group. Career paths are influenced by family traditions and social backgrounds. Undoubtedly, there is still a strong element of socio-professional heredity in the civil service, which has developed especially through the higher levels of the career structure. It applies to 45 per cent of officials in category A and operates as a means of social reproduction.

Belonging to civil service – and furthermore to a *grand corps* – allows individuals to distinguish themselves and produces mutual esteem. But Luc Rouban (1998b) stresses that nowadays, various processes have undermined the homogeneity of the group. The question arises whether civil servants are any different from their counterparts in the private sector. Although it is difficult to measure differences in behaviour and in self-image between the two groups, it seems that the civil service is gradually losing part of its distinctiveness.

An important issue is democratisation which has failed in part. Despite the existence of internal recruitment procedures (see above), the ENA, in particular, has been subject to much criticism for not having fulfilled the aim pursued by its founding father, Michel Debré. Social basis for the recruitment of the ENA has narrowed since the 1970s[12] and opportunities for upward mobility through the civil service has decreased. Internal recruitment, especially, has been diverted from its aim. There are many reasons for this collapse but is seems that the economic crisis has played a key role.

It should be emphasised that 'representative administration' is not an issue in France. Recruitment and careers are based on the merit principle and a strict enforcement of Article 6 of the Declaration of Human Rights which provides for equal access to public rewards and jobs, notwithstanding race, sex, religion or opinion. This conception prohibits all forms of positive discrimination.

Women in the Civil Service

An important characteristic of the French civil service is its increasing feminisation. In central government, the proportion of women exceeds 55 per cent of civil servants. But a deeper analysis reveals important discrepancies between categories: more than 80 per cent of clerical workers in the civil service are female but only 65 per cent of the middle ranks are female (see Table 8.4).

Table 8.4   The proportion of women in the state civil service

1996	National education (%)	Other ministries (%)	Total (statutory civil servants) (%)
Category A	56.3	33.4	53.1
Category B	77.4	49.2	68.1
Category C	66.4	45.3	51.8
Total	63.1	44.1	56.3

Source: Ministère de la fonction publique 1998.

Table 8.5 demonstrates the small proportion of women at the higher positions (June 1997).

At the higher level, the average proportion is about 45 per cent (including secondary school teachers) but women occupying the most senior positions number only 12 per cent (this figure was 9.2 per cent in 1992). Similarly more than 80 per cent of the *grand corps* are male.

The following figures show the proportions of women in the state civil service:

Table 8.5   The proportion of women at the higher positions

	%
Ministerial department directors	7.7
Rectors	12.9
Ambassadors	6.4
Council of state	16.4
Court of Audit	13.1
General finance inspectorate	6.8
Deputy directors, heads of services	19.1

Source: Ministère de la fonction publique 1998.

POLITICISATION

The relationship between administration and politics has passed through several phases since World War II. The decline of politics in favour of technocracy characterised the first part of the Fifth Republic. During this period, the administrative elite was in charge of the economic growth and the modernisation of the society.

Since the 1980s, their influence and expertise have been called into serious question. This evolution has not gone as far in France as in certain other countries. Several reasons can be suggested, particularly the fact that in France, administration remains the way for social promotion (Rouban 1998b).

Nevertheless, politicisation has increased at least in some of its symptoms. The term of politicisation can be understood in different ways:

1. An official's involvement in political life, and presence in the parliament or in the government;
2. A civil servant's political attitudes;
3. Political control on appointments and careers.

With regard to the first way, in France, there is no obstacle to civil servants competing for elections and the statutes provide for a special position of temporary leave which allows them to hold a political office (for example deputy) for several legislatures without losing the advantage of belonging to the civil service (they are not obliged to resign). Moreover, according to critics, there is a growing trend to consider the ENA as the way for a political career. The ministerial cabinets afford access to the summit of the power and 'good' constituencies to be landed on, provided that the voters do not rebel (which occurs).

But the picture should not be exaggerated. While it is true that 40 per cent of the deputies elected in 1997 are civil servants (which corresponds to the average proportion during the last decades), only 6.4 per cent are *enarques* (former students of the ENA) and 4 per cent members of the *grand corps*; a large majority of the civil servants elected at the parliament are teachers (Rouban 1988b). Furthermore this 'over-representation' of the civil service in parliament cannot be generalised to all the elected assemblies where local notables dominate.

During the Fifth Republic, the proportion of civil servants within the government[13] has evolved between 32 per cent (first Juppé cabinet 1995) and 66 per cent (Messmer cabinet in 1973 and Cresson cabinet in 1991). The socialist cabinet of Jospin counts 53.8 per cent civil servants, which is within the average; but the proportion of *enarques*, 30.7 per cent, is quite exceptional (the *enarques* were only 9.5 per cent in the Fabius cabinet in 1984 and the proportion is usually near 20 per cent).

Judging the relationship between civil service and politics should also be tempered by looking at the background of politicians. In many cases, they spent only a few years in the civil service before starting a political career to which they devoted their lives (Jacques Chirac or Lionel Jospin, for example).

In the second instance, the public sector as a whole is more unionised than the private sector and votes more frequently in favour of left parties.[14] Nevertheless the position in the hierarchy has a decisive influence on the vote and the values shared by civil servants.

Furthermore, civil servants are closer to political parties than private sector employees but the differences are not considerable. The same remark can be made if we examine civil servants' attitudes towards values: liberal values are supported by 53.7 per cent of senior civil servants and by 73.7 per cent of private sector executives; Europe by 61 per cent of state civil servants, and by 59.8 per cent of private sector employees (Rouban 1998b).

The last issue is the degree of political control over appointments and careers. The career system leaves only limited room for politicisation of the civil service. Recruitment through different schools, including the ENA, is not politicised. It entitles one to a career in a corps, the members of which enjoy equal rights to promotion. Moreover, the distinction between the grade and the post allows some flexibility in dissociating career progress – according to the special statute of the corps – and appointments to a certain position. Nevertheless, politicisation of careers takes place through different procedures and practices.

- The role of the *cabinets ministériels*: their members are recruited either in the civil service (most common) or in the private sector, at the discretion of the minister, on criteria of personal confidence added to political and/or technical skills. There is evidence that service in a ministerial cabinet provides for significant support either to start a political career or to get a discretionary appointment.

- Discretionary appointments: for the most senior positions (or *emplois à la discrétion du gouvernement*), appointments are decided by decree taken in the council of ministers (prefects, rectors, ministerial department directors, and so on); 40 to 50 per cent of the ministerial departments' directors are usually replaced during the period of one or two years following a political change of the majority (82.5 per cent in 1986–87); yet this rotation takes place in a system where mobility plays an essential role in the career of top civil servants.

- There is a legal basis for external recruitment (*tour extérieur*) at mid-career to ministerial inspectorates and to the *grand corps*, in a proportion of one-fourth or of one-third of the regular promotions: these nominations which provide for some ventilation of the high civil service are discretionary; yet a procedure has been established to limit the risk of abuse by requiring the consultation of a committee (the opinion of the committee may not be followed by the government, but the government is usually reluctant to go against it and there are only a few examples of an opinion being overruled).

CONCLUDING REMARKS

To what extent has the New Public Management affected the French civil service? Formulated in such broad terms, the question receives a denial. Undoubtedly, privatisation has been carried out, and monopolies have been gradually abolished in accordance with European law. While the mission of state and public services has been called into question, that is their organisation and capacity to meet the social needs, their essence remains intact.

In contrast to anti-statist ideology, the circular of the prime minister of 26 July 1995 on the preparation and implementation of the reform of the state (established by Alain Juppé) reaffirmed the role of the state and the public service values.

The reduction of influence or privileges of the civil service has never been the aim of the modernisation policy, and only a narrow wing of the political class advocates such an action. Neither the managerialism ideology nor concepts of 'market testing' or 'value for money' have penetrated the French civil service.

The reasons for this reluctance to embrace the most radical version of NPM are numerous and refer to the historic and institutional background of the French civil service. Yet, it should be emphasised that unlike the British civil service, the French one can rely on a strong support in the political class (see the proportion of civil servants in the government and in the parliament).

It is true that the public criticises administration, the complexity and slowness of procedures. But, despite recurrent campaigns and popular ridicule to which it is subjected, the civil service offers socially attractive employment and is viewed as a dispenser of services essential to social cohesion. Most public polls show that citizens like the teacher, the postman, the nurse, etc. and consider their numbers insufficient (the civil servants in the ministries or in some local administrations may not enjoy such a good reputation).

Still, this does not signify a consensus. The role of the higher civil service (which is reproached for being cut off from reality), the decentralisation, the frequency of strikes in the public services, and the comparison of salaries and conditions of employment with the private sector, for example, are subject to debate.

But the French civil service has evolved according to its own values, in an attempt to reconcile the basis principles of a career system resulting from general statute and the introduction of modern management techniques. Of course, this is not an easy task.

The civil service involvement in modernisation policies has been viewed in an experimental and pragmatic way. One the main innovations is the development of autonomous units on the basis of a quasi contractual agreement, (*centres de responsabilité and contrats de service*). These aim at allowing greater management flexibility in return for a commitment to improving services to users and adopting rigorous monitoring procedures. Attempts to promote professional training, modern human resources management methods, and evaluation procedures have been significant (the Equipment ministry has been a leader in these reforms) and cultural renewal is noticeable.

Nevertheless, the impact of these changes has been limited by several obstacles which are not the result of statute nor strong trade union opposition. First, modernisation policy has encountered the corporatism and the strategies dominated by the vested interests of the corps. Second, the most innovative actors have been discouraged by a lack of consideration from the state towards its financial agreements: resources have been cut notwithstanding the objectives assigned or the results, and schemes allowing a 'collective return for modernisation' have been abandoned. Third, adhesion to new management methods has been unequal. If senior officials, especially those in the field services, appreciated their increasing autonomy, middle level managers have been quite reluctant in implementing new policies. Moreover, important differences persist between sectors and institutional barriers have remained an important obstacle.

The State Reform Programme of 1995 has widened the perspective and drawn the main orientations of the modernisation of human resources management: forward-looking staff management, the development of in-service training, a renewal of appraisal procedures, the delegation of management.

How successful will these ambitions prove to be in the future? Undoubtedly, important changes have occurred, but the difficulty is to move from sectoral experiences to a global transformation of management and procedures including structures and financial management.

Regarding the evolution of the civil service, two points should be stressed. First, the increase of mobility and polyvalence – by merging or grouping together different corps into professional paths (*filières*) – allows more room for flexibility and is probably the most interesting perspective in order to move the whole structure. Second, the introduction of some differentiation in careers according to performance by rewarding good results and imposing sanctions on shortcomings would require not only the establishment of a true performance appraisal system but also the possibility of drawing concrete conclusions from the evaluation. But such a differentiation is hardly compatible with the principles of the civil service statute – which is based on equality – and with the existence of the joint commissions which push towards an increasing homogenisation of careers. Furthermore, such an evolution would require an increase in the responsibility of heads of service in managing the careers of their staff; managers themselves would be subject to a rigorous appraisal of their results (with rewards and sanctions). Up to now, attempts at such performance assessment have been very tentative and senior management has been resistant to it (Chevallier 1996b, Rouban 1998a).

In the end, if the French civil service has avoided a radical upheaval of its missions and operation, it has proved – in continuity with its history – that is has a remarkable capacity to adapt to external and internal pressure such as European integration, public expenditure limitations and evolving social demands. Relying on a strong tradition, it has been able to transform its culture and process without giving up its values. The debate on their 'privileges' – security of tenure, retirement plans – is recurrent and tensions may rise. There is no reason why the civil service should not be able to face the challenge and adapt to the demands of society.

NOTES

1. It is also true of most economic and financial enterprises and cultural institutions.
2. The Court of Cassation (*Cour de Cassation*) is the supreme Judicial Court, and the Council of State is the supreme Administration Court (since 1987, there have been three tiers of courts in the administrative order).

3. Traditionally French administration law makes a distinction between these two concepts: *déconcentration* is a transfer of powers and resources from the ministerial departments to the state local services: the state still acts through its civil servants but the decisions are closer to the citizens; *décentralisation* is more radical and political: powers and resources are transferred from the state administration to the autonomous local authorities, elected and subject to limited judicial review and control of accounts only in cases of legal violation.

4. The pension is 75 per cent of the last salary, after 37.5 years of contributions. These figures are taken of the 1996 payment statistics (real staff); which might be slightly different from the budgetary staff. (*Ministère de la fonction publique* 1998).

5. During the *Ancien Régime*, collecting taxes was not a task of the monarch administration but was entrusted to the members of a corporation called *Fermiers généraux*.

6. Including post and telecommunications which have been excluded from civil servant statistics since 1990.

7. These figures are constructed from the 1996 payment statistics and consider the 'real' staff or staff in function which might be slightly different from the budgetary staff (*Ministère de la fonction publique* 1998).

8. This includes not only teachers but also administrative staff; it excludes universities (109 204).

9. Ministère de la fonction publique, 1998.

10. Category D has been gradually suppressed at the beginning of the 1990s by the Durafour agreement.

11. The indexation of the wage-scale has been abandoned since the early 1980s.

12. The proportion of students whose father is a senior executive or a member a liberal profession rose from 38 per cent at the beginning of the 1960s to 65 per cent 20 years later. During the same period, the proportion of working class children has decreased from 4.9 per cent to 3.6 per cent (Kesler 1985).

13. Ministers, delegated ministers and State secretaries.

14. An inquiry was carried out by the CEVIPOF (*Fondation nationale des sciences politiques, Paris*) in 1997 (Rouban 1998b).

BIBLIOGRAPHY

Braibant, G. (1998), 'An overview of the French administration in F. Gallouedec-Genuys' (ed.), *About French Administration*, Paris: La Documentation française.

Les Cahiers de la Fonction publique et de l'administration (1998), *La Rémunération des fonctionnaires, no. 165*, Paris: Berger Levrault.

Chevallier, J. (1996a), 'La politique de modernisation administrative', in *L'État de droit, Mélanges en l'honneur de Guy Braibant*, Paris: Dalloz.

Chevallier J. (1996b), 'La Réforme de l'Etat et la conception française du service public', *Revue française d'administration publique*, 77.

Claisse, A. and M.-C. Meininger (1994), *Fonctions publiques en Europe*, Paris: Montchrestien, coll. Clefs.

Institut international d'administration publique (1996), *An Introduction to French Administration*, Paris: La Documentation française, Getting to know French Administration

Kesler, J.-F. (1985), *L'ENA, la société, l'Etat*, Paris: Berger-Levrault.

Kessler, M.-C. (1986), *Les Grands Corps de l'État*, Paris: Presses de la Fondation nationale des sciences politiques.

Legendre, P. (1968), *Histoire de l'administration française de 1750 à nos jours*, Paris: Presses universitaires de France.

Meininger, M.–C. (1998), 'Public service: the public service', in F. Gallouedec-Genuys: *About French Administration*, Paris: La Documentation française.

Meininger, M.–C. (1999), 'Remarques sur le concept de Gouvernance et le système politico-administratif français', in J. Corkery (ed.) *Governance: Concepts and applications*, Brussels: IISA.

Meny, Y. (1998), *The French Political System*, Paris: Institut international d'administration publique, La Documentation française, coll. Getting to know French Administration.

Ministère de la fonction publique, de la réforme de l'État et de la décentralisation (1998), La Fonction publique de l'État, annual rapport, March 1997–March 1998, Paris: La Documentation française.

Röhr, J.A. (1995), 'What a différence a state makes: reflections on governance in France', in G.L. Wamsley and J.F. Wolf, *Refounding Democratic Public Administration*, Thousand Oaks/London/New Delhi: Sage.

Rouban, L. (1996), 'Des cadres supérieurs en devenir', *Revue française d'administration publique, 70*.

Rouban, L. (1998a), *The French Civil Service*, Paris: Institut international d'administration publique, La Documentation française, coll. Getting to know French Administration.

Rouban, L. (1998b), 'La politisation des fonctionnaires en France: obstacle ou nécessité?', *Revue française d'administration publique, 86*.

Ziller, J. (1988), *Egalité et mérite: Institut européen d'administration publique*, Brussels: Bruylant.

Ziller J. (1993), *Administration comparée*, Paris: Montchrestien.

9. The Development and Current Features of the Italian Civil Service System

Rudolf Lewansky

INTRODUCTION

The Italian civil service cannot be understood without considering the political system. After World War II, Italy, previously a monarchy, became a parliamentary republic. In the long period between the late 1940s and the early 1990s, the political scene underwent very little substantive change: a large Catholic party (Democrazia Cristiana, the DC) was continually in power, in various coalitions with minor centrist parties, and since the late 1960s with an increasingly moderate medium-size socialist party. Opposition was represented by a small Fascist party to the extreme right of the political spectrum, and by the largest Communist party in the west to its left. Thus, political competition was, in fact, more apparent than real, 'blocked' as it was by internal and international factors – the east–west confrontation. It was impossible for the major opposition party, the PCI, to formally take part in the formation of a government, although it held very moderate positions and strove to distinguish itself from the USSR, a strategy that allowed it to gain increasing shares of electoral consensus (up to approximately one third in the 1980s).

Coupled with features of the national political culture, especially in the southern areas of the country, such as 'amoral familism' (Banfield 1958), the DC and its allies were able to gain consensus by establishing clientelistic relationships with specific groups or individuals to whom benefits were distributed. Civil service posts themselves, in a country with high unemployment rates, were handed out according to this mode of consensus generation. Such a system hardly required an effective or efficient public administration for its legitimation. Even when social protests that rocked Italian society during the late 1960s and the 1970s (that is beyond their leftist ideological façade, as a demand of modernisation of the state, and especially of a greater capability of the public sector to 'deliver'), the political-administrative system responded by adopting a number of limited measures, especially concerning decentralisation (namely the creation of the ordinary regions in 1970).

The post-war Italian economy, until then primarily based on agriculture, underwent a process of rapid industrialisation; in terms of GNP (1 101 billion dollars in 1994) and of industrial production (317 billion dollars in 1993), it constituted the fifth largest economy in the world (*The Economist* 1996), even though the southern parts of the country benefited much less from the process.[1] Notwithstanding such societal developments, the administrative system followed an evolution of its own. Italian bureaucracy featured a strongly juridical-formalistic and pre-industrial organisational culture and a patrimonial concept of posts held by its members (also due to the social-geographic origins of many civil servants, coming from the less developed southern regions); furthermore, it lacked a well-trained, technically competent, ambitious and motivated administrative élite; an *esprit de corps* was completely absent.

Not surprisingly, the service delivery and policy implementation capabilities of such an administration were decidedly low. The civil service was however able to externalise the costs of its inefficiency and avoid bearing the responsibility of its (non)actions (Cerase 1990: 13). Though dissatisfaction for the poor performance of the public sector has always been widespread, governments and politicians have been able to leave things as they were by paying lip-service to the need for reform and efficiency, and by adopting symbolic measures (special committees, and departments in charge of studying and promoting reform were set up, and qualified reports were produced). In fact, in its relationship with the political system, the civil service gladly renounced power and prestige in exchange for security of post and career. On this basis, personnel policies were the result of benevolent legislation, decisions of the administrative courts – biased in favour of personnel – and pressure from trade unions, who enjoyed inside access to policymaking in this field. On the other hand, although society in general certainly suffered from the ineffectiveness of the administration, many individuals have gained consistent advantages from such situation (suffice it to say that tax evasion is estimated to be around 15 per cent, as compared to 1–2 per cent in other developed countries). Thus, public administration has not carried out a role of leadership, much less support, in the development of the national economy and in the process of modernisation. On the contrary, it has governed the rearguard, in the sense of simply mitigating the social effects of industrialisation (Melis 1996: 12). The Italian case could be metaphorically described as a 'time warp' situation in which a society with a highly developed economy finds itself is entangled in the 'swamps' of a pre-modern civil service.

In the early 1990s four different, albeit tightly connected, factors converged to upset this long-lasting situation:

1. the end of the east-west confrontation;
2. the explosion of the '*Tangentopoli*' scandal that brought into the open the deep corruption that affected both the political and the administrative systems and confirmed the majority of Italians in their low opinion of public administration; it also deeply changed the political situation allowing first a coalition of centre-right parties and then one of the centre-left to take power (since 1996 the country has been governed by a centre-left majority including the previous communist party);
3. the appearance on the political scene of the *Lega Nord* that, among other things, can be seen as the expression of the dissatisfaction of productive strata of Northern Italian society caused by the inefficiency of the administration;[2]
4. the situation of the economy, and especially the serious situation of public finances requiring a consistent cut in public expenditure and an increase in effectiveness of the public sector, in order to keep pace with the process of European integration, coupled with the growing levels of unemployment making the privileges of civil servants unacceptable in the eyes of the majority of the population (D'Orta and Diamanti 1994: 54). As a consequence, besides the considerable impact on the political system, a number of ambitious attempts to reform the administration in general, and the civil service in particular, have been enacted during recent years, though only time will tell what their final outcomes might be.

THE DEVELOPMENT OF THE CIVIL SERVICE SYSTEM

Present public administration represents the result of a process of incremental 'sedimentation' (Sepe 1987: 44) on top of a model that has its roots in the reform put into place in the kingdom of Sardinia (actually Piedmont) in 1853, along the Napoleonic model (filtered through the Belgian experience) based on ministries. The organisational structure was strongly hierarchical and centralised, being conceived of as a machine that was supposed to 'mechanically' execute the directives issued by political decision-makers. This model was subsequently extended to the rest of the country as Piedmont annexed the other states of the peninsula and a unitary national state was created in 1860.

This basic structure still characterises central state administration today, though a number of significant changes have occurred. From the late 1800s, other types of organisational models began to appear as the public sector undertook new types of activities that went beyond the typical 'order' functions (defence, internal order, taxation): *aziende autonome* (independent firms), *enti pubblici* (public bodies) and *partecipazioni statali* (state-owned firms), operating under more flexible procedures, rules and controls, were created to carry out economic and welfare activities. Such 'parallel administrations' also represented a way to recruit personnel (typically featuring a technocratic and efficiency oriented culture) with characteristics different from those of the ministerial civil servants. It is important to keep this aspect in mind since such evolution has also brought about considerable variations as far as the civil service is concerned, in terms of working conditions, features of personnel and so on.

Personnel numbers have grown considerably during the more than 130 years of existence of Italy as a unified political entity, both in absolute terms and in relation to the population. When the country was unified in 1860, there was 1 state employee for every 145 inhabitants; at present there is 1 for every 11 inhabitants (Cassese 1983: 32). Growth, however, has not occurred in a linear fashion: there have been phases of rapid expansion (1910–20, and the 1930s) and others in which increases have been modest. In two periods (the end of the nineteenth century and the mid 1920s) there has even been a decrease in absolute terms. Personnel employed by the *aziende* reached a maximum of 425 100 in 1979 (Cassese 1983: 388).

After that date, numbers started to decline because of the change in legal status or privatisation (in 1995 the figure was down to less than 44 000). One should also remember personnel that, though formally belonging to the private sector, depend on firms that are part of the state-owned firms (in 1980, 713 000). In 1980 the public sector, in its widest meaning, included some five million jobs (Cassese 1983: 114).

Major increases have occurred in this century. Since 1900 the population has doubled, whereas public personnel has increased 30 times (Sepe 1995: 292–3). Contrary to other European nations, an 'administrative revolution in government' (Melis 1996: 12), for example its increase in terms of functions, organisational dimensions and personnel, did not occur simultaneously with the creation of a unified national state. Rather, it took place at the beginning of the twentieth century as the state progressively took responsibility for welfare, infrastructure (such as railways, nationalised in 1905) and productive activities. In 1900, the ratio personnel/population (0.53) was actually lower than in 1861 (0.6). By 1910 state expenditure had reached 14 per cent of GNP, and 21.4 per cent between 1921 and 1930 (as compared to 10 per cent in 1862) (Sepe 1995: 56). By 1923 there were 509 000 civil servants (more than 1 300 for every 100 000 inhabitants) (Cassese 1983: 380); this was also a result of the expansion during World War I.

The Fascist regime was somewhat contradictory towards the expansion of the administration. After an initial reduction of personnel (a minimum 503 000 units in 1925), justified by the imperative of cutting public expenditure, the numbers grew considerably during the 1930s and 1940s as the regime attributed new functions to the state, and thus to the administration, especially in the welfare and economic fields (Melis 1996: 330) as a part of its strategies to boost its internal consensus as well as its international standing (527 000 in 1930, 638 000 in 1932, for example more than 1500 civil servants per 100 000 inhabitants, 722 000 in 1937, 839 000 in 1939 and 140 000 in 1943).

In the aftermath of World War II, personnel again grew considerably, first through temporary positions that were transformed into permanent ones over time. In the face of the economic crisis, the administration performed as a 'social shock-absorber' offering jobs, albeit poorly paid at that time since salaries in the public sector had lost much of their value compared to the prewar levels (Melis 1996: 417 ff.). The 'enlarged' public sector in 1991 represented 7.4 per cent of the population and 17.9 per cent of the overall labour force (PCM 1993: 214).

Personnel continued to grow until the late 1980s, when consistent efforts to reduce the extension of the public sector in general and to reduce personnel in particular have, more or less successfully, been put into place. Several laws have limited turnover; other provisions have actually frozen hiring completely for periods of time.

REPRESENTATIVENESS

Senior executives typically are male, come from urban areas (according to the results of the research by Aberbach et al. 1981, 74 per cent come from small towns – a figure higher than any other country included in the survey), are rather old in age and belong to the middle classes. In this last respect, the research by these authors (ibid. 1981: 64), in the early 1970s showed that the Italian administrative élites are 'distinctively unrepresentative in social origins' due to the closure to recruitment from the lower classes. As far as age is concerned, in the early 1970s, Italian top level civil servants were older and had a longer period of service in the administration as compared to their counterparts in other European nations (Putnam 1975: 98). In 1989, out of a total of 6 660 managers, 26 per cent were over 60 years of age; 43 per cent between 50 and 59; 27 per cent in their forties, and only 1 per cent below the age of 40. However the trend which dominated until the 1980s might be changing if the data collected in a recent survey in three ministries are representative. According to these, 21.8 per cent of top managers are younger than 50 years old (Chiarini 1995: 140).

With regard to gender, in the last decades of the previous century and in the beginning of this one, women working in the public sector were confined to such sectors as the telegraphs and telephones. They began to enter into the public sector massively in the years before World War I, although they were confined to the lower levels with repetitive tasks. In the aftermath of that war, the associations of public employees and of the veterans developed a strong campaign against women working in general, arguing that they should return to their homes and take care of the family (Melis 1996: 267). Fascism, also because of its masculine and 'imperial' ideology – that assigned women the role of mothers of numerous children for the regime – reduced female presence among the public personnel (a decree of 1938 limited it to 10 per cent of total personnel).

After World War II, an increasing feminisation took place: 26 per cent in 1969, 33 per cent in 1980, 51.4 per cent in 1985 and 49.9 per cent in 1991 of total personnel (central and local) (PCM 1993: 235). Many women today see public employment as a job compatible with traditional social roles of housewives, thanks to the sort working houres. The differences in absentee-ism in the ministries between men (4.9 per cent) and women (13.1 per cent) is meaningful in this respect (though the data also include maternity leave); it seems plausible that the pro-family ideology of the dominant Catholic party has consciously favoured the 'social' use of public employment under this respect.

The consideration that women represent at least half of total personnel (if not the majority) can be deceptive. First of all, school personnel (where women are particularly numerous) alone accounts for approximately half of total state employees, so if this sector is excluded, the total female presence would be lower. Second, women generally occupy medium-lower level posi-tions (Pipan 1992: 130), though the number of female senior executives is certainly growing. Out of a total of 6 660 managers, women represented only 9.7 per cent in 1989; furthermore, at a closer look, it appears that female managers are concentrated in the lower echelons of the managerial career (12.5 per cent of the *primi dirigenti*, the lowest level; 7.6 per cent of the *dirigenti superiori*, the intermediate level; but only 1.5 per cent of the *diri-genti generali*) (ISTAT 1992: 46).

The only case in which an issue of ethnic representativeness can be found is that of the Süd Tirol/Alto Adige Province (on the border with Austria). In order to suppress tensions that were degenerating into violent actions carried out by the German-speaking language group in the 1960s, an agreement between the Italian and Austrian governments ('De Gasperi-Gruber') pro-vided for a proportional division of all public resources (including posts in the administration) to each linguistic group (German, with the majority in the area, Italian and Ladin). Knowledge of German is required to access to any position in the administration. Though problems arise in the application of the agreement, generally speaking the solution has brought about a liveable peace among the linguistic groups.

The major issue pertaining to representativeness concerns the geographical origin of civil servants, for example the fact that the majority come from southern Italy. After unification of the country in 1860, the administration of the newly-formed nation was mainly entrusted to personnel coming from the Piedmont administration, especially as far as the higher echelons were concerned (Melis 1996: 37 ff.). The common origin represented a significant element of internal cohesion during the phase of building the nation-state. The Piedmontese predominance continued throughout the nineteenth century.

By the beginning of the twentieth century however, recruitment shifted towards the southern regions; a process which started from the lower levels and gradually crept up the hierarchy (Sepe 1995: 307). By 1930 the process of '*meridionalization*' was well advanced, and it became even more acute during the 1950s and 1960s, especially in national level administrations (whereas it occurred much less in local administrations). At present, 51.6 per cent of civil servants come from the southern regions (where 36.7 per cent of the total population resides); another 19.8 per cent come from the area of Rome (8.9 per cent of the population) whereas only 28.4 per cent come from the north (54.4 per cent of the total population) (D'Orta and Diamanti 1994: 59). The phenomenon is even stronger in the case of senior executives: 62.6 per cent from the south versus 24.4 per cent from central Italy and only 11 per cent from the north (Cassese 1983: 65 and 1984: 40, Melis 1996: 477); similar results are confirmed by a recent survey of the senior civil servants belonging to three ministries (Industry, Labour, Interior) (Chiarini 1995: 128-9).

The basis of this historical phenomenon is rather simple: the lack of alternative sources of jobs in the southern regions which have not benefited by a process of economic development comparable to that of the north. Thus the public sector has become the major employer. Furthermore, even though salaries were generally lower than in the private sector, a position in the administration was often perceived as an opportunity of social promotion. As far as the middle classes in particular are concerned, starting at the turn of the century a clear split became evident: the northerners were increasingly attracted by technical degrees that offered lucrative professional opportunities in the growing private sector, whereas the southerners would pursue a degree in law which offered access to the public sector.

The '*meridionalization*' of the administration has had a number of relevant consequences. First of all, it fostered a patrimonial conception of their post among personnel since the role of the administration is perceived as that of offering jobs and income rather than that of producing collective goods of some sort. Security of posts and careers are held at a premium as compared to other possible values (responsibility, high earnings, power, professional satisfaction, service to the public and so on), and a modern result-oriented and productive culture is absent. Also, this situation contributes to low levels of motivation of civil servants towards their jobs since they have entered the administration because of the lack of alternatives, rather than as the result of a positive choice.

Also, the difference in background and basic cultural orientation have created a significative gap between the economic sector and the public one. The civil service – including its top levels – is permeated by a pre-industrial culture that is hardly representative of the more advanced areas and sectors of present Italian society (Guarnieri 1988: 98). The phenomenon is one of the causes of the present legitimacy crisis of the Italian political system mentioned above.

Another relevant consequence is presented by the irrational distribution of personnel across the country: 40.6 per cent of civil servants are located in the northern part of the country (6.6 employees for every 100 inhabitants); 22.7 in the Centre (9.1 per 100 inhabitants – highest due to the presence of the central bureaux of the ministries located in the capital, Rome); and 36.7 in the south (7.3 per 100 inhabitants) (RGS 1992; Cerase 1994: 28; PCM 1993: 40). The increase in positions in the post-war period has, in general, been stronger in the southern regions (Serrani 1979: 35). Southerners are often hired for positions in the north. Approximately one-fourth of state civil servants working in the north were born in southern Italy (Cerase 1994: 34). As soon as possible, they strive to get transferred back to their regions of origin, which causes a deficit of personnel in the administrations located in the northern parts of the country.[3]

On the other hand, one must consider that employment in the public sector was used more or less consciously as a means to contain the restlessness and gain the consensus of the educated middle class of the southern regions that were excluded from the benefits of economic development concentrated in the north (Melis 1996: 185) by offering them a sort of compensation (Cassese 1977: 96).

THE INTERNAL LABOUR MARKET

The 1853 reform introduced in Piedmont marked a transition for personnel from the status of 'servants of the crown' to that of 'servants of the state' by establishing the principle that its position (rights and duties) would be regulated by law (Benvenuti 1977: 345 ff.). In practice, however, employees were still considered to be without rights. Somewhat paradoxically, this was a consequence of the 'constitutionalisation' of the state. Since the ministers were responsible for their acts in front of parliament, they were supposed to be able to exert authoritarian control over their staff, even though this implied depriving them of the rights that were conceded to the rest of society members (Melis 1996: 29).

When the country was unified in 1860, the administration was made up of a limited number of personnel, highly homogeneous. The internal structure was strongly hierarchical. By the early 1900s, the situation had changed substantially. First of all the sheer numbers had expanded to a point that personal relationships were no longer sufficient to ensure the functioning of the organisation. Second, homogeneity had been lost: personnel came from different areas of the country and social classes. Personnel began to have a voice heard after 1876 (when budgetary problems became less acute and the 'left', headed by Depretis, took over government from the right). The diffusion of socialist ideology and the influence of trade unions produced higher levels of social tension also within the public sector. By the beginning of this century, personnel were already organised in numerous unions in all the sectors of the administration.

The expansion of functions carried out by the state since the beginning of the century as well as the growth in numbers had important effects on the relationships between the state and its personnel. Clearly an authoritarian style of personnel management was inadequate, posing the need of an explicit regulation based on new principles. Starting in 1904, the Giolitti government passed a vast number of laws concerning civil servants in order to accommodate the requests coming from this sector and reduce tensions within the administration. Though promised since 1876, on the example of Bismarckian Germany (Melis 1996: 117), a unitary source of regulation of the relationships between the state and its personnel fixing clear rules concerning the guarantees (of job, career, salary) as well as the duties of civil servants was finally approved for the first time in 1908. The statute marks a turn towards a 'protected service'.

A second statute of civil service was passed by minister De Stefani at the beginning of the Fascist period in 1923. It imposed more strict internal hierarchical principles and stressed the authoritarian traits of the organisation (imitating the military hierarchy). In this respect, all in all, it represented a return to the traditional conception of public administration, typical of the previous century (Melis 1996: 297 ff.). The statute also restricted possibilities of promotion and made them more selective, and reduced personnel. In 1919, personnel had managed to obtain assurances that advancements in careers could be conceded even in the absence of posts at that level ('*ruolo aperto*') in order to ensure rises in salary; the new legislation abolished such a provision ('*ruolo chiuso*').

A third statute was passed in 1957. Essentially it constituted a softening up of the 1923 statute on the basis of the jurisprudence of the administrative tribunals (the *Consiglio di Stato,* Guarnieri 1988: 85). Careers were divided into levels on the basis of uniform and rigid criteria that did not reflect the actual functions carried out by each specific administration. The principle of the '*ruoli chiusi*' was maintained and salaries were tied to career advancements (*de facto* this caused the creation of new administrations in order to satisfy the requests for promotions).

A feature that characterises Italian civil service is the fact that public personnel has always been disciplined by special provisions belonging to administrative law, separate from those of ordinary civil law applying to personnel of the private sector (D'Amico 1992: 80). This approach represented the logical consequence of the dominant juridical doctrine according to which the state could not be set on the same level as private entities, and thus its decisions should have an authoritative nature. Civil servants are simply considered the human component of the administrative organisation, and are therefore subordinated to the special supremacy of the administration; the relationship is unilateral, exempting the state from the obligations and rights that normally apply to other workers (D'Orta and Diamanti 1994: 52, Rusciano 1978: 125). Thus working conditions and labour relations in the public sector were, in fact, increasingly regulated by law on the one hand, and by administrative jurisprudence on the other, which has played an increasingly important role in defining the regulation of public employees through its decisions (Melis 1996: 199) since the beginning of the twentieth century.

Due to their monopolistic competence over all controversies concerning public personnel, specialised administrative courts (at present the Regional Administrative Tribunals, TARs, and the *Consiglio di Stato*, the final appeal level of administrative justice) have become increasingly influential in defining rules applying to personnel, with profound consequences not only on personnel management, but on public administration in general. Due to the fact that components of such courts themselves come from administrative ranks, they tend to consider matters brought before them with a perspective biased in favour of personnel (Cassese 1983: 50).

Only very recently, has the public sector been brought under the same legislation that regulates the private sector. One consequence is that, beginning in 1998, personnel controversies are to be decided by the ordinary judge rather than the administrative courts (however the latter remains competent for the 'public' aspects of the labour relationship, which results in a great deal of uncertainty; also, ordinary courts are already burdened with a heavy backlog, so it is not clear how they will be able to cope with some additional 60 000 cases each year...).

As far as personnel working conditions are concerned, these were traditionally established unilaterally by the state through laws. Starting in the 1970s, however, such an approach has undergone a gradual, but substantial transformation towards an industrial relations system similar to the one existing between employers and employees in the private sector, based on bilateral agreements resulting from collective bargaining with the unions recognised as counterparts. Three different levels of bargaining have been established:

1. the entire public sector;
2. each of the eight compartments (ministries, research institutions, universities, schools, and *aziende autonome* at the national level, plus health services, regions and local government at the sub-national level);
3. the decentralised level: only some matters (organisation, recruitment, numbers of personnel, discipline of rights and duties) are still to be regulated by law, whereas the economic aspects are to be decided through (triennial) negotiated agreements. According to legislation passed in 1993 (Act No 29) a special agency, ARAN (*Agenzia per le Relazioni Sindacali*), based in the prime minister's office, is charged with bargaining with unions in a role similar to that of a private employer. The authorisation of the government is still required to sign a contract in order to assure the availability of necessary financial resources in the state budget. The goal of this approach is to enable the government to respect expenditure limitations imposed by the situation of public finance, an objective often missed in the past due to the 'permeability' of the political system to the pressures coming from the civil service.

Only specific categories such as top level managers (*dirigente generale*), police, judges, prefects, diplomats and university professors, have been excluded from such process.

Since the late 1960s, the trade unions (especially the three major ones which are strong among private sector workers, CGIL (left), CISL (Catholic) and UIL (centre), became heavily involved in personnel management decisions. Their representatives were included in the commissions internal to each administration responsible for such affairs; thus, their role had become blurred with that of the state itself (the phenomenon went under the term of '*cogestione*' (co-management) (Melis 1996: 497). One notable implication of the privatisation trend previously discussed is also that unions are resuming their role of a real counterpart rather than one of '*cogestione*' of personnel.

In the late 1960s and 1970s trade unions become very strong in Italian society in general, and in the public sector as well. In the 1970s, levels of membership were quite high (55–60 per cent compared to 36 per cent of industry) (D'Amico 1992: 85) even though considerable internal differences existed (for example 80 per cent among the railway personnel, 40 per cent among school teachers). Membership has, however, seriously declined since the 1980s: only 42 per cent of those interviewed in a recent survey (Cerase 1994: 185) declared that they belonged to a union, and small sectorial unions, with a narrow corporatist perspective, became quite diffused.

Job Classification

Until the mid-1970s personnel was divided into four 'careers' (reflecting the hierarchical model at the basis of the De Stefani reform of 1923, and substantially maintained in the *Statuto* of 1957): auxiliary, executive, 'conceptual' (employee) and directive, according to the functions carried out and the level of studies accomplished. Each career was divided into a number of '*qualifiche*'. This system created a number of serious difficulties: pressure to obtain advancements in order to secure increases in pay were very strong; also, there was an extreme division of job assignments. A fifth – managerial or *dirigenziale* – career was added in 1972 which is divided into five levels, three of which are to be found in all ministries: *primo dirigente, dirigente superiore* (subsequently eliminated by Act No 29/93) and *dirigente generale*.

A different system, based on so-called *qualifiche funzionali*, already proposed in the 1950s and foreseen by legislation in the late 1960s, was in fact introduced only in 1975 in the *aziende autonome* and in 1980 for ministerial personnel. There were originally eight *qualifiche*, later increased to nine, excluding managerial personnel. The aim of the reform was to obtain a correspondence between the levels assigned and the functions actually carried out. Furthermore, it was intended to reduce the salary and regulatory 'jungle' that existed between similar tasks among the different areas (the senate had previously instituted a special inquiry commission to investigate just such a 'jungle') by grouping tasks with homogeneous contents and responsibilities, and to pay the same salary to each *qualifica*, each comprising a number of professional profiles (based on the type of professional task, the degree of autonomy, the requirements required). The new system allows for salary increases according to a number of levels within each *qualifica*, with periodical increases, thus attempting to reduce the pressure of employees for promotion and the creation of new positions at higher levels as the only way to obtain a wage rise.

In fact, the results were very different from the original intentions: salary increases and advancements did not result in the desired increase in performance, and pressure to obtain increases in pay through career advancements continued. Also, the 'jungle', though considerably simplified, still remained to some extent. In the ministries 'compartment' for example, the situation in 1994 was the following, starting from the 'top': *dirigente generale* (with three levels A, B and C); *dirigente superiore*; *primo dirigente*; general inspector, division director; levels nine to two (level one has been abolished). The situation in other compartments of the state administration (school, police and so on) is very different from the one that applies to ministries.

Salaries

During the 1960s, salaries were relatively high, whereas in the following decade, increases in salaries remained behind those of the private sector, also because of the high rate of inflation that plagued the Italian economy since the oil crisis. Over the last five years, pay increases in the public sector have just kept pace with inflation (16.7 per cent over five years), whereas increases in real salaries in the industrial sector have been higher (19 per cent).

In 1980, the average salary in the central administration was equivalent to US$12 000 (the ratio between this and the per capita income was 1.88). To have a comparative perspective, according to the same source the figures were US$18 540 (with a ratio of 1.64) for the United States, US$21 164 (ratio 2.14) for Japan, US$25 982 (ratio 2.10) for Germany, and US$15 366 (ratio 1.60) for the United Kingdom (Heller and Tait 1989: 249).

The gap between the lowest and the highest level salaries has been decreasing. In 1961 the ratio between the highest and the lowest level was 1 to 8, in 1971 it was 1 to 5, and became 1 to 3 in 1979 (Cassese 1983: 68). In particular Act No 312/80 flattened differences in salary levels and damaged the higher echelons. Managers however can supplement their salary considerably in a number of ways, e.g. by sitting in the boards of public agencies (Allum 1976: 216).

Since 1956, salary increases were tied not to merit, but simply to seniority in service (provided one did not have 'demerits' on the job, in fact an extremely rare event). Incentives aimed at increasing productivity have been introduced since 1987, but have hardly been successful due to their small amount (maximum 0.80 per cent of salary) and the reluctance to distribute them in a strongly differentiated manner. The recent (November 1996) contract of the top civil servants includes the possibility of consistent differences in salary according to responsibilities and tasks carried out, and results obtained. Measures aimed at increasing productivity and cutting costs (Pipan 1992: 132), such as the creation of *ad hoc* staff offices, have produced very meagre results.

Civil servants benefit from a number of other advantages: a secure position (tenure), handsome retirements (with fewer years of work as compared to the private sector), long holidays and short working hours and high rates of absenteeism. Surveys carried out in the ministries indicate that in average employees work 2–3 hours a day *de facto* (Cassese 1983: 119). This allows many to have a second job (however the present government is putting a stop to this, unless civil servants choose a part-time position), or to study in order to obtain a higher education degree and be able to obtain a better position within the administration. Recent provisions also attempt to modify the organisation of work in order to have offices open on afternoons (the typical opening hours until now have been 8 a.m. to 2 p.m., 6 days a week); however

27 per cent of public offices are still closed in the afternoon.

Civil servants are satisfied with the contents of their work and their relationships on the job, much less so of working conditions and especially of salaries. Opportunity to change any aspect of their present situation (place, contents of work, working hours) is very low (Cerase 1984: 19, 134 and 146).

Low morale, a patrimonial conception of posts and relatively low salaries can push civil servants to increase their earnings by accepting bribes, a quite diffused phenomenon known as '*Tangentopoli*' exists, thanks to complex and hardly 'transparent' procedures that attribute high levels of discretion to bureaucrats – notwithstanding the cumbersome controls and procedures intended to prevent this.

As mentioned previously, security of positions in civil service has become an asset to which personnel, especially those coming from situations featuring a lack of alternative employment, attribute considerable value. The level of security has, until now, been extremely high, due to the impossibility *de facto* of dismissing civil servants – even in cases where someone was responsible for serious crimes against the administration. Something, albeit with great difficulty, has started to change recently under this respect. A sentence of the *Consiglio di Stato* issued in 1996 stated that a civil servant could be fired if this was needed to ensure the efficiency and the economic soundness of a public administration (in the case under consideration, the cost of personnel was too costly for the administration and not justified by the amount of work to be carried out).[4] Another sign of change in this respect is represented by the latest contract of the top civil servants (some 4 600 individuals) established that the latter can be dismissed if they do not ensure adequate performance and results.

Deployment

The sclerotic trait of Italian bureaucrats, as compared to other European countries, is well known. They spend practically their entire working career in the public sector, and within the latter inside the same department (actually in the same branch, for example Directorate-General) (Putnam 1975: 98). An even stronger image of sclerosis emerges if one considers that numerous bureaucrats come from families in which a tie with the public sector already exists. In 41 per cent of the cases, a parent is a civil servant;[5] in this respect too Italy scores first in comparison with the other nations included in the survey (Aberbach et al. 1981: 74).

The survey carried out by Aberbach et al. (1981: 70–1) concluded that Italian (senior) bureaucracy fits 'the model of guild recruitment almost perfectly': once a civil servant enters the administration (in their sample, at the average age of 22), he or she will very probably pass the next 35 years of their professional life within the same administration (80 per cent in one single ministry); lateral entrance is 'virtually non-existent'; only 2 per cent of their sample has passed one-fourth of their adult life outside national government (compared to 37 per cent of the sample examined in France and 49 per cent in Germany).

Levels of horizontal mobility (that is among ministries/administrations) as well as external mobility (that is exchange with the private sector) are extremely low. A recent survey of senior civil servants (*dirigenti generali* and similar) belonging to three ministries evidences a differentiated situation existing among administrations. The careers of prefects occur entirely within the Interior Ministry by gradually climbing the hierarchical ladder. In the case of the Ministry of Industry, a part (30 per cent) of top managers come from public agencies (*enti pubblici*), that however are tightly connected to the ministry itself. The 'external' component – coming from other ministries, local authorities but also from trade unions – is even stronger (almost half) in the case of the Ministry of Labour (Chiarini 1995: 129–30). However, even in such cases, executive personnel comes from public or 'semi-public' sectors tightly connected with the administration, whereas managers coming from the private economy 'are so rare that they can be quoted by name' (Cassese 1984: 56).

According to another survey which considers personnel in general, 42 per cent of interviewed personnel have never changed the type of job carried out; 62 per cent have never moved from the same municipality; those who do move, do so mainly for personal reasons rather than for requirements of their organisation or for career advancements (Cerase 1994: 95 and 115 ff.).

'Traditionally', transfers to other locations occurred on the basis of wishes of individuals themselves (nearer to place of origin, typically in the south, as mentioned previously; Cerase 1994: 18). Efforts to promote geographic mobility (also due to the above-mentioned imbalance in the distribution of personnel between north and south), either on a voluntary or compulsory basis, have been carried out since the late 1980s, albeit with considerable difficulty; at the end of 1992 only approximately 7 000 individuals had been transferred.

Italian administration has not always been characterised by this situation of extremely low mobility. During the second half of the nineteenth century, after unification, mobility was considered a part of the normal *cursus honorum* that brought civil servants to the top of the hierarchical pyramid (Melis 1996: 62). The reasons for the present situation can be found, in part, in the search for security connected to *meridionalization* of the administration, and also in part, in the career system that rewards permanence within the same administration rather than mobility. The principal point in this last respect is that careers are, to a large extent, determined by automatic mechanisms, that is agreements negotiated with unions or 'internal' examinations where 'insiders' are greatly favoured, mainly on the basis of seniority in service, rather than on the basis of an evaluation of actual performance or as a reward for merits, responsibilities, professional capabilities or training (Cerase 1994: 18). Quite often, vertical mobility has also been decided by the administrative tribunals that have promoted single individuals or categories of personnel to higher posts on the basis of juridical interpretations (PCM 1993: 44). According to a recent survey, less than one-fourth of civil servants advanced in their careers through competitive tests. Competition among colleagues and promotions based on merit are considered unfavourably in the organisational culture of the public sector (Cassese 1983: 66). On average, 15 to 20 years are required to reach the top positions.

Greater organisational flexibility has been achieved in recent years thanks to the introduction of part-time jobs and contracts for limited numbers of years and changes in working hours and tasks.

The recruitment methods are also responsible for low levels of mobility. Access to positions within the civil service takes place through an examination (*concorso*), a method, established by the constitution, that, in principle, is intended to offer equal opportunities to all assuring that the most suitable candidates are hired (Pipan 1992: 126). In practice the procedural obligations to be followed in carrying out such *concorsi* are not only cumbersome and expensive, but are rarely effective in ascertaining the actual capabilities of the candidates. Furthermore, exceptions and derogations to this system are frequent so that administrations have high margins of discretion in defining the manner of hiring personnel and the actual basis of competition, which can be more or less open. According to one survey, in fact less than half of personnel entered into the administration through an examination, while the remainder was initially hired through a temporary appointment (6.3 per cent of personnel in 1995), that was subsequently transformed into a permanent one by special law or other mechanisms that do not imply a competitive test (Cerase 1994: 109). Thus, it is clear that a consistent portion of civil servants have not undergone a selective process.

As far as the executive levels are concerned, Italy has never had channels of recruitment similar to those of the *grands corps* in France or of British 'Oxbridge', though there are several training institutions, such as the Scuola Superiore della Pubblica Amministrazione (Higher School of Public Administration) created in 1957 with the original intention of creating an institution similar to the French ENA; the FORMEZ, originally created to train personnel in the southern areas of the country and recently charged with focusing on local government personnel; and the schools of several ministries (Interior, Revenue, Defence, Cultural Heritage). A governmental directive of 1993 defines the themes which are to be given priority (informatisation, relations with the public, relations with the unions, organisational and procedural analysis, manager training, foreign languages).

In 1972 an original recruitment channel (*corso-concorso*) was introduced for the lowest level of the executive career (*primo dirigente*). A certain number of selected candidates from *within* the administration would be admitted to a 14-month course, after which they would undergo a competitive examination carried out by the staff of the school itself (rather than by ministerial personnel) for admission to the civil service (Cassese 1984: 50). The system was not implemented due to the resistance of the bureaucracy itself and a subsequent law in fact, allowed the ministries to decide appointments at that level. More recently a similar channel – a four–year (including a two-year stage in a public or private organisation) course followed by an examination – has been introduced to recruit *external* personnel for managerial positions and the first *corso-concorso* has actually started.

The features of the recruitment and career systems in use should clarify why so little exchange between private and public labour markets occurs: the two markets are almost completely separated. Individuals enter the public sector at the lower levels, and access to the subsequent levels occurs through internal mechanisms. Access from the private sector is extremely rare, although things have started to change in this respect as far as the senior executives are concerned, due to recent reforms, especially in local governments. On the other hand, in some cases medium and higher level civil servants can find opportunities in the private sector, typically after an early retirement and especially from such ministries as Finance (fiscal consulting) and Defence (armaments industry; in this case the positions offered to senior armed forces officers constitute a typical case of '*pantouflage*').

Training

The levels of schooling required for each 'functional qualification' are specified by law (elementary school for first and seond; lower secondary/ intermediate school for third and fourth; higher secondary for fifth and sixth; university degree for seventh and eighth). However, personnel already belonging to the civil service have the advantage that they can compete for a higher qualification with a lower educational level (Cerase 1994: 72).

Among the personnel of ministries, 34.1 per cent has completed compulsory schooling (8 years), and 49.6 per cent holds a high school diploma, 15.2 per cent have a university degree (*laurea*, usually corresponding to four years of university) (RGS 1994: vol. (1): 143). Among personnel possessing a university degree, the dominance of a legal background has continued to grow over time (35 per cent in 1954, 40 per cent in 1961), though it must be noted that the situation can vary from one area of the administration to another. A strong presence of economic and technical backgrounds can be found in the Ministry of Labour and in the Ministry of Industry (Chiarini 1995: 138–9); obviously enough, non-legal preparation is also frequent in specialised branches such as the school system and the health service (Cerase 1994: 56). About 15 per cent obtained their university degree *after* entering the administration (which is possibly thanks to the fact that class attendance is generally not required in Italian universities). In such cases, the degree is instrumental in obtaining access to a higher qualification (also due to the value accorded to degrees in Italy). On the other hand, civil servants, especially those coming from the south, often hold education qualifications that exceed requirements of the positions they cover (Cerase 1994: 15).

Participation in on-the-job training is very limited (Cassese 1983: 118). In 1992, 14 906 employees (0.40 per cent of the total) had attended courses offered by the public administration schools mentioned above – small numbers indeed, and even more so if one considers that the courses are very short (PCM 1993: 371). In other sectors however, such as the health and school sectors, additional training is more significant (Cerase 1994: 63).

ORGANISATIONAL CULTURE

The pre-modern character of Italian bureaucracy results clearly from the organisational culture that permeates it. Italian bureaucracy features a lack of *esprit de corps*, social status and motivation; it is permeated by clientelism, and not infrequently, corruption; and it follows criteria of legal rationality, whereas concern for effectiveness, achieving results and solving problems is weak if not absent (La Spina and Sciortino 1993: 217). Such a description certainly does not fit the entire public administration, but is representative of the general situation.

As far as rationality is concerned, as the functions of the administration began growing in complexity beginning in the 1880s, a process of professionalisation took place; new and more qualified capabilities were required: medical doctors, geographers, statisticians, engineers, accountants. In 1882 there was an explicit attempt to create a civilian engineering corps (*Genio civile*), inspired by the French model of the technical *grand corps*. The statistical service represented another example of a qualified technical sector of the administration (Melis 1996: 104 ff.). Even disciplines such as public administration and organisational theory exerted some influence on the training of public personnel around the beginning of this century. In sum, in this period Italian bureaucracy still had a professional orientation and a concern for performance.

Starting however with the beginning of the twentieth century, under the influence of the public – and administrative – law school founded by V.E. Orlando in the 1880s, grafting German legal doctrine onto the French administrative tradition, (Dente 1988: 6), legal culture gradually became predominant. A law degree was required to access the higher posts within the administration. The administration became an interpreter of laws and regulations and the activity of the state was completely 'legalised' through the notion of 'administrative act' (Melis 1996: 13 and 213) and technical careers became marginal. The Fascist regime further encouraged this trend by fostering formalism as a goal in its own right; furthermore, the level of preparation of civil servants seriously declined during the Fascist regime (Cassese 1984: 59).

The system put into place since 1869, carried out through control of the accounts (by the *Corte dei Conti and the Ragioneria Generale dello Stato*) and of the formal legitimacy of decisions, further strengthened this trend and caused a loss of responsibility on the part of the administration (nor are such forms of control capable of hindering corruption, as '*Tangentopoli*' has shown).[6]

Thus, legal aspects were promoted to the detriment of those connected to effectiveness (Freddi 1989: 54; D'Amico 1992: 46), to an extent that it can be said that 'administrative law – based on procedural legitimacy, pervasiveness of preventive controls, uniform interpretation of provisions, distribution of tasks by law, lack of discretion – actually is Italian administrative culture'[7] (Dente 1988: 5). Both the political and administrative spheres appear to be a 'monopoly of the jurists'.[8] The conception bureaucrats have of their job is that it consists of interpreting and 'applying norms and regulations precisely' (Putnam 1975: 102), not of obtaining results; thus policies passed by politicians are often sabotaged *de facto*, albeit generally not as explicit expression of opposition from the bureaucracy, causing serious implementation deficits. Italian bureaucracy appears 'old and formalistic, lacks modern technical skills, is entangled in its procedures, doubts its own efficacy' (Passigli 1975: 233). The legal orientation also constitutes an effective screen that allows civil servants to protect themselves from unwanted intrusions from the outside and in a manner to enhance their self-interests.

Personnel training, typically legal, is partly related to this feature. However, the relevant point is not the type of education *per se*: legal training is typical of roman-law countries (Aberbach et al. 1981: 51–2); the relevant point in the Italian case is that the formalistic-legal culture has deeply permeated the entire structure of Italian administration, influencing the mentality and the operations of civil servants.

Other factors are relevant in forming the organisational culture, such as the fact mentioned above that careers typically take place within only one administration, producing a parochial vision that excludes consideration of issues from the point of view of other administrations (Minelli 1990: 189); discourages innovation and the circulation of new approaches; and encourages personnel to develop a 'patrimonial' conception of their post. The hierarchical and co-optation practices that govern access to higher levels of the career, coupled with the advanced age of executives on average, favour conformism rather than innovation (D'Auria 1990: 125). The importance attributed by personnel to security of post and salary, as discussed above, causes prejudice to other values such as performance, effectiveness, personal success, professional capabilities, interpersonal and inter-organisational competition. And finally, one should also note the high levels of frustration, lack of responsibility and alienation towards their tasks typical of a large number of civil servants.

As a way to overcome the difficulties posed by a civil service presenting such traits, the political system created the 'parallel administration' mentioned above; these special agencies presented a less legalistic and more result-oriented organisational culture as early as the 1920s and 1930s and still do to some extent in post-war Italy. In these special agencies, employees hold degrees in scientific and economic disciplines, are much more professionally competent, mobile and more achievement-oriented, and are more representative of the different areas of the country than the traditional bureaucrat (Passigli 1975: 232).

POLITICISATION

The Historical Evolution of Relationships Between Political and Bureaucratic Personnel

Notwithstanding the changes that have characterised the political system (constitutional monarchy, expansion of voting rights, Fascism, democratic Republic) over the more than 130 years since unification of the country, the administrative system has, generally speaking, remained insulated from the political domain, in the double sense of its connections with the latter and of being tempted to exert a political role itself.

The origins of the such separation date back to the 1853 reform that, among other issues, dealt with the relationships between the political and administrative spheres. Political personnel – the ministers – appointed by the king were put in charge of directing the administration and were solely responsible for their activities in front of the parliament; the ministers were also supposed to ensure the unity of administrative activities in terms both of policymaking and implementation (to use modern terminology). According to such a model, a *Segretario Generale* (usually of political extraction) acted as a *liaison* between the minister and the bureaucracy (Cassese 1983: 28–9). Civil servants were subordinated to both the ministers and the 'secretary general'. In 1888 the latter was substituted by a figure similar to the British parliamentary secretary, whose powers were decided upon by the minister, thus leaving something of a void between the political and the administrative élites, that eventually was filled during the first decades of 1900 by the heads of the *Direzioni Generali*, who became increasingly independent *vis-à-vis* the ministers.

Notwithstanding the cleavage introduced by such reform, and thanks to the relatively small size of the kingdom of Piedmont, the administrative and political élites remained deeply connected by personal ties, and even the intermediate levels of the bureaucracy presented a high degree of 'osmosis' with political personnel (Melis 1996: 48–50). In the larger unified nation, this feature was eventually lost: civil servants were recruited from different areas and social classes; the administration therefore could no longer be managed simply through shared values and personal ties. The progressive extension of voting rights and the rise of popular (Catholic and Socialist) parties further eroded the comfortable relationship between political and administrative élites (Cassese 1983: 67; Sepe 1987: 45). Whereas 'mixed' administrative/political careers were still frequent in the first 20 years after unification, they became increasingly rare even in the last decades of the 1800s. The cases of ministers coming from the bureaucratic ranks became less frequent. There were exceptions to this trend. Giolitti in the first decade of 1900 co-opted a number of highly competent top bureaucrats into his cabinet, and they acquired considerable influence. In the period between the end of the World War I and the rise of the fascist regime, the Nitti government relied heavily on a 'technocratic' top level bureaucracy, especially in the 'parallel administration', tightly connected with the ruling class that played an important political role in making important policies and promoting relevant pieces of legislation (Sepe 1987: 45).

The growing dimensions of ministries and the increasing protection conceded to employees by legislation made it increasingly difficult for the ministers to direct the organisations and personnel they were in charge of. Even in the statute of 1908, it is clear that employees were concerned with protecting themselves against interferences from the political sphere (this principle can be found in all personnel regulation since).

The Fascist regime abstained from excessive ideological intrusions into the administration (an important difference with the Nazi regime) beyond the propaganda façade, provided civil servants did not oppose the regime; politics and administration remained essentially separated (although the latter was subordinated to the former), also thanks to the role of the crown and the conception of the administration as politically neutral fostered by the Liberal (in the European sense of the word) ideology of the *Consiglio di Stato* (Guarnieri 1988: 75). It is true that all personnel had to be members of the Fascist party, but just because membership was compulsory, it did not imply a real selection of those ideologically supporting the regime (Guarnieri 1988: 76). Rather the regime left the direction of the administration to the internal hierarchy, strengthened by the De Stefani reform of 1923. All in all, Fascism gained consensus among public personnel by offering stability and status (connected to the role attributed in the Fascist ideology to the 'state', of which the civil service was part), while it had suffered in both respects during the previous period of war and economic crisis. The major exception was the prefects. In this case the regime, immediately after taking power, wanted to be sure it could count on the men in charge at the periphery (though it did not get to the point of including them into the party hierarchy as did the German Nazis). Nor did the regime extensively use the distribution of posts in the logic of a spoils system as far as the state administration proper was concerned. Only access to political posts was reserved to persons connected to the regime. In the case of the 'parallel administrations', the situation varied. While positions in those operating in the welfare field were often used to compensate the 'friends' of the regime, the financial-economic agencies set up by A. Beneduce – such as IMI and IRI – were often headed by managers coming from the private sector and staffed by highly specialised personnel with a technical background.

The Fascist period represented the definitive turning point in the relationships between the political and the bureaucratic systems, based on mutual non-interference into each others' spheres of influence. The fact that the administration was able to maintain a certain degree of autonomy from the regime fostered the idea within bureaucracy that it represented the 'continuity' of the state, whatever the political regime of the moment might be (Guarnieri 1988: 79).

No integration between the administrative and political élites exists at present (Cassese 1984: 36). It is very unusual for civil servants to engage in a political career, though legislation is extremely permissive in this respect (civil servants elected to representative bodies are entitled to a leave of absence). 'The number of civil servants present in the political arena in Italy is certainly one of the lowest among Western countries' (Cassese 1984: 38). Only 3–5 per cent of elected members of parliament come from the administration (plus 10 to 15 per cent of teachers).

Relationships between bureaucrats and politicians are characterised by considerable mistrust (Cassese 1984: 44). The former despise politics and fear that the latter might invade their sphere. Italian bureaucrats seem to be readier to criticise parties, politicians and parliament, and more worried about social conflict, less sympathetic towards political liberties and political 'pluralism' in general compared to their colleagues in other industrialised countries (Aberbach et al. 1981: 179–81).[9]

The post-war republican constitution appears to be mainly inspired by the will to separate the political and administrative spheres as much as possible, in order to avoid the risk that the administration could become a tool in the hands of a totalitarian regime. Also, the constitution of 1948 appears to be deeply influenced by the ideology of 'administrative neutrality and impartiality' (Melis 1996: 414), which also explains why it reserved the power to determine the structure and the functions of the administration to the parliament, rather than to the government. Thus the administration is subjected to two masters, government and parliament, but this by no means implies that it receives adequate guidance (Cassese 1984: 37).

Bureaucracy in the Policy Process

The idea that decisions are taken by the politicians and their implementation is the affair of the bureaucrats appears to be largely predominant. This, however, is not so much the effect of a 'Weberian conception of the role of bureaucracy' (Cerase 1990: 24), but rather the result of the peculiar evolution of bureaucracy in Italy and of the reciprocal rationalities of the two actors and the roles that each has chosen to play.

As a result of the above-described cleavage that has come into being between civil service and the political system, their relationship is based on an exchange, never explicitly formalised, but very clear to both parties. On one hand the administration abstains from interfering (unless requested to provide its input) from the policymaking processes. A number of analyses agree that Italian bureaucrats have a weak role and are not autonomous from political actors in policy formulation processes (Dente 1995: 45; Pasquino 1993: 12). As a result, civil servants typically hold a neutral posture towards policy decisions to the extent that they shy away even from appearing in public roles, for example in the media and so on (Regonini 1993: 47). A good example is offered by the prefects: unlike their French counterparts, Italian prefects have proven unable to carry out interest mediation between centre and periphery, so it must, therefore, occur through political channels (Melis 1996: 77-80; Tarrow 1977).

In exchange, the political system never seriously interferes with affairs concerning the civil service without its agreement (at least until recently). Management of careers (assignment to posts, promotions, deployment) is the domain of the administrations, of the unions and of the administrative courts, with minimum interference by the ministers; such activities represent the main concern of the civil service, interested only in safeguarding, and possibly increasing, its privileges and benefits (Cassese 1984: 43–5). The only area in which bureaucrats intervene directly in policymaking is when personnel policies are at stake (Pasquino 1993: 26): civil servants 'despise politics, but make use of it' (Cassese quoted in Aberbach et al. 1981: 233). A typical goal displacement phenomenon thus characterises Italian administration: personnel management has become its dominant task (Pipan 1992: 122). For the greater part of the last 50 years or so, most of the changes introduced in Italian administration have been focused on personnel (two-thirds of provisions on the public administration concern personnel), and these have always taken the interests of civil servants themselves into careful consideration either in the legislation, or in its implementation, while the system has been incapable of modifying the other variables that determine administrative performance (Capano 1993: 266).[10]

One piece of legislation, Act No 748/72, exemplifies this point very clearly. The provision aims at creating a managerial career distinct from the rest of the bureaucracy and attributing powers to it which are autonomous from those of the minister. In exchange for increased responsibilities, a 90 per cent increase in salaries was granted. In fact managers took the money, but refused to accept responsibilities and shied away from taking decisions, preferring the protection of hierarchy. Ministers themselves, who were supposed to issue general directives to their managers seldom did so (Cassese 1984: 53). The Act also gave the ministers the power to appoint top level executives (*dirigenti generali*), a power intended to create a trust relationship. In fact designation by government is used mainly to obtain consent and submission from the bureaucracy (a threat to obtain co-operation), rather than to put capable persons in charge of the administration. Also, the appointments usually simply follow the rules of the game established by the bureaucracy itself (that is seniority). Ministers prefer to rely heavily on their cabinets and on the legislative offices, formed by personnel chosen by the ministers personally, typically from special public bodies as the *Consiglio di Stato*, a 'nursery' of senior civil servants (Cassese 1984: 62) and the *Corte dei Conti* (Audit Court) and on commissions of experts, or on qualified experts 'borrowed' from public agencies and universities.

On the other hand the government was given the power to dismiss managers, but even this tool has been rarely used.[11] In fact, a minister who wants to get rid of a manager simply promotes him to one of several special bodies such as the Corte dei Conti or the Consiglio di Stato, where they are usually happy to go, due to the handsome salaries connected to such posts. All in all, the provision represented the price paid to top level bureaucracy in exchange for the powers transferred to the newly instituted regions, in order to maintain the co-operative relationship with the politicians in power (Cassese 1984: 49, D'Auria 1990: 135). The attempt to create an élite with autonomous decision powers, status and professional prestige failed (Capano 1992b: 241 ff.).

Another attempt in the same direction was made some 20 years later (Act No 29/93) by empowering managers with a general authority over administrative affairs (Capano 1993: 275, D'Orta and Diamanti 1994: 48). While political personnel is responsible for issuing the general objectives and directives of administrative action and assigning the necessary resources, managers are responsible for administrative, technical and financial management, and are empowered to adopt all necessary acts. They are also subject to a periodic evaluation of the results obtained. Once again, managers seem to be avoiding the role assigned by the legislator (D'Alberti 1994: 132 ff.), but recent governments continue to persist in their quest for means capable of making managers take responsibility and to be held accountable for results.

Summing up on this point, the basis of the relationship, at least until recently, can be described as an exchange of power and prestige for security of post and career. The two parties reached a *modus vivendi* based on a policy of reciprocal self-restraint. It is symptomatic that overt conflicts between ministers and higher bureaucrats are a rare event (Cassese 1984: 54–7). Politicians, as mentioned above, also buy off the consensus of top bureaucrats by granting additional benefits that can double or triple their income, such as the substantial indemnities deriving from being nominated as members of the boards of public bodies, which imply little additional work and power 'money against power' Cassese 1983: 73.

This 'arrangement' however is not without consequence. Politicians try to direct the activity of the administration towards their policy targets through laws and regulations. The culture of political personnel generally attributes scarce importance to administrative affairs; getting laws passed is considered sufficient: implementation will somehow follow. The bureaucracy however adopts a 'stick-to-the-rules' attitude in the implementation of policies, partly because this reflects its legalistic culture, partly because it tends to avoid any risks in carrying out activities that might jeopardise job security and career advancements, and partly also because it is suspicious of possible political intrusions.

Each new attempt by politicians to obtain desired behaviour from the administration only strengthens its legalistic attitude. In the end, procedures become extremely cumbersome and slow, increasing inefficiency; the situation can become even more entangled if the judiciary intervenes, as is often the case. The bureaucracy maintains its power thanks to the possibility of interpreting provisions at its discretion (and can exchange favours with politicians on this basis); the role chosen for itself of 'interpreters of the law' gives it considerable leeway and power. The process becomes a vicious circle (Cassese 1983: 69), in which the bureaucracy is a machine out of control, resisting any attempt to guide it (Regonini 1993: 32). This tendency has been further strengthened by the characteristic short tenure of ministers in their posts (less than 1 year in the past) and fragmentation in the political system which have encouraged the bureaucracy to 'rise above politics' and become fundamentally unresponsive.

At first glance, such a situation appears to be untenable since it would create a legitimacy crisis in the eyes of society, undermine the effectiveness of public policies and limit the system's capability to produce required innovations (as demonstrated by the failure of attempts to introduce substantial reforms in Italian society during the 1970s and 1980s (Cassese 1983: 70)). In fact, however, for part of the political system – that in power – the situation has offered considerable advantages (at least until the early 1990s) for a number of reasons. First of all, the polity could bypass the ineffective ministerial administration by resorting to the parallel administrations, more available to be influenced by the political system (Guarnieri 1988: 100) when it needed specific policies to be carried out.

Second, the satisfaction of regulatory or economic requests (increase in salaries, creation of new positions and new organisations that favoured promotions, and so on) of civil servants brought vast amounts of votes to the Democrazia Cristiana (and to a lesser extent to its minor allies).Thanks to its long permanence in power, the DC gradually managed to penetrate the ministerial administration, and vast sectors of the bureaucracy have supported the party.[12]

Also, the inertia of the administration made it possible to block policies that were unwelcome to social groups which supported the DC. Most important, the dominating party (and its internal fractions) was able to use the administration to support its clientelistic style of generating consensus in its own favour by creating a 'political market' based on the exchange of political support for either the procurement of posts within the administration itself, or of benefits (especially in the welfare field; Cassese 1984: 58) granted to clients through the manipulation of the bureaucratic apparatus (justified ideologically by the need to keep out the communist danger).

LaPalombara (1964) has showed how sectorial interest groups established clientelistic relationships with specific ministries based on the exchange of information and co-operation (the weakness of the administration put it in a subordinate position). This was the case of the powerful Confindustria – the national association of industrial firms – with the Ministry of Industry, or the union of school teachers with the Ministry of Education.

In other sectors the relationship could instead be defined as one of 'parentele' between the DC and organisations with the same (Catholic) ideology operating in specific sectors (e.g. agriculture). In such cases the DC obtained decisions and measures from the bureaucracy in favour of the organisations it supported (Allum 1976: 147-8). The administration eventually 'learned' from the political system to adjust its actions to the consensus of relevant interest groups. The point to be noted, however, is that this system did not aim at producing a diffused social consensus, but rather at satisfying a vast and incoherent array of 'corporative' and sectorial interests (Amato 1975: 492), that in return offered their support to the DC and its allies. Thus, in order to increase their influence, the politicians would typically either penetrate the administration down to the lower echelons, or bypass it all together directly carrying out tasks that should have belonged to the administration (Melis 1996: 516, Ferrera 1984: 202), depending on the specific situation.

Civil servants were willing to accept the intrusions in the administrative proceedings by politicians (both members of government and of parliament, as shown by Aberbach et al. 1981: 230) in order to satisfy their constituencies, in exchange of privileges and benefits (D'Amico 1992: 93). Due to this attitude, the bureaucrats have lost awareness of the group identity that had allowed them to remain somewhat autonomous even from the Fascist regime (Melis 1996: 499).

Last, but by no means least, not infrequently the use of the administration involved it in illegal activities and corruption (Melis, 1996: 515), also thanks to the weakness of controls and of the judiciary (paradoxically, the excess of laws – passed with the intention of preventing corruption – in effect allowed bureaucracy to manipulate them discretionally), as shown by '*Tangentopoli*' (1993); the financial resources extracted from such activities could go either to individuals or to political parties.

NOTES

1. Which explains why in terms of yearly *per capita* GNP, Italy is only number 19 (US$19 268).
2. An eloquent indicator of the anti-administration 'mood' of many Italians is represented by the results of national referenda held in March 1993; three (out of eight) of these concerned specific ministries (Agriculture, Tourism and *Partecipazioni Statali* responsible for state-controlled firms). A vast majority of citizens (respectively 70.1, 82.2 and 90.1 per cent) on this occasion voted in favour of the abolition of the ministries as a way to express a more general dissatisfaction towards public administration.
3. The prefect of Milan, for example, recently estimated that the state offices in his province (the economic capital of the country) were lacking 30 per cent of the required personnel (Sepe 1995: 305).
4. However, a subsequent sentence of January 1997 concerning another group of personnel took an opposite stand.
5. The data might be even higher: according to research carried out in 1960, more than 50 per cent were sons/daughters of civil servants (Allum 1976: 215).
6. The previously mentioned De Stefani reform of 1923, that aimed at cutting public expenditure, strengthened the accounting control of *the Ragioneria Generale* of the Finance Ministry over the other ministries. Parallel administrations represent an attempt to escape from the accountability and control system typical of the administration proper.
7. In a country like Italy where the level of interpersonal trust in the political culture is low (Guarnieri 1988: 102), this type of culture might also have a positive function insofar as it reassures citizens excluded from other channels of access (such as clientelism).
8. In this respect, it is worth noting that the actors of the reform policy are mainly specialists in public and administrative law rather than economists or social scientists (Dente 1988: 20).
9. However, this conclusion should be considered with caution due to the small size of the sample included in the survey, but especially considering the period in which the survey was carried out; no recent data are available, but it is possible that the generational turn-over might well have substantially modified executives' attitudes.
10. Only in recent years, has the focus been shifted from personnel to a broader reform of administrative performance and greater attention has been paid to serving the 'clients'. For example Act No 241/90 disciplined, for the first time, administrative procedures and consistently modified the relationship between citizens and civil servants (a recognition of 'administrative citizenship'; Melis 1996: 528) by means of such provisions as those indicating that

an identifiable employee responsible for the procedures concerning a specific act must be designated (a truly revolutionary change in the culture of Italian administration) and by regulating the right of access to administrative documents.

11. One of these cases occurred very recently when the Minister of Finance forced the General Director of State Monopolies to resign because of several mistakes committed.

12. Methods employed to assure conformity to the dominating political party were sometimes more brutal: rather than purging bureaucrats close to the previous Fascist regime, in the early fifties the government purged thousands of members of the leftist trade unions from the administration.

BIBLIOGRAPHY

Aberbach, J., R. Putnam and B. Rockman (1981*)*, *Bureaucrats and Politicians in Western Democracies*, Cambridge, MA: Harvard University Press.

Allum, P. (1976), *Anatomia di una Repubblica*, Milan: Feltrinelli.

Amato, G. (1975) La burocrazia nei processi decisionali, *Rivista Trimestrale Di Pubblico*, 2: 488–501.

Banfield, E.C. (1958), *The Moral Basis of a Backward Society*, New York: Free Press.

Benvenuti, F. (1962), 'La riorganizzazione del pubblico impiego in Italia', *Il Politico*, 2 (17): 342–57.

Capano, G. (1992a), 'La riforma del pubblico impiego', *Amministrare*, 2: 265–95.

Capano, G. (1992b), *L'improbabile riforma: Le politiche della riforma amministrativa nell'Italia repubblicana*, Bologna: Il Mulino.

Capano, G. (1993), 'Il decreto 29/93: 'La riforma del pubblico impiego', *Amministrare*, 13 (2): 265–95.

Cassese, S. (1977), *Questione amministrativa e questione meridionale*, Milan: Giuffré.

Cassese, S. (1983), *Il sistema amministrativo italiano*, Bologna: Il Mulino.

Cassese, S. (1984), 'The higher civil service in Italy', in E. Suleiman (ed.), *Bureaucrats and Policy Making: A Comparative Analysis*, New York: Holmes and Meier, 35–71.

Cassese, S. (1994), 'Aggiornamento sulla riforma amministrativa nel 1993–4', in S. Cassese and C. Franchini (eds), *L'amministrazione pubblica italiana: Un profilo*, Bologna: Il Mulino, 239–59.

Cerase, F. (1990), *Un'amministrazione bloccata*, Milan: F. Angeli.

Cerase, F. (1992), 'Organizzazione e cultura nella pubblica amministrazione italiana', *Rassegna italiana di Sociologia*, 33 (4): 507–34.

Cerase, F. (1993), 'Gli impiegati pubblici', in M. Paci (ed.), *Le dimensioni della diseguaglianza*, Bologna: Il Mulino.

Cerase, F. (1994), *I dipendenti pubblici*, Bologna: Il Mulino.

Chiarini, R. (1995), 'L'alta burocrazia ministeriale: Modelli di reclutamento e carriera', *Rivista Trimestrale di Scienza Politica*, 1 (15)(April): 119–54.

D'Alberti, M. (1994), 'L'alta burocrazia in Italia', in M. D'Alberti (ed.), *L'alta burocrazia*, Bologna: Il Mulino, 131–71.

D'Amico, R. (ed.) (1992), *Manuale di Scienza dell'amministrazione*, Rome: Edizioni Lavoro.

D'Auria, G. (1990), 'La politica di riforma amministrativa', in B. Dente (ed.), *Le politiche pubbliche in Italia*, Bologna: Il Mulino, 119–53.

Dente, B. (1988), *La cultura amministrativa italiana negli ultimi 40 anni*, proceedings of the conference on Culture and Politics in the Italian Republic, Bellagio: Rockefeller Center.

Dente, B. (1994), *I caratteri generali del processo di riforma*, proceedings of the conference "Reinventare la Pubblica Amministrazione", Turin: Fondazione G. Agnelli, December 2–3.

Dente, B. (1995), *In un diverso stato*, Bologna: Il Mulino.

D'Orta, C. and E. Diamanti (1994), 'Il pubblico impiego', in S. Cassese and C. Franchini (eds), *L'amministrazione pubblica italiana: Un profilo*, Bologna: Il Mulino, 45–64.

Ferrera, M. (1984), *Il Welfare state in Italia*, Bologna: Il Mulino.

Freddi, G. (1989), 'Burocrazia: Democrazia e governabilità', in G. Freddi (ed.), *Scienza dell'amministrazione e politiche pubbliche*, Rome: NIS, 19–66.

Guarnieri, C. (1988), 'Burocrazie pubbliche e consolidamento democratico: Il caso italiano', *Rivista Italian de Scienze Politica*, **1**: 73–103.

Heller, P. and A. Tait (1989), 'Raffronti internazionali sull'occupazione e le retribuzioni nella pubblica amministrazione', *FORMEZ, Le retribuzioni nel pubblico impiego*, **14**: 145–298 (Government, Employment and Pay: Some International Comparaisons, Documents of the IMF, Occasional Paper no. 24, april 1983).

ISTAT (1992), *Annuario statistico italiano*, Rome: ISTAT.

La Palombara, J. (1964), *Interest Groups in Italian Politics*, Princeton, NJ: Princeton University Press. (Clientela e parentela, Milano, edizioni Comunità).

La Spina, A. and G. Sciortino (1993), 'Common agenda, southern rules: European integration and environmental change in the Mediterranean states', in D. Liefferink, P. Lowe, and J. Mol (eds), *European Integration and Environmental Policy*, London: Belhaven, 217–36.

Lacava, C. and G. Vecchi (1994), *L'amministrazione nella XI legislatura, proceedings of the conference "Reinventare la Pubblica Amministrazione"* Turin: Fondazione G. Agnelli,.

Melis, G. (1996), *Storia dell'amministrazione italiana 1861–1993*, Bologna: Il Mulino.

Minelli, A. (1990), *Amministrazione, Politica, Società: Un'analisi comparata di sistemi amministrativi in azione*, Milan: F. Angeli.

Pasquino, G. (1993), 'I rapporti fra politici e burocrati', in G. Pasquino (ed.), *Politici e burocrati*, CNR and Istituto C. Cattaneo, 9–30.

Passigli, S. (1975), 'The ordinary and special bureaucracies in Italy', in M. Dogan (ed.), *The Mandarins of Western Europe: The Political Role of Top Civil Servants*, New York: J. Wiley, 226–37.

Pipan, T. (1992), 'La gestione del personale nel pubblico impiego', *Rivista Trimestale di Scienza dell'Amministrazione, 2*.

PCM (Presidenza Consiglio dei Ministri, Dipartimento per la Funzione Pubblica) (1993), *Rapporto sulle condizioni delle pubbliche amministrazioni*, Rome.

Putnam, R. (1975), 'The political attitudes of senior civil servants in Britain, Germany, and Italy', in M. Dogan, *The Mandarins of Western Europe: The Political Role of Top Civil Servants*, New York: J. Wiley, 87–126.

Putnam, R. (1993), *La tradizione civica nelle regioni italiane*, Milan: Mondadori. (*Making Democracy Work*, 1994 Princeton, NJ: Princeton University Press).

RGS (Ragioneria Generale dello Stato), Ministero del Tesoro (1992), *Conto annuale 1992: Il personale delle amministrazioni*, Rome: Istituto Poligrafico e Zecca dello Stato.

Ragioneria Generale dello Stato (RGS), Ministero del Tesoro (1994), *Conto annuale 1994: Il personale delle amministrazioni statali*, Rome: Istituto Poligrafico e Zecca dello Stato.

Regonini, G. (1993), 'Politici, burocrati, politiche pubbliche', in G. Pasquino (ed.), *Politici e burocrati*, CNR and Istituto C. Cattaneo, 31–58.

Rusciano, M. (1978), *L'impiego pubblico in Italia*, Bologna: Il Mulino.

Sepe, S. (1987), 'Il peso della tradizione e i problemi presenti: A proposito delle vicende storiche dell'Amministrazione centrale', *Rivista Trimestrale di Diritto Pubblico*, **2**: 41–82.

Sepe, S. (1995), *Amministrazione e storia*, Rimini: Maggioli.

Serrani, D. (1979), *L'organizzazione per ministeri*, Rome: Officina.

Tarrow, S. (1977), Between Center and Periphery: Grassroots Politicians in Italy and France, New Haven, CT: Yale University Press.

APPENDIX 9A

Table 9A.1 Development of the Italian state civil service over time in relation to population

Year	a Total number of state civil servants	b Population (000s)	b/a Ratio
1861	50 000 [a]	25 756	515
1881	64 992 [b]	29 278	450
1891	126 343	n.a.	
1901	n.a.	33 370	
1910	376 777 [c]	35 695 [g]	94.6
1921	519 440 [d]	37 404	72
1931	543 737 [e]	40 582	74.6
1941	1 139 774 [f]	n.a.	
1951	1 097 209	47 159	42.9
1961	1 296 136	49 904	38.5
1971	1 779 004	53 745	30.2
1981	1 963 360	56 336	28.6
1991	2 312 657	56 765	24.5

Notes:
a Figures are imprecise in the first decades due to the fact that the numbers of personnel with permanent positions were low, but activities were carried out by individuals who worked on temporary or even a voluntary basis, hoping to obtain a post subsequently (Melis 1996: 70).
b Excluding judges.
c Including personnel of *aziende autonome*.
d Including railway personnel.
e Including judges from here on.
f Since 1932 teachers of the elementary schools become state personnel.
g Figure for 1911.
Sources: Cassese 1983, 380 ff; PCM 1993: 225.

Table 9A.2 Size of state civil service and local and health service personnel on 31 December 1995

"Compartment"	Absolute numbers	Percentage of total civil servants
Ministries	286 783	8.7
School	1 031 122	29.6
Universities	109 420	3.2
Diplomats	901	0.03
Judges	9 685	0.3
Perfects	1 797	0.06
Police[b]	322 318	9.4
Military	139 590	3.8
Aziende autonome[a]	43 792	1.2
Total central state	1 945 408 [a]	
Local government	698 815	20
Health service	685 572	20.9
Other agencies	88 639	2.5
Total	3 418 434	–

Notes: a AIMA (agriculture surplus), Monopolies (tobacco, and so on), Fire Department, Cassa Depositi e Prestiti (loans to public bodies)
b Including: police, carabinieri, Guardia di Finanza, prison guards, forest guards, military chaplains.
Source: (RGS 1995: Vol. II p. 41–6) RGS December 31 1995, (2): 4–6.

Table 9A.3 'Enlarged' public sector (000s)

Year	1970[a]	1981	1991
Ministries	1 366	1 700	1 946
Aziende auto-nome	185	234	266
National welfare agencies	87	57	61
Electricity board (ENEL)	104	117	111
Municipal agencies	114	146	158
Local government	751	1 339	1 472
Other local bodies	424	638	745

Note: a Estimated figures
Source: PCM 1993: 213.

Table 9A.4 Women as per cent of civil servants

Ministries	44.8
Aziende Autonome	35.7
School	71.7
Health service	52.1
Local government	40.8
Non economic agencies	43.1
Research institutions	33.2
Average on total	51.8

Source: RGS 1992 Cerase 1994: 26.

Table 9A.5 Distribution of ministerial personnel among levels (percentage) at the end of 1994

Levels	Total	Women
Senior executives	0.15	0.01
Middle managers	1.67	0.33
Lower managers (Director Divisions)	0.4	0.06
Level 9	5.80	1.92
Level 8	2.58	1.15
Level 7	21.23	10.33
Level 6	7.5	3.52
Level 5	31.91	16.89
Level 4	19.12	5.89
Level 3	9.21	3.0
Level 2	0.25	0.1

Source: RGS 1994 Vol. (1): 96.

Table 9A.6 Salaries at various levels for different categories of state personnel in 1995 (first data: in lire; second data in US$)

Compartment/Levels	Senior Executive (*Dirigente Generale* A,B,C)	Middle manager (*Primo dirigente* or *dir. superiore*)	Professional (ninth *livello*)	Clerk (fourth *livello*)	Lowest position (second *livello*)
Ministries	129 822 000 / 81 138	79 373 000 / 49 608	52 160 000 / 32 600	30 254 000 / 18 908	28 863 00 / 18 03
School (75.8% of personnel are teachers)	61 244 000 / 38 277 (school principal)	46 243 000 / 28 901 (higher level teacher)	34 436 000 / 21 522 (lower level teacher)	37 896 000 / 23 685	24 454 00 / 15 28
Universities (44.25% of personnel are professors)	116 037 000 / 72 523 (full prof.)	82 431 000 / 51 519	50 751 000 / 31 719	27 773 000 / 17 358	23 761 00 / 14 85
Judges	303 220 000 / 189 512 (highest rank)	–	–	–	57 599 00 / 35 99 (lowest rank)
Prefects	103 327 000 / 64 579	78 781 000 / 49 238	41 381 000 / 25 863	–	–
Diplomats	524 458 000 / 327 786 (ambassador)	234 090 000 / 146 306	195 910 000 / 122 443 (average lower level embassy personnel)	–	–
Police	103 802 000 / 64 8762	84 008 000 / 52 505	59 094 000 / 36 933	35 283 000 / 22 051	–
Military	112 872 000 / 70 545 (Gen. to Col.)	73 455 000 / 45 909 (Lieutenant)	81 014 000 / 50 633	31 885 000 / 19 928 (V level)	–
Aziende autonome	149 807 000 / 93 629	79 823 000 / 49 889	50 758 000 / 31 723	32 384 000 / 20 240	24 986 00 / 15 61

Note: The Italian lire have been transformed into US$ at a rate of 1600 lire per dollar.
Source: RGS 1995.

Table 9A.7   Real salaries (index numbers: 1861=100)

Year	1881	1908	1923	1939	1956
Directive career	103.9	110.8	74.3	99.4	92
Employee career	98.5	134.5	82	108.2	109.1

Note: in the same period per capita GNP passed from 100 to 233
Source: Sepe 1995:345.

10. The Development and Current Features of the Spanish Civil Service System

Salvador Parrado Díez

INTRODUCTION

While the Spanish administrative system owes much of its present character to the French administration exported by Napoleon, other administrative traditions have also influenced the Spanish system giving the administration and civil service its distinctiveness. Spain has evolved from one unitary state into seventeen unitary states (*Comunidades Autónomas*) that have followed in a mimetic fashion the patterns of the ministries and civil service based in Madrid. The 'quasi-federal' status achieved by the system is very similar to that of Germany. Management techniques and new administrative fashions coming from Anglo-Saxon countries have been translated into Iberian administrative organisations with little success so far, and the most important reform of the Spanish public administration has nothing to do with the wave of 'New Public Management', but rather with the territorial devolution of political power.

In less than two decades, the system has evolved from a unitarian centralised state to a regional state. During the transition phase from Franco's dictatorship to democracy, the founders of the 1978 constitution decided to create, *ex novo*, a regional autonomous level. In doing so the nationalist political leaders from the Basque Lands and Catalonia (mostly of the latter) were accommodated and the present autonomic state (*Estado de las Autonomías*) was formed. The seventeen Autonomous Communities (AC) were created with their own parliaments, government and administrations. According to Agranoff (1994), and at the risk of over-simplification, some features of this regional level of government should be mentioned:

1. The agreements on autonomy were established from the very beginning on a bipartisan regional-national basis. The first agreements were made with the Basque and Catalan regions. The people in these areas have historically pressured the centre for autonomy. These negotiations-patterns formed the basis for future discussions with the other regions which desired the same degree of autonomy.
2. Attaining autonomy through the acquisition of functions by the ACs should be considered a 'process' and not as a 'system'. The construction of the autonomous state has followed an evolutionary pattern. Instead of getting an overarching agreement whereby certain central government functions were passed onto regional authorities from the very beginning, the transfer of services is still evolving in response to problems as they are encountered. In addition, personnel are still being transferred to the ACs.
3. Asymmetry is a working strategy for the historical regional authorities (in particular the Basque and Catalan regions). The constitution made it possible for the three historic territories of the Basque country, Catalonia, and Galicia to acquire autonomy by a faster route than other territories. These three regions, excluding Andalucía which is under a special constitutional provision, reached autonomy before the other communities. The rest acquired autonomy later and were originally granted more limited powers and subjected to a set of uniform conditions (e.g. size of cabinet, election dates, no-confidence votes).
4. Regarding the transfer of functions, legislation can be either exclusively a central government task or it can be shared with the ACs. If it is shared with the ACs, the basic legislation is considered a central governmental task while the detailed legislation falls in the domains of the ACs. The ACs normally carry out the implementation.

Due to the restriction of space, this chapter will focus only on the national service. None the less, the basic information for the national service on entry requirements, mobility and salary system is the same for the regional civil services as well. Therefore, much of this chapter can be considered accurate for the regional level.

The national Spanish civil service has been shaped throughout the last two hundred years, and owes much of its present nature to the role of political actors. Throughout history, the political context has influenced civil service reforms, sometimes stressing the improvement of performance in order to legitimise government activity and on occasion reinforcing political governance. Reforms have shown a power dynamic between the political and bureaucratic realms. Politicians have tried to control bureaucracy and to increase legitimacy by providing services more effectively. At the same time, bureaucrats have tried to avoid political control by creating groups of civil servants, corps, with self-ruling capacity and autonomy from political power.

The corps constitutes an organisational element of the Spanish civil service in several senses. They are the gateway for entry into public administration, and administrative careers have historically depended on the corps. The corps also operate as social-pressure groups within the public sector. Their role as pressure groups depends, according to Gutiérrez-Reñón (1987), on their numbers, internal cohesion and access to power centres. While the origins of corps and their primary goal was oriented on job security, the evolution of their objectives included increasing their administrative power by 'owning' sectors of the organisation, pursuing corporatist self-regulation, and controlling financing systems. The appearance of political parties and trade unions with the advent of full democracy in 1978 and with specific 1984 legislation has not undermined the strength of corps or their ability to dominate the administrative arena.

Spanish public sector personnel systems at all levels are regulated by the same basic legislation with a combination of tenured civil servants and staff contracted under labour regulations, an employment system combined with a career system and a co-existence of corps of functionaries with the employment system.

Most changes in the civil service have occurred in the form of transitions outlined by Heady (1996), from a military and ruler-responsive to a majority-party-responsive civil service; from a corporatist socio-economic context to a pluralist competitive environment; from civil servants as mission guiders to policy-responsive public servants; from a decentralised personnel management system to a division of personnel functions in a centralised fashion. These transitions occurred thanks to the political transition from Franco's dictatorship to democracy. Scholars agree that the transition from the former regime to the parliamentarian democracy occurred between 1975, with Franco's death, and 1978, with the endorsement of constitutional law. None the less, we propose in this text that the transition in public administration – and especially within the civil service – ended between 1982, with the entry of the Socialist government, and 1984, with the draft of new civil service legislation. The Socialist government which entered office in 1982 was the first democratic government whose members came from outside the state machinery. During Franco's reign, most cadres came from the state machinery and 40 per cent had held politically appointed positions with Franco. This changed in 1982 when the cadres of the Socialist Party originated from outside the bureaucracy and only 5 per cent of political appointments had held previous political offices with Franco and 15 per cent with the previous transitional government (Parrado Díez 1996). The reform that shaped the civil service into its present nature was approved by parliament in 1984. This civil service reform must be considered since transformations in the Spanish civil service have mostly taken place after its inception.

In this chapter, four topics are examined. The first section is devoted to the history of the Spanish civil service. The second section deals with internal labour market relations. The third section focuses on the issue of politicisation. Section four depicts the social image of civil servants using survey data. In the conclusion, we relate the several transformations experienced by the Spanish civil service to the configurations designed by Heady (1996).

THE DEVELOPMENT OF THE CIVIL SERVICE SYSTEM

The Spanish civil service has evolved through a piecemeal process lasting several centuries. To define the Spanish civil service as a unified body may present an inaccurate impression since most steps, reforms, evolutions and involutions have occurred without considering the system as a whole. While reforms have attempted to address the civil service system as an homogeneous entity, civil servants have organised into autonomous corps, established parallel organisational structures, avoided general rules and sought at most times to maintain and promote their own privileges.

Origins: The Servants of the King (Eleventh–Eighteenth Centuries)

Antecedents of the Spanish civil servants can be found in the servants working for the monarchy under the command of the ruler from the eleventh and twelfth centuries. The importance of those servants within the machinery of the monarchy depended mainly on the control of the ruler over the territory and on the relationships between the king's private household and the administration of the territory under its power. Unlike other European territories where the monarch had very limited powers during medieval times, Castillian kings centralised all territorial forces to expel the Arabians from the Iberian lands during the Reconquista. A handful of feudal lords without a strong king would probably not have succeeded in the enterprise. The continuous war conditions of former Spanish kingdoms made monarchs strong against feudal lords (Beneyto 1958). In this first phase, civil servants can be fully identified as personal servants according to the terminology of Raadschelders and Rutgers (1996), in the sense they were personal servants of the ruler, and they managed both the monarch's household and the state's household at the same time.

During the thirteenth century, efforts of Spanish kings to distinguish among personal activities and administrative tasks began to appear. Some officials performed administrative tasks and personal duties for the king, but regulations to differentiate public and private responsibilities were drafted and a legal profile protecting ethical principles appeared (Beneyto 1958). Somehow during the thirteenth century, civil servants became state servants.

In other countries, this happened during the seventeenth and eighteenth centuries (Raadschelders and Rutgers 1996). The church entered the administrative domain of the absolutist state. Many influential posts were held by clergymen who disputed offices with lawyers even in the field of administration of justice (Beneyto 1958).

The transformation of the Spanish crown into an empire and a power during the sixteenth and eighteenth centuries brought about the concomitant increase of the monarchy's tasks. Meanwhile a distinction between political or high rank posts and technical or middle rank posts began to take place. Top offices were mostly held by clergymen while medium level posts were destined for lawyers. Nevertheless, it would be premature to consider civil servants of the period as public servants. According to the definition of Raadschelders and Rutgers (1996), the division of the political and the administrative sphere and the circulation of theories about public office at universities (Beneyto 1958) hint at the appearance of public servants as a coherent category.

The Beginnings: The Spoils System and Civil Service Reforms (Nineteenth Century)

Regulations and developments in the nineteenth century shaped the civil service as an embryo of the present system. During this period, two factors were continuously present: militarisation and political control of the civil service. Regarding the military element, the nineteenth century was a convulsive period of continuous wars and decolonisation of Spanish domains in Latin America. The soldiers who returned from Latin America, where they were no longer needed, came back to Spain and were always offered an administrative post. This militarisation process took place at the administrative level and in the political arena. Several coups d'etat and military uprisings throughout this century brought military cadres into top political executive positions. The influence of the military culture was so strong that many behaviour patterns of the military regime were transferred to administration and, for certain periods, administrative officeholders had to wear an uniform during duty hours (Jiménez-Asensio 1989).

Concerning the politicisation of the civil service, two influences of politics on civil service must be considered: (1) the spoils system and purges encouraged by alternative political parties in government, military uprisings and dictatorships; and (2) the role of civil servants in elections. Although, military culture is supposed to be less political in nature, the continuous engagement of military cadres through the multiple upsurges of the nineteenth century made officers in top levels more politically aware. This politicisation of military cadres was compatible with a militarisation of administration at lower levels.

The spoils system version, which appeared in the constitutional text of 1812, lasted until 1918, and compelled all employers appointed by a previous government to leave office with the entrance of a new government. Moreover, office leavers could not be offered another job elsewhere. This phenomenon was labelled *cesantía*. The opposite phenomenon, *empleomanía*, describes a situation where partisans expect to receive a job as a reward for their dedication to the political cause, that is the bureaucracy was the patrimony of the government. In fact, it was the post, or rather the employment, and not the employee which was the subject of transaction. The job was the good to be rented or sold (Nieto 1986), and when the formation of cabinets was a consequence of military risings, there was a clear link between militarisation and the spoils system.

Civil servants played an important role in elections. During the alternation system between liberals and conservatives in the period from 1875 to 1917, governments stayed in office for relatively short periods of time (from several months to three or four years) and elections became the rule. Civil servants were allowed to vote and were capable of guaranteeing the continuity of the political party already in power. Jiménez-Asensio (1989) shows that electoral rolls were altered to favour the number of civil servants to be included in the limited suffrage. In addition, civil servants voted in groups, decorated their uniforms (el pucherazo) to make their choice apparent, the governmental choice, more evident.

Since the spoils system placed job security at risk, most civil service reforms during the nineteenth century and the first two decades of the twentieth century attempted to tackle this problem. The civil service has experienced five reforms since the beginning of the nineteenth century. The first two, the reform of the treasury administration by López Ballesteros (1827) and the reform of Bravo Murillo (1852) will be addressed in this section, while the remaining three, Estatuto de los Funcionarios (1918), Ley articulada de Funcionarios Civiles del Estado (1964), and Ley 30/1984 de Medidas para la Reforma de la Función Pública will be dealt with in subsequent sections.

Some similarities and differences can be found between the two reforms of the first half of the nineteenth century. Reforms were not embedded in a general restructuring movement of the state machinery. While their goals aimed at covering the whole civil service, the specialised corps avoided inclusion in the reform. The departmentalisation of Spanish administration and the formation of specialised corps became obstacles to global reforms. A multiple system was formed throughout the nineteenth century: a general system for relative small numbers of civil servants and specialised systems with the creation of autonomous bodies of functionaries (corps), for whom the general rules did not apply.

Reforms had a rather nominal effect since in administrative reality, most statements were continuously reverted to the former situation. This happened, for instance, with the declarations on the spoils system – cesantías – on numerous occasions.

In Ingraham's terminology (1996), the dominant tradition of both reforms was the management tradition, since efficiency and economic rationality of the civil service prevailed over governance and political legitimacy, although the attempt of Bravo Murillo (1852) was directed toward achieving political legitimacy. According to Nieto (1986), Bravo Murillo was the first technocrat and member of the government who viewed the bureaucracy as an independent power because he aimed for the reform of the civil service without the intervention of parliament. He desired to use bureaucracy as a means of governing the country.

The second half of the nineteenth century and the first decade of the twentieth century was void of general reforms. Global legislation required strong and long lasting governments and the political turnover was too intense to launch a reform. To overcome this obstacle, annual budgetary laws were frequently used to introduce some measures in the civil service. In the Budgetary Law of 1864, for instance, the division between politics and administration within the executive was established. At that time, only civil servants could be politically appointed without *merit concours*. Later on, outsiders were considered for appointments.

Consolidation: Bureaucratisation of Public Offices (1900–80)

World War I, with its political, social and economical crisis, brought about a considerable change in governmental policy related to the civil service, even though Spain did not take part in the conflict. Low-level functionaries and workers of private enterprises were severely hit by the economic crisis. Civil servants also participated in uprisings and strikes during 1917 and 1918. The government reacted with the launch of the Estatuto de Funcionarios (1918). Top civil servants did not participate in the uprisings, in fact, they attempted to help repress the movement to some extent, since this revolutionary upsurge did not conform to their needs (Nieto 1986).

The three most relevant goals of the 1918 reform aimed at increasing the salary of civil servants, achieving job security and using open competitive exams for recruitment thereby burying the spoils system. These measures were applied to all civil servants who were not grouped into special corps since the members of these corps had already achieved tenure and open competitive exams was the rule for their recruitment.

The 1918 reform differs from the previous ones in two relevant aspects. First, the reform had real effects, that is the spoils system was abolished and job security was guaranteed. Second, the governance tradition prevailed over managerial principles since politicians were interested in controlling bureaucracy and in making government effective. Nevertheless, since there was a dual system, the legislation only affected those who did not belong to a corps. The civil servants who belonged to a corps had a distinct and ad hoc set of regulations. This dual system prevailed until 1984.

The 1918 legislation ended the spoils system and tenure of office became a feature for all civil servants. In spite of the legislation, the spoils system was re-adopted during the dictatorships of both Primo de Rivera (1923–1931) and Franco (1939–75) by purges. In the former case, university professors were dismissed for opposition to the dictator, while in Franco's regime, all civil servants who had been identified with the Republican government or had shown a non-active compliance with the principles of the political movement had to leave office. With the purges, job security and tenures were temporarily abolished. The need for new cadres during the post civil war period (1936–39) brought a group of individuals to the adminis-tration who were politically identified with the new regime but not always professionally competent. The political class was also replaced by an inexperienced group of politicians who lacked knowledge about politics and the bureaucracy.

The 1964 civil service reform coincided with the economic boom (Ley articulada de Funcionarios Civiles del Estado). It created a centralised body to deal with personnel matters (Comisión Superior de Personal) and a job classification system to combine with the corps. A career system was introduced, but the results were far from satisfactory (Baena 1993). Although the combination of a position structure and corps on which to pursue an adminis-trative career was attempted, it was not evident that legislation was aimed at achieving the fusion of all specialised systems of grand corps, that is those corps requiring a university degree.

The 1964 reform diverged from previous reforms in several aspects. The act was concomitant to other reforms of the 1960s which aimed at changing some procedures and basic laws concerning the administration. Those reforms attempted to legalise the state in the absence of democracy. The civil service reform complied with the efficiency and the governance tradition. On the one hand, it focused on the management tradition of increasing the efficiency of the civil service; on the other hand, the 1964 act perpetuated the power of grand corps that also dominated political power. Most political posts of the executive were occupied by members of the major corps: ministers, 80 per cent; under secretaries, 92 per cent; and general directors, 90 per cent (Alvárez 1984). Bureaucrats also controlled the Cortes, the House of parliament, installed by Franco in 1943 (Linz and De Miguel 1975; Bañón 1978). Moreover, bureaucrats held a variety of positions in public and private enterprises at the same time (Baena 1977). This helps to explain the great power of bureaucrats who embodied the core of a power elite (Mills 1956), and suggests that the 1964 reform was one which increased political governance on behalf of a few.

Reform and Attempt of Modernisation (1980s–90s)

The current civil service system was finally formed after the 1984 act of parliament of the socialist government with some amendments that have been added during the last years. Attempts to reform the system have been negotiated at the executive level with regional authorities. The newest piece of legislation, which is likely to pass through parliament, grants more freedom to each individual regional authority to regulate its civil service. This procedure makes personnel systems more operational and more responsive to local needs; however, it also poses a question of state cohesion since mobility within the administration will be severely restricted.

The main goal of the 1984 civil service reform was to undermine the power of corps. Basically, three components of corps power can be identified during Franco's dictatorship: (1) they had a self-financing capacity through special taxes they charged citizens for the services they provided; (2) they had a self-governing capacity to protect their interests; and (3) they could veto proposals of politicians in personnel matters. Corps had an independent power and they used it to treat the administrative organisation as a part of their patrimony. In fact, the socialist government tried what previous governments never dared: to challenge the grand corps, those whose members have a university degree. In this sense, the 1984 reform could be considered historical. Although the attack on corps strength was the avowed objective of government, Suay thinks that it was not necessary to use new legislation to undermine corps power because they had already lost it. Suay gives two reasons for this belief: (1) 1965 legislation forbade civil servants from charging citizens for the services they provided; and (2) the transition from dictatorship to democracy in 1975, brought political parties and trade unions into the scene and they were attempting to replace the grand corps in the exercise of power.

The 1984 reform should finally establish an open system based upon posts over a close system defined through an administrative career that had been dominated by corps in the past. The content of the reform can be reduced to a number of principles. A post system was established and, based on a 1988 law that modified 1984 legislation, only those posts placed at the lowest levels of the hierarchy could be given under labour contracts. The rest should be granted to civil servants. Second, the constitutional tribunal states that the normal provision of vacancies should not be filled using labour contracts. Posts would no longer be assigned to a particular corps. Members of any corps could apply for the job if they possessed the required educational level and personal grade. Those corps that performed similar functions were combined into one; for instance, several corps of tax comptrollers became one corps. Finally, corps would only have influence upon entry into public administration and they would no longer be relevant for salaries, which would be related primarily to the job in the future.

When interviewed about the reform, grand corps members shared the criticism against corps and applauded the main principles of the reform: they preferred to be paid according to the post they hold and not based on the corps they belonged to. They would accept a more rigid system of incompatibilities, they thought that there were too many corps whose differences, in fact, only served to hide the privileges they enjoyed. None the less, those interviewed suggested that any criticism was more accurately directed to other corps and not to their own (Beltrán 1985).

The 1984 act was meant to be provisional until the principles of the system were more precisely defined. The Modernisation Programme (MP) of public administration that the socialist government designed during the late 1980s and early 1990s could have made the provisional status of the 1984 Act definitive in the sense that the relationship between payment and job performance required a different type of organisation.

The MP was the commitment of the government to improve and reinvent the public sector. It was launched in the late 1980s with the aim of introducing more efficient and effective delivery of public services and goods to citizens. The ultimate objective of the MP, with regard to human resources, was the introduction of a 'new managerialism'. It was envisaged that 'new public managers', responsible for the execution of public programmes, would be operational at the end of the modernisation process. This involved organisational redesign, the introduction of budgeting by objectives and human resources reorganisation. However, the attempt to reinvent government failed and only some of the organisations which became agencies have overcome bureaucratic rigidity to provide more efficient services.

THE INTERNAL LABOUR MARKET

The Size and Distribution of the Civil Service

In 1996, almost two million public servants worked at the national (43.6 per cent), regional (33.2 per cent) and local level (23.2 per cent). As a result of the decentralisation process, the greatest bulk of civil servants is slowly being transferred to the regional level (MAP, 1998). The division between civil servants and those contracted under labour legislation varies enormously for the national and the regional levels. If doctors, nurses and teachers are not considered, the proportion of civil servants in ministries at the national level (76 per cent) is higher than at the regional level (see Table 10.1).

At the local level, an important distinction is made in Table 10.1. In local corporations, there are some civil servants who are recruited at the national level (that is secretary of the city council) but the percentage (1.4 per cent), like its role, is small. At the local level, locally employed public servants with civil service status or with labour contracts (98.6 per cent) make up the greatest bulk of local personnel.

Table 10.1   Size of the Spanish national civil service (1996)

Level	Number	Percentage
Central level[a]	798 668	43.5
Central ministries and autonomous bodies[b] (100%)	438 147	23.9
a) Civil servants (76%)	332 991	18.2
b) Labour contracts (19.4%)	85 000	4.6
c) Others (4.6%)	20 154	1.1
– Civil staff of military ministry	37 249	2.0
– Security forces	125 088	6.8
– Doctors and nurses	132 234	7.2
– Public corporations	65 950	3.6
Regional autonomous administration	608 926	33.2
– Regional ministries and autonomous bodies (100 %)	233 291	12.7
(a) Civil servants (52.9%)	123 291	6.7
(b) Labour contracts (47.1%)	110 000	6.0
– Others	375635	20.5
Local administration (100%)	425 156	23.2
– Nationally recruited civil servants (1.4%)	5 723	0.3
– Locally employed personnel (98.6%)	419 433	22.9
Total = 100%	1832 750	

Notes: a 80 765 staff (teaching and administrative) members of universities are not included.
        b Public servants of Independent Agencies and Social Security Administration staff
          are included.
Source: MAP 1996.

Civil servants who were not transferred from the central level to the regional authorities were mostly engaged in service delivery functions. The new planning and coordinating role of the central level compels civil servants to adapt themselves to the new situation. As a consequence of this, the distribution of human resources is geographically and functionally unequal in Spanish central administration (MAP 1998). There are ministries and provinces which are overstaffed. For example, in the Ministry of Agriculture and in the province of Madrid, civil servants were not transferred to Autonomous Communities (ACs) and coordinating and planning functions have remained in these organisations. Other ministries and agencies which deliver services (Traffic

Agency, Police Forces) have considerable personnel deficits. The workload in such agencies is greater and the pay is lower than in other public organisations which have coordinating functions. These issues are being reviewed by central bodies when considering issues of entry and mobility.

Entry and Formal Mobility

The civil service system must be regulated by law and not by administrative functioning with regard to the following issues: acquisition and loss of civil servant status, administrative career, incompatibilities, rights, duties and responsibilities, disciplinary rules, the creation of corps.

The Spanish civil service is a mixture of several contradictory dimensions. Human resources are composed of tenured functionaries and employees permanently contracted under labour regulations with a predominance of the former (76 per cent) over the latter at the national level in 1996. The distribution at the regional level is more even with civil servants comprising 52.9 per cent, and labour contracts comprising 47.1 per cent (see Table 10.1). Yet, an employment system organised in a hierarchical manner in order to promote career advancement based on job performance is combined with the corps system for the civil servants which still attempts to influence the administrative career of their members. Neither features the generalisation of an administrative career open to the entire public sector, especially in regional governments, where less than half of employees have civil service status. It is in this context that entry and mobility are to be understood.

Entry to public administration is achieved through an open competitive exam which normally consists of testing memory on several dozen topics and examining reasoning skills by way of a practical exercise. Before the 1984 legislation, each corps used to decide when new members should be recruited, and the evaluation commission of the exam was monopolised by corps members. Nowadays, access to the civil service is annually centralised through the Public Employment Offer, for which ministries advance proposals about their needs of new staff and corps members may not be in majority in the evaluation commission of exams. Entry has been restricted as a consequence of a policy to cut down public sector expenditure. Between 1990 and 1997, only 8 000 new employees entered the central administration (MAP 1998). The central civil service unit is imposing tight control on recruitment, so that only agencies at the central level which are understaffed are allowed to increase their personnel. However, before recruiting outside staff, central units of the civil service are bargaining with trade unions about the compulsory mobility among central ministries from over-staffed agencies whose functions have already been devolved to under-staffed agencies at the regional level which still deliver services to citizens (post offices, employment offices, social security and the like). Agencies have reacted against this policy by intensively using temporary contracts for jobs of structural nature.

Once the exam has been passed, a civil servant receives an initial grade. Each grade can be 'consolidated' in the personal record after two years in the post of the same level or of a higher level. No matter how many levels higher the post is than the personal grade, a civil servant can only 'consolidate' two grades each two years. For instance, if the difference between the level of the post and the grade is six grades, this individual must stay in this post at least six years in order to 'consolidate' the level of the post as a personal grade. Advances up the administrative ladder constitute the career opportunity for the civil servant. Educational requirements are established for entry into any corps (see Table 10.2).

Table 10.2   Distribution of civil servants among groups of entry according to educational title

Groups	Educational title	Minimum level	Maximum level
A	4–6 years at university	20	30
B	3 years at university	16	26
C	A levels	11	22
D	16 years education	9	18
E	14 years education	7	14

Source: R.D. 364/1995, art. 71.1.

Public sector mobility among different administrative levels (central, regional and local) has been allowed since the 1984 Act, although it will depend on the job requirements. During the devolution process of central functions and services to regional authorities, personnel was also transferred with the services, although top central civil servants were reluctant to work for regional authorities because they feared that salary would be lower and career perspectives narrower. There are also opportunities for vertical mobility (intra-departmental) and for horizontal mobility (inter-departmental) within central level. The most important requirement one must take into account is the administrative level of the vacancy. If the level corresponds to a group (A, B, C, D, E) higher than the group of the corps a civil servant belongs to, he must do a public competition exam prior to entry in the corps of the higher group. The civil servant of a lower group has an advantage in the exam because a percentage of jobs is reserved for internal promotion. If the applicant for a vacancy is in the range of administrative levels he could apply for, the normal mobility rules apply.

In the past, the members of the grand corps attempted to colonise a domain of the administration and prevent other corps members from working in that area. For instance, diplomats did not allow economists or civil administrators to work in the Ministry of Foreign Affairs. This practice was abolished by 1984 legislation. The 1984 reform tried to weaken the grand corps through the introduction of a 'post' system, grouping posts into levels or ranks (7 to 30) and establishing educational requirements for entry into those levels (see Table 2). Up to level 29, posts are filled through *merit concours*, whilst posts at level 30 are filled through a non-meritocratic process. The incumbent of a post in level 30 must leave office at the will of the recruiter or an incoming superior post-holder. The civil servant who holds an office at this level may be downgraded to an inferior post but still retains grade 30 status, if he or she has been in post for at least two years.

Another important issue dealt with by legislation was regulating the ability of civil servants to hold two or more jobs. The presence of bureaucrats in public and private enterprises, as well as membership of the Cortes permitted under Franco was outlawed in 1984 (Ley 53 de Incompatibilidades). Civil servants cannot hold more than one public sector job and restrictions are also placed on holding posts in the private sector. The restrictions are mainly related to the posting allowances that the civil servant receives and with the type of activity to be undertaken in the private sector. These provisions hinder the mobility between private and public sector.

In Spain, managers have been allowed to spend several years in the private sector. After a limited period outside, they must return to their previous positions or they lose their rights and privileges. Until 1996, there was restrictive legislation regarding career leaves. After fifteen years in the private sector – considering the most favourable cases – civil servants should return to public administration, otherwise they would lose the status of public servants. Those civil servants may have to enter administration against their will and their entry may also cause uneasiness in the organisation as they choose where they want to work (regardless of the amount of staff in that particular organisation) and perhaps in a period of severe recruitment constraints. Although there are no data to illustrate this problem, it was a concern of MAP for several years before a solution was found. Legislation in 1996 (Ley 13/1996 de Medidas Fiscales, Administrativas y del Orden Social) has abolished the maximum period of time that civil servants may remain at the private sector.

The Salary System

The group in which the corps is included and the personal grade of civil servants are relevant for salary. The payment system is common to all civil servants while the department determines pay scales for contractual and blue-collar workers. Payment depends mainly upon the post held and not upon the corps, as was the case before 1984. Before 1984, as Seage points out, salary depended on membership in a determined corps and the coefficient used in working out the salary amount was rather discretionary since it was conditioned by the power that the corps enjoyed. Furthermore, the payment system was not competitive with private sector enterprises nor with other public organisations like local corporations that could always attract civil servants from the national level. Legislation since 1984 should ultimately overcome these problems. In the present system, there are four main components: basic salary and *trienios* represent 30 to 50 per cent of total remuneration depending on the administrative level and post held (see Table 10.3 and Figure 10.1).

Table 10.3   Annual distribution of salary and allowances in US$ (1997)
(1$=140 ptas)

	Salary	Trienios[a]	Rank	Post[b,c]	PRP[d] (*)	Total
30-A	13 031.7	2 502.0	11 443.1	19 542.8	5 314.2	51 834.0
26-B	11 060.4	2 001.4	8 247.3	7 367.8	4 714.2	33 391.3
22-C	8 244.7	1 502.1	6 022.1	478.6	3 257.2	19 504.7
18-D	6 741.5	1 002.8	4 663.1	478.6	3 000.0	15 885.9
14-E	6 154.4	752.1	3 602.2	478.6	2 571.4	13 558.8

Notes:
a Each three years there is an annual amount to add. For this table, it is considered that a civil servant has 5 trienios, which is average in a relatively ageing public administration.
b Average post allowance.
c 15 per cent of 22, 18 and 14 post holders receive a higher post allowance. Here, only the minimum is considered.
d Performance related pay.
Source: Ley de Presupuestos 1997; data estimated for Post and (*) PRP (Performance Related Payment).
This table pertains to civil servants at the top levels (30, 26, 22, 18, 14) of each educational group (A, B,C, D, E).

Trienio is a fixed amount of money granted every three years of service. Guaranteed allowances make the second major bulk of the whole salary. Important components are the rank allowance (depending on the personal grade or on the level of the post being held), the post allowance (depending on the particular features of the job) and the individual allowance (similar to the concept of performance-related payment (PRP) which depends upon the productivity of the person). For all hierarchical levels, salary and rank allowance are established in an Annual Budgetary Law, whilst posting allowance and individual allowance are determined by each ministry. In reality, however, the individual allowance is normally agreed upon with the relevant trade union for each administrative level and only in extreme cases will the superior deny the PRP complement to a public servant.

Figure 10.1   Distribution among salary and allowances (1997) (per cent)

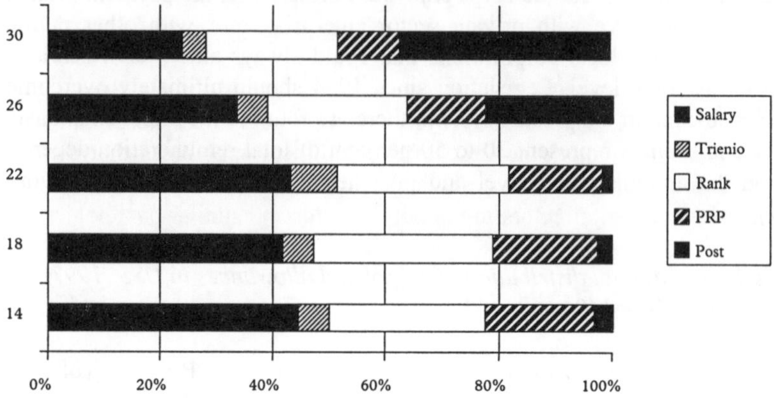

Source: (Ley de Presupuestos 1997; data estimated for Post and PRP).

Trade unions play different roles in salary negotiations according to employment status. Pay for civil servants is negotiated centrally while salaries for contractual staff is negotiated at the ministry level. The most relevant factor in adjusting pay is the forecast rate of inflation and negotiations are made on annual basis. Trade unions' bargaining powers are mostly deployed to assist contractual staff although all public servants benefit from the results if government agrees on general issues. Top civil servants will receive relatively little benefit from negotiations since their representation in trade unions is practically non-existent (Ortega 1992).

The public sector harms its position in the labour market since it traditionally offers lower pay conditions than private enterprises for managers with the same type of rank and functions, as Gutiérrez-Reñón and Labrado-Fernández (1988) observed when comparing trends of public and private sector pay in 1987 (see Figure 10.2). Although the study is more than ten years old, most of the results are believed to hold true nowadays as well.

The assessment of posts in private and public sector undertaken by Hay Management Consultants was based on the analysis of the knowledge required to carry out the functions associated with the post, on the capacity to solve problems and on the responsibilities linked to the functions of the post. Each factor was assigned a value between 50 and 1 640 points. General directors, next rank to top civil servants of level 30 and politically appointed are included in the illustration. According to Gutiérrez-Reñón and Labrado-Fernández (1988), one can see four basic trends in public pay: (1) generally speaking, salary in the private sector is higher than in the public sector if jobs with similar content and responsibilities are considered; (2) in the first range of the x axis (200–700 points), responsibilities, job content and salary increase accordingly; (3) in the second range (700–1200 points), civil servants in levels 29 and 30, the rather small salary increase does not relate to an increase of technical difficulty and responsibilities; (4) in the third range (1300–1600 points), the increase of responsibility does not correspond in the case of general director (the first level of political appointees that can be recruited from outside the civil service) with an increase of salary, and the gap between general directors in the public sector and similar post holders in the private sector was of US$5000 in 1987.

Figure 10.2   Annual wages in the private and public sectors according to post assessment (1987) (in million pesetas)

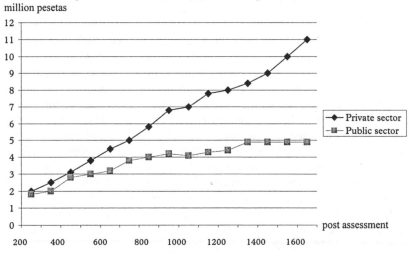

Source: Gutiérrez-Reñón and Labrado-Fernández, 1987, p. 96. The post assessment of Hay Consultants has been used. Equivalence in US$ (1$= 140 ptas) for Figure 10.2.

Since public sector salaries cannot compete with private enterprise for high rank officials, there has been a process of 'agencification' in the Spanish system since the budgetary law of 1991. As a result, more than 30 agencies, for example the National Airports Association, Post and the Tax Agency among others, have been created to operate under private law regarding human resources and contracts with providers. This shift allows agencies to contract personnel for top positions and to assign different salaries for all staff. Agency salaries are able to compete with private enterprise payments.

Real Mobility: Functioning of the System

Informal rules modify substantially legal provisions for mobility and payment. In comparative terms, the salary level and salary increases between posts of different responsibilities in the public sector are far behind the private sector (see Figure 10.2), however it helps to understand how administrative careers operate in the Spanish civil service system. In fact, advances up the administrative ladder imply a combination of acquiring a higher echelon in the hierarchy and better post allowances in the new post. The post system can be used, theoretically, to allocate human resources in a more rational way by promoting based on merit. However, there are two major aspects still controlled by corps.

One, the corps is still effective in obtaining favourable initial posts for their members. Members from Group A normally enter at level 20 (see Table 10.2), but in influential corps, such as civil administrators, diplomats and finance comptrollers, level 26 or 28 is common for beginners. The implication of the first dimension is that the administrative career for top civil servants, those that belong to a corps in Group A, is rather short. In less than six or eight years, a well-placed civil servant who has connections within the corps could reach level 30, the peak of his career. The appointment to level 30 posts is based on the discretionary powers of the general director (a politically appointed official), who will recruit the deputy general directors (level 30) among civil servants. Since more than 80 per cent of general directors belongs to a grand corps (Parrado Díez 1996), contacts within the corps will be very useful for those civil servants placed at the best positions in the ministry who also belong to the same corps of the general director. Level 30 post holders can be dismissed through the same mechanism and can be downgraded on the administrative ladder, although he may have consolidated personal grade 30 and the correspondent salary allowances will be paid while the posting allowance will be a smaller sum of money.

On the other hand, the corps lobby effectively to obtain posts with special salary allowances for extra responsibilities (posting allowance). As can be seen from Figure 10.2, post allowance grows with the increase of the personal grade or administrative level applied to the civil servant. The basic remuneration for upper level posts are based mostly on post allowance, while the basic remuneration for lower level posts depend on salary. The use of post allowance counterbalances the non-distributory effects of the basic salary established in the annual budgetary law. Posting allowances differ considerably among posts for which a person with the same consolidated grade is required. In some way, the search for posts with better salary constitutes an informal career of civil servants. In some cases, post allowances of deputy general directors are higher than the same salary complement of general directors, who are politically appointed to a higher level. The political appointment is not an incentive from the salary perspective for civil servants.

In most cases, the only competitive dimension of public sector employment is job security. The first avowed reason to work for the public sector for 86.3 per cent of the interviewees of a citizen's survey was job security (CIS, 1993a). Other incentives to work for the public sector score rather weakly. Salaries for high rank officials cannot compete with salaries in private enterprises; to prepare and successfully pass a public competition exam takes between one and three years (without any governmental support); there is no real administrative career and, finally, the performed job is not really assessed and paid accordingly.

POLITICISATION

Positioned above the Spanish civil service is a sphere occupied by political appointees. This area between pure politics and pure administration helps to increase political democracy in Aberbach and Rockmans' (1988) words. Political democracy implies reinforcement of the political rationality in which responsibility and political leadership are valued. The existence of political appointees helps the government to put the most realistic goals of the winning political party manifesto during elections into practice. The disposition of this area of the executive allows understanding the relationships between the Spanish civil servants and the realm of politics. The Spanish political appointment area of the executive summit enjoys following features: (1) political appointees of the summit are responsible for decision making, implementation and/or political assessment of public policies of nation-wide coverage; (2) recruitment is decided according to non-meritocratic criteria and the recruits belong either to the civil service or to the private sector.

This is not the place to describe the composition of the Spanish political-administrative area in detail. It will suffice for the purposes of this chapter to mention that it is composed of three broad tiers: minister, secretary of state and general director. The questions to be answered in relation with the politicisation topic are: (1) what organisational devices has the government deployed in order to gain control over bureaucracy?; (2) to what extent are civil servants or outsiders appointed for posts at the apex of the executive?; and (3) how many of those appointed civil servants possess the party book?

First, socialist (1982–96) and conservative (1996–) governments have enlarged the political-administrative sphere by increasing the number of politically appointed positions even though a parallel process of power, functions and service devolution to the regional authorities has been taking place during the 1980s and the 1990s. Although there are no constitutional or legal provisions in the Spanish system requiring political appointees to leave their positions once a new political party or coalition forms government, the entry of socialists in 1982 and of conservatives in 1996 brought about the termination and new appointment of three-quarters of the political summit in the first case (Parrado Díez 1996) and it is presumed that the same happened in the latter case.

The second question is whether the political-administrative sphere is filled primarily with outsiders or civil servants. Legal provisions have allow private sector expertise to be appointed for administering the summit since the middle of the nineteenth century. The period of Franco's dictatorship was dominated by the grand corps of civil servants that, in the absence of a party system and in the absence of a strong political party of the regime, controlled most sources of power: non-democratic parliament, public and some private corporations and the political executive. For instance, more than 90 per cent of state secretaries (*subsecretarios*) and general directors who worked in the executive belonged to a grand corps (Alvárez 1984). The most represented corps during this period were diplomats, public prosecutors, attorneys general, judges, notaries, university professors and engineers (Alba 1984). The regime was engaged in constructing a legal state and undertaking public works in order to reduce unemployment. This high proportion of civil servants (more than 90 per cent) in the political-administrative sphere was reduced to 66.2 per cent among second tier office holders – secretaries of state – and to 78.2 per cent among general directors during the socialist period (Parrado Díez 1996). As can be seen from the data, possibilities for outsiders are not very large.

Third, it is necessary to explore the issue of political party membership. Although the information collected for this issue during the socialist governments between 1982 and 1991 is based on biographical data and informal sources, some trends can be suggested. From the analysis of the data, one-third of political appointments were reserved for party members. There were some differences among secretaries of state (50 per cent of post holders had the party book) and general directors (30.2 per cent). Among all civil servants that held a political appointment in the analysed period, only 12 per cent belonged to the socialist party and the number of political party cadres that entered political office was insignificant (Parrado Díez 1996).

Further, one can conclude that the posts at the apex of the executive are not very attractive from the point of view of the professional career. There are several reasons for this. First, the general director salary, for instance, cannot compare to salaries of similar positions in the private sector (see Figure 10.1). Second, the tenure of political appointments lasted an average 3.2 years during the period 1982–91 and the return to previous activity is not always easy. In the former case, there are relatively severe legal restrictions for political office incumbents to work in the same functional field of his public office during the following two years after termination and the termination is not followed by indemnity sums as in private enterprises. For the civil servants, the prestige of having held a political office can be seen as the only reward and incentive to accept appointment. On the one hand, the salary of general directors is lower than that of some deputy general directors (civil servants in level 30 offices). Moreover, the 'indemnification' that all political appointees with civil service status receive for life as a part of the salary is quite small.

Third, a clear party identification of civil servants does not help them later on in their administrative career. The post-career of former government political appointees will not automatically be rewarded with an office of level 30, for which discretionary powers of the recruiter (a political appointee) may be used. In some cases, posts of level 29 or 28 are searched if a post of level 30 is offered; it will probably be a second rank position of an advisory nature where posting allowances are not that attractive. This third argument aids in understanding why the level of political party commitment of civil servants is not very high. Not only is affiliation poor but public activity of civil servants in meetings and party conventions also seems to be negligible.

Although civil servants do not appear to be highly committed to political parties, political appointees use civil servants' expertise during political campaign time. Civil servants will have to contribute, for instance, to writing reports in which achievements of the government in office are highlighted, while critical aspects of service delivery are omitted. Political appointees send these reports to the headquarters of the political party in government and the information will be intensively used in political marketing. Although the principle of neutrality forms part of the Spanish constitution, top civil servants do not seem to disobey the master's command. Generally speaking, however, Spanish civil servants seem to be more neutral in terms of party politics than citizens like to think, although further research is necessary to prove this hypothesis.

The Public Opinion Image of Civil Servants

The social image of civil servants can help in assessing the extent to which government performance is legitimised through its actions and inactions. The information presented in this section offers some ideas about how citizens perceive civil servants who work for the community. Unfortunately, there are no historical data. All data used here result from ad hoc questions included in surveys for other purposes or to the only questionnaire on the social image of Spanish civil servants. All surveys except one have been carried out by CIS (Centro de Investigaciones Sociológicas, the governmental Centre for Socio-logical Research). The information will be presented in four groups: (1) how civil servants are perceived when dealing with citizens; (2) how civil servants perform in comparison to their counterparts in private enterprises; (3) how civil servants are perceived in comparison with politicians; and (4) how the citizen was treated during his/her last experience in a public office.

First, according to citizens, civil servants do not treat them very well. Respondents agreed or strongly agreed with the following statements: Spanish civil servants are authoritarian with the citizen (42.1 per cent); they are strict in complying with administrative rules (52.4 per cent); they are slow (56.7 per cent) and not really effective. Furthermore, civil servants are not willing to serve the citizen (only 20.7 per cent of respondents think they are) and only 23 per cent believe that civil servants flexibly meet citizens' demands. The only positive statement to support civil servants' performance was that they are good professionals (39.7 per cent strongly agreed or agreed). Moreover, the public service was not perceived by interviewees as consistent when dealing with different groups. Some groups receive worse treatment than others: illiterates (53.4 per cent agreed with this answer), lower-income individuals (54.4 per cent) and gypsies (63.2 per cent) while higher-income individuals received better treatment (70.9 per cent agreed with this answer) as did members of the civil servant's family or acquaintances (86.3 per cent). To have a 'friend' in a public office is a guarantee that the matter will be dealt with appropriately. Citizens strongly believe (74.5 per cent) that administrative affairs are sped up and taken care of if the citizen knows someone behind the counter. This opinion has no basis in practice since 75.5 per cent had no family members working for the public sector and 59 per cent had no friends in public office.

Second, there are some differences between private and public sector workers. In CIS surveys (1996 and 1993a), almost half of the interviewees declared that civil servants were less concerned than private sector workers, less motivated to carry out their jobs and less productive. The other half was divided among the following categories: more, equal and no response. In a 1992 CIRES (Centro de Investigaciones sobre la Realidad Social, the (private) Centre for Research on Social Reality) survey, a negative perception of public sector servants in comparison with private sector workers predominated in the only question on public service. More than one third considers that functionaries are not very devoted to their job, while the figure in the case of private sector workers was 15.6 per cent.

Third, the relatively poor perception that citizens have of the civil service could be explained by a certain political cynicism in the sense that people have little confidence in politics in general. In two surveys carried out by CIS (1993[a,b], 1994), the average degree of empathy declared by interviewees to several professionals showed that civil servants were positioned in the middle of the scale (5.1 in a scale from 0 to 10 in 1994). Only four groups averaged lower than civil servants (top bank managers, 4.0; military cadres, 4.8; trade unionists, 4.6; and politicians, 3.2). Although no blame has been placed on civil servants in the corruption cases which have appeared in the executive during the previous socialist governments, no representative of the state and the realm of politics and administration is viewed with empathy by citizens, except policemen (6.1).

However, when individual experiences are considered, the social image of civil servants is considerably ameliorated. Thus, 74.3 per cent of citizens had no problems the last time they directly received a public service; 74.9 per cent received the level of service they expected; 87.2 per cent were not handled in a discriminatory manner in comparison with others and the treatment was not unfair.

The environment of corruption, the perceived necessity of internal connections, and rather authoritarian and low quality service have considerably influenced the image of civil servants. The contradiction between civil servants considered as a whole and individual civil servants shows that the image inherits most of the bad traits of a bureaucracy, while civil servants are performing well and are able to get Spain out of the dark times of dictatorship when the quality and the amount of services provided was much lower.

CONCLUDING REMARKS

In this section, we relate the information discussed above to the conceptual configurations designed by Heady (1996) in order to describe the transition from the civil service of Franco's regime to the current civil service in the Spanish democracy. Heady considers the assumption that organisational entities have a natural tendency to coalesce into 'configurations'. Conceptually speaking, configurations are defined on the basis of a theoretical framework or a synthesis of the literature. The configurations that Heady uses for defining the national civil service are related to the political regime (responsiveness to a governing body), to the socio-economic context (decision making on socio-economic issues), the place of the personnel management system within the whole political system, the qualification requirements for entry into the service and the sense of mission of the civil service.

Although the dictatorship ended well over twenty years ago, an examination of the transition of configurations that occurred in the intervening period can help us better understand the present situation. In some dimensions, the transitional process from one configuration into another has been fully completed while in other dimensions, the process is in the final stage. The relevant transitions for the Spanish case are: (1) from a military and ruler responsive to a majority-party-responsive civil service; (2) from a corporatist socio-economic context to a pluralist competitive environment; (3) from civil servants as mission guiders to policy-responsive public servants; and (4) from a decentralised personnel management system to a rather centralised system with a division of personnel functions in some cases.

First, a transition from a military and ruler-responsive to a majority-party-responsive civil service has taken place. In relation to the political regime, the responsiveness of the civil service system to the Francoist political elite was rather mixed and shared by the model of ruler responsiveness and responsiveness to the military cadres. General Franco took power with his army and transferred power to military officers by appointing them to the war ministries and some civilian ministries at the very beginning. The military was unlikely to be seen as superior cadres in civilian positions since Franco mistrusted officers (Alba 1984). Moreover, the coalition between military professionals and civil servants was stronger at the beginning of the dictatorship in the post-civil-war period. Once purges had been carried out to rid the government of the official collaborators with the previous Republican governments and a new bureaucratic elite was emerging to permeate all state structures, the configuration of the civil service transformed into the ruler-responsive model, with slight modifications. Political power resided in the hands of a ruling group, commanded by Franco, and the same members of the ruled groups composed this ruling group: bureaucrats. The relative charismatic image of the dictator was the basis for legitimacy and it was clearly perceived by all social components from within the state machinery and from outside that the leader could not easily be replaced by another leader. In spite of the dictator's efforts to self-perpetuate the regime, his goal was doomed to fail: (1) the appointed successor to the presidency, general Carrero Blanco, was killed by a terrorist bomb in 1973, two year's prior to Franco's death; (2) the monarch 'appointed' to conduct the destiny of the Spaniards decided to take the democratic route once Franco disappeared.

After this period of mixed ruler-military responsiveness, civil servants became responsive to the governing party or the coalition of parties in a Spanish parliamentary system. None the less, Heady's proposals must be slightly amended in the Spanish case since a pattern of patronage appointments emerged which was similar to presidential systems even though political party membership had not yet been intensively developed or used for political appointments. With each change of the governing political party or coalition of parties, most political appointees are dismissed even though the legal system does not include a provision requiring this.

Second, considering the socio-economic environment, there has also been a transformation of the corporatist state ruled by bureaucratic corps that also permeated large private corporations and channelled the representation of interests to a pluralist competitive context. Civil servants of grand corps had become the masters of the system during the dictatorship. The freedom to operate in the economy was restricted and there were no other groups able to compete with civil servants in the exercise of power. The official trade union and the political movement of the regime could not wield enough power to counterbalance grand corps' influence. With the advent of democracy, political parties and trade unions replaced the corps in state machinery and in other institutions. The opening of the system to different groups, different interests and different parties contributed to shaping the environment into a pluralist competitive one. Although the role of trade unions is still weak in public services, their influence has grown considerably in recent years. The newly proposed act of parliament (not yet passed) would grant trade unions considerable bargaining power.

Third, with regards to the sense of mission, there has also been a transition in the Spanish civil service from a guidance mission during the dictatorship to policy responsiveness starting with the advent of democracy. During Franco's regime, the civil servants viewed themselves as entitled to assume the leadership role in the political system. In the absence of political parties, civil servants were the leaders of society. They knew what was right for the state machinery and for society. With the appearance of political parties, the civil servants became responsive to political leadership. The political party involvement of civil servants is secondary to their public service role and the general image they convey is that of professionalism and party neutrality.

Finally, the entrance of socialists in government in 1982 brought about an important change. The existence of a multiple system is one of the most relevant features of Spanish government from the middle of the nineteenth century until the 1984 Act. The multiple system consisted of a combination of the timid efforts of politicians to launch reforms that would apply to all civil servants without undermining and affecting special corps of functionaries and the power of these groups to preserve and gain more privileges. Special corps always avoided general legislation and reinforced their privileges throughout the second half of the nineteenth century and more than three-quarters of the twentieth century. Personnel functions were decentralised on a ministry-by-ministry basis and corps controlled not only entry into the civil service, but also the administrative career of its members, the salary and the like. The unique point of reference for any civil servant was the corps they belonged to. There were as many systems as corps. Besides this, the general system that applied only to general corps should be considered.

The multiple system has not yet been entirely replaced by a unified system. The 1984 act was drafted with the main objective of undermining corps' power. This action was perhaps unnecessary since corps were replaced by political parties in the exercise of power. The role of corps in shaping the administrative life of its members has been notably diminished since then. The formal functions left in hands of corps are restricted to the entry process: civil servants must enter into public administration through a corps and no more than two corps members will be included in the evaluatory commission that examine applicant performance. Multiple actors share the personnel management functions. Among them one must consider the Ministry of Finance and Treasury, the Ministry for Public Administration and, to a minor extent, the department where civil servants are performing their tasks. Thus, there is a division in the assignment of responsibilities among different bodies with an attempt to abolish corps influence. None the less, the power wielded by corps can still be noticed in some aspects: some corps are able to get a relatively high administrative level for starters (level 26 or 28) instead of assigning newcomers with the top minimum for group A (level 20). Also, some corps are able to acquire advantages in mobility processes, even though restrictions have been established in the 1984 act.

Since 1996, however, and thanks to government's need to decrease public expenditure, central units of the civil service are highly centralising and controlling the entry and the internal distribution of public servants within the national level. In this context, it is difficult to envisage the transition from traditional administrators working in a centralised organisation to new public managers who are responsible for the resources they use, promoted on merit, and act like their counterparts in the private sector. The Spanish civil service still combines traditional and modern aspects and a drastic change is not likely to occur as we enter the twenty-first century since the present government is not committed to changing the rules.

For the next century, however, the Spanish government must continue to concentrate on establishing an operational and cohesive framework of the civil service for the national and the regional level of government. So far, the same regulations are applied to the civil service at the central level and all regional authorities. A piece of legislation that is currently being discussed in parliament concerns the extent to which civil services from various autonomous communities may differ to adapt to the need of their community without jeopardising the cohesion of the state. Once this decision has been made, each civil service may have to undergo a transition from a traditional administration to a new administration which is more citizen-oriented and more efficient.

BIBLIOGRAPHY

Aberbach, J. and B. Rockman (1988), 'Mandates or mandarins? control and discretion in the modern administrative state', *PAR*, (48): 606–12.

Agranoff, R. (1994), 'Asymmetrical federalism in Spain: design and outcomes', Paper presented at the sixteenth World Congress of the International Political Science Association in Berlin.

Alba, C. (1984), 'Bürokratie und Politik: Hohe Beamte im Franco-Regime (1938–1975)', in P.W. Waldman, W.L. Bernecker and F. López-Casero (eds), *Sozialer Wandel und Herrschaft im Spanien Francos*, Munich: Ferdinand Schöningh.

Alvárez, J. (1984), *Burocracia y poder político en el régimen franquista*, Madrid: INAP.

Baena, M. (1977), 'El poder económico de la burocracia en España', *Información Comercial Española*, **522**: 12–21.

Baena, M. (1993), *Curso de Ciencia de la Administración, vol. 1*, Madrid: Tecnos.

Bañón, R. (1978), *Poder de la burocracia y Cortes franquistas 1943–1971*, Madrid: INAP.

Beltrán, M. (1964), 'Datos para el estudio de los funcionarios públicos en España', in *Documentación Administrativa,* **83**: 9–ff.

Beltrán, M. (1985), *Los funcionarios ante la reforma de la Administración,* Madrid: CIS.

Beneyto, J. (1958), *Historia de la Administración española e hispanoamericana,* Madrid: Aguila.

CIRES (Centro de Investigaciones sobre la Realidad Social) (1992): *Sample, 1200 interviews.*

CIS (1983), *Barómetro de marzo,* Estudio 1334, Sample, 2500 interviews.

CIS (1993a), *Imagen social de los funcionarios,* Estudio 2054, Sample, 2500 interviews.

CIS (Centro de Investigaciones Sociológicas) (1996), *Barómetro de octubre,* Estudio 2225, Sample, 2500 interviews.

CIS (1993b), *Barómetro de diciembre,* Estudio 2076, Sample, 2500 interviews.

CIS (1994), *Barómetro de diciembre,* Estudio 2127, Sample, 2500 interviews.

Cos-Gayón, F. (1851), *Historia de la Administración española,* Madrid: Instituto de Ciencas Juridicas.

Derlien, H-U. (1985), 'Politicization of the civil service in the Federal Republic of Germany: facts and fables', in F. Meyer (ed.), *La Politisation de l'Administration, Bruxelles: Institut International des Sciences Administratives,* 1–39.

Dirección General de la Función Pública (1974*), Evolución y previsión de efectivos en la Administración civil del Estado,* Madrid: Dirección General de la Función Pública.

Fernández, P., 'Relaciones laborales. Sistemas de representación y participación en la administración pública', *Temas de Gerencia Púbica para las oposiciones de TAC,* **76**: s.f.

Gutiérrez-Reñón, A. (1969), 'The Spanish Public Service', *International Review of Public Administration,* Brussels, 133–40.

Gutiérrez-Reñón, A. (1987), 'La carrera administrativa en España: Evolución histórica y perspectivas', *Documentación Administrativa,* **210/211** (May/September): 29–70.

Gutiérrez-Reñón, A. (1990), 'Función del cuerpo en un sistema de carrera', *Revista Vasca de Administración Pública,* **26**: 83–9.

Gutiérrez-Reñón, A. and M. Labrado-Fernández (1988), *La experiencia de la evaluación de puestos de trabajo en la Administración Pública,* Madrid: Ministerio para las Administraciones Públicas (MAP).

Heady, F. (1996), 'Configurations of civil service systems', in A.J.G.M. Bekke, J.L. Perry and Th.A.J. Toonen (eds), *Civil Service Systems in Comparative Perspective,* Bloomington/Indiana: Indiana University Press, 207–27.

Jiménez-Asensio, R. (1989), *Políticas de selección en la Función Pública española (1808–1978),* Madrid: INAP (Instituto Nacional de Administración Pública).

Linz, J. J. and J. M. de Miguel (1975), 'Las Cortes españolas: 1943–1970', *Sistema,* **9** (8): 103–24.

Mény, Y. (1993), *Politique comparée,* Paris: Montchrestien.

Mills, W. R. (1956), *The Power Elite,* New York: Oxford University Press.

Ministerio de Economía y Hacienda (MEH) (1992*), Personal al servicio del sector público estatal,* Madrid: Inspección General de la Administración del Estado, Ministerio de Economía y Hacienda.

MAP (Ministerio para las Administraciones Públicas) (1996), *Boletín Estadístico del Registro Central de Personal,* Madrid: MAP.

MAP (Ministerio para las Administraciones Públicas) (1998), *Planificación de Recursos Humanos en la Administración General del Estado,* Madrid: MAP (Secretaría de Estado para la Administración Pública) (mimeo).

Nieto, A. (1986), *Estudios históricos sobre Administración y Derecho Administrativo,* Madrid: INAP.

Ortega, L. (1992), 'La reforma de la alta burocracia en España', *Revista Sistema,* **107**: 5–20.

Parrado Díez, S. (1996), *Las élites de la Administración Central: Estudio general y pautas de reclutamiento*, Seville: Instituto Andaluz de Administración Pública.

Raadschelders, J.C.N. and M.R. Rutgers (1996), 'The evolution of civil service systems' in A.J.G.M. Bekke, J.L. Perry and Th.A.J. Toonen (eds), *Civil Service Systems in Comparative Perspective*, Bloomington/Indiana: Indiana University Press, 67–100.

Seage, J., 'Los sistemas de retribución: Las retribuciones en la Administración Pública', *Temas de Gerencia Púbica para las oposiciones de TAC*, 72: s.f.

Suay, J. (1987), 'La reforma de la Función Pública: Su impacto sobre la burocracia española', *Revista Española de Derecho Administrativo, Civitas*, 56 (October/December).

11. West European Civil Service Systems: Variations and Similarities

Hans A.G.M. Bekke and
Frits M. van der Meer

INTRODUCTION

Eight West European civil service systems have been analysed in this volume using the theoretical framework presented in Chapter 1. In this conclusion, we examine the level of variation between West European civil service systems by comparing the findings from the eight chapters. In addition, we discuss various explanations for patterns in the development and design of civil service systems in this region.

In order to address these issues, an important question – one that has been carefully avoided up to now – has to be answered. What is the rationale for using a predominantly geographical approach for comparing civil service systems? In Chapter 1 we mentioned that this West European volume is part of a wider civil service systems research project. This project consists of a series of five comparative studies. Volumes have been published or are being prepared on Africa, the 'Anglo-Saxon' countries outside Europe, Asia and Eastern Europe. The implicit presumption has been that the label 'West European' refers to something more than a geographical location in space. What then could that 'something more' be? Civil service systems are embedded in a wider political and societal context. The design of civil service systems and changes in that design over time are closely related to political and societal developments in the same period. For centuries, these West European countries have belonged to a distinct political, economic and social environment. At the same time each country, some more than others, has developed its own identity due to its particular historical and cultural evolution. Discerning these explanations requires a historical-institutional approach.

For this final chapter, we use the framework mentioned above as a structure. In Section 2, the historical development of civil service systems is examined. We discuss the internal labour market systems in Section 3. Since
civil service systems operate in a predominantly political environment, we
survey political-administrative relations in Section 4 by exploring the level of
politicisation. The relationship between civil service systems and the wider
societal context is explored by tackling the issues of representativeness (Section 5) and public opinion (Section 6). In Section 7, the issue of civil service
reform is addressed. We wrap things up in the final conclusions.

THE HISTORICAL DEVELOPMENT OF CIVIL SERVICE SYSTEMS IN WESTERN EUROPE

Raadschelders and Rutgers identify five more or less separate stages in the
evolution of civil service systems. These phases have been described in our
introduction. Their model centres around the close relationship between civil
service system development and the formation of the modern state. In this
model, modern is conceived as a state governed by the 'Rechtsstaat' or rule-
of-law principle. The Raadschelders/Rutgers model is in essence an historical-institutional approach to civil service evolution. A major difficulty in any
historical-institutional approach is where to begin the analysis. Although
Peters calls this the weak spot of historical-institutionalism, on closer inspection this criticism should not be all too deadly (Peters 1999). The problematic
part is the framing of the issue, otherwise we end up trying to answer 'the
chicken or the egg' questions. Institutional development really suggests
institutional transformation by processes of institutionalisation and de-
institutionalisation (Bekke 1999). That process of transformation might render institutions almost unrecognisable over a longer period of time.

In political and administrative history, the depersonalisation of authority
relations within the state is considered a major departure from traditional
modes of government. Our analysis starts at this breaking-point in civil service history. In all cases, and particularly in Britain, France, Prussia and
Spain, the emergence of a central state in combination with the centralisation
of authority is considered an important explanatory factor in the growing
reliance of rulers on both military and civilian officials. The multiplication of
government tasks and the increasing level of administrative specialisation
eventually made the separation of the personal and the administrative household of the ruler inevitable (stage 1). It was initially an organisational division, but it also symbolised a profound change in authority relationships.
These changing roles represent an important institutional shift, as the authority relations of civil servants towards the ruler (gradually) became less personalised (stage 2). Civil servants gradually evolved from personal servants

in the service of the ruler to servants of the state. While it began as a practical necessity, in modern times it became a norm for 'good governance'. This norm reinforced the process of depersonalising intrastatal authority relations.

This generic portrayal of these early stages in civil service development needs some refinement since state development shows degrees of local and temporal variation. Although territorial integration was realised in Britain, resistance to centralisation of authority by the monarchy proved substantial quite early in its history. See for instance the Civil War and the Glorious Revolution in the seventeenth century. These had slowing effects on the process of bureaucratisation. Britain had a more unique position in the development of its civil service system. That uniqueness was only reinforced later on by Britain's ability to fend off French domination in the Napoleonic era. The transition mentioned by Raadschelders and Rutgers certainly also occurred in the areas covered by present-day Belgium, Ireland, Italy, the Netherlands and Norway. Conditions here have been more complex since these countries, with the exception of the Netherlands, did not enjoy independent statehood until the nineteenth and early twentieth century. To an important extent, these areas have experienced the same development as the states they were a part of. The confederate Dutch Republic, the predecessor of the Netherlands, came into existence as a result of a revolt caused by the centralisation policies of their Spanish Habsburg rulers.

The transition from state towards public oriented civil servants (stage 3), as Raadschelders and Rutgers call it, was a gradual process. In many European countries, an aspiration for political and state reform developed in the late eighteenth century that was often inspired by predominantly French political thinking. Changes on the continent were actually realised as a consequence of the 'Napoleonic' wars and conquests. Political-administrative renewal was either imported or imposed (see for instance Belgium, the Netherlands, Italy and Spain) or introduced by reconstructing administration. Instrumental in effectuating these changes was the establishment of the Rechtsstaat or in Anglo-Saxon terms the rule of law. The Rechtsstaat principle involves regulating the relationship between the state and the citizens by defining the respective right and duties. This powerful idea had implications for the relations between government and the civil service system. In the slipstream of the Rechtsstaat, a legal-rational bureaucracy developed (Page and Wright 1999).

Step-by-step, the legal position of civil servants in all countries included in this volume was formalised and standardised. Apart from defining the legal position, the reforms pertained to improving recruitment and selection procedures. Civil service employment might be honourable but should not involve honorary offices. Merit instead of prerogative and privilege was becoming the guiding principle. During the nineteenth century and the first half of the twentieth century, rules and regulations relating to the position of civil servants towards the political officeholders were adopted. The civil service evolved into a protected service (stage 4). Alongside the development of a protected civil service, the nature of employment changed drastically. Due to a rapid increase in the size and range of government activity, the number of government officials and the qualitative demands on those civil servants rose dramatically. In this sense, the civil service increasingly became 'professionalised' and civil servants became professional. In the later part of the twentieth century, they became more autonomous players in policymaking processes (stage 5). The word 'professional' has different meanings in different civil service systems and it varies over time. The most extensive connotation is that the officials are 'up to the job'. The adjectives 'merit' and professionalism' are closely associated in this particular meaning. What 'professional' exactly means therefore depends on the merit criteria in a certain civil service system for a given period. To name two extremes, in France, the civil service became characterised by officials trained in specific professions while in Britain, the generalist senior civil servant became the ideal of a civil service professional.

Comparing the Raadschelders/Rutgers model to the empirical evidence in the previous country chapters, a first conclusion is that this model helps further our understanding of the historical transformation of these civil service systems. Nevertheless Fry, for instance, concludes that this model is only applicable in general terms. Apart from the problem that 'historical models' and particularly evolutionary models can be quite impressive with respect to their empirical applicability, some comments can be made with respect to the successive nature of the last three stages. The civil service as a protected service (stage 4) and the civil service as a professional service (stage 5) can be considered as two dimensions of their third stage (the public-oriented civil service). Furthermore this model depends very much on the development of the Rechtsstaat or the rule of law. In essence, it describes the changes to the civil service as a response to the creation of (in a classical sense) the liberal state. Two major problems arise. First, although the concepts of the Rechtsstaat and the rule of law may be a dominant normative force in all of the countries included in this volume, more traditional relationships, for instance of a clientelistic nature, may persist. The Belgian and Italian cases are two examples of this which produce a seemingly intra-contradictory (almost prismatic) institutional design. A second issue is that although the development of a protected and professional civil service went hand in hand, a tension between these two dimensions arose particularly during the (second half of the) twentieth century. The importance of the civil service as a professional and increasingly autonomous entity turned political-administrative relations (and particular political control) and – in some countries – the representativeness of the civil service into important topics. At the same time, the (often perceived inflexible) protected nature of the civil service was causing problems with the issue of how to manage these professionals.

THE INTERNAL LABOUR MARKET

In the later part of the nineteenth and the first half of the twentieth century, many of the present day features of the internal labour market (ILM) came into existence. The legal position, the reward structure, recruitment and selection procedures, etc., were increasingly regulated and standardised. The personnel management system became increasingly bureaucratised. At the same time, most European civil service systems experienced a growing tension between these bureaucratic (and sometimes perceived rigid) personnel management regulations and practices on the one hand and the objective of achieving flexible labour relationships on the other. Particularly from the 1980s, initiatives have been undertaken to introduce more flexibility in personnel management. These last reforms have come to be known under the label New Public Management (NPM). That perceived rigidity in government personnel management systems pertains not only to the issues mentioned above but also to a lack of mobility and adaptation to internal and external changes in the environment of government. This need to modernise personnel management in the public sector has led to a wide array of human resource management initiatives. For instance, initiatives to limit the terms of office of senior civil servants introduced in Belgium, Ireland, and the Netherlands are a first example for this drive towards flexible labour relationships in core administration.

The same efforts are and were paid to the introduction of merit pay and flexible reward schemes. Many of these initiatives are either in their early stages of implementation or have produced rather disappointing results. These difficulties can be explained by either outright resistance (see for instance the Italian case) or to a shortage of financial means and political determination. In a situation of financial austerity merit pay seems difficult to implement. At the same time, the special (political) nature of government employment limits the implementation of 'private sector management' practices. In addition, hiving off government agencies and the privatisation of executive tasks have also resulted in more flexibility in labour relations, legal status and remuneration of officials.

On another level, tensions continue to exist between 'managerial' (be it bureaucratic or flexible by nature) and 'political' considerations relating to human resource management in the public sector. These tensions are extensively discussed in the section on politicisation. We should remark that these managerial and political dimensions are powerful symbols of good governance. Although they are not conflicting as abstract symbols on this particular level, this is not necessarily the case on the collective choice and the operational levels. We will return to this tension in the sections on politicisation and representativeness.

Wise has stated that the ILM construct pertains to more or less coherent labour markets. From the previous chapters, it has become apparent that not only between countries but even within a particular national civil service system, different internal labour markets can co-exist. Roughly, three different systems of deployment can be distinguished: a decentralised system of recruitment and selection, a general career and a specialised career system.

The decentralised system of recruitment and selection highly resembles what is practised in the private sector. The Norwegian and Dutch (below the very senior level) civil service systems can be considered examples of these decentralised systems. Personnel management issues are handled by ministerial departments and decentralised units within these departments. An exception is made with respect to pay settlements, but even here in recent years these pay packages (in line with the increasing flexibility of labour relations) can be custom-made to the individual needs of the department and their employees. Since a central personnel management office is absent, one can easily speak of loosely coupled ministerial internal labour markets. As a side-effect, interdepartmental mobility is low in these systems. In principle these systems are open to the outside world, in practice, little mobility to and from the private sector is exhibited. During their working life, most civil servants stay in their respective organisations. This implies that in practice, civil servants have a non-formalised career in government and most frequently in their own organisation. Since civil servants are normally recruited for a job instead of a career, the emphasis is on (a high level of) pre-entry education.

In contrast to the decentralised function-oriented system is the career system. The career system has two subspecies. One is the general career system which is widely associated to the senior civil service operating in the United Kingdom. It has recently been implemented in the Netherlands for the top ranking officials. This type of career system involves generalist civil servants or general administrators. By nature, this career system applies to the senior levels of the civil service.

The so-called corps structure is the professional/specialised variant of the career system. These structures are mainly dominant in France and Spain. Civil servants belong to certain professional corps or bodies. They enter these corps after specialised education. For instance in France the Ecole Nationale d'administration and the Ecole Polytechnique are the elite schools for accessing the most prestigious corps from which civil servants are selected to secure their postings. Because of the nature of these corps, interdepartmental mobility is the exception rather than the rule.

Each of these deployment systems can exist in a particular civil service system. For instance in Britain and the Netherlands, the general career system applies to the top-level grades whereas the 'lower' grades fall under the decentralised system. One of (the relatively less prestigious) French corps is that of the general administrators. The police, the judiciary, the military and the Foreign Service in most countries can be considered specialised career systems.

POLITICISATION

By its very existence, civil service systems are political creations. Relations at the political apex of government have merited much attention over the last decades, but they have also been subjected to a high degree of (conceptual) cloudiness. In discussions on political-administrative relations, two different strands of enquiry can be distinguished. First, there is the issue of accountability – more particularly the issue of ministerial responsibility. Second, research and discussions have focused on the actual division of work and power relationships between political and administrative officeholders. Although these issues are interrelated, the topic of political-administrative relations in terms of accountability and responsibility is usually analysed from a constitutional and mainly normative starting point while the latter is studied from a political science perspective which stresses the empirical aspects of the relationship.

The normative perspective, the Weberian ideal type of 'neutral' civil servant, is still very much the accepted point of view in the countries discussed here. The separate roles and procedures of selection and recruitment are founded in the constitutional legal structure. This legal constitutional approach emphasises the principle that political authority should be invested in elected and/or accountable officeholders. Depending on the nature of the political regime, these officeholders should be accountable to the legitimate source of power. Because of the nature of their permanent position, civil servants do not fall in this category. Civil servants should work under and within the guidelines of these elected officials. The ability to serve, counsel and advise the political officeholders requires recruitment and selection on basis of 'merit'. What the concept 'merit' means in this respect is rather complex and varies from country to country and position to position. With respect to permanent positions, 'merit' is still defined by the professional qualities. The separation between political and administrative roles and patterns of recruitment and selection is considered both an instruction norm and at the same time it is an important symbol for assessing the legitimacy of government.

Particularly in the political science tradition, the issue of politicisation is defined in terms of a tendency towards a growing osmosis between the political and administrative systems. The very word politicisation relates to a trend that administration, or for that matter the civil service, is becoming more political in nature. This can pertain to the role of the civil service in the policymaking process. From our discussion above it has become clear that during the course of the last century or so, the importance of the civil service has greatly increased. Members have become powerful, professional players on the political-administrative scene. What can be learned from all cases is that integration of political and administrative officeholders at the political-administrative apex is considered in all countries (perhaps with the exception of Norway) a serious issue.

The issue of politicisation can be seen as an answer to this integration problem. Viewed from this perspective, actors in the 'political' system are employing a repertoire of instruments to control the civil service. Without giving a full overview, instruments can include (party) political considerations in recruitment and selection procedures, the use of intermediary political-administrative structures, the use of alternative sources of policy advice and alternative modes of service provisions (see for instance, Italy). Starting with the existence and emergence of so-called intermediary structures, they have been created in order to provide government control over the standing bureaucracy. These structures can be formalised, as is the case of Belgium and France. Policy advice is given by ministerial cabinets. The cabinets are filled by political appointees of whom the majority is recruited from the civil service. In other countries structures are less defined. In Spain there is also a grey zone between politics and administration occupied by political appointees. In Germany, appointment to the top grades is open to the discretion of the government of the day. In the other countries, the issue is even less defined. This absence of formal rules doesn't mean that increasingly political (sometimes called media) advisors are appointed. In the Italian case, the involvement of the regular civil service is even avoided when using extra-bureaucratic structures such as independent agencies and outside advisors.

One might get the impression that in the cases of Britain, Norway and the Netherlands, and to a lesser degree Germany and Ireland, political control mechanisms are less manifest. One should add that for instance in the Netherlands (non-substantiated) claims have been made about partial party-politically motivated appointments to top-level positions in the civil service. One possible explanation is that the existing civil service ethos in these countries includes an emphasis on a general compliance to the political system.

REPRESENTATIVENESS

The issue of civil service representativeness is often perceived in terms of insuring the legitimacy of the civil service in society. Like the issue of politicisation, this issue has become more important due to the perceived increase of civil service power. The average (higher) civil servant is claimed to be a white, middle-class and male professional. This research confirms this standard image although interesting discrepancies do exist. While we can point to major (but decreasing) differences in educational background of civil servants, they nevertheless belong to the various national professional elites in that particular country.

The empirical analysis of the representativeness of West European civil service systems is very much linked to the normative/policy aspects. The normative aspects become manifest in policy towards making the civil service more representative. Opinions in the various countries widely differ with respect to the normative importance of representativeness. Active policies directed to create 'mirror-image' representativeness are rather rare. The scale and influence of policies to increase the inclusion of females, and in some cases ethnic minorities, by using instruments like positive-discrimination are rather limited, but such policies do exist. Belgium is an exception. The cleavage structure in Belgium society and the high degree of political and societal distrust can be held responsible. In Belgium, representativeness should be considered a means for securing the national integration of a socially fragmented state.

The principle of equal opportunity is dominant in the approach to civil service representativeness. Government employment should be subject to democratic and legal principles concerning fundamental values such as equity, merit and openness. These principles function as powerful symbols of the democratic and legal nature of the state. Nevertheless, the concept of equal opportunities is somewhat ambivalent. Equal opportunities might signify an open access to the civil service. This means that recruitment and selection are (formally) not discriminatory in nature. Only job related criteria are used in the selection. In the formal systems, this principle of open access is installed in all countries. In many European countries, it is enshrined in the constitution. As signatories to the Convention to Civil and Political Rights, these countries are required to guarantee this open access. Equal opportunities in recruitment and selection does not imply equal opportunities in society, and it doesn't imply that there might be self-selecting mechanisms in society at work (see for instance the meriodinalisation in Italy).

Factors that are relevant in explaining representativeness are the level of homogeneity in a country, the relevant constitutional and legislative framework, the role and perception of the state, the territorial system of the state, the educational system, and the state of the labour market. Homogeneity relates to the number of issues that divide a country. Norway, for instance, is considered a fairly homogeneous country without many or deep crosscutting cleavages. The same is the case with Ireland. Two issues which remain are female representation and the representation of people with a lower level of education. That homogeneity is certainly not the case with Belgium. Relevant topics (in addition to feminisation and education) in Belgium are language, religion and politics. Representativeness is seen as a policy to pacify the different sectional interests. Every group gets what it is proportionally entitled to. Representativeness can be seen as the means of insuring a balance of power and the preservation of the Belgium state. In addition, the territorial system of the country is another important factor for explaining the level of representativeness. Regionalisation and federalisation are instruments to promote the level of representativeness. This is not so much realised on the national or federal level but by transferring power to the 'regional' authorities. There is then more dependence on regional homogeneity. Given the fact that educational qualifications are still unevenly distributed amongst society, policies which are directed to narrow the scope of government to the formulation and preparation of policy, diminish the societal inclusiveness of civil service system.

PUBLIC OPINION

In the preceding country chapters, we encountered a wide divergence in citizens' views on the performance of civil servants. When asked their opinion on civil service performance in general, citizens are more negative than when asked to evaluate 'real life' encounters with civil servants during actual public service delivery. The results affirm what is maintained in the available opinion literature. General opinion on the performance and legitimacy of the civil service is, to say the least, indifferent or even negative. The concept of the incompetent bureaucrat indulging in red tape is (still) a powerful image in many West European countries. On closer inspection, there is more cross-national variation than a cursory overview reveals.

For instance, in the Irish and Norwegian cases, the general attitude towards the civil service is much more positive than average public opinion in Europe. To a lesser extent the same can be said for the Netherlands. In looking at cases such as Spain, and particularly Italy and Belgium, the picture becomes bleaker. In Spain, Italy and Belgium, complaints are made with respect to the endemic nature of favouritism and patronage. In other European countries, these complaints are absent or substantially lower. Notwithstanding these variations, public opinion in all West European countries shows a deteriorating tendency in the past decades.

In contrast to general perception, public opinion towards specific groups of civil servants is more positive. (The only exceptions are the United Kingdom, Italy and Belgium.) As has been said in the case of the Netherlands, an explanation for this difference is that concrete encounters or experiences with civil servants can dispel existing stereotypes or, in the cases of Britain, Italy and Belgium, can confirm them.

A variety of explanations have been provided on the history of this predominantly negative view on civil services and civil servants. A first explanation is a perceived deficiency or breakdown in civil service performance. Many of the countries included in this volume have had their share of political and administrative scandals. These scandals have influenced the standing of politics and administration. In addition to these scandals, it should be observed that standards have actually been lowered over time, but that the actual performance is not meeting the standards expected by the population.

As a consequence, there is a growing lack of confidence in and disenchantment with the political system as a whole. This general attitude to the political administrative system also influences public opinion of the civil service. Growing political cynicism has had its effect. It should be added that this cynicism is prevalent and is also directed at political institutions such as parliament and the political executive as well as the civil service.

In explaining this political cynicism, we have to distinguish between a traditional and a more dynamic variant. The dynamic variant has been described above, and deficient government performance is responsible for this. The traditional static variant has to do with a low level of national collective integration. In the case of Belgium, Hondeghem mentioned institutionalised mistrust in central authority. The same conclusion is applicable to the Italian political administrative system. Both countries share a history of frequent foreign domination. This history of foreign domination created a sharp division between state and (local) community. To a certain extent, nation building was lacking in the formation of the formal institutions of state. In recent years, emerging crises in the political administrative systems in Belgium and Italy have only reinforced this attitude. Using Mary Douglas' phraseology in the Belgian and Italian cases, we have fatalist societies with high grid/low group situations leading to the distrust in the political administrative system as described above. Alternatively, the egalitarian culture in Norway can help to explain the relatively small distance between government and society resulting in a better public opinion in that country. The Irish case tends to suggest the influence of religion, as Roman Catholics tend to be more favourable to the civil service than Protestants and people of a non-denominal background. The Belgian, Spanish and Italian cases refute this relation between Catholicism and trust in the civil service. Without going into too much detail, the explanation could be the particular nature of Irish Catholicism perhaps in relation to the national identity.

REFORM

Civil service systems are exposed to marked processes of change and transformation. From the early 1980s, a new wave of reform has been launched. Looking at the stream of policy documents and studies published by scholars, and issued by governments and international organisations like the OECD, the IMF and the World Bank, one can easily get the feeling that administrative reform has become endemic. The words 'new public management' are often used to label the new approach to managing government organisations. This reform epidemic engulfing the nations of the world has led the scientific community to wonder where these reforms stem from, what basic reasons explain their ascension and whether these reforms are actually identical in content (Hood 1998).

The role and functioning of government in most nations in the world has come under scrutiny primarily due to a combination of a rapid and pervasive transformation of the economic and social structure of society and a growing disenchantment with actual government performance. Social-economic change and transformation are regarded as strong forces for reforming government regardless of the exact outline and results of the reform. These forces for reform are strengthened by the recommendations and pressures of the above mentioned international organisations. In the 1980s, particular attention was focused on improving performance in terms of emphasising the need for efficiency and effectiveness. This 'new' managerial approach consisted of using private sector techniques and objectives such as changing administrative techniques, emphasising output control, increasing attention for a more flexible system of employment and introducing competition within the public sector. The issue of legitimacy primarily concerns the interaction between government and citizen. Although the issue of legitimacy was part of the 1980s version of NPM – being mainly embodied in the drive for a 'customer orientation' – the very effects of the NPM policies in that period led again in the 1990s to a renewed interest in civil service ethics and responsiveness.

As a remarkable aspect of these reforms of public organisations can be considered the rapid and world-wide diffusion of ideas and concepts. Hannan and Caroll (1992) refer to the density (the extent) of diffusion of particular ideas about new organisational outlines. It can be seen as a function of the legitimacy and the degree of institutionalisation of these ideas. However, the speed of these transformations may have prevented a more steady development of institutionalisation processes. Berger and Luckmann (1966) distinguish three sequential stages of institutionalisation. The first stage is habitualization in which new structural arrangements are generated in response to a specific organizational problem. The second stage, the semi-institutionalisation stage of objectification, includes the appearance of some degree of social consensus among decision-makers concerning the value of structure and the increasing adoption of that structure. The last full institutionalisation stage is sedimentation when the complete spread of structures and the perpetuation of structures over a period of time can be seen (Bekke 1999). Transformations of public organisations, also as they appear in this volume, show such rapid institutionalisation processes that the stages of habitualization and objectification can hardly be found.

Tolbert and Zucker (1996) distinguish between two models of diffusion of civil service reform: a regulative one, in which the nation state enforces new forms of public administration on subaltern governmental bodies; and a normative one, in which a broad social movement or trend provides for diffusion. The latter model is well known in institutional theory as the process of institutional isomorphism: (public) organisations develop into a situation of similarity and communality of organisational shape by conforming to normative pressures and expectations from their institutional environments (DiMaggio and Powell 1983).

CONCLUSIONS

Two important trends during the course of Western European history have been crucial to civil service design. The first trend has been the foundation a depersonalised state and the establishment of the rule of law. The second trend involves the shaping of national identity. Starting with the first trend, explaining differences and similarities, political science and public administration have traditionally pointed to the steady development of the state. A common feature in Western Europe (may it happened sooner or later) is a process of state integration supported and manifest by the centralisation of power. That centralisation produced the formation of state institutions. The relation to societal unification has been rather complicated. In many cases, there is a twofold relationship. This is particularly true from the nineteenth century onwards. National identity (with its shared culture, beliefs, rules etc.) depends very much on a shared historical experience. For instance, it is well established that a shared French identity became strongly reinforced by military conscription and the extension of compulsory education. At the same time, nineteenth century romantic nationalism provided the idea of a believed national identity as a stepping stone for state formation. Beliefs about the state and its role are the product of this intertwined process of state and societal formation.

This volume has compared civil services in West European nation states by using a neo-institutional approach. The central theme has been that civil service systems can be viewed as systems of institutionalised structures, norms and procedures that mediate the mobilisation of human resources in the service of the state. In doing so, we suggest that the uni-dimensional concept of bureaucracy is not a useful object of analysis for the purpose of general comparative research (Bekke et al. 1996). What can we learn by applying this research methodology?

First of all, by using some basic elements of institutional arrangements of norms, values, procedures and rules (the successive general concepts of historical development, internal labour market, politicisation, representativeness, public opinion and reform) we are able to avoid the 'coins and flags' method used in much comparative research by which one only can gather some singular data without the social, cultural and political environment in which these data have to be understood. Institutional analysis implies the notion of systems ruled by norms, culture and traditions rather than by organisational goals and rational perspectives. Institutions are embedded in societal environments and as structuring processes of input and output between segments of society and wider societal life. By viewing civil service systems as institutional arrangements instead of as bureaucratic unities, we may analyse how they solidify or change traditional beliefs, how order is given to and change is initiated from these arrangements and how general societal institutions affect the way civil service systems service the state's goal: how they give a certain order to political and administrative processes, how they bring personnel into the state organisation, how they transfer democratic values from society into the administration and how they control behaviour in it. In many ways, civil service systems are shaped and stabilised by formal or informal norms and values, historically developed and adapted to particular societal experiences and beliefs. This implies that they can be described by elements of their static position: structures, habits, norms and rules. At the same time, institutions are mechanisms for shaping and transforming actions, rules, beliefs and structures. In the institution concept both order and transformation are concentrated (Bekke 1999).

In this volume, we find many examples for these connotations. Despite the – in many respects common – Western European tradition and history of the countries presented in this book, there are many differences, that can be attributed to particular social and cultural circumstances and traditions. But there are as many similarities which are caused by common backgrounds, political and cultural interrelations and – not least – a shared classical Greek-Roman origin which means that many institutional arrangements are grounded in the political philosophy of Greek-Latin ancestors.

REFERENCES

Aberbach, J.D., R.D. Putnam and B.A. Rockham (1981), *Bureaucrats and Politicians in Western Democracies*, Cambridge, MA: Harvard University Press.

Bekke, A.J.G.M. (1999), 'Studying the development and transformation of civil service systems', in J.D. White and J.L. Perry (eds), *Research in Public Administration*, vol. 5, Stamford: Jai Press, 1–18.

Bekke, A.J.G.M., Jim L. Perry, Th.A.J. Toonen (1993), 'Comparing civil service systems', *Research in Public Administration*, 191–211.

Bekke, A.J.G.M., Jim. L. Perry, Th.A.J. Toonen (eds) (1996), *Civil Service Systems in Comparative Perspective*, Bloomington: Indiana University Press.

Berger, P.L. and Th. Luckmann (1966), *The Social Construction of Reality*, New York: Doubleday Anchor.

DiMaggio, P and W.W. Powell (1983), 'The iron cage revisited: institutional isomorphism and collective rationality in organizational fields', *American Sociological Review*, **48**, 147–60.

Douglas, M. (1982), *In The Active Voice*, London: Routledge & Kegan Paul.

Douglas, M. (1989), *How Organisations Think*, London: Routledge.

Farazmand, A. (1997), *Modern Systems of Government: Exploring the Role of Bureaucracy*, Thousand Oaks, CA: Sage.

Hannan, M.T. and G. Caroll (1992), *Dynamics of Organizational Populations: Density, Legitimation and Competition*, New York: Oxford University Press.

Hood, Christopher (1998), *The Art of the State; Culture, Rhetoric and Public Management*, Oxford: Clarendon Press.

Kiser, L.L. and E. Ostrom (1982), 'The three world of action. A meta-theoretical synthesis of institutional approaches', in E. Ostrom (ed.), *Strategies of Political Enquiry*, Beverly Hills, CA: Sage, 179–222.

Krasner, S.D (ed.) (1983), *International regimes*, Ithaca, NJ: Cornell University Press.

Morgan, E.P and J.L. Perry (1988), 'Re-orienting the comparative study of civil service systems' *Review of public personnel administration*, 84–95.

North, D.C. (1990), *Institutions, Institutional Change and Economic Performance*, New York/Cambridge: Cambridge University Press.

Olsen, J.P. (1996), 'The changing political organization of Europe: an institutional perspective on the role of comprehensive reform efforts', in J.J. Hesse and Th.A.J. Toonen (eds), *The European Yearbook of Comparative Government and Public Administration*, Baden Baden: Nomos Verlag, Baden-Baden.

Page. Edward C. (1992), *Political Authority and Bureaucratic Power: A Comparative Analysis*, New York: Harvester Wheatsheaf.

Page, Edward C. and Vincent Wright (eds) (1999), *Bureaucratic Elites in Western European States. A Comparative Analysis of Top Officials*, Oxford: Oxford University Press.

Perry, J.L. and J.C.N. Raadschelders (1995), *Protocol for Comparative Studies of National Civil Service Systems*, Bloomington/Leiden.

Peters, B.G.. (1988), *Comparing Public Bureaucracies: Problems of Theory and Method*, Tuscaloosa: University of Alabama Press.

Peters, B. Guy (1999), *Institutional Theory in Political Science: the New Institutionalism*, London: Pinter.

Pierre, Jon (ed.) (1995), *Bureaucracy in the Modern State: An Introduction to Comparative Administration*, Aldershot: Edward Elgar.

Raadschelders, J.C.N. (1998*), Handbook of Administrative History*, New Brunswick, NJ: Transaction.

Rose, R. (1984), *Understanding Big Government. The Programme Approach*, London/Beverly Hills/New Delhi: Sage.

Rose, R., 'Public employment in Western nations', Cambridge: Cambridge University Press.

Rouban, L. (1995), 'The civil service culture and administrative reform', in B.G. Peters and D.J. Savoie (eds), *Governance in a Changing Environment*, Montreal/Kingston: McGill-Queen's University Press.

Tolbert, P.S. and Zucker, L.G. (1996), 'The Institutionalization of Institutional Theory', in Clegg, Hardy and Nord (eds), Handbook of Organization Studies, London: Sage.

Toonen, Th.A.J. and J.C.N. Raadschelders (1997), *Public Sector Reform in Western Europe*, Report for the Comparative Research Project on Public Sector Reform in Central, Eastern and Western Europe, Department of Public Administration, Leiden.

Weber, M. (1972), *Wirtschaft und Gesellschaft*, Tuebingen: J.C. Mohr.

Index